THE
HEIGHTS
OF
MOUNTAINS

THE HEIGHTS OF MOUNTAINS

GUY FRANKS

Copyright © 2024 by Guy Franks.

All rights reserved. No part of this publication may be reproduced, distributed, or transmitted in any form or by any electronic or mechanical means, including information storage and retrieval systems, without a prior written permission from the publisher, except by reviewers, who may quote brief passages in a review, and certain other noncommercial uses permitted by the copyright law.

Library of Congress Control Number: 2024908065

ISBN: 979-8-89228-085-3   (Paperback)
ISBN: 979-8-89228-087-7   (Hardcover)
ISBN: 979-8-89228-086-0   (eBook)

Printed in the United States of America

For Bobbie Ellen

What the pattern describes is not a trait, such as greed, or an innovation, such as derivatives, but a cultural devolution—a generalized decline in standards.

Origins of the Crash
by Roger Lowenstein

I'd been a fool about many things, but just when I thought everything would turn out all right, it went wrong.

Dream Merchants
by Harold Robbins.

Book One

Chapter 1

It was nearly midnight and the five of us sat around in a circle in the middle of Marty's studio apartment. None of us were tired. The business of founding a multi-million-dollar corporation filled us with a kind of effervescent energy. We were like inventors in the basement, oblivious of time, putting the finishing touches on an experiment that would bring us fame and fortune.

Stuart Baum was talking. We called him Stu, and he sat on a foldout chair in front of a small table that contained a briefcase filled with legal documents, marketing data, colored graphs, and operational plans. Stu was a corporate lawyer and had come with us from Metropolitan Fiber Systems.

"Thanks to Marty and Eccel Partners, we have our first $3.8 million in venture capital," said Stu. He talked like a lawyer; his words were carefully chosen and spoken with a dry arrogance.

"That will be more than sufficient to set up our offices, start hiring, and get our proof of concept rolled out. We just signed a lease for five thousand square feet of office space—with potential to grow a lot more—over at Rio Seco Business Park in San Jose, and we can start moving in…what? —starting Tuesday. Right, Marty?"

Stu glanced over at Marty, who nodded and added, "Yeah, around Tuesday… It's right off Montague Expressway."

"Doesn't Rio Seco mean dry river?" I asked with a slight grin. "Couldn't we have found a more colorful place—like Rio Bravo?"

The other three chuckled at my little joke but Stu ignored it and continued talking.

• 3

"Now's the time to keep our eye on the ball. We've got enough money to gear up and make it through the first half of the year but we'll need more capital, and quickly, to make it through the second half. Marty and I have meetings set up with VCs on Sand Hill Road to make that happen, and I'm confident we can raise another two to four million in the coming weeks. Wouldn't you say so, Marty?"

Stu was referring to venture capitalists (VCs), and again, he glanced over at Marty, who nodded in agreement and added, "Yeah… The time is ripe."

"Exactly! The time is ripe," continued Stu. "With deregulation, low-interest rates, and the exponential growth of the Internet—hell, even Greenspan has jumped on the bandwagon—*the time is ripe.* Everybody's hot to back the Internet pony."

"Too bad we can't add a dot-com to our name," I said. "It'd be worth another five mil in venture capital."

The other three chuckled again at my quip, and even Stu raised an eyebrow and smiled.

"Yeah, too bad," he said. "But I think CrestPoint Communications Group Incorporated fits the bill nicely. It clearly identifies us as a Telecom provider. Without us, there is no high-speed Internet. Even the VCs get that. We bring the bats and balls to the game. Without us, there is no game…"

I tuned Stu out for a moment—he with his platitudes and sports metaphors—and reviewed this moment in my head, savoring it like the glass of Cabernet Sauvignon I held in my hand.

CrestPoint Communications Group Incorporated.

That was quite a mouthful. There'd been a lively debate over the name of our new company but we'd finally taken it from the street sign out front of Marty's apartment, *Crestpoint Drive*. The name embodied all the hipper elements we were looking for. It rolled off the tongue, evoked the image of a mountain top, implied high achievement, and hung out there as something of an inside joke. Marty quickly gave it a little style by capitalizing the "P", and after running it through the copyright and legal mill, our grand endeavor became officially known as *CrestPoint Communications Group Incorporated.*

And I thought I knew everything there was to know about starting up a company. *Ha! Not even close.* To create a Competitive Local Exchange Carrier, or CLEC (pronounced *see-lec*), business plans had to be developed, venture capital raised, FCC and PUC reviews completed, state and city certifications approved (unfortunately every state and city had own their specific set of requirements), franchise agreements secured, collocation and interconnection contracts signed with the Baby Bells[1], and an endless list of boxes to check. Then there was all the internal stuff like hiring plans, the choice of operational support systems, contracts with equipment vendors, contracts with installers, concept testing, marketing and sales strategies, pencils and paper, and of course, a logo to choose from.

Despite the daunting list, we were finally in the home stretch. Just four months ago, the five of us had been working for Metropolitan Fiber Systems building the Information Super-Highway. We were part of their West Coast Broadband Deployment, each of us with a VP-level position, working our butts off, day and night, building fiber optic systems in Tier 1 cities. Ubiquitous broadband, high-speed Internet—that was the dream. Then WorldCom acquired MFS at the end of last year and the dream got "re-prioritized," so we each pulled the rip cord on our golden parachutes and split.

I liked to think that I was the inspiration for CrestPoint or at least the guiding hand that nudged Marty in the right direction. Marty was a natural leader and a technical genius, both an innovator and a tireless entrepreneur, and he and I had become friends at MFS. When we left MFS, it was with one goal in mind—to start our own company. That it had to be connected with the Internet went without saying. But building fiber systems was out of the question; ringing a city with fiber optic cables *à la* MFS cost millions of dollars and showed little return on investment. We needed something cheaper yet more elegant.

---

[1] Independent regional Bell Operating Companies (RBOCs) are nicknamed Baby Bells like AT&T, NYEX, Bell Atlantic, etc.

Digital Subscriber Line, or DSL, had been around for years. It was a technology that allowed you to deliver high-speed Internet over a regular phone line at a speed 30 times faster than a dial-up modem. It was already deployed in the UK and Belgium, and Marty and I had been involved in its budding development over at MFS. We understood the science behind it and the technical logistics involved in rolling it out. And it didn't take fiber cable or expensive optical carrier equipment to deploy. It was cheap yet elegant.

It was during a game of racquetball one day that the idea came to me. I was kicking Marty's butt as usual, and when we stepped outside the court to wipe off and re-hydrate, I bent down to pick up my water bottle, stood up, and said, "How about DSL?"

Marty looked at me and I could see the wheels spinning behind his amber eyes. He was off and running. "We lease the lines from the Baby Bells," he said, somewhat out of breath. "Re-sell them to the ISPs, who do the marketing and sales, and we play the CLEC without the overhead. We're on the hook for collocation and a DSL box—but that's it, partner. It's pure gold!"

And so, as they say, the rest was history.

Marty quickly recruited his team from other MFS expatriates, each one highly intelligent and an expert in his field, and each one as hungry as Marty and me to open up the Internet to everybody in America and make millions of dollars doing it. We chose the Bay Area for our corporate headquarters since it was the hub of the *Internet gold rush*, and we staked our claim in Marty's small living room on Crestpoint Drive in San Jose and started digging our gold mine.

It was now March of 1997, and after four months of toil and preparation, we were ready to launch *CrestPoint Communications Group Inc.* Tonight was the final assembly and pre-flight checklist. Marty had a bottle of champagne on ice, along with five glasses, and we were almost to the point of popping the cork.

I tuned Stu back in.

"We'll have losses the first couple years. The investment community expects that. But the key to our success is to get big fast-- market shares over profit. It used to be that you had to show five, even ten years of profit before you could go public, but not anymore. The Internet has changed everything. The old rules are out the window. The smart strategy today is rapid growth. Growth, not profit, but especially revenue growth. We all understand that?"

"Yeah," I said. "We need to be the *firstest* with the *mostest*." I glanced over at Marty who winked at me with a smile. He appreciated it when I simplified things.

"I figure we have to be EBITA positive[2] at the end of three years," continued Stu. "Until then, investors and analysts are going to measure us like the CATV[3] industry, using a fully discounted cash flow. But that's to our advantage. So getting market share into the first seventeen cities we've identified—the NFL cities—is going to be critical... *Critical*... Marty?"

"I think you said it," replied Marty with a nod. "To that end, we've struck tentative agreements with eight Internet Service Providers, including Fastcom and Telocity, and we've got more in queue."

The mention of Internet Service Providers—the ISPs—put me in mind of a quote by Churchill: *It is one thing to see the forward path and another to be able to take it.* And we're just about to yank them onto the forward path, I thought to myself. Our neat little DSL product will force them to dismantle their wonky old modem pools and become our middleman. We're about to shake up the industry. Dial-up modems are the buggy whips of yesteryear and we're the automobile. It's called creative-destruction and we are its agents.

"But let's recap, then go around the room," continued Marty in a buoyant mood. "You've all got your titles and signed off on your equity shares. In two years, we'll go public and you'll all be millionaires. But only if we execute—execute on our business plan and execute on our operational plan... Russ, as Executive Vice President and Chief Development Officer, where are we in nailing down the technology and rolling things out?"

---

[2] Earnings Before Interest Taxes and Amortization.
[3] Cable Television

That was my cue. "We've contracts with Copper Mountain and Netopia for the DSL equipment, and Cisco for the backend. They're all giving us volume discounts. I'm just about to sign a deal with Lucent for the installation, but I'm going to need a steely-eyed missile man to drive it all home."

"Got anyone in mind?" asked Marty.

"I do. I'm interviewing him this weekend… But getting the equipment is not going to be the choke point. We'll have the equipment and the crews to put them in. The key is going to be collocation and getting an order to flow through from end to end."

Marty turned to C.V. Chandrasekar. "Chandra, as EVP and Chief Information Officer, where do we sit in getting our orders to flow through?"

C.V. Chandrasekar, or Chandra as we called him, was in his mid-thirties, slightly balding, and always seemed to have an amused twinkle in his brown eyes. Born in India but raised in the U.S., Chandra spoke English without a trace of an accent despite having grown up with Hindi-speaking parents. He was an impeccable dresser and his choice of colors, which were often bright reds and yellows, always paired well with his mocha-colored complexion. He was married to an attractive blonde but had no kids.

"When we place an order with SBC, for example," said Chandra, "there will actually be three orders." He went on to explain the intricacies of placing a DSL order with an RBOC (pronounced r-bock), which were the Regional Bell Operating Companies, also known as Baby Bells, who were being forced by the government to lease parts of their network to competitors like us. They weren't too happy about it. There would be resistance and difficulty, stated Chandra, but nothing we couldn't deal with.

Chandra finished his summary and Marty nodded solemnly. "And what about our corporate LAN?" he asked Chandra.

"Up and working when we move in. We just need butts in the seats."

"And that brings us to our EVP and Chief Operating Officer," said Marty. "Mister Lau, where do we stand on our hiring plans?"

Ron Lau was a second-generation Chinese-American who was fluent in both Mandarin and English. He spoke English with a slight accent and, on occasion, tended to truncate his sentences, but he spoke rapidly and to the point. Also in his mid-thirties, Ron was short, slight of build, with a thick head of dark hair that was beginning to show some streaks of whitish-gray. In his dress, he preferred black slacks and white shirts, and he always wore a tie. He was a devout Christian and always carried a thumb-worn bible in his briefcase. Ron was married with two kids.

"I think we can be to fifty butts by end of month," said Ron. "Most admin and project managers." He went on to explain our hiring strategy, which was to target ex-Bell people since they knew the business and order processes we needed to contend with. The local Baby Bell SBC was helping us out by laying off employees. As a result, there was something of a bidding war out there, but we were offering a $1000 bonus plus stock options at a couple of dollars a share. This "strike price" per share would only go up the longer they delayed, so they were incented to jump on board now. As for bringing in mid-managers, something more might be needed, suggested Ron. "We can sweeten the pot there," he said. "Offer them VP rights, fatten the bonus, and increase stock options. They walk in, two by two, just as Noah's ark."

"Yeah, the VP title gets them every time," chuckled Marty. "Thanks, Ron... Stu, as EVP and Chief Financial Officer, is there anything else you wanted to add to what you already told us?"

Stuart Baum was also in his mid-thirties and looked like a tall and rather barrel-chested version of Dustin Hoffman. He wore pressed slacks with wingtips and tended towards V-neck sweaters with a collared shirt underneath, usually with a tie. Invariably he rolled up his sleeves, exposing his thick and hairy forearms. Born and raised in Brooklyn (a fact he reminded us of frequently), he still retained an edgy, Brooklyn accent after all these years. I think he had a family but I wasn't sure since he never mentioned them. To be truthful, Stu was not my favorite of the four. He was a top-notch legal mind and knew finances inside and out, but for some reason, I didn't cotton to him. The fact that I'd once seen him bring a woman manager to tears in a staff meeting at MFS probably had something to do with it.

"One more point I'd like to make," replied Stu. "As a start-up, we need to think outside the box. That includes expanding beyond just our traditional roles and doing what it takes to get the job done. Elasticity and a certain relentlessness are going to define our role. Take my role for example—CFO and Corporate Lawyer. I see myself more like a ball player who can play multiple positions—wherever the team needs me to win. I could just as easily add Chief Business Officer to my title since I'll be allocating company resources to meet our financial goals or Chief Investment Officer since I'm managing our portfolio of assets and working with investors. You could even add Chief Compliance Officer given the fact I'm riding point on regulatory compliance. There're probably other titles I could—"

"Don't forget chief cook and bottle washer," I said.

Both Chandra and Ron laughed loudly at that. I always enjoyed taking Stu down a notch when the opportunity presented itself.

"My point is," replied Stu, unamused, "we have many hats to wear."

"Exactly," interrupted Marty. "We're going to wear many hats. So let's wear them well. We're a start-up, not a lumbering giant like AT&T or some Baby Bell like SBC who can't take a shit unless it's approved by four levels of management, documented in their standards and practices, and blessed by the PUC."

We all laughed at that depiction, since it was so right-on. All of us had worked for Ma Bell or a Baby Bell at some point in our careers, and the one thing we were sure of was *we didn't want to be like them.*

And nobody knew that better than Martin Madrid. Like the other three men, Marty was also in his mid-thirties. (At age forty-four, I was the old-timer of the group.) He was rather short, only about five-foot-eight, but he was a formidable presence, and his amber eyes, almost gold in hue, were keen and penetrating. It used to be that CEOs were low-key and faceless, the men in the gray flannel suits, but nowadays they were more like rock stars. Marty certainly fit that role. He was handsome, charismatic, and could talk a bird out of a tree. And he dressed the role. Blue jeans and polo shirts were his uniform of choice, though he would occasionally don a corduroy sports coat, even a tie, on more formal occasions. His sandy blonde hair was styled in the fashion of Jon Bon Jovi and he kept himself clean-shaven. Despite the rock star trimmings, I found Marty refreshingly down-to-earth. Unlike me, he was a devoted family man. His wife was pregnant with their first child, and she remained in their house up in Marin while he searched for a new home for them in Silicon Valley. He kept a large picture of the two of them in his apartment, and it was one of those antique tintypes you can get at the Boardwalk where everyone dresses up like cowboys and saloon girls. In it, he's wearing two six guns with a funny hat on his head and has a big grin on his face.

Marty's true genius was in applied science, specifically in figuring out things that worked for people. The old way of doing things didn't appeal to him. CrestPoint Communications was something new and innovative. We were going to deliver high-speed Internet to the common man. Sure, it was a risk. We were gambling everything. Our savings, our reputations—it was all on the line. But there was no one I'd rather take that gamble with than Six-gun Marty.

———

Marty popped the cork on the champagne bottle and poured out five glasses. We each took a glass and held it out, waiting for Marty's toast.

He paused a moment, raised his head in thought, then said, "In the words of the Grateful Dead, '*Without love in a dream, it will never come true*'... I love this dream and I hope you love it too, because without our love it ain't gonna come true. It's the Information Age and we're its Knights of the Round Table. With high-speed Internet for all, we're gonna create a worldwide community. Distances will be conquered. Borders will cease to exist. National hatreds will disappear and the world will become one. That's our *holy grail*... So, here's to us, to CrestPoint Communications, to our success and the building of our one world!"

We responded with "here-here" and drank from our glasses. I chuckled to myself at the Grateful Dead quote. Marty was a tie-dyed in the wool Deadhead and never missed a Grateful Dead concert if he could help it. And the choice of words—'worldwide community' and 'national hatreds'—he was really getting his Al Gore on. I knew he had political aspirations and in my heart I wished him the best of luck. Governor Madrid had a nice ring to it.

"I'd like to say a prayer to our endeavor," said Ron.

There was a moment of awkward silence.

"Of course," said Marty with a smile. "It's only appropriate. Go ahead, Ron." Marty bowed his head and we all followed suit.

Ron held his bible in one hand and spoke his prayer. "Lord God in heaven, in your mercy, please watch over us and bless this great endeavor—"

I half-listened to the rest of Ron's benediction. As something of an agnostic, I was slightly embarrassed by the moment and my participation in it. I wasn't sure about Stu and Chandra's religious beliefs, but I was certain that Marty, who was a man of science like myself, was also a skeptic. But his sense of largesse had prevailed and I bowed to its logic. In moments like this, form and tradition were everything.

"Amen," said Ron.

"Amen," we all repeated.

And there we stood, silent for the moment, basking in the afterglow of Ron's benediction. Five men. The Gang of Five. We were the product of America's most prestigious institutions, graduates of Cornell, Harvard, MIT, and Stanford; the wiz-kids at companies like AT&T, Bell Labs, General Motors, and MFS. Each of us a top performer, driven and ambitious. Yes, God bless CrestPoint Communications! Without a mountain to climb or a world to conquer, what would men like us be doing but wreaking havoc someplace else?

"Any other toasts," asked Marty. "Words of wisdom... Russ? I know you've got something to say."

"I do." I raised my glass and glanced around at their faces. I wondered if all these big egos would get along together. We would see. "Ambition, not so much for vulgar ends, but for fame, glints in every mind."

The Heights of Mountains

"Here-here."

"Churchill, I suppose," said Marty.

"Hmm."

We shook hands all around and began to gather up our things. It was after one o'clock in the morning. Marty came over and put his arm around me.

"Kind of late," he said. "You can crash out here if you want."

"Nah. Thanks anyhow. This time of night, it's not even a half-hour drive."

———

The drive up 101 to Redwood City was a breeze. I parked my car in the Westpoint Harbor parking lot, unlocked the wrought iron gate, and walked down the dock to my boat. It was quiet. The rows of boats were dark and sat still in the water. Everyone was sleeping.

I came to my boat and went aboard. It was actually classified as a motor yacht—a forty-five-foot Bayliner 4587 Motoryacht with twin diesels that I had souped-up to get an extra ten horsepower and almost four more knots of cruising speed. I bought it new in '95 and named it *Danny Boy*, after my son.

I walked through the cockpit and turned on the light to my living room. I had blinds installed on the bay windows and all the slats were tilted in such a way that I could see out but nobody could see in. I grabbed a cold beer out of the fridge, hit the power button on my CD player, sat back in my recliner, and listened to Sinatra sing about his funny little valentine.

I was still keyed up from the day's events and I needed some time to wind down before going to bed. A person appeared in the doorway. It was Cybil. She was barefoot and wore tight, short trunks that showed off her long, shapely legs. Her shirt was cut above her navel and she was bra-less, which highlighted her pert nipples. She held my cat Clementine in her arms. On seeing me, the marmalade-colored cat jumped down, alighted across the floor, and leaped gracefully into my lap where she curled up.

"I didn't think you'd ever get home," said Cybil. She walked over to me and grabbed the beer out of my hand, took a long swig, and then walked over to the bar. "Want a real drink?" she asked coolly.

"Sure." I gently stroked Clementine's neck as she purred softly.

I watched her make my drink—Johnnie Walker Red over ice with a splash of water. Cybil was thirty-one with a trim and pleasing figure which she enjoyed showing off with tight-fitting clothes. Her dark hair was cut short, revealing a graceful neck, and with a turned-up nose, big brown eyes, and a small mouth, she was more cute than beautiful. She reminded me of Playboy's Miss December 1989, only not as stacked.

She was a bit of a free spirit. In a rather odd arrangement, she lived on a sailboat with her ex-husband and together, she claimed, they were sailing around the world in fits and starts. Two months ago, she came on board while I was working on my engines, and after talking to me for an hour straight she decided to have an affair with me. I made no objections. She was a kick in bed, something of a randy beatnik, who came and went as she pleased. I really didn't expect much more than a few months of fun out of it. My nickname for her was Quiz-Game Girl because she talked in questions.

She handed me my drink and stood there looking me over. "Out late with the boys, huh?" she said. "What? Starting your little company, right?"

"Hmm."

"Are you the head honcho? Top dog? What's the name of your company?"

I took a sip of my drink and gave her a quick summary, not forgetting to give her my full title of Executive Vice President and Chief Development Officer. I knew that would rile her.

"Fancy," she breathed out with some sarcasm. She sat down on the edge of the coffee table and eyed me. "So what now? You wear suits and ties, work sixteen hours a day, get up-go to work, come home-go to bed, work your ass off, and die of a heart attack at fifty? Is that it?"

"Sounds like fun."

"You have a strange sense of fun."

"So I've been told."

"Are you one of those A-type personalities?"

"A-minus."

She looked down at her empty beer bottle and began to peel off the label. "Oh," she said, looking back up. "You got a message on your machine. Your ex-wife's reminding you that you got a meeting at your son's rehab tomorrow… I didn't know your son was in rehab."

"Cause it's none of your business."

I saw the hurt in her eyes but it faded quickly. She stood up and went over to the fridge to get a fresh beer. "Wanna smoke a joint?" she asked.

"No."

She stood there studying me, and after a moment she said, "Bob and I are sailing down to San Diego tomorrow. We're blowing this pop stand."

"Bon voyage."

"Is that your polite way of saying 'good riddance'?"

"Not at all," I replied. "I'm gonna miss you." It was true. I found her amusing and I would miss her, at least for a few days.

"That's nice to hear." She took a long swig of her beer and then waltzed over to me as Sinatra sang about the girl next door. She stood in front of me gently swaying back and forth to the music.

"I bet you're ridin' high," she said. "Ridin' high in April, shot down in May. Isn't that a Sinatra song?" She finished off her beer with a lusty chug and set it down on the coffee table. "It's time for the icing on the cake… A good fuck would top this whole night off for you, wouldn't it? It'd be the cherry on top. Don't you think? … I'll be in the bedroom waiting." She said this last part in a throaty whisper.

As she walked past me, she took off her shirt and tossed it in my lap. It scared Clementine, who jumped off my lap and scampered across the room. I heard Cybil laugh as she went into the master bedroom.

The thought of her lying naked on my bed made it impossible for me to finish my drink, so I got up, turned the lights off, and followed her in. She lay nude on her stomach, stretched across the bed, reading an article in one of my Playboy magazines. Her smooth, deeply tanned skin showed no bikini lines. I whipped off my clothes and crawled up behind her, playfully biting her on the ass as I went, and then came up to her head and kissed her neck. She tossed the magazine aside and twisted around underneath me so we were face to face.

"I've never been fucked by an Executive Vice President," she said.

"It's your lucky day."

Our lips locked together and her eager tongue danced around in my mouth. She reached down, found me, and guided me in as she spread her legs. She was warm and moist and I thrust deeply into her. She moaned—then started talking.

And this was really why I called her Quiz-Game Girl because for the next ten minutes, as she quickly came and then came again, she peppered me with questions.

"Oh, you like it there? Don't you?... Just like that, don't you?... Deeper... You want me?... You want me?... Say it... Can you feel me cum?... Ohhhh!... Can you feel that?... Want my legs up? Put my legs up... Is that better?... Ohhh, God! Yes!... Your're sooo big... You like it when I talk dirty? Don't you?... Yesss, I know you do... Cum inside me. Do you want to cum inside me?... Ohhh..."

All I could do was grunt my answers to these questions while I thrust into her, until I finally climaxed and dropped down into her arms. She hugged me tight around my neck and whispered more questions into my ear. I grunted my answers and waited for her to loosen her grip before I rolled over onto my back. She curled up beside me with her lips pressed against my shoulder and lay quiet.

I closed my eyes and breathed in the moment. She was right. This was the icing on the cake. I had gambled everything, started a business, and now taken this woman. A primordial power welled up inside me and made me feel invincible. It was like planting a flag on top of Mount Everest.

The feeling morphed into a warm glow and it quickly lulled me to sleep. I got up once during the night to go to the bathroom and covered us both with a blanket as I got back into bed. When I fell back asleep, I had a dream.

I'm at the foot of a mountain. It isn't Mount Everest; it's smaller, more like Mount Hamilton where I used to cycle. I'm gathered there with Marty, Ron, Stu, and Chandra. Without speaking, Marty begins to lead us up the hill. He's wearing two six guns and has a funny hat on. Everything has the look of an old tintype photograph—the grass, the trees, the sky, even the way we're dressed—and there is kind of a copper hue to everything. I feel a pressing sense of urgency. Something important is at the top of the mountain and we have only a short time to get there. Stu keeps complaining that we're not going fast enough.

At one point, I glance back and see my son Dan, only he's a young teenager and not a twenty-two-year-old adult. I wave at him to hurry up but he doesn't pay any attention to me. I'm torn between waiting for him or keeping up with the group. He's walking slowly, hardly trying to keep up, and I begin to get angry. I try to yell at him but nothing comes out so I wave at him more frantically. At that, he stops and reaches into his pocket. Even at this long distance between us, I can see it is a syringe, and he crouches down and turns his back to me. I can't stop what he's about to do. Frustrated, I let him go and run to catch up with the group. We walk for hours but don't seem to get any closer to the top, and when I glance back, Dan is nowhere to be seen.

When I woke up Cybil was gone. I put my robe on and walked out into the galley to fix a cup of coffee. There was a note by the coffee machine and I picked it up and read it.

Will you miss me? Bon voyage and have your fun.
Cybil

I smiled at that. Even her goodbye note was in the form of a question.

Chapter 2

I shifted uncomfortably in my chair and re-crossed my legs. They were the same kind of metal chairs you found in a school auditorium—fold out, enamel gray, hard as nails—and I wondered if they'd been chosen purposely to make every one of us feel as uncomfortable as hell.

It wouldn't have surprised me. Everything in this facility, from the color paint on the walls to the potted plants to the food in the cafeteria, all seemed calculated to evoke a mood. I imagined it all came out of some conference of psychotherapists. After days of earnest and educated debate, they had issued their list of recommendations on how best to design a Drug Rehabilitation Center—then published it to the world. They were probably Germans.

This was my second visit to my son's rehab facility, not counting the day we checked him in over a month ago. My first visit, with my ex-wife Janet, was an indoctrination session conducted by two of the therapists, a man and a woman tag-team, who told us about the process, the journey, and the need for patience and understanding, emphasizing to us that no one was to blame for our son's heroin addiction. I listened politely while holding Janet's hand. Frankly, I'd heard it all before. Heroin was cheaper and stronger than ever, and heroin addiction had become an epidemic in white, middle-class communities. Pop culture made it glamorous. It could be smoked or snorted, and rock stars OD'd on the stuff all the time, gaining instant immortality. Our son was just another statistic.

This was my son Daniel's second stint in rehab—the first at age nineteen, and now the second at twenty-two—and I was an old hand at the game. The drug rehab environment was a world turned upside down, where black was white and up was down. Inside these walls, language turned to jabberwocky. For instance, using words that passed judgment, words like "loser" or "deadbeat," especially if they were targeted at the victimized addict, were strictly verboten. If one wanted to call an addict out for the wreckage they'd caused in everyone's life, the best you could do was suggest that they had "made some poor decisions" or "chosen a life path that was destructive to yourself and others."

And it didn't stop there. I had once sat in a group counseling session where a divorced couple got into a screaming match with one another, dropping f-bombs, calling each other "cocksucker!" and "shit bag!" while their teenage daughter sat in her chair and glanced around at the other group members with a 'see-what-I-have-to-put-up-with' look on her face. The counselor, a soft colorless woman in her forties, sat with her head down and let the shouting match play itself out. Yet later this same counselor took offense at a parent who used the term "retard," quickly cutting him off and telling him that "we don't use hateful terms like that." The chastised parent duly apologized while I laughed to myself at the utter absurdity of it all.

The lesson here was that an addict was a victim of a sickness. The cure for the sickness was detox treatment along with cognitive behavioral therapy, which included exploring painful memories and emotions in order to purge one's demons. In many ways it seemed similar to religion; one got baptized as a victim, exorcized their demons through ritual counseling sessions, and then went back into the turmoil of life with a cleansed soul and armed with a dogma of beliefs to help you make it through your day. It exchanged one opiate for another.

But here I was, back again. Today's visit was the result of Jan's pleading and persistence. Dan wanted me in this session, she said, and it would mean a lot to him if I would attend. So, I agreed. And despite my skepticism over the whole process, I had decided to approach it all like *Pascal's Wager*. I couldn't prove it was totally useless, nor could I absolutely prove it was helpful, but there was more to be gained on betting it was helpful than not.

I sat next to Jan in our metal chairs in a circle with eight other participants. The counselor was a woman in her late twenties, an ex-addict, who was slender with long black hair and looked partly Native American. She was talking to a female patient and her lesbian lover who were on the outs due to the former's lies and drug use. The counselor Fala was trying to find common ground between the two while the rest of us sat patiently and listened.

Dan sat across from us. At six-two, he was nearly as tall as me and had my reddish-brown hair, but other than that he resembled his mother with his blue eyes, high cheekbones, and narrow chin. He sported a short and scraggly beard that clashed with his combed and neatly parted hair. Dan's lanky frame leaned forward in his chair, his elbows resting on his legs, but it was a position that didn't last long as he continually shifted up and down, from side to side, while his eyes roamed around the room. He was always high-strung, but he seemed more nervous than usual.

My son was the same age I was when Jan told me she was pregnant. I was twenty-two, in my first year of grad school at Stanford, and pursuing my Master of Science in Mechanical Engineering. Jan was an undergraduate majoring in History. We met at a mixer and immediately hit it off, and we dated exclusively for the next three months. In those three months, we screwed like rabbits, up-down, sideways, backwards, in her dorm room, in the back of my Toyota, anywhere we could be alone, and we got along swimmingly. Then at the end of three months, she told me she was pregnant.

"How can that be?" I asked in disbelief. "You're on the pill."

"I was—I am," she replied, tears coming to her eyes. "I don't know what happened... Maybe I missed a day... I don't know."

I was shocked, a little angry, and a whole lot confused. How did a highly intelligent woman involved in a sex-filled relationship *forget* to take the pill? It was mindboggling. But all I could manage to say was "What now?"

"What do you mean?"

"I have my master's program. You have a bachelor's degree to finish. We each have plans... And I don't see where a child fits in. Not at this point." I watched her reaction and waited. I wasn't going to bring up an abortion, I'd let her do that, but it seemed the only logical choice.

She wiped the tears from her eyes and stared at me. I could see she was collecting her thoughts—that my reaction to this news was not what she had expected—and now she had to regroup.

"I'm having the child," she said finally. Her voice had a hint of angry defiance in it. After a pause, she added, "You can do what you want."

That was the end of our discussion. A week later and after some heavy soul-searching, I asked her to marry me because, quite frankly, it seemed the right thing to do. She accepted without hesitation, and if she had any second thoughts she never shared them. My parents stepped in and helped us out financially so I could stay on track, and a year later I completed my master's and got hired by Bell Labs. Jan finished her senior year, gave birth to our son Daniel, and stayed home to care for him in our two-bedroom apartment in New Jersey. Five years later we were divorced.

After the divorce, Jan moved back to the Bay Area and took Danny with her, but in those first five years, I had nurtured my son, played with him, and loved him as best I could. He was an average child, playful and fun-loving, but early on I could see there were no traits of genius or brilliance emerging. He was also overly sensitive to rebukes and disappointments, sometimes crouching in a corner with his back to us or stalking the house with a scowl on his face until he finally settled down.

With Danny gone to live in California, I found that I missed my son, and after a year I was able to transfer from Bell Labs over to AT&T Pacific Bell as a Director of Network Planning with an office in San Francisco. This put me close to Danny and I was able to work out a custody agreement with Jan that allowed me to be with him every other weekend. We usually spent those weekends on my boat—a twenty-six-foot Searay V-260 cabin cruiser—touring the bay, fishing off the coast, and taking excursions out to the Farallon Islands. I bought him a brass pocket compass and every so often I would call out, "What's our heading, Danny boy?" He would quickly dig the compass out of his pocket, take a reading, and yell out "South by southeast!"

"Right!" I would yell back. "South by southeast. Steady as she goes."

But, as the years passed, I found we had less and less in common. What drove me did not drive him; what I found interesting or fascinating he found difficult or boring. And my talents and expertise were simply not things he ever exhibited. At ten, I designed an aerodynamic, soap box car that I raced in the soap box derby. At ten, Dan collected comic books and rode his skateboard. At fifteen I won my high school district's science fair, while at fifteen Dan was sneaking out of his mother's house to attend rock concerts and smoke dope. And at nineteen, I carried a 4.8 GPA at Stanford while my son spent his nineteenth year getting hooked on heroin.

And here he was, twenty-two, and back in rehab.

"And what would you like to say to Pat now that you know these things?" asked Fala. She was addressing the patient's girlfriend who seemed afraid to answer. "Go ahead. Talk to her," said Fala in a soft authoritative voice. "How important is she to you?"

"Very."

"Then talk to her. Tell her how you feel."

The woman hesitated a moment then stammered forth an avalanche of emotional exclamations. *It was her fault. If only she had listened and paid attention. She loved her and didn't want to lose her. Together they could work it out.* Now they were both standing up, begging forgiveness, professing their undying love and came together in a hug as most of the group sighed "Ahh."

I glanced at the clock. There was only thirty minutes to go.

Fala was looking at me. I had not "Ahh'd" or clapped my hands like the others in the group and she studied me with a slight frown on her face.

"Dan," she said, turning towards my son. He quickly straightened up and looked at her. "There are some things you wanted to say to your dad? Here's your chance… Russ, there are a few things your son would like to share with you—if you're willing to listen."

"I'm all ears," I replied with a thin smile. She had a definite anti-dad vibe going but I wasn't going to let it throw me off stride.

"Dan?" repeated Fala.

"Yes," he replied, a bit tentatively. Fala slowly closed and opened her eyes to express compassion, and Dan took the cue and cleared his throat. He scratched his beard in thought then crossed his arms, exposing the myriad of tattoos across his forearms which were *de rigueur* for junkies and convicts.

It started out with "My whole life I've tried to please you" and ended up with "I guess that's all I have to say," and in between and for the next fifteen minutes I listened to him accuse me of judging and belittling him his whole life. Nothing he ever did was good enough for me. I never praised him, he could not live up to my expectations, and heroin was a way of dealing with the pain of being a disappointment to me. His complaint was illustrated with anecdotes, some of which were exaggerated or twisted beyond recognition, and I sat there and listened to it all without interrupting him.

When he finished talking, Fala took over and began reviewing the highlights of his speech like a district attorney going over the evidence of a crime. When she re-quoted some of Dan's accusations, my objections of "that's not quite accurate" or "that never happened," were quickly cut off. She finally completed her summation and stared at me with undisguised malice.

"What do you have to say to all that?" asked Fala. "How does it make you feel?"

I glanced around the group. Everyone was staring at me—all except Dan, who was leaning forward with his head down. I caught the eye of another father sitting across from me and his face showed sympathy for my plight.

"Sad," I said. "It makes me feel sad… It's a tough job being a father, especially a part-time one, and it's sad to hear that my son thinks I did such a lousy job of it."

"And this is the fallout of that," said Fala, nodding towards my son.

There it was—I stood accused in the Court of Jabberwocky of driving my son into drug addiction. Fala, in all her Comanche rage, planned to roast me on the skewer of public opinion, as small as it was, and strike a blow against all the thoughtless and cruel fathers of the world. She would make us pay.

But I wasn't going down without a fight.

"If you say so… But I find it even sadder that you—a trained psychotherapist—would buy into this fiction, into this collection of lies and exaggerations and patented excuses. I would have thought they trained you better than that—"

"I don't think—"

"Hold on—it's my turn to talk. Respect my voice. Isn't that your credo here? As I was saying, I would have thought they trained you better than that. Trained you to spot prevarication. Trained you to identify projections and compulsive lying. Sadly, you're willing to run with this picture my son has painted without once giving it a critical eye. Come on, Fala. You're better than that."

There was dead silence.

"See what I mean," my son suddenly said. "How he turns things around?"

"Respect my voice, that's true," replied Fala. I could hear the anger in her voice. "You should try it. Your son opened up to you and all you want to do is dump on him."

"Rubbish."

"It's not *rubbish* to him. Perhaps you didn't listen—listen carefully. That doesn't appear to be a strong point of yours. What he spoke was the truth to him. Maybe it's true for others… Jan, what are your thoughts on this—on what your son said about his father?"

Jan sat calmly, and after a moment she simply replied, "I'm not taking sides in this."

"That's because she's afraid," said Dan.

"Afraid how?" asked Fala quickly. She leaned forward, her eyes bright with excitement, and glanced from Jan to my son and then back to Jan again. "Why are you afraid, Jan? Are you afraid of this man? Is he abusive? Tell us the truth. You're safe here… Dan, what is she afraid of?"

All eyes turned to Dan. Fala remained breathless, on the edge of her chair, as though she were about to uncover a horrible truth. I also looked at my son. He leaned forward with his arms on his knees and returned my look with a slight smile. Suddenly a cold shuddering thought pierced my brain. It would be so easy for him to say I abused his mom, or that I abused him as a kid, and here in this room I would stand accused and convicted. Police would be called. An investigation launched. My career ruined. Was reality that damn fragile, I wondered.

I waited for my son to speak.

"Dan?... What kind of abuse are we talking about here? Physical abuse?... Sexual?"

Dan soaked up the anticipation—then finally replied, "Nah, it's nothing like that... She's still in love with him and's afraid to say anything negative about him."

There were some murmurs amongst the group and a few chuckles.

"I mean, they've been divorced seventeen years and she still thinks they're gonna get back together. It's *pathetic*... And she still jumps in bed with him whenever he whistles..."

"My sex life is nobody's business," said Jan.

"*Sorry*, mom."

I glanced around the room to confirm the sudden shift in mood. There was general amusement as everyone relaxed in their hard metal chairs. Fala leaned back in her chair as the air went out of her balloon. She'd aimed and missed, but I was sure she would try to get the last word in.

"Okay... Well, then," said Fala as she quickly regrouped. "I just want to remind everyone here—patients and loved ones alike—that you don't need to be afraid to speak the truth here. This is a safe zone. And if you're uncomfortable speaking up in front of the group, you can always come to me in private. With anything. Is that understood?... Good... Now, I just wanted to reinforce with you, Russ, the importance of listening. Listen to your son. I think that would do a world of good for both of you."

"Thank you, Fala," I replied. "I think that's great advice, and this's been very educational. I'm sure my son and I will benefit greatly from it." It sounded patronizing because it was.

Fala nodded curtly and turned her attention to another patient. "We only have a few minutes left. Ray, we haven't heard from you yet."

I sat with Jan in a booth at Denny's and sipped my coffee. We hadn't spoken for a while—just sipped our coffee and reflected on the evening's events—when she suddenly broke the silence and said, "Thanks again for stopping. I know it's late… But I hate eating alone."

"No problem." I smiled and studied her face. At forty-three, she was still a very attractive woman. Her smooth complexion was absent any crow's feet, or other tell-tale signs of aging, and her blue eyes still held the color of robin's eggs. When she smiled, there were lines on her cheeks that had lengthened over the years but they gave her face a deeper, more mature look. Her light brown hair showed no gray, and if she touched it up, I couldn't tell. She'd put on a little weight over the years but it didn't really show, though she was bigger in the bust than when I first met her. That was in '74 and she immediately reminded me of Miss August 1970, who later became Playmate of the Year in 1971. Neither was beautiful. They were pretty and sexy, with cheerful smiles, and Jan shared the same great body with sporty tits, a slim-curved body, and even the same bikini tan lines. Jan was twenty then and I couldn't get enough of her.

She wore a loose blouse, light blue in color, that was unbuttoned enough to show the beginning of her cleavage, and a pendant rested just above it that was in the shape of an owl, her favorite animal. I was a bit surprised to find her in white shorts today, given it was a rehab meeting. Most of the women wore jeans or slacks to these counseling sessions but not Jan. More than once I caught myself admiring her legs as she sat in her chair next to me.

"How's the job going?" I asked. She worked at Hewlett Packard in Palo Alto and had been there over ten years.

"Good. Growing leaps and bounds… Got a nice bonus end of last year."

"I bought one of your laser printers the other day."

"Jeez, you should'a told me. I could'a got you a discount."

"Dang," I laughed. "I'll remember that next time… So all's good? You dating anyone?"

"No," she answered as she glanced down, slightly blushing. "I mean I'm not dating at the moment, but I'm fine, good, except for this thing with our son. It stresses me out."

"I know."

"You don't think it's genetic, do you? I mean, with Danny. I've been thinking a lot about this lately. My granddad was an alcoholic. And on your side—what?—your mom was hooked on pain pills, wasn't she?"

"That was to deal with the pain from the cancer. I wouldn't call it an addiction."

"Well, it's got to be something. It has to come from somewhere."

"Maybe it's just a weakness. A character flaw."

"I don't want to believe that… Something had to trigger it. A child with a good upbringing, with loving parents, with every advantage, doesn't start sticking needles in his arm unless something drives him to it… I mean—and I know we've talked about this before, and they tell us not to take the blame—but maybe it was us, maybe it was me."

"Don't say that."

"But when I sit in those sessions and hear him talk, and hear the therapist talk, they make me feel it's my fault."

"Well, certainly that Fala creature wants you to think that."

She laughed at that, quickly regaining her composure. "Yes, Fala," she said with a wry smile. "She certainly had it in for you."

"For a second there I thought she was going to have me drawn and quartered—that whole abuse thing. She *wanted* to hear the worst. I felt like I was in front of the Grand Inquisitor—what's his name? Tor-something."

"Torquemada."

"Right. And Dan could have said anything at that point and she would have believed him… Madness."

She looked at me with an amused tenderness. "I wouldn't have let it go that far," she assured me.

"That's good to hear."

"Yeah, sorry about that. I didn't know it was going to be an ambush, or else I wouldn't have asked you to come... But you held your own, as I knew you would."

I shrugged my shoulders as if to say, "no biggie," and sipped my coffee. I wanted to change the topic. "Do you really jump in bed with me whenever I whistle?" I asked her with a mischievous grin.

She laughed. "I think it's me who does the whistling," she said.

"Hmm... But it's been a while."

"Last Christmas."

"That's right..." I remembered last Christmas. Her parents had invited me over for dinner. Dan was there. We exchanged presents and enjoyed a pleasant evening together, and afterwards Jan followed me home to my boat where we immediately jumped in the sack together. We were not your normal divorced couple. Even though I'd hurt her badly—and I took full blame for our divorce—we remained close through the years and occasionally, when the stars and planets aligned just right, we had sex together. We knew each other's bodies in detail, knew what pleased the other, and our trysts together were always enjoyable. Afterward, we would kiss goodbye and say something like "Talk to you soon" and go back to our separate lives.

But I knew she still loved me. I didn't need Danny's indiscreet announcement in rehab that "she's still in love with him" to know that. But she understood better than anyone that loving me was a zero-sum game, and she'd learned over the years to keep her passion in check as though it were precious keepsake hidden in a drawer. She lived her own life, and from what I could tell it was a full life. She dated—was even engaged once—and took her life one day at a time.

"How many women have you *dated* since then?" she asked. I shrugged my shoulders and turned up my palms in answer. "How many were over twenty-five?" she added.

"A few."

Her last question was a bit of a dig. Yes, I was a womanizer—she knew it, I knew it, hell, everybody knew it. It went without saying. It was my philandering that destroyed our marriage. She once accused me of marrying her out of a sense of honor, and she was probably right, but my actions after our marriage were less than honorable. My first infidelity was with her best friend. After that, I made a steady diet of attractive young women, both at work and in our social circle, doing my best to keep it a secret, but she soon learned the truth. At first she pretended to ignore it like some mobster's wife over his gumads, but after countless indiscretions on my part, anonymous phone calls, and a growing sense of humiliation, she finally kicked me out, accusing me of being "some kind of dumb-ass Hugh Hefner." Really, she did me a favor.

I was simply not the marrying kind.

The waitress came and asked us if we wanted refills on our coffees. We replied no and she set our check down on the table. "Thank you," I said.

"You haven't told me about your company," she said, changing the subject. "What's it called? CrestPoint Communications, right? What's happening with it?"

"Technically, we're in business now," I answered. She looked genuinely interested, and I still had half a cup of coffee left, so I gave her a quick summary, finishing it off with the bold prediction that in a couple of years, if all went well right, we would go public and have the capital to expand globally.

"Still chasing after the Golden Fleece," she said with a smile.

I smiled back at her. She liked to use historical allusions when she talked. That was the History major in her. I found her to be a romantic—in the philosophical sense. She believed that history made sense and taught us lessons, that events happened for a reason and that all of history was leading us inevitably to a better world. I thought it charming to think that way.

"Just remember what happened to Jason," she added.

"He died a beggar, I believe."

"Well, he lost everything—his family, his friends, even his fame and fortune. He roamed the earth a beggar, finally taking refuge underneath the rotting hull of the great ship Argo—the ship he used to sail after the Golden Fleece. It collapsed on him and killed him."

"I'll try my best to avoid that fate."

"I'm sure you will," she replied with a wink. "Just keep that boat of yours shipshape."

"You can bet on it." I finished the last of my coffee and picked up the check. "You ready?" We got up together and I paid the check and left.

It was a cool clear night. We were in Campbell, at the foot of the Santa Cruz Mountains, and I breathed in and caught the fragrance of pine trees in the distance. Jan lived nearby and I walked her to her car and hugged her.

"You don't need to go back there," she said, referring to rehab, "but it would be nice if you could call him once in a while to check on how he's doing."

"Of course."

"Maybe it will work this time. Maybe he'll stay clean and live a normal life—I pray to God."

She was still in my arms and I hugged her again, feeling her breasts press up against me and the warmth of her skin. "I hope so," I whispered.

"Bye… I'll call you."

I kissed her on the lips and turned to walk over to my car, a '77 Triumph Spitfire 1500. As I fished for my car keys I heard a noise, a sort of soft screeching sound, and I stopped and listened. It was gone—but as I took another step I heard it again, this time louder. I turned back towards Jan and saw her standing next to her car watching me. She tried to whistle again and I laughed.

I acknowledged her whistle with a nod, got in my car, and followed her home.

Chapter 3

Known to Russ Chappel, and only one other person on earth, was the uncomfortable truth that he'd had an affair with a married woman seven years ago. To compound matters, she was the wife of one of his employees (though they were separated at the time). He didn't make a practice of bedding married women, in fact, quite the opposite. Call it a code of conduct. Married women were an unnecessary complication to be avoided, and given there were so many single, beautiful women in the world to choose from, he found it best to keep married women, no matter how desirable, at arm's length. But this particular woman created a set of circumstances that caused him to violate that code (not that he didn't help her along the way).

Her name was Ronnie and she was the spitting image of Miss July 1983 with her blonde hair, five-foot-five shapely frame, 35-inch bust, and heart-shaped lips. Russ first met her at a Christmas party in 1986, and even though he was with an attractive blonde of his own, he couldn't keep his eyes off of her. And more than once she caught him looking at her. Later that night, after he shook hands with her husband, she stepped forward and hugged him saying, "Nice to meet you."

He continued to run into her over the years at company functions and family barbecues, and they became friendly. She would stop and talk with him, always listening intently to anything he had to say, and she would lightly touch his arm or leg (if they were sitting) to emphasize a point. He even invited the two of them out on his boat for the sole pleasure of seeing her in a bikini, and he always sensed she noted and appreciated his admiration for her beauty. But if there was anything between them, it remained unsaid; she was the mother of two young kids, her husband was a man he liked and admired, and they seemed happily married, so Russ was content to admire her from across the room and fantasize about her in his head.

That all changed a few years later. At a company picnic Russ threw every summer for his employees, she snuggled up next to him at a table and they talked for a good hour while her husband played horseshoes. She was a talkative woman with a seductively husky voice and he enjoyed listening to her. The conversation was warm and light-hearted, and whenever one of her kids came up asking for something she'd shoo them off and tell them to "talk to daddy." There were no hints or subtleties in their conversation, just a convivial flow of words, back and forth, and she complimented him on how well he listened. Then she mentioned that her husband was traveling a lot.

"Yeah," he replied sympathetically. "He's heading up that project for us down in L.A. Hopefully he can wrap it up in another week or two."

"Hmm," she hummed indifferently.

It was then he put two and two together. Her husband Mark had pushed hard to take on this project even though it entailed considerable time in Los Angeles, and Russ had given it to him along with a promise of promotion if it went well. He flew back home every Friday night to spend the weekend with his family, but Russ perceived now for the first time that this arrangement had put some strain on their marriage. This perception was reinforced by the fact that not once during this day-long picnic had Russ seen her and her husband kiss, hold hands, or even talk to each other. When it came time to say goodbye, she came up and hugged Russ as usual but this time she lightly scratched his back with her manicured fingernails.

That little scratch on the back played in his head for days. Not that he wondered what it meant—he knew exactly what that little signal meant—but coming as it did from a married woman, from a playmate look-alike and the wife of his employee, there was a certain forbidden-fruit flavor to it he couldn't get out of his mouth. A week later she called him at his office in San Ramon. She was shopping nearby in Danville and wanted to know if he was free for lunch. Sure, he said.

Russ met her at an Italian restaurant where they hugged hello and she gave him another suggestive scratch on his shoulder, this time ever so lightly. He ordered the linguini with clams, she had the chicken Caesar salad, and all the time she kept up a running commentary on her shopping chores. She wore a red, low-cut blouse with a tight-fitting black skirt and he couldn't keep his eyes off her tender neckline and inviting cleavage the whole lunch. He decided to test the waters by telling her that her husband's project was due to wrap up next week, so things would be going back to normal.

"That's good to hear," she said. The indifference in her voice was thunderous.

They finished lunch and he walked her out to her car, a blue mini-van, and they hugged. This time her manicured nails skated across his back with an evocative swirl. When they came apart, she held on to his arms and looked up at him with hungry eyes and a half-open mouth. He pulled her back in and kissed her hard. She gave as well as she got, but after a long ten seconds she suddenly turned her head and pushed away.

"I can't," she stammered. "I'm sorry…"

"It's all my fault," he said, knowing that was a lie. He reached out to take her hand but she pulled it away as though from a hot flame.

"No… I'm sorry. I have to go." And with that she jumped into her car while he stood and watched her start up the mini-van and pull out. As she drove by, she glanced over at him with a wonderfully guilty smile on her face.

It was then he knew exactly what he was going to do, and to his everlasting regret he did it the very next day—he pulled a David and Bathsheba. Just as King David sent the husband of Bathsheba into the front line of battle to get rid of him, Russ easily created a set of circumstances that caused Ronnie's husband to stay in Los Angeles for another month. But her husband didn't welcome the news like Uriah and instead was stoical and slightly bummed at the prospect of spending another month in L.A., but Russ reminded him of the promotion awaiting him at the end of the tunnel. This promise along with the man's sense of loyalty swayed the argument, and when he told Russ that he'd stay the course, even thanking him, a twinge of guilt that would grow to something bigger passed over Russ.

Two days later, Ronnie called him and said, "I need to talk to you." Her seductively husky voice made it sound like an invitation, and he suggested they meet later that night on his boat. She was hesitant at first but Russ persisted. Suddenly she blurted out, "Mark and I are separated."

"Bloody hell. Sorry to hear that," he said. "Come to my boat. I'll whip up a little dinner and we can talk. Just the two of us. No interruptions… You must tell me what's going on; I want to hear it all. Say you'll come."

"Okay."

Over the next three weeks they screwed exactly three times. Due to school, soccer practice, and babysitters, they could only meet on Wednesday nights. The first time was fresh and exciting and a night to remember. After a couple glasses of wine, she let her guard down, and when he took her into his arms she didn't resist and let him guide her into the bedroom where she suddenly came alive, nearly tearing his shirt off and diving into his pants. They fell onto the bed, their clothes half off, and went at it like they were on a timer. She fucked with a guilty pleasure, as though the whole thing was sinful—a sinfulness she would drink to the last drop like a savory wine. When they were done, she dressed quickly, kissed him goodnight, and hurried off saying she had to take the babysitter home.

The second time something was missing, a small thing like an eager smile, but he could feel it nevertheless. It was in her touch—the abandon was gone—but she still seemed to enjoy herself, coming fiercely with a loud moan as he poured into her. Afterward, she left in a hurry again to go drive the babysitter home and feed the family dog, this time leaving without a kiss goodbye. As Russ lay there in bed, the seed of guilt he'd felt weeks ago began to grow, and he got up and made himself a drink.

By the third time, he knew it was over. After fucking in almost a business-like manner, it was obvious that her guilty pleasure had worn itself out and all that was left was just the guilt. And like the clap, she had given that guilt to him. She also knew his reputation—knew that there was no future with him. The best she could hope for was a long-drawn-out fling before he moved on to someone else. And Russ really had no energy to try and draw it out any further, which was a decision made easier by the fact she didn't give head. He'd offered himself to her a couple of times, once pushing her down gently towards his erection and the other time walking up to her face as she sat on the bed, and both times she turned her head away. He found it rather disappointing.

Gorgeous as she was, she was a soccer mom who didn't give head, and he had a date with a breath-taking redhead the following night who he knew gave great blow-jobs. So, they said goodbye without a kiss or a scratch on the back, and two days later she called him to end it.

"Mark can never know about us," she said dramatically. *"Never-ever!* Do you hear me?"

"Of course."

"And one more thing?"

"What's that?"

"Give me my husband back."

After they hung up, Russ made a few calls and wrapped the L.A. project up to everyone's satisfaction. Her husband was happy and thankful to hear he was going home, and never once did he mention or complain to Russ that he was separated from his wife. Russ admired his unruffled poise.

He also gave him his promotion.

CHAPTER 4

Russ buzzed him in at the gate and Mark walked down the dock to where *Danny Boy* was moored. As he approached, he saw Russ standing in the stern of the boat and the tanned, lean, six-foot-four frame that he remembered so well reached up and waved him on. He waved back and hurried his walk.

"Hey, Russ. Good to see you," said Mark with a big smile. "Permission to come aboard."

"Permission granted."

They warmly shook hands. If Russ Chappel looked the same to Mark after all these years, then Mark Kirkland looked pretty much the same to Russ. "Here, let me look at you," said Russ as he let go of Mark's hand and stepped back to appraise his old employee.

Mark was nearly six feet tall with thick blonde hair and wide shoulders. He had a hardy, Scandinavian look about him, handsome and soft-spoken, with the same dark green eyes of an artist or poet. At close range, Russ detected some ash coloring around Mark's temples, but other than that he looked younger than the forty-year-old he knew him to be. He wore blue jeans and a green polo shirt that was tucked in, accentuating his flat stomach.

"Still hitting the gym, I see," said Russ.

"I try… Still riding your bike?"

"Not so much—still playing racquetball. Did you bring your racquet?"

"*Nooo*," replied Mark, rolling his eyes. "And if I did, I wouldn't admit it. I still have painful memories of getting my butt kicked by you."

Years ago, Russ had been an excellent racquetball player and Mark was sure he still was.

Russ laughed at that. "So, what's it been?" he asked Mark. "Seven years? I still had the Sea Ray back then. How do you like this baby?"

Mark glanced around the motor yacht. "Quite a set-up, Russ," he said. "Where's the crew? On leave?"

"It's just me... Let me give you the dime tour."

Mark followed Russ as the latter took him around the boat. Russ was most interested in showing him the twin diesel engines and explaining the modifications he'd made to the fuel injection system to increase engine efficiency to over 55%. Both men were mechanical engineers by education and training, and the topics of compression ignition and torque adjustment were discussed and easily understood. As they talked about air-fuel ratio, Mark got an opportunity to get a closer look at his old boss.

Besides being tall and lean with a russet-brown tan, Russ was one of the most impressive men Mark had ever run across. Along with his charm and intelligence, the man was strikingly good-looking. It was almost a classic, Hollywood handsomeness with symmetrical features, chiseled cheekbones, and gray insightful eyes. At forty-four, he still reminded Russ of the 1930s actor Errol Flynn, but now older and more distinguished-looking, as though someone had carefully etched his face to give it just the right touch of weathered refinement. He wore a neatly trimmed mustache above his thin, expressive lips, and his reddish-brown hair, now slightly receding, was cut short and parted neatly on the left. He moved with the tactful grace of an English Gentleman—never rushing, using deft hand movements, sitting cross-legged—and it was an image Mark was sure he cultivated.

They went through the cockpit and into the cabin as Russ pointed out interesting features along the way. The cabin, which looked like a studio apartment with a couch, recliner and coffee table, was surprisingly large and Mark applauded the décor with a *"Niiice!"* as he scanned the room. A few things caught his eye: framed prints of nudes, tastefully done, one by Goya and two others by Vargas, hung on the wall. There was a bust of

Winston Churchill, which Mark remembered from years ago, an antique sextant, shelves that contained handsome, leather-bound books, including books by Churchill, the Hornblower series by C.S. Forester, Moby Dick, as well as a couple of best-sellers by Harold Robbins. Next to the bookcase sat a nice little bar that appeared to be well-stocked. On the coffee table were some technical magazines along with the latest edition of *Playboy*.

Russ also showed him the sleeping quarters, one room that contained two bunkbeds for guests and the other a master bedroom. He quickly swung the door open and close on the master bedroom, giving Mark just a brief glimpse of the interior. It was enough time for Mark to note the queen-sized bed and a painting of an English fox hunt above it.

Mark smiled to himself at that—the hounds chasing the fox. Some things never changed. Russ was still the Grand Bachelor and this floating pad was proof of it. Russ' reputation as a lady's man was legendary. Back in the day when Mark worked for him, his rep was well-known, and their friends and colleagues privately referred to him as a smooth operator, a skirt-chaser, and a *Don Juan*. His combination of charm and good looks, along with a deep, strong, masculine voice seemed to act as an elixir on women. And not just any women. When they worked together and attended social functions, Mark always saw him with an attractive woman on his arm. And not just attractive but beautiful—Playboy caliber. Yet he never brought the same woman twice to an event or seemed to date any one woman more than a couple of months. It was a lifestyle that seemed to fit him, like Wilt Chamberlain or his look-alike Errol Flynn who had made an art form out of it.

"Let's settle in here," said Russ. He pointed Mark to a spot on the couch while he sat down across from him in the recliner. "Like anything to drink? Soda, beer?"

"No thanks."

Russ nodded and regarded Mark for a moment. He really wanted this man for the job but luring him away from SBC was going to be a challenge. How much he would have to offer to secure his talents would soon become apparent. His motives for going after this man were complicated; it was partly an appreciation of Mark's abilities, their history together, and perhaps even a little bit of guilt was involved.

The two men first met twelve years ago in 1985 at a meeting in San Francisco. This was right after the break-up of Ma Bell, and they both worked for Pacific Bell who, like the other Baby Bells, were now in business for themselves. Russ was a director, on the shortlist for VP promotion, who brought an impressive resume with him (Stanford grad, Bell Labs, Pac Bell Executive). He had a reputation for making the complicated simple, and for finding talent. Mark, on the other hand, hired into AT&T out of high school and worked his way up the ladder. He had a reputation for being smart and driven, and for getting things done.

At that meeting, each man got a taste of the other's talents. There was Russ' strategic thinking, his ability to extrapolate, and his uncanny knack for explaining the complicated in simplified terms. There was Mark's operational acumen, his ability to deconstruct a problem and his gift for driving workable solutions. In a way, they complimented one another, and over a short time and several shared meetings, they struck up a rapport and, with it, a desire to one day work together. Russ saw in Mark a quick-thinking dynamo which he could use in his organization to get things done. While Mark saw in Russ an astute leader, a clear thinker, and someone who could help him advance his career.

Russ was soon made a Vice President of a new, expanded organization, and he recruited Mark to come over and take on one of the key positions. Mark worked for Russ for the next four years until Russ abruptly left to go work for Metropolitan Fiber Systems, but during that time Mark learned a lot and successfully took on any challenge Russ threw at him. Mark viewed Russ as his mentor, and Russ, for his part, groomed the younger man for advancement. And true to his word, Russ promoted Mark to director level before leaving to go to MFS.

That was seven years ago.

"How are the kids?" asked Russ.

"Great. Lacy just turned fourteen and is a freshman at Sacred Heart. Brandon's twelve. Both doing the normal stuff—homework, sports, watching too much TV, keeping their grades up—knock on wood… How's your son? What's he now, in his twenties?"

"Twenty-two. He's fine… And your wife? How's Ronnie doing?"

"Great," replied Mark with a smile. "Works part-time at Nordstrom. She's big into aerobics these days and works out all the time. She wants to teach a class."

"Good to hear," said Russ. At his question about Ronnie, he had closely watched Mark's body language, carefully looking for signs that Mark might know or perhaps suspect the truth. It only took a few moments for Russ to confirm what he hoped for. After seven years, she'd kept her secret safe.

They made small talk for another couple of minutes before Russ cut to the point of their meeting. "I need you on my team, Mark," he said.

"I'm flattered."

"Just a fact. We're in a race up the mountain, and the first one to establish market share across America is going to win. Proof of concept will be in six cities, four on the west coast and two in the Midwest. This is where we prove to the investors we can do what we say we can do. Then after that, we're targeting seventeen major market areas to begin with, some thirty-six cities in all. The key is going to be speed to market, and that means establishing collocation and installing the equipment. Your forte—driving deployment plans, meeting aggressive deadlines, and getting it done. That's Mark Kirkland."

"You mentioned on the phone you've hired Lucent to do the installation… I know them. And Copper Mountain's your supplier?... I don't know them."

"They're solid. We did our research."

"Anyone else?"

"Cisco for the backend—to tie into the operational support systems."

"*Cisco*… I wish I had stock in Cisco right now."

"You'll have stock in CrestPoint, which is even better—and a VP title to go with it. You can hand-pick your own team."

"Where's all this capital coming from?"

"Venture capitalists. There's a boom happening right now. I'm sure you're seeing it as well. Everybody's pouring capital into the Internet. If you're an Internet provider or got a dot-com after your name, you're golden. They're throwing gobs of money at you and expecting a big payoff down the line."

"Like the transcontinental railroad?"

"Precisely, only this time it's the Information Superhighway."

"Well, everyone's throwing capital at it except SBC.

"Baby Bells aren't tailored to deliver a groundbreaking product in such a short amount of time. Look at how long it took them to roll out touch-tone dialing—even after they had the technology. Like twenty years."

"Tell me about it. You've heard about the ADSL product we're developing. Our version of your product. I got the engineering piece of it but the Product Team is just spinning its wheels."

"Let me guess. You've broken down the systems you need, the resources required, and the money it's gonna take to do it properly but nobody will listen. Nobody wants to commit resources; I.T. says it will take two million and two years to deliver the systems to support it; and the result will be half-measures and kluge solutions. And in a year from now, when CrestPoint starts selling DSL to customers and is front page news, your upper management will go ape-shit and demand to know why your product isn't ready to go. Everybody will start pointing fingers, and it'll be CYA time. In the end, after heads have rolled, they'll pour the money and resources into it that they should'a done in the first place, but it'll be a day late and a dollar short."

"Sounds about right."

"We don't have that problem. We're a start-up—without all that heavy baggage. We'll be at the top of the mountain looking down while SBC's still putting their shoes on."

"I can see the advantages, but start-up companies are risky, even if they are well-funded."

"True, it's a bit of a gamble. So was the railroad. But it's not like we're trying to open a bookstore in a neighborhood full of bookstores. This is DSL—high-speed internet—and nobody else is doing it. Not even the other CLECs. We've got the brain trust, the telecom experience—we've got the vision. Marty Madrid is our CEO. He's our vision-guy. Wait till you meet him; he'll blow you away… Trust me when I tell you we're assembling the best and the brightest. And everyone's all in, Mark. No half measures."

Russ paused for a moment and studied Mark's reaction. It had been reserved and mildly curious up to this point, but it lacked the enthusiasm he'd hoped for. But he knew Mark well enough to bank on two things: he loved a challenge and he wasn't happy where he was. Russ was sure of this latter fact because he'd kept tabs on Mark over the years through his contacts at SBC. The man was well-respected, but after seven years, he was still a director. His career was languishing, and there was a general perception that he was growing restless. It was this restlessness that Russ was banking on.

"I wouldn't expect anything less," replied Mark. "But the gamble remains..." His voice trailed off as he noticed a boat motoring by. It was all rigged up for deep-sea fishing and heading for open waters.

"You just had a downsizing last month," said Russ. "That couldn't have been any fun."

"No... I hate 'em. The rating and ranking—well, you know. You end up letting good, hard-working people go, and it's no fun. It's the one part of the job I truly hate."

"Probably another one coming mid-year."

"Very likely. It's SBC's formula for bumping up the stock price."

"Well, you'd be stepping into a situation where you're hiring people. Maybe even some of those good people you had to let go last month. We're ramping up to about a hundred employees this year, then probably five hundred into next year. You'd be right in the middle of that—hiring, growing—building a network for high-speed Internet."

"I like the sound of that. It's been a long time since I've built a team."

"You might like the sound of this as well—Vice President of Deployment. Your VP title will come with a commensurate salary along with a stock option plan that could make you a wealthy man in a couple years when we go public. No guarantees there—we have to perform—but just as an example, when MFS went public in '93..."

Mark half-listened to Russ' tale of how MFS went public and how Russ and his peers made out financially after their Initial Public Offering (or IPO). Mark's real attention was on his own misgivings, not about CrestPoint Communications. He was sure it was everything

Russ said it was. Nor was he confused by the task at hand—it sounded challenging and exciting. No, his biggest misgiving was the time away from his family a job like this would entail. To succeed, he would have to sell out and go all-in, and that meant long hours, eating and sleeping the job, and staying in pit-bull mode most of the day. Not that this necessarily worried him; as long he came home every night to his wife and kids, he was certain he could manage it. But it was the travel. That was the kicker. They were targeting thirty-six cities and that meant travel, possibly extensive travel, likely for weeks at a time. That was a non-starter for him. Seven years ago—in fact, when he was working for Russ—he had led a project down in L.A. that kept him away from his family for months. The strain had nearly wrecked his marriage, and he wasn't going to let that happen again.

Russ was handing him a folder. Mark came out of his reverie and reached over and took it.

"I've laid the numbers out for you," said Russ. "Your salary, your stock options—take a look at it."

Mark studied the sheet of paper. It was professionally made up and contained his full name, birth date, and proposed new title of Vice President of Deployment along with a projected start date. The salary was about ten grand more than he made now and the stock option plan was broken down by the number of shares and his current stock price. As he reviewed the tempting offer, he caught the tune of a song coming into the cabin from outside. He lifted his head and listened, recognizing the tune at once as *Oh Happy Day* by The Edwin Hawkins Singers.

"What's that?" Mark asked.

"It's a bloody nuisance is what it is," replied Ross as he walked over to the window. "We have some holy rollers a couple berths down and every Sunday they like to crank up their gospel music." He slid the window shut, muffling the song, but Mark could still hear about the happy day when Jesus washed our sins away.

"There," said Russ as he returned to his seat. "What do you think about the numbers in front of you?"

Mark paused, feeling the moment at hand. Why did that song float into the cabin just now, he wondered to himself—just when I was reviewing an opportunity of a lifetime? *Oh Happy Day*. It was an omen and a good one. He felt a tingle up the back of his neck as though his guardian angel (and he was sure he had a guardian angel) was trying to tell him something. He wasn't looking at the numbers anymore—they were a blur on a white piece of paper—and instead waited for logic and his engineer's mind to calm his inner emotions.

To Russ, it looked like Mark was impressed by the numbers and was collecting his thoughts before he answered. He felt confident the answer was going to be yes.

"The numbers are attractive," said Mark in a flat tone. "I'd be lying if I said they didn't interest me. They do. But there's a lot to digest here…" He set the folder down and looked Russ square in the eyes. "Do I think it's an exciting challenge?—I do. Do I think CrestPoint has a solid business plan?—I do. DSL is going to sell like hotcakes. But am I willing to give up on SBC, a company I've worked at for over twenty-one years with great benefits and relative security? Am I willing to give up on all that to take this gamble with you, a man I respect and admire?"

"Thank you, Mark. That means a lot to me… You know the salary is negotiable" Russ added this last part with an ingratiating smile.

The man had a way about him, thought Mark. He knew how to put people at ease and how to flatter and entice without coming off as smarmy or pushy. Yet the push was there, hidden underneath the charm, and it was tenderly persistent and almost seductive. He could see why women were attracted to him.

"We can talk money… But it really comes down to one thing, Russ. Travel. You're talking thirty-six cities—across the country… I've got growing kids and a wife that wants me at home. The last time I was away from home for an extended time was that project of ours down in L.A. and it almost cost me my marriage. I don't want to go through that again. So, we can talk money, but if I'm expected as VP of Deployment to crisscross the country and spend weeks away from home… well, that's a non-starter."

Russ cleared his throat before replying: "I don't want my VP of Deployment crisscrossing the country. I expect you to put together a team that will do that for you. We'll have a national presence, but your office will be in San Jose. But straight up—at first—will you need to travel? Probably. You need to assemble your team and get your hands dirty in the initial roll-outs, but we're talking two-to-three-day trips max then back home to your family. After that, there shouldn't be any travel, not unless something goes completely wonky and you have to fly out to give it your personal attention."

Mark nodded his understanding. He could hear the muffled lyrics of another gospel tune coming through the closed window. It sounded like Whitney Houston and was something about holding on, God is on his way. "I report directly to you and no one else?" he asked confidently. "And I pick my own team—no interference, no second guessing?"

"Absolutely."

"Give me a day or two. I need to talk to my wife… Today's Sunday. Give me till Tuesday to give you an answer."

"Take the week if you need it."

"Tuesday."

"Very good… Now, we're moving into our offices Tuesday, so page me and I'll call you right back."

"Will do."

Russ got up and walked over to the bar. "Want a cold one?" he asked

"Love one."

Russ returned and handed Mark a cold bottle of beer. "Cheers," he said. Mark returned the "Cheers" as they clicked bottles. Russ sat down and they enjoyed their cold beer, reminiscing a little about their days together back with Pacific Bell. As they talked, part of Russ' brain took inventory of their meeting. He was confident that Mark would say yes—that after talking to Ronnie, comparing dollars and prospects, and envisioning himself building a team and leading a national deployment, he would pull the trigger. It only needed to soak in for a day or two, and he would say yes. Luring Mark Kirkland away from SBC would be a big win for CrestPoint Communications; it would demonstrate that they could draw top-notch talent into their ranks based solely on the power of their business plan. He had a good feeling about it.

Mark, for his part, assessed his chances of taking the job at about 60-40, slightly in favor. It would depend greatly on Ronnie's reaction since he put great store in her opinion. The money was good, the stock options incredible, the job itself a tantalizing mountain to climb, but it was a risk. All start-up companies were a risk. So, why take the chance, he asked himself. But he already knew the answer to that question. There was another reason pushing him towards this job that he didn't like to admit to himself. Yet it was there nevertheless, like a black dog following him through the neighborhood, and he couldn't shake it. Maybe this job was the antidote to a kind of malaise that had settled into his soul. It was a vague and growing discontent with his life that was becoming noticeable, and perhaps, just maybe, this job was God's answer to that problem.

They talked for a half hour and Mark finished his beer. "Gotta run," he said, getting up. Russ stood up with him and the two men shook hands. "Sunday dinner at my mom's," he added as an explanation. "And much to think about."

"Like I said, take your time. It's one of those crossroads decisions and I want you to be certain."

"Appreciate that."

They walked out to the stern of the boat where they shook hands again before Mark stepped down onto the dock. Russ gave a quick salute and headed back into the cabin.

Mark breathed in the brine-scented air and smiled to himself. He was feeling pretty good. He would talk this over with Ronnie, run it by a couple of trusted colleagues back at SBC, and make a decision. He was certain that the right decision would reveal itself.

Two berths down he came upon a smaller cabin cruiser that was playing the gospel music. He slowed his walk and glanced down to read the name of the boat. It was the *Sea of Galilee*. Glancing up he saw above the cockpit a worn and weathered sign, carved in wood, which said "Follow me, and I will make you fishers of men." He sniffed a laugh at the harmonious wit of it all.

"How's it going?" sang out a cheerful voice.

There was a man about Mark's age sitting cross-legged on the roof of the cabin that he hadn't noticed before. The man was shirtless.

"Doin' good. How 'bout yourself?"

"Couldn't be better! You have a blessed day!"

"Thanks! You, too."

Mark walked on, his already buoyant mood fortified by the man's cheerful sincerity. Once in his car, Mark popped in a cassette tape, *Simon and Garfunkel's Greatest Hits,* turned up the volume, and sang the lyrics out loud as he drove home.

Chapter 5

❦

"How did Russ look?" asked Ronnie.

"Pretty much the same," replied Mark. "Still tan and fit-looking… He's got a bigger boat—a motor yacht. It's like forty-five feet long."

"Wow. Did you guys take it out?"

"No, we sat in the cabin and talked about the job."

The Kirklands were returning from Sunday dinner at his mom's house. Mark was driving the mini-van while Ronnie sat in the passenger's seat. Their kids sat in the back seat. Lacy, the older daughter, listened to music through her headphones and watched the traffic out the window. Her brother Brandon was absorbed in his hand-held video game. It was about a half-hour drive home and this was the first chance Mark and Ronnie had all day to talk about his job interview.

"So tell me more about CrestPoint Communications. They're gonna sell high-speed Internet, right? ADSL—the same product you're developing at SBC. How's it different?"

Mark smiled to himself. He appreciated how his wife listened to him when he talked about his work, and she knew the right questions to ask. "You're right, it's the same technology, but at the current rate it will take SBC five years to bring it to market while CrestPoint will do it in one."

"Okay, I can see that. And you said it's, what, like thirty times faster than our dial-up modem?"

"Right—only it's loop-limited. I didn't explain that before, but basically you only get those higher speeds the closer you live to the central office where the equipment is. The farther out the worse it gets until you don't get it at all."

"Will we get it where we live?"

"I'd have to calculate the distance… but maybe."

She hated their dial-up modem system. It was always going down and it took forever to download anything big like pictures or videos. Something faster would be great—she could see why people would buy it—but it'd be ironic if her husband helped build this product and they ended up not being able to get it.

"He wants you to lead the team that installs the equipment across the country," she said more as a statement than a question. "What would your title be?"

"Vice President of Deployment."

"It's a promotion then?"

"Yeah, and more money." He told her what his new salary would be and carefully explained how the stock options worked. This is what she'd been waiting to hear, he knew, and all their discussion leading up to this point had been foreplay. "But we're talking two to three years before going public," he continued. "And no guarantees—the company could go belly-up. But if all goes well and the company makes it big, then we're talking a major payday. We couldn't cash in right away. Legally you have to wait like six months, but—again—if all went well, we could see a lot of money."

"What's a lot?"

"Millions."

"Wow." Ronnie looked out the window as her mind quickly tallied up and calculated all the ways becoming a millionaire could improve their lives. They weren't exactly poor but they were stretched, what with mortgage payments on their house, Catholic schools for the kids, and numerous other expenditures that came with maintaining an upper-middle-class lifestyle. They couldn't travel much and drove used cars, and many home renovations remained undone due to lack of funds. Even her wardrobe suffered from the restrictions she put on her own spending. All that could change with millions of dollars.

Ronnie Kirkland was born Veronica Lynn Roth to a Jewish father and Irish-Catholic mother. Her father was a rich and powerful executive at United Airlines and settled his family in a large estate in Hillsborough, California, which was an upscale town nestled in the peninsula foothills and included the likes of Bing Crosby, the Hearsts, and other famous millionaires. Besides being from a rich family, she was a knockout from a very early age, and hers was a life of plenty—plenty of playthings, plenty of boyfriends, and plenty of freedom. But at seventeen she got pregnant. Her parents took her out of school during her pregnancy and arranged for her to give up the baby for adoption. Afterward, she could feel the great disappointment and shame emanating from her parents like a kind of oppressive chill, and at eighteen she moved out and got a job at a travel agency (with the help of her dad) and rented her own apartment.

Though they never disowned her, Ronnie still felt ostracized by her family. She attended birthday parties and holiday dinners but there was always a coolness, that aloof affection from her parents that made her feel estranged and unwanted. It became her goal in life to win her family back and reclaim the life she deserved. She would prove to her parents she was a woman of substance. To that end, she dedicated herself to her own self-improvement, working hard at her job, taking night classes, and only dating the right men. Given her looks and intelligence, dating the right men should have been easy, but it wasn't. Most men she wanted to date—men with high-paying jobs or from rich families—just wanted to screw and move on, especially when they learned she had a daughter floating around somewhere. But she kept her focus, enjoying a good lay now and then, knowing the right man would eventually show up.

She met Mark at a night class on Business Fundamentals. She thought him good-looking and found he was sharp and well-spoken when he talked in class. And he noticed her. Soon they were dating, and she swiftly learned that he was intelligent and driven, had a great job, and was good in bed. He also didn't give a damn about her teenage pregnancy. After a month of dating, she did the unprecedented and invited him over to her parents for Thanksgiving. To her delight,

Mark and her dad hit it off, and she saw that both her parents were impressed by his drive and intellect. He won their hearts and minds permanently a month later at Christmas dinner when he got down on his knee in front of her entire family, opened the box containing a large diamond ring, and asked her to marry him.

Her mother insisted on a big Catholic wedding, which her parents paid for, and they honeymooned in Ireland. Upon their return home, she found herself pregnant and lobbied hard to get them out of their one-bedroom apartment and into their own home. That it had to be in Hillsborough went without saying, even if it was way out of their price range, for it would symbolize her return and prove to herself that all her hard work had paid off. She asked her parents to give her an advance on her trust while simultaneously prodding Mark to talk to her dad about helping out with a loan. In the end, she got her house, gave birth to two kids, and kept her early marriage problems hidden from friends and family. But her marriage was rock solid now, and her quest to achieve the life she truly wanted—rich and full and admired by others—was nearly complete.

"What are you thinking?" he asked.

She heard the question and pulled out of her daydream. "The money would be nice," she replied evenly, hiding her excitement. "It would help with their school… We could pay off the mortgage. Do other things we've put off for years… But the real question, dear, is what do you think?"

Her business-like tone didn't fool him. He knew exactly what she was thinking. She was excited at the prospect of becoming rich and was already spending the money in her head. This didn't make her greedy or mercenary; he understood her better than that. She was a woman who had a clear picture in her head of the kind of life she wanted for her and her family, and she kept that picture in focus, working towards it in increments, daily, like an artist painting on a large canvas. She was a good person who knew what she wanted, and he admired her for that.

"It's a big commitment," he said. "At a level deeper than what I'm at now. I'd have to put together a team then build out a national network from scratch. We're talkin' long hours, long days, weekends, even some travel in the first year. And that's my biggest concern—I can't go into it half-ass; it has to be all or nothing—and my biggest concern is the time away from you and the kids… Remember what happened last time."

"And we learned from that."

"We did," he agreed, his mind racing back to seven years ago and the *lesson* they had learned. There had been growing fights over his time away from home and then, one day, she turned it off, went cold, and started treating him like a stranger, and he was sure their marriage was over. But then, almost like a miracle, she was crying and wanting him back, and then suddenly he was back home and all was good again. But he wasn't sure what *lesson* was learned from it all other than to stay close to home.

He reached over and squeezed her hand, and she smiled back at him. They drove awhile in silence, both glancing at a line of billboards along the side of the freeway. The odd collection of billboards had been there for years along Highway 101, sitting across the road from the city of San Carlos, having sprouted up in the bay marshlands like so many weird saltwater giants. Until recently, they had advertised local Ford and Chevy dealerships, appliance stores, and restaurants, but now reflected the growing Internet and dot-com boom by displaying giant ads from companies like America Online, Prodigy, @Home Network, Ask.com, and others. They were colorful and eye-catching but when they got to the end of the line, Russ caught a glimpse of a smaller billboard, set back from the others, that simply read 'Jesus Saves'.

It suddenly reminded him of the gospel songs that floated into his ear during his interview with Russ. They were like some divine-sent message, and he wondered if he should tell her about it. But he decided against it. Oddly enough, during fourteen years of marriage, they had never talked about God, and he didn't want to start now. He'd stick to practical matters.

"There's also no going back—to SBC," he said, breaking the lull. "If this thing doesn't pan out, there's no going back to my old job. I'd be resigning. So that's the risk—with a start-up like CrestPoint, that would be the risk."

"It's not like you don't have marketable skills—and a great reputation in the business," she replied quickly. "If it came to that, you could step into a job at AT&T or Atlantis or some other firm like that. They'd love to have you… So I'm not too worried about that, and you shouldn't be either." As she continued along this vein, building up his rep and minimizing the risk, she sensed that he was leaning against taking the job. He was throwing out a lot of negatives and not many positives. Why is that, she wondered to herself. Does it have something to do with Russ? Does he know about our fling seven years ago? Does he suspect something? No, deep down in the pit of her soul she was sure he didn't suspect… But still.

She had hidden her nervous surprise when Mark told her about Russ calling him out of the blue and wanting to hire him. At first she thought Russ might be trying to insinuate himself back into her life, but she quickly discarded that thought like a stale piece of bread. She hadn't spoken to him since their last night together on his boat and she was sure that Russ, like herself, regarded the short affair as a stupid mistake.

She knew why it happened; she'd been lonely, feeling neglected, and halfway suspected that Mark was cheating on her with someone down in L.A. Russ was an easy choice. He had a reputation as a playboy; he was handsome with a polished masculinity, and she'd caught him several times admiring her body. So, she made it happen. But halfway into the affair she realized her mistake, and it wasn't so much her conscience as it was her own prudent good sense that caught up with her. Russ was never-ever going to be anything more than a good fuck, and risking marriage and respectability for that was downright idiotic. It didn't add up. So she wrapped up her affair with Russ as though she were closing out an empty bank account, took stock of her feelings for Mark (yes, she loved him, still loved him, and would always love him), and put things right again because she possessed the power to do so.

Mark drove on, listening to her talk. This was their usual dynamic—she talking, he listening—and it felt comfortable to him. Her monologues could go on for five to ten minutes, even get interrupted in spots, but never lose their expressive rhythm or general theme. She was like a smooth jazz artist, pleasing to the ear, and she was never more pleasing to Mark than when she built him up and made him feel special.

He exited the freeway at 3rd Avenue and drove onto their house while he listened to her talk about how Russ, who prized his talents, was obviously cherry-picking him for the job because he was the only one Russ trusted to do it right.

Their house sat on Gramercy Drive, right on the border of Hillsborough and San Mateo, and he pulled into the driveway reminded of the fact that they lived on the Hillsborough side of the border—not the San Mateo side—and how important that fact had meant to Ronnie when they bought the house.

It was nighttime, nearly time for the kids to go to bed, and they piled out of the mini-van in relative quiet listening to their dog whine in the backyard. Mark glanced up at the roof. It was over thirty years old and needed replacement, and he thought how he could pay for a new roof if he took the job. They went inside and commenced their well-practiced routines: the dog was let in and fed, messages listened to, garbage taken out, homework assignments checked, the TV turned off, pajamas put on, teeth brushed, and kisses goodnight made.

———

Ronnie sat on the edge of the bed in her bra and panties listening to Mark pee in the bathroom. It was a loud, steady stream and sounded like a horse peeing in a wet field. It was a sound she had heard a hundred times before and her thoughts wandered off with it.

She really wanted him to take this job but she knew better than to push him. The money was good, but that wouldn't be enough to convince him. He valued her opinion and would do almost anything to please her, but not even that would be enough to uproot him from a secure job he'd had for over twenty years unless he was inspired. She felt he was close to being inspired. He just needed a spark.

He finished peeing and she could hear the sounds of him brushing his teeth at the sink in their bathroom. There was one other reason he needed to take this job, she thought, and she hadn't brought it up to him yet because she wasn't quite sure what it was or how to express it. That was because she only sensed it—like a deep, underwater current she had only a slight sensation of it from the surface of his personality. But it was there nonetheless. And it wasn't a discontent—she didn't like that word—but it was something like that, something akin to restlessness or even boredom. Not that he was bored with her or their life. If she was sure of one thing and one thing only when it came to Mark, it was that he loved her and the kids with his heart and soul. It was a different kind of boredom, and she'd seen it with her father. It was just that hole inside men that always needed filling up.

He walked into the bedroom in his boxers and she stood up to greet him, coming into his arms to kiss him tenderly on the lips. He grabbed her tight, finding her tongue, swirling them together, then kissing her neck as he reached behind and unfastened her bra. She arched forward, slipping out of her bra, and he bent his head down to kiss her lavish breasts before sliding his lips back up to her waiting lips. He began to maneuver her onto the bed where they could lie down and make love, but she surprised him by gently yet firmly pushing him back so she could sit down on the bed facing him.

A wonderful whim flitted into her head, a timely inspiration—a gift she hadn't given him in years—and she went with it, looking up at him with eyes filled with carnal submission, and pulled his boxers down. She grabbed his erect cock like a baton and started giving him head.

His initial shock at this sudden turn of events filled his mind with passing thoughts (*she never did this; yes, when they dated, when they were first married, then she stopped; but it didn't matter to him; she was ablaze in bed, so he didn't care; and unlike other women her age with two kids she loved sex, so he counted his blessings*) but these thoughts were quickly eclipsed by the sweet sensations erupting in his head.

She went gently at first and then slowly picked up the pace while he spread his legs slightly so she could play with his balls. It didn't take long—no more than two exquisite minutes—before he came in her mouth, a bolt of pleasure soaring up his spine and into his brain where it burst like a multi-colored missile.

With a mouthful, she got up, humming happily past his ear, and went into the bathroom where she spit out his cum and washed her mouth out. Drained and happy, he pulled his boxers up and fell face-first onto the bed.

She came back in and snuggled up next to him in bed. "You like that?"

"Hmm... that was great."

"Thought you'd like it. Now get some sleep... And remember this when you dream—you need something to fill you up... Something more."

"Hmm... Something more."

He felt her kiss him on the cheek and say "I love you, babe." He hummed it dreamily back and quickly fell asleep. An hour later, he was deep into an oddly-shaped dream.

First he is on Russ's boat—the old one from years ago, then the new one—and Russ is showing him the engines which look like something from a souped-up muscle car. There are other people there who all seem to know him but he doesn't know them. Ronnie is also there sitting in a corner, watching him closely. A woman in a Playboy bunny outfit walks around carrying a drink tray... Next he's out on the bay, just he and Russ, and Russ asks him to take the helm. The wheel is shaped like a large, chrome-plated fish with the letters IXOYE inside it. He's seen the letters before but can't remember their meaning.

"Look there!" yells Russ. Mark glances off the port side and sees the outline of a giant, whitish whale swimming next to them. Russ says it's a rare creature and they need to follow it, and rapidly Mark steers around islands and rocks in pursuit of the creature as Russ cheers him on. This goes on for a while with dogged persistence... But now he's standing on the dock. Evening is setting in. Next to him is

moored the Sea of Galilee and a man sitting cross-legged on the roof of the cabin is inviting him on board. The man is shirtless with long hair. He has wonderfully serene eyes and his calming voice beckons Mark to come aboard. Mark takes a step towards the boat but stops when he feels a hand on his crotch. It's Ronnie and she's behind him and she's reaching around to massage his crotch while she whispers in his ear. Quickly he gets a hard-on.

When he woke up, he found Ronnie playing with his cock, giving him an engorged, aching hard-on. Groggy, not sure if he was still dreaming, he came fully awake when she slipped off his boxers and climbed on top of him, sliding down onto his erection with a pleasured gasp. He held on to her hips and let her do all the work, and after she came, he turned her onto her back and took over. They went hard at it, breaking into a sweat, giving each other their all, whispering, breathless, until finally, feeling himself close, he flipped her legs up over his shoulders so he could drive home even deeper. Within moments she grabbed a pillow to muffle her loud moan, and he followed right behind her with his own orgasm. He lowered her legs and eased himself down into her arms where their warm, wet bodies slid into a locked embrace.

"I love you so much," she whispered, breathing in the heavy masculine aroma of his body.

"I love you."

"It doesn't matter what you do—I'll always love you... Do what you have to. Fill yourself up. You know I'll always be here for you."

"I know."

They remained like that, locked in their embrace, man and wife, whispering to one another in a duet of soulful words until the pauses between the words grew longer, the silence in-between more exquisite, and they fell asleep in each other's arms.

Chapter 6

The offices of CrestPoint Communications Inc in Rio Seco Business Park, located off Montague Expressway in San Jose California, in the heart of Silicon Valley, were in controlled disarray. Desks, chairs, and office furniture sat unpacked across the carpeted floor, either delivered to their spot or parked off to the side on the way to their destination. The debris of moving in—cardboard boxes, bubble wrap, Styrofoam, and binding straps—lay in piles off to the side, leaving a clear path for the movers to continue their delivery. Mixed in with the movers were telephone installers laden with heavy tool belts, IT techs running Ethernet cables and setting up computers, new employees carrying in boxes, and the occasional pizza delivery man.

Marty Madrid felt like a kid in a candy store. His candy store. He'd been in the new offices since six this morning, bouncing from one small project to another, helping move a desk, supervising a cable installation, testing phones, talking with everyone he met, and now at almost one o-clock he paused and stood, his short-sleeved shirt heavy with perspiration, and took in the buzz of activity.

This was fun, he thought. The beginning with all its hopes and energies and sprouting possibilities was always fun, though it wasn't like him to stop and think about having fun when he was in the middle of it. But the high he felt made him reflective, like a carpenter contemplating a stack of fresh-cut lumber.

"Hey, no rest for the wicked," joked Russ as he passed by carrying a box to his new office.

"Ha!" laughed Marty as he watched Russ whisk by. Like everyone else, Russ sported the day's attire—blue jeans, a short-sleeved shirt, and tennis shoes—but as always, he dressed in a way that seemed coolly unperturbed. Marty noted that his shirt was still nicely tucked in and his jeans, which fit snugly around his buttocks, seemed almost tailored to his frame. "Hey, is your phone working yet?" he called after Russ.

"Not yet."

"I'm on the case, Watson," called out Marty.

"The game's afoot," Russ yelled back as he disappeared into his office.

Just ten minutes before, the telephone guy had assured Marty that all the phones would be up within the hour, that the problem wasn't the wiring in the building but rather at the "office end" of the business PBX, and not to worry. "What, me worry?" he had replied to the installer with his best Alfred E. Newman smile. The joke was lost on the young man.

Paused in reflection, self-communing, Marty's mind generated electrically charged tendrils of thought, some connected, others seemingly random, in a self-perpetuating current of activity… *Where's that installer, the one who looks like Luke Skywalker with a goatee? May the force be with you. He's merely a drone in this hard-wired world. At the mercy of the Empire. Why can't it all be wireless? That day is coming, I'm sure of it. Wireless local area networks. Shared frequencies and overcrowding are the problem—solved by wireless routers and multiple antennas in a star configuration. The architecture is clear. Or IP Telephony—that's the future. But probably years away. Our LAN is a wired morass of copper tentacles, like wisteria that creeps and coils itself through the building. Ethernet—invented by Robert Metcalfe, the same guy who predicted the internet would collapse in 1996. Foolish prediction. Chandra is giving us 10BASE-T, at 10 Mbs, in a bus topology. Plenty of speed to give birth to our DSL baby. And my wife is due any day now. Back home in San Anselmo, the hills of Rose Valley, stored away in our condo like a ripe watermelon. And the watermelon is a boy, or so the sonogram says. The magic of TV. Hana is probably in her recliner right now watching TV, drinking whole milk and munching on chocolate chip cookies…*

The thought of his wife brought a small wave of guilt but he shook it off and walked out towards the reception lobby. There he found their new receptionist Shawna—trim, attractive, and slightly harried-looking from the day's hectic activity—and gave her a smile. She beamed back at him like a lighthouse in a storm.

"Did you get some lunch?" he asked her.

"Yeah, a piece of pizza."

"Breakfast of champions. Have you heard from Gordons yet?" Gordons was the art gallery where he had purchased a large picture of Jerry Garcia. It was an illustration of the Grateful Dead guitarist with a colorful graffiti-style overlay to it. Perfect for his office.

"They said by three."

"Awesome." Marty glanced out the large windows and saw Stuart Baum standing out front. He was smoking a cigarette. The double doors were propped open for the movers and Marty walked outside to speak to Stu.

There were two other people standing with Stu, all of them smoking. This was a common sight in front of business across America—small, huddled groups of smokers, exiled outdoors, getting their nicotine fix before their break was over.

"Phone working yet?" he asked Stu.

"No… Computer's up."

"Really? CFO gets his computer fired up before the CEO. How's that happen?"

"It's who you know, not what you know," replied Stu with a smile, flicking his cigarette. He raised his other hand up which held his Nokia cell phone. "Just talked to the Sand Hill people and confirmed 10 am on Thursday."

"Good. I want to include Russ in our presentation this time round."

"Why?"

"For some of the technical stuff."

"You know it as well as he does."

"True—but he's got a knack for making it simple." He watched Stu shrug his shoulders. It wasn't lost on him that Stu didn't care much for

The Heights of Mountains

Russ and vice versa. "Pow-wow in my office in a half an hour. Just the five of us. Let Ron and Chandra know if you see 'em."

"Got it."

Marty walked back in and crossed the large floor—the large floor where cubicles and workstations were being assembled—and headed towards his new office. On the way, he passed by Russ' office, rapped on the door jamb to catch his attention, and told Russ about the meeting in a half hour before continuing to his own office. Marty's office was the biggest one in the building. It already contained a small conference table with six chairs, a white board, and a counter that would eventually hold a coffee machine and small refrigerator. The office sat in the northwest corner of the building and overlooked a dry creek, manicured bushes, and a couple of large oak trees where squirrels romped and played. He sat down at his desk, an expansive, mahogany model with a glossy finish, and leaned back in his leather chair.

His multi-line phone was powered on and he picked up the receiver and put it to his ear. Still no dial tone. He set the receiver back and swiveled his chair to the left to face his computer screen and keyboard. His desk was ergonomically designed to allow him to face his computer screen and keyboard with a straight back. One click of the mouse turned the black screen into a bright start-up window. Another click told him there was no Internet connection. "Shit!" he said to himself.

He thought about chasing down an IT tech—even finding Chandra if need be—to get his computer up and working, but instead he got up from his chair and went over to the white board. There was a black marker and an eraser ready to go. He drew a sideways 8—the infinity symbol—then erased it to ensure the marker and eraser worked as advertised. After that, he began writing on the board.

He wrote out five bullet points. They were the five goals from *Thriving on Chaos* by Tom Peters, a top-selling management-philosophy book from 1987. Despite being ten years old, Marty firmly believed that the tenets preached in the book on how to build a winning company were as relevant now as then. The five goals, which he had committed to memory, were written out in a flowing cursive style:

• 61

- *Creating Total Customer Responsiveness*
- *Pursuing Fast-Paced Innovation*
- *Achieving Flexibility by Empowering People*
- *Learning to Love Change*
- *Building Systems for a World Turned Upside Down*

Finished, he stepped back and admired his handiwork. Just then an IT tech appeared in the doorway. "Just need to put on an RJ-45 connector and you'll be good to go," said the tech.

"Have at it," replied Marty. The young man looked to be around twenty-two with a smooth complexion, like melted French-vanilla ice cream, that contrasted with a shock of jet-black hair. Marty met him at the desk and bent down with him as the tech fished for the end of the Ethernet cable. Like his wife, the young man was Asian. As the tech grabbed the cable, he smiled over at Marty who was barely a foot away from him. The suggestive smile and soft coffee-colored eyes confirmed what Marty suspected.

The tech cut the end of the cable, prepped it, and crimped on a connector as Marty silently watched him. "Nice work," complimented Marty. The young man smelled of sweat and a hint of Aqua Velva after shave. "What's your name?"

"David."

The tech reached under the desk and plugged the cable into the hard drive then stood up. "May I?" he asked Marty, indicating the chair in front of the computer.

"Be my guest."

David slid smoothly into the chair and lined up with the keyboard. After a few mouse clicks and keystrokes, he had Marty's home page up. "That should do it," he said.

Marty put his hand on the young man's shoulder and peered in at the screen. "Hit the browser," he said, and David immediately clicked on the browser icon. The search screen quickly popped up. "Excellent," he said, gently squeezing David's shoulder.

The Heights of Mountains

"Hey, Marty!" He abruptly let go of David's shoulder and turned towards the door to see C.V. Chandrasekar. "Computer up?" asked Chandra. "Good—David, go set up Mr. Chappel. The other corner office. He's next." The tech popped up out of Marty's chair and left the office without a word.

"Give her a drive," said Chandra, then watched as Marty sat down at his computer and started clicking away.

"It's fast," commented Marty with a grin.

"Better be. We're paying enough for it… Stu said there was a meeting at 1:30—in ten minutes. I'm going to get a soda. Want something?"

"Ahh, yeah—Diet Pepsi."

Chandra left to find the newly installed and stocked soda machine in the break room while Marty accessed his email. There was nothing new, just day-old emails from Wolf Partners, a venture capitalist, and one each from an analyst at The Yankee Group and a reporter at PC/Computing, both wanting to interview him. Chandra returned in five minutes and handed him a Diet Pepsi. He opened the can of soda and sat down with Chandra at the conference table, making small talk until Russ, Stu, and Ron wandered in and sat down with them.

Russ glanced at the whiteboard, quickly scanning the five points. "Peters," he said simply.

"Yeah!" replied Marty loudly, capturing everyone's attention. "I know we've talked at length about the nuts and bolts of our company, but we've talked very little about management philosophy and I wanted to make sure we're all on the same page. *Thriving on Chaos*—brilliant book by Peters, and I'm sure you've all read it." (Everyone nodded in the affirmative.) "I can't think of a better playbook for us—in terms of creating the right management practice and organizational structure. We need to become revolutionary and remain revolutionary—on the cutting edge—quickly adaptable to change, and always-always *creating*—whether it's creating new product opportunities or creating value to existing products. This really needs to be ingrained into our business culture, one where we reward risk and innovation and abhor stagnation. I want our work environment—out there" (He pointed out the door.) "I want it to reflect our philosophy. It should be part play and part hard work. A place where people feel free to express themselves... like what they have at HP and Apple..."

"Now that Jobs is back," added Stu.

"And it's the little things that count," continued Marty. "A breakroom that's got great coffee—maybe Peet's or Starbucks—and vending machines with Drake's coffee cakes, Toblerone Chocolate or those Kettle Cooked chips instead of the run-of-the-mill garbage."

"Or Utz," chimed in Ron with a smile. "Ever had Utz potato chips? Yum."

"Then we'll stock Utz—and other delicacies to delight the palate. This will be a place where people wake up in the morning and *can't wait* to get to work—a place that balances work and play, that's fast-paced, open to ideas, and a cool hang-out. Kick your shoes off, walk around in your slippers, come to work in blue jeans and t-shirts if you want. Stuffy dress codes are for AT&T and GM—not CrestPoint. And our job is to create that environment. We need to nurture it, cultivate it, walk the talk—each one of us."

"We need a reward and recognition program that means something," added Chandra. "Not just trinkets and rhetoric. Something with meat on the bone, that has some lasting impact."

"Money," said Marty. "And not chump change. If you score a big sale with an ISP or deliver ahead of time on your installation dates—*boom*, a thousand-dollar bonus. Your name in lights. And group recognition as well. If all of us—and I mean the five of us here and everyone out there—if we work our asses off and deliver on our business plan then, *boom*, we take everyone down to Disneyland or Hawaii, with their families, and we say thank you properly."

"Let's start making money first," interrupted Stu with a rueful grim.

All five men chuckled at this remark as Marty pointed at Stu and nodded as if to say, "Point well-taken." Despite the mild admonishment, Russ, Chandra, Ron, and even Stu were caught up in Marty's energy. When Marty got worked up, animated like now, he was like a gifted evangelist who was both inspiring and entertaining to listen to.

"I want to board some key points here," said Marty as he got up from his chair and walked over to the white board. He drew a line down the center of the board separating the five points he'd already captured from a new list he was about to start. "Russ, let's start with you. Looking for key management principles we want to emulate—to cultivate a winning work environment. How do we empower people and make them feel valued?"

"Besides paying them on time?" quipped Russ, but his demeanor quickly turned more serious as he added: "If we're really sincere about empowering people, in making them feel valued, then it starts with a thing I call 'generous listening'. If we want to connect with our employees, *really* connect and make them feel engaged, then we must *listen* to them, deeply, with our full attention and interest. Don't come at them with preconceived ideas or with an attitude that you know better than they do. Open your mind and listen for the gems they have to offer you. No one-way streets or drill sergeants." On this last note, Russ shot a quick glance at Stu.

"No drill sergeants," echoed Marty.

"And what I find works well for me—in group sessions or conference calls—when you're trying to work through a problem, is the Count Basie Principle…"

"Count Basie? *The jazz musician?*" asked Stu with slight sarcasm in his voice.

"Hmm. That guy. It's the Count Basie Principle versus the Gene Krupa Principle. Both were big band leaders but with totally different styles. Krupa was a drummer and every one of his numbers features a big drum solo. The spotlight's on him. His band serves him. Basie, on the other hand, sits in the background delicately playing on his piano, keeping time, and every so often comes in with a brief solo, something short and eloquent, then lets the band go back to doing its thing. Everyone's in it together. Everyone gets their spotlight—and it makes for better music. So… we should manage the big band more like Count Basie, subtle and inclusive—and less like Krupa." On this last note, Russ shot another quick glance at Stu.

"Not like Krupa," echoed Marty. He had captured three points on the whiteboard that read:

- *Generous Listening*
- *No drill sergeants*
- *Basie over Krupa*

Suddenly a beeper went off. Russ reached down to his belt and pulled his beeper off, read it, then stuck it back on his belt. "Got to get this," he said, standing up. "Be right back—if I can find a working phone."

"My office," said Chandra.

"Got it." Russ left the room and Marty went back to his discussion, tagging Stu this time to give his input.

In less than ten minutes Russ returned to the room with a big smile on his face. Stu was still talking—at this moment about taking responsibility for the common good—when everyone's attention turned to Russ.

"What's up?" asked Marty. "Good news?"

"CrestPoint just scored big!" replied Russ. "We just hired our new VP of Deployment."

"Outstanding!"

"What's his name? When's he start?"

"Mark Kirkland," replied Russ. "Director-Network Engineering at SBC. He submitted his resignation, effective in two weeks."

"I know him," said Ron, who seemed very pleased by this announcement. "When MFS went into the Bay Area, he help fix problems with renting conduit space. Good man... This is a big thing. Some think we're taking cast-offs from the RBOCs, but now we took a top man away from SBC."

"Cream of the crop," agreed Russ.

"It shows we can lure top talent away from our competitors based on our business plan and potential," said Stu. "Analysts love that sort of thing."

Marty agreed with this perception and added that Kirkland's hiring couldn't have come at a better time given their upcoming meeting with venture capitalists. But with that, he quickly brought his team of officers around to the task at hand—flushing out and defining their innovative management style.

After another hour, and more bullet points on the whiteboard, CrestPoint's management style began to take shape. It was a blend of philosophies that started with the tenets of business gurus Peter Drucker and Tom Peters, along with a heavy dose of *Kaisen* (a Japanese business strategy they all heartily subscribed to). Also in the brew was a dash of Sun Tzu, a hint of Machiavelli, a sprinkling of Steve Jobs, as well as a splash of Captain Picard from the starship Enterprise. It contained such concepts as Continuous Improvement, Embracing Change, Management By Walking Around (MBWA), and a small potpourri of pop psychology and feel-good add-ons.

Pleased with the outcome, Marty would take about a day to whip the piece-parts into a cohesive whole and lay it out in a professional-looking PowerPoint presentation. From there it would be handed-off to his officers to roll out to their respective teams in a concerted effort to impart their philosophy to all their employees. Then everyone would be on the same page.

Marty checked his watch. It was six-thirty. He'd been in the new offices for over twelve hours, but he had no desire to go back to his studio apartment. Plus, he needed to call his wife and check on her. He'd put that call off long enough, telling himself he wanted to call her on his new office line and not on his wonky cell phone. But now his office phone was up and working and had been for the last hour.

He punched up the number and Hana answered on the first ring.

"Hey, Sweetie," he said.

"Marty!" answered his wife in dramatic surprise. "Where have you been? I called you a couple times on your cell phone. Didn't you get my messages? What number is this you're calling from?"

Immediately, Marty was put on the defensive by her questions that were less questions and more like soft accusations. She had a knack for that, he thought. Without skipping a beat, he launched into his explanation—yes, he saw she called, even listened to her messages to make sure it wasn't an emergency, but he didn't like talking on his cell phone, what with the delay and the sketchy audio, and had been waiting all day for them to install his work phone, which was what he was calling her on now. "And how are you feeling?" he asked, wrapping up his excuse.

She told him in elaborate detail, like a dental patient who explains all the worrisome specks and spots they found during her oral examination, and he listened patiently, sometimes responding with a comforting word or two.

"Is your sister there?" he asked.

"Yes, she's here. My mom was here earlier but she left. We're going to order some take-out for dinner. Have you eaten yet? You know I don't like it when you forget to eat. It's not healthy…"

Marty assured her he was going to eat and not to worry. She needn't worry. And after fifteen minutes of conversation, which consisted mostly of Hana describing her day, he finally got the information he was looking for, the information he could have gotten in the first ten seconds of their conversation. She was not experiencing any labor pains; she was uncomfortable but okay.

Satisfied that the baby wasn't coming in the next hour, and sensitive that Hana just needed a little TLC, Marty took over the conversation. As he talked, he could picture her sitting back in her recliner, the receiver to her ear with a slight smile, nodding and humming answers to his comments. He didn't know what kind of take-out she and her sister Miya were getting but she had to remember her diet, he reminded her. Keep your iron up and your blood sugar down. And you're taking your vitamins, right? Promise? "I know it's not easy right now," he continued. "It's like being married to a doctor, only I'm giving birth to CrestPoint Communications, and I have to be here for the delivery… Yes, everything is going well. I'm excited. You should be too. But not too excited. I need you to rest. Once we have our son, I'll move you down here into a house. I've looked at some places already—I think you'll love the area—and the three of us will be together.

The Heights of Mountains

"Remember, I'm only an hour away—an hour and a half at the most. Plenty of time for me to get up there for the delivery. We're going to do this together. Trust me. *Together*. Right? *Together*. Do you have faith in me?... Good, because you're the most important thing in my life and I love you. You know I love you?"

"I know, I know. I love you, too, darling. More than anything."

He could hear the warm satisfaction in her voice, and he took that as his cue to wrap up their conversation. Go eat your dinner, he told her, and he needed to eat, too—in fact he was starving. He'd call her before he went to bed. He promised. "Love you, Sweetie," he said. "I'll call you later... Love you, too... Gotta go... Bye, Sweetie."

As he hung up the phone, he noticed a figure come into the doorway. It was Stu. He must have been waiting outside the door for his conversation to end, which meant he heard the whole thing.

"Hey, Stu. What's up? You still here?"

"Oh, yeah," replied Stu as he entered the room. He had an assertive manner about him and walked as though he were stalking his prey. "Lots to do... How's your wife doing?"

"You heard all that, did ya? She's fine. Very pregnant... You have kids, right?"

"Yeah."

Marty waited for more but it wasn't forthcoming. He found it slightly odd that Stu, whom he knew to be married, never talked about his family. "Is Russ still here?" he asked, picking up the slack.

"Nah, went home. Banker's hours."

"Make sure he gets a copy of our slide show for Thursday. He may have some upgrades."

"Sure."

Marty knew from experience that there was more to this little visit than a friendly chat. Stu did not disappoint.

"We need to think about bringing on a Human Resource person sooner than later," he said. "Probably an EVP. Somebody to handle all the state and federal mandates, like sexual harassment training and workplace safety. It's a long list and all needs to be documented and made available to regulators. I know I don't want to do it, and I know you don't want to do it. And this department also needs to be responsible for hiring and staffing, contractors, and all that stuff."

"What does Ron have to say about it?"

"He's in total agreement."

"Okay. I know we've talked about this before, but I thought we were going to wait a bit. Until we got our core group in place."

"Yeah, I thought so, too. But some of this training, like sexual harassment and fair hiring practices are contingent on our business license. It can't wait."

"Hmm, got ya. Any candidates in mind?"

"Yeah, a few. It needs to be a woman or someone of color. That's another quota box we need to check. But it doesn't need to be a woman of color. Just one or the other."

Marty sniffed a bit of a laugh at that. "Right," he said. "You got my blessing, but we need to run it by the rest of the team. Especially if we're going to make her an EVP... Get this list of candidates to me. We'll let Ron do the initial screening, but the team will make the final decision."

"You got it."

"Good... Anything else percolating in that bean of yours?"

"Nah, that's it," replied Stu with a short laugh. "See you tomorrow."

He watched Stu stalk away and then he turned back to his keyboard to start shutting things down. He was *very* hungry, he realized. There was a restaurant he'd discovered, just across the freeway, called Athena's Grill that specialized in Greek and Mediterranean food. Their Gyro Plate with the seasoned beef and tzatziki sauce was his favorite. And they did take-out. He'd order ahead and pick it up and his way home. Pair it with a nice glass of Pinot Noir. The whole delicious prospect made him hungrier, and he finished logging off his computer, called 411 to get Athena's number, placed his order over the phone, and got ready to leave. He checked his watch and saw it was past 7:00 pm.

Another figure loomed in the doorway.

What now, he thought, but when he looked up, he saw that it was the IT tech, David.

"Still here?"

"Thought I'd check in one last time," said the young man. "See if you need anything."

Marty regarded David for a moment, letting the possibilities dance through his head. They both knew. And there the young man stood, framed in the doorway, with his soft eyes, French vanilla complexion, and jet-black hair. An engraved invitation. With just a word he could make it happen, and within the hour they would be lounging around naked in his studio apartment playing with each other's body. Tempting. *Very tempting.* But with this delectable urge came a sobering counterpoint, as Marty was a man who never lost sight of the big picture. He had a pregnant wife, and he owed her a call at bedtime. With success at CrestPoint and good publicity came great opportunities. A political career. Perhaps even a run at the governorship. And little flings like this brought liabilities. Not that he believed the young man would kiss and tell, but little chances like this added up and increased the risk. There were just too many unknowns with David. The risk was too great.

These thoughts played out in Marty's head in less than five seconds, and in the end the sobering counterpoint splashed cold water on his growing erection.

"No, I'm good," he replied, turning his back on those soft eyes and French vanilla cheeks.

"You sure?"

He heard the disappointment in the young man's voice. "Yeah, I'm sure," he said firmly. He could feel the figure linger a moment in the doorway and then disappear, and when he turned around David was gone.

Marty took a deep breath through his nose to clear his head and thought about his Gyro Plate. He'd pair it with a nice Pinot.

Chapter 7

Starting around 10:00 am, the break room at CrestPoint Communications began to see life as employees hit their morning break. It was slightly oversized for a staff of only twenty-one employees, most of whom had come from established corporations and were programmed to take their morning break at ten, their lunch at noon, and another break at three. They were used to seeing an active and bustling break room. But the traffic was minimal, for now. Some folks came in to grab an energy drink or a fresh cup of coffee and returned to their desk while a few lingered to shoot the bull and gossip.

"I heard they were going to put a Peet's Coffee in here."

"I thought it was gonna be Starbucks."

"No—no Starbucks. They wanted some exorbitant fee to set up a kiosk in here."

"Who told you that?"

"Ron Lau."

"No loss. They're from Seattle. Nothing good ever comes out of Seattle."

"Jimi Hendrix, Nirvana… Kenny G."

"Microsoft."

"I rest my case."

"What? Are you an Apple guy?"

"Yeah, I gotta Mac… Take a Mac over Compaq and Windows 97 any day."

"Don't let Chandra hear you say that."

"I know… What made him go with Compaq when he could'a gone with Mac?"

"Compaq is the number one selling PC in America, and 'cause he knows Apple's about to go bankrupt."

"Where'd you hear that? I thought Steve Jobs was back."

"As an advisor."

"Yeah, as an advisor, which means Scully is probably on his way out. Just look at their stock price. They're in trouble."

"Yeah, my sister works over there and says they're in trouble. There was a good article in Sunday's Merc about it. They got Macintosh clones on the market that are eating into their profits, plus they fell into development hell with their new software and got nothing to show for it."

"Watch Gates buy 'em up."

"Wouldn't be surprised. Then he'll be master of the universe."

"Not our universe, unless he plans on getting into the DSL business."

"Wouldn't put it past him—though we got enough competition as it is."

"Just Nomad, right?"

"And some company named Pulse Netconnections. Russ was telling me about them this morning. They're brand new like us, only out of Colorado. Got the same business plan with DSL, selling it through ISPs."

"Then that makes three of us…"

"Russ thinks that'll be it for now. The industry will wait to see how we do and who comes out on top—Hey, Craig. Giants win last night?"

"Yeah, three-two. Bonds homered."

"He's finally gettin' it going… And so Pulse makes three, and now we're gonna see who's Michael Jordan and the Bulls and who's the Utah Jazz."

"What we doing standing here for? We better get our ass in gear."

There was general laughter at this last remark. One of the four employees who had been talking peeled off, coffee cup in hand, while another joined the group.

"What you talkin' about? See Leno last night?"

"No, missed it. Why?"

"He was jokin' about this whole Eddie Murphy thing."

"Jeez, that didn't take long."

"The Eddie Murphy thing? You mean getting pulled over with a prostitute in his car?"

"Not just any prostitute—a transexual prostitute. And it was like four in the morning. He told the cops he was just giving the gal a ride home, and they let him go."

"Just performing a public service—cruising around at four in the morning giving people rides home."

"A Good Samaritan through and through."

"No doubt... Hey—I finally saw *The English Patient*. Rented it last night."

"Whatcha think?"

"Ehh... How did it win Best Picture? I don't get it."

"Didn't like it, huh? You and Elaine Benes."

"Elaine Benes?"

"Yeah, didn't you ever see that *Seinfeld* episode where she trashes the movie? Everyone is raving about *The English Patient*—gotta see *The English Patient*—and Jerry, I think it's Jerry, takes her to see it and she hates it. Then she gets dragged to see it again by girlfriends who disown her after she trashes the film."

"Then her boss Peterman makes her go see it."

"Yeah, it's a crack-up."

"If you want to crack-up, go see *Liar Liar* with Jim Carey."

"Yeah, I heard it was funny."

"It's hilarious."

"I'll have to check it out... Gotta get back on the phone with Telocity."

"How's that going?"

"They want to treat our order like a dial-up modem. It's DSL, dummies. Not dial-up modems. It's a whole new language to them."

"Hang in there. They'll get it sooner or later."

"Yeah, it better be sooner than later or else Marty'll sic the dogs on them."

The Heights of Mountains

"The dogs? You mean Stuart Baum?"
"Yep... Anyhow, gotta run."
"Later."
At this, the break room confab broke up and everyone headed back to their desks.

———

Barry was twenty-six and still lived with his parents. He was a manager at Blockbuster Video, which gave him enough of a salary to pay rent (a generously low $100 a month), keep his '85 Honda Accord running, and pour the rest into his state-of-the-art computer station where he spent most of his free hours surfing the web, hanging out in chat rooms, and trying to develop his hacking skills.

Today was a special day, and he had planned it out in detail with his other techie buddies. At exactly 10:00 am, Metallica tickets went on sale. At 9:45, he logged into the ticket website and, like thousands of other people, waited for the countdown. His two other buddies—Ender and Mo (short for Maurice)—were also logged in and awaiting the countdown. They were all on 28k modems, actually 28.8 kbits/s, 3200 baud, V.34 modems, and between the three of them, one of them was bound to score three tickets.

At 9:58, he got ready to click on the Buy button by poising his cursor over the red arrow. Click too soon and he'd get an error screen, thus losing precious time before he could get back to the Buy button again. Click too late and hundreds of others would beat him into the waiting queue. It was an art that required precision timing. But Barry was confident he would succeed. He had alerted his parents to stay off the phone for the next hour. That would eliminate the chance of his mom picking up the receiver on their shared line and causing his modem connection to go belly-up. He would have preferred a dedicated modem line but his attempts at convincing his parents to install a second phone line had failed. But he felt confident the line would stay clear, plus he used AOL, which had proved pretty dependable in the past.

• 75

At exactly 10:00 by his atomic clock (given to him by his parents on his twenty-fifth birthday), Barry clicked on the Buy button. He watched the download begin, and in less than fifteen seconds—bingo—he was in. The next step required him to choose the date (the twenty-second), the number of tickets (three), their seat location (Lawn), then hit Next and wait. Another excruciating twenty seconds went by before a message popped up telling him the tickets were available and please confirm your purchase. He clicked on the Confirm button and waited again. And waited. Over a minute passed without success.

He began to worry and checked his connection. It looked solid. The download seemed in order, but it looked like his screen was buffering. Another minute passed. He toyed with the idea of hitting the Back button—an act of desperation—but forced himself to wait it out. It wasn't time to panic yet. He took a deep breath to calm himself and patiently stared at the screen as though it were a work of modern art he didn't quite understand. After another minute and a half, the screen renewed itself with a message asking him to input his account password again.

That didn't make any sense, he thought, but he obeyed the command without hesitation. He quickly typed in his password and hit Enter. After another excruciating minute passed, he came back to the Confirm screen. Luckily, his order was still active—three lawn seats for the twenty-second—and he re-clicked the Confirm button and waited. A popup message told him he had four minutes and twenty-five seconds to complete his order. He was sure now that his order was processing.

At exactly the three minutes and ten seconds mark, his screen froze up as he saw his line go busy. Someone had picked up the receiver! He bolted from his chair and yelled out his doorway, "Get off the phone! Mom! I told you, get off the phone!"

He heard someone abruptly hang up the receiver, followed by his mother's voice, suddenly contrite and apologetic. "Oops, sorry... I'm *sooo* sorry. I forgot."

"Criminy, mom!" he yelled back at her. He quickly returned to his computer to assess the damage. His connection was lost. He plopped back down in his chair, frustrated by the turn of events but determined to prevail, and re-established his Internet connection. After five minutes, he was back at the Buy screen. After clicking on three lawn tickets for the twenty-second, he hit the Buy button and quickly got a message that all tickets were sold out.

"Shit!" he shouted, arching back in his chair.

After he calmed down, he checked in with his buddies (his back-up plan). They had fared no better. Now they were at the mercy of scalpers if they wanted tickets. The three of them commiserated through AOL Instant Messenger.

"It was the connection, Dude," typed Mo. "28.8k is too slow, and ur not even getting 28.8."

"Earthlink is offering 56k next month," typed Ender. "We'd have to change over and get new modems but that wood solve it."

"Its not the speed," countered Barry. "We need dedicated modem lines."

"Dude ain't gonna happen."

"Yeah good luck with that."

"We need DSL," typed Barry.

"DSL?" answered Ender. "Heard of it. Digital Subscriber Line. Right?"

"Right. Besides being like 30 times faster than a modem it shares the same phone line without interference."

"Dude! That solves it. How much?"

"Not available yet. Like next year sometime."

"Bummer Dude!"

"Cant wait."

Chapter 8

Marty stood at the head of the long conference table ready to speak. Both Stuart and Russ sat poised to listen along with four executives from Wolf Partners, a market analyst from World Markets named Frank Altobello, and another analyst Teri Starr from The Yankee Group in Boston. The spacious conference room looked out over Sand Hill Road in Menlo Park—the home of venture capitalists.

"Thank you, John, for the opportunity to come talk with you today," said Marty in his polished speaking voice. One of the suits from Wolf Partners nodded back at Marty. "The dynamic here is pretty straightforward—we're looking for money and you're looking to invest money. Match dot com couldn't have found a better match. Wolf Partners is looking to invest in the next best thing and we—CrestPoint Communications—*are* the next best thing. Now, that may sound like a boast, but it's not a boast if we can prove it—and that's just what we intend to do in the next hour… Stu."

Marty glanced at Stu who took the cue and clicked the mouse on the laptop that controlled their PowerPoint presentation. The laptop was connected to a projection screen that displayed the slides as Marty talked.

For the next fifteen minutes, Marty covered the history and the set of circumstances that had brought CrestPoint Communications into being. First, there was the Telecommunications Act of 1996 that opened up the local loop for competition, forcing the Baby Bells to share parts of their vast network at wholesale prices. This had given rise to hundreds of Competitive Local Exchange Carriers (CLECs) across the nation, each with similar business plans that included re-selling dial

The Heights of Mountains

tone to local phone customers and providing T1s, ISDN, and other digital services to business customers. Many had started building their own switches, laying in costly fiber optic equipment, and constructing cable TV networks.

"CrestPoint Communications is a CLEC," declared Marty. "Though some folks are calling us a DLEC—a Data Local Exchange Carrier. Why? Because our product is low-cost, high-speed Internet access." And this, he explained, brought them all to the second key driver: The Internet.

The Internet was everything. Even Bill Gates was saying the Internet was the most important thing. Just look at the exponential growth of home computers; the percentage of households in the U.S. owning computers had increased from 15% to 35% since 1990. And the Dot Coms were piling on, offering everything from books and CDs to clothes and dog food for online purchases. Our whole economy was now based on information technology, and having a home computer was no longer a luxury—it was becoming a necessity.

"And what does every one of those online buyers want?" asked Marty with a knowing look in his eye. "They want low-cost, high-speed Internet access. And that's where CrestPoint Communications comes into the picture."

Russ listened as Marty talked about the Information Age and how CrestPoint was poised to break the mold for Internet providers. Stu sat across from him looking every bit the Corporate Lawyer/CFO/CIO/CCO (and anything else he imagined himself to be) in his dark gray suit and red power tie. Russ leafed through a hard copy of the PowerPoint presentation to familiarize himself with the slides he was going to speak to. Stu had handed him the hard copy right before their departure with a half-ass apology for not getting it to him sooner. But it didn't matter. Russ knew the material inside and out.

His real attention was on Teri Starr. The market analyst from Boston appeared to be in her early thirties and reminded him just a bit of Miss October 1990 with her shoulder-length auburn hair and dark, manicured eyebrows. She sat with her notepad, looking every bit the Ivy

League grad in her dark blue, pin-striped dress with matching blazer, and the white blouse she wore underneath the blazer was unbuttoned just enough to make a glance worthwhile. Upon being introduced, her handshake lingered as she looked him up and down with an approving smile. Since that moment they had been playing eye tag with one another, and he was certain the sexual attraction was mutual.

Teri doodled on her notepad, half-listening to Marty's history lesson, as she continued sizing up Russ Chappel. He was certainly a tall drink of a man. He was tan and handsome with symmetrical features that reminded her a bit of an old actor whose name she couldn't recall at the moment. She saw poise and confidence in his bearing, and his brown, corduroy sports coat over a turtleneck sweater extenuated his lean, athletic frame. She guessed him to be in his early forties and full of experience, and there was no doubt in her mind that he was interested in her. The Yankee Group had sent her out here to the venture capital of the world to get a firsthand look at the movers and shakers, and there was no reason she couldn't have a little fun of her own while she was at it.

This instant chemistry between Russ and Teri was not lost on Stu. He quickly noticed the two checking each other out. That was just like Chappel, he thought. Couldn't keep his dick in his pants. Always on the lookout for poontang. It was the man's fatal flaw and a flaw he would use one day to take him down. But in the meantime, this could work to their benefit. A little fling, a romantic interlude, might incline Ms. Starr to encourage her company to give CrestPoint a high-buy rating right before our IPO. It might mean a few dollars more on our stock price. So plug away, Chappel—plug away.

"And now I'd like to hand things over to Russ Chappel, our Chief Development Officer, to talk about the science behind DSL."

At the sound of his name, Russ took his attention away from Ms. Starr and nodded at Marty. He walked to the front with a swashbuckling stride and faced his audience with a winning smile (at least, that's how Teri saw it), then told a joke about two scientists (who walked into a bar) that everyone laughed at before he launched into his presentation.

Russ covered the basics: DSL worked over the same twisted copper pair that your phone worked over. It wasn't expensive fiber optics, coax, or wireless, and required no trenching or costly towers. It was the same twisted copper pair that your modem line came over—only it was twenty-five to thirty times faster than a dial-up modem at around 7 Mbps downstream with 640 Kbps upstream, and 1.1 Mbps in both directions. And it was a clean, uninterrupted connection. This was possible because DSL split the frequency with the phone line.

"But it's distance limited, correct?" remarked Frank Altobello. Like Teri Starr, he'd been sent out to Sand Hill Road to "get his nose in the middle" of what was going on.

"Yes, it's distance-limited," replied Russ, "with data rates diminishing the farther out from the central office you get. But we've calculated that CrestPoint can deliver dependable DSL service out to a radius of thirteen thousand feet. According to our analysis, this covers nearly 90% of businesses and homes."

"That jives with our analysis," said Teri, smiling up at Russ.

Frank nodded at this and tried to make eye contact with Teri, but her attention was locked in on this Chappel guy. He'd met her before, back east. She was unmarried with a reputation for enjoying men—rich, intelligent, and powerful men—but had turned down his invitation to dinner despite his best efforts. Now it was obvious she had her sights set on this Chappel guy and it slightly irritated him.

Russ paused, waiting on another question, then launched into a description of how the equipment worked. It started with a small box (a DSLAM[4]) that would be placed in a collocation rack in the central office. A slide illustrated how everything connected end to end. This triggered another question from Frank.

"What's this all going to run?" he asked. "I mean, you got to lease the line, pay for collocation, install the box—what's your estimate on cost? What are you running with in your cost/benefit analysis?"

Russ didn't have a number yet—that would all be flushed out in their proof-of-concept trials—but before he could respond, Stu jumped in.

---

[4] Digital subscriber line access multiplexer

"Fifty-thousand… per collocation site," said Stu.

Russ had never heard that number before and had no idea where it came from. But he kept quiet.

"Fifty-thousand," echoed Frank. "Seems kind of low."

"Based on what?" replied Stu. "Talk to our competitors—talk to Nomad—and I think you'll find they're running with the same number."

"I will. Thanks… *Fifty-thousand.* Hmm." Frank wrote $50,000 down on his notepad for all to see.

Russ would talk to Stu and Marty about that number. He didn't much appreciate Stu throwing it out without running it by him first, but Marty didn't seem bothered by it. Perhaps they knew something he didn't. Despite the surprise, he remained unruffled and continued his presentation without a hitch. When it ended, he handed the podium back to Marty and glanced over at Teri as he headed back to his seat. She smiled approvingly at him.

It was time for Marty to deliver the coup de gras.

"Today, Internet Service Providers like AOL have these giant modem pools in every city," declared Marty, pointing to a slide that illustrated his point. They use dedicated services like T-1 lines and aggregate all this Internet traffic somewhere else before transporting it to other cities." Here Marty paused and waved his hand like a magic wand, revealing a new slide that painted a different picture. "In the future, ISPs won't have to do any of that. Instead, they'll become sales and marketing companies for us… We will sell them DSL. They, in turn, will take our high-speed data service and resell it to small and medium-sized businesses and residential customers across the country."

Marty took a breath, and with a fiery passion in his eyes, pointed out at his audience like a rock and roll performer up on stage. *"With your funding*—with Wolf Partners' *help*—CrestPoint can build this DSL network, operate it, and maintain it. This will free Internet providers to concentrate on finding customers, operating E-mail and the World Wide Web network, and selling the service at retail prices. They'll also answer the phone if anything goes wrong…"

The Heights of Mountains

Here Marty paused again for dramatic effect before hitting the high note in his performance. "CrestPoint will build a DSL network at wholesale prices, mark it up, and sell it to ISPs. And they—not us—will resell it to a data-hungry population looking for fast and reliable Internet service. CrestPoint will do all this without cumbersome inventories, warehouses, or large Sales and Marketing divisions. We are the elegant solution enabling the world to exploit the full potential of the Internet... Any questions?"

There were nods and pleased smiles all around the room. Except for Frank Altobello. It was obvious to him that Wolf Partners was going to back this venture. In fact, everyone from VCs to investment bankers were falling over each other to pour money into companies like this one. Even his own company was on the bandwagon, so he certainly wasn't going to get in front of that freight train. But he would try to show that it wasn't quite as rosy as this guy Madrid was making out.

"What are your assets?" he asked Marty.

"Our employees," sang out Marty, his voice filling with pride. "That's our greatest asset—the talented and creative people who will take CrestPoint Communications to the top of the mountain."

"Capital assets."

"Minimal—that's the whole point. The small box Russ mentioned will be installed in central offices across the country, even internationally. Collocated... So, in that regard, collocation will be our capital asset."

"Then everything else will be leased or outsourced. If I'm understanding you right?" asked Frank, pressing on before Marty could respond. "You'll rent collocation space from the Baby Bells, which they don't want to give up, lease their copper lines, which they also don't want to give up, and hand it all off to the ISPs to sell and troubleshoot?"

"Exactly!" replied Marty with a knowing smile. "But in the words of Jerry Garcia, 'It's all part of it, man'" He used a slightly stoned voice to quote Jerry, which elicited some chuckles from the other attendees, but he quickly turned his tone back again. "Will the Baby Bells make it difficult? They'll try. But they're obligated by law to comply, and we have one of the best corporate lawyers in the country to make sure they do" (Here he nodded towards Stuart Baum.) "We also have people on our team—people like Russ—who come from the Bell companies and know them inside and out and know how to beat them at their own game. So, we're very confident we have a winning formula."

"But your business model—and correct me if I'm wrong—is based on speedier downloads," said Frank, giving Marty a knowing smile right back to him. "To be successful, you're betting that everyone in the world is going to want speedier downloads."

"I know I do," stated Teri sharply. "The timing is right."

"Correct, the timing's perfect," echoed one of the suits from Wolf Partners.

"I agree the timing is right," replied Frank. "That's not my point. My point is you don't have any other products to fall back on. Unlike the other CLECs, who offer multiple products, you just have DSL. Correct?"

"Correct," replied Marty with a shrug. His demeanor could change on cue, from showman to serious businessman to starving artist, and now he took on the role of the tolerant college professor who must now draw pictures to make an obvious point to his dull student. "And IBM *just* sells computers. It's not just speed… DSL will be a faster, cheaper, and more reliable product than anything on the market. It's a knockout punch. And, in time, our product line will grow, and our footprint will become global."

"You use words like 'global' and 'international'," said Frank. "Are you planning field trials in other countries?"

"Yes," replied Marty, his voice turning confidential. "I'm in negotiations with a large consortium in Europe—I can't mention any names at this point—but we're looking at opportunities to take CrestPoint Communications global."

This statement surprised Russ, and he shot a glance over at Stu, who kept his head down. Did he know something about this, he wondered? In chats with Marty and in discussions in their staff meetings, this topic of negotiations with some international consortium had never come up. Was Marty just ad-libbing, or was there really something going on he didn't know about?

The Heights of Mountains

"Interesting," said Frank. He scribbled in his notepad and looked back up at Marty. "Sounds exciting." That was all he had to say. The body language around the room was decidedly against him and he could read it loud and clear.

John, the head honcho from Wolf Partners, cleared his throat to speak. He hadn't much appreciated Frank's line of questioning and he intended to clear the air. "Thank you, Marty," he said. "I know we don't have any questions. You covered the ground very thoroughly, and we appreciate your time and effort... Our goal here at Wolf Partners is the creation of wealth. We accomplish that goal by identifying a big problem—and we believe that costly, slow, and unreliable access to the Internet is a big problem—then match it to an elegant solution that solves the problem. You've given us that. We're absolutely convinced that DSL will solve this problem in an affordable and efficient manner. It just takes someone to do it. Which brings us to the next step in reaching our goal—finding an entrepreneur and his team that can make it happen... I can say, and I speak for all of us here at Wolf Partners, that you, Marty, are that entrepreneur, and CrestPoint Communications is that team. Congratulations."

There were pleased smiles all around. In short order, the conference room was cleared except for Marty and Stu, along with John and one of his lieutenants. They would talk money while the others waited in a plush anteroom.

Frank Altobello admired the burgundy leather furniture in the waiting lounge and wondered how much it cost. He talked with the two suits from Wolf Partners about price-earnings ratio and the New Economy while watching Teri and that Chappel guy out of the corner of his eye. They looked awfully chummy together.

After a half hour, the four men came out of the conference room smiling and shaking each other's hands. Marty winked at Russ and Russ took that as a sign that they had got what they'd come for—at least two million in funding. He excused himself from Teri's presence and peeled off to talk with Marty and Stu. Marty quickly confirmed that

• 85

Wolf Partners had committed $2.1 million in capital to their venture. It was a big win.

"What was all that about some large consortium you're negotiating with in Europe?" asked Russ, keeping his voice low.

Marty shrugged and smiled mischievously. "A creative lie," he said.

"So, it's not true?"

"It will be true."

Russ glanced over at Stu but Stu, again, avoided his eyes by looking down. It was all a little bothersome—this 'creative lying'—but he supposed it hadn't done any harm. Just as long as it didn't become a habit.

"Look, guys," he said, quickly changing the subject. "I'm having lunch with Teri and we're taking her car, so I'll get a ride back with her."

"What took you so long?" joked Marty. "Meanwhile, I think we'll see what Mr. Altobello is doing for lunch. See if we can't tune him up."

Their plans set, they broke up their huddle and pursued their targets.

———

Marty pushed a piece of scampi around his plate with his fork as he talked to Frank Altobello. Stu listened, adding a comment here and there. The three of them sat eating lunch in an upscale restaurant in downtown Menlo Park. It was an Italian restaurant, but instead of ordering linguini or fettuccine, Frank had ordered a gourmet burger, oversized and stacked with goodies, that he ate with a knife and fork.

"This funding we got today, along with the three-dot-eight we got from Eccel, will go into developing our initial recipes," said Marty. "We gotta show that the dogs are gonna eat the dog food… This first year is focused on end-to-end provisioning and working out the ordering process—establishing a footprint with interconnection agreements and collocation… End-to-end provisioning entails logistical planning, as well as battles with both the RBOCs and ISPs to achieve acceptable intervals. After that, we figure out the difference between what we're gonna have to pay the RBOCs to lease their network and what we're gonna charge the ISP to buy DSL from us."

"Gross margin," clarified Stu.

"And there's a lot more in the first year. I haven't even mentioned all the regulatory issues, both at the state and city levels, that have to be worked out. So, yes, our eyes are wide open, Frank. This first round of funding is considered risky. Wolf Partners knows that. But it's not quite as risky as you're making out—certainly not with the team we've put together."

"You misunderstand me, Marty," replied Stu as he stabbed his burger with his fork and cut off a large bite. "I don't doubt your team… I don't doubt you'll do everything you say you're gonna do—in the first year… It's your business model I doubt. It's all based on DSL. As I said before, you don't have other products to fall back on. You're a kind of a one-trick pony."

"If you want to look at it that way," said Marty as he watched Frank move the fork into his mouth. "We prefer to look at it differently. DSL is our foothold—then we grow. Take Amazon—they started out just selling books. That was their foothold. Now they're branching out to CDs and videos."

"Hmm," agreed Frank, chewing the large bite of his gourmet burger. He swallowed before continuing. "But that's web commerce—not telecom. Right? You guys have to go out and raid the local loop."

"Yep," laughed Marty. "Just call us 'Raiders of the Local Loop.'"

Frank smiled briefly at the joke as he began cutting into another piece of his burger. "I just think it's gonna be difficult to generate long-term success in the telecom business by leasing communications capacity from others."

"That remains to be seen," said Stu. "On the other side of the equation, we have Internet traffic that is doubling every hundred days."

"I've heard that stat before," replied Frank. "I think it's a marketing ruse—a number that CNBC threw out there without any real data to support it… But it might be true."

Marty sipped thoughtfully on his iced tea and watched Frank daintily move the fork of burger from his plate to his mouth. "I'm not hearing you say that DSL isn't gonna sell," said Marty. Frank nodded as he chewed, agreeing with Marty. "And not just sell but sell like beanie babies. DSL hits the sweet spot, Frank. For regular Internet providers like Fastcom and Telocity, the ones squeezed between AOL on the consumer side and international giants on the big-business side, CrestPoint offers a compelling alternative. They're going to line-up to buy our DSL service…"

"How many years before you see yourself turning a profit?"

"Three," replied Stu. He paused to take the measure of Frank Altobello, and he was sure he had sized him up correctly. "And two years before we go public. When that happens, small fortunes will be made—for our investors, for our employees, and for our favored clients who won't have to wait for trading to start on the open market."

"Hmm," nodded Frank, feigning innocence. But he knew exactly what this CFO guy meant. It was a very carefully worded bribe. If he—if World Markets—gave CrestPoint Communications a high buy rating right before their IPO, he could put himself in a position to make lots of money by buying their stock at a reduced price before it hit the open market and skyrocketed.

"I see," he replied evenly, letting slip a small smile.

"So, can we count on you, Frank?" asked Marty. "Can we count on World Markets? Take our story back. Tell them all about—"

Marty was interrupted by the ring of his cell phone. "Excuse me a sec," he said as he reached into his pocket and read the number. "Gotta take this… Hi, Hana. What's up? — I'm in the middle of… What? Now?... How far apart are your labor pains?... Okay… Okay, where's your sister?... Good. I'm leaving now. I'm on my way… Love you, too."

Marty hung up the call and looked meaningfully at Stu and Frank. "Gentlemen, I'm about to have a baby. Gotta run."

Stu and Frank congratulated him. It was quickly agreed that it would be faster for Marty to leave the restaurant. Frank would give Stu a ride back to CrestPoint. Marty thanked them and absent-mindedly shook their hand before dashing off in a cloud of impending fatherhood. Stu and Frank finished their lunch and Stu picked up the check.

Lunch with Teri Starr led to an invitation from Russ to go boating with him on Sunday. She accepted, and come Sunday they cruised up to Sausalito on *Danny Boy* and had lunch at Scoma's. They both ordered the Crab Louie, which came piled high with fresh Dungeness crab, and paired it with a delightful bottle of buttery chardonnay from the Napa Valley.

Their conversation was light and playful with an undercurrent of sexual anticipation. Russ talked very little about CrestPoint Communications and Teri talked even less about Internet market strategies. Instead, their discussion bounced from one topic to another—fine wines, yachting, life on the East Coast, love of baseball—and they found they had a lot in common. They ordered a second bottle of chardonnay and shared a chocolate tiramisu.

Russ was used to dating young, attractive women and he felt very comfortable in Teri's company. He knew she had a tightly curved body, so he wasn't surprised when she came on board this morning and quickly stripped down to her bikini, revealing her heart-shaped ass and a thirty-five-inch bust packed nicely into her black bikini top. At nine in the morning, it was still chilly out, and when they got underway she put on a long-sleeved shirt, tying it at the waist like Ursula Andress in *Dr. No*. For lunch, she donned a pair of shorts and flip-flops, and when they sat down at their table, he realized she had taken off her bikini top and was bra-less underneath her white shirt. If he looked hard enough, which he did, he could make out the dark areolas of her breasts. And while his eyes roamed from her breasts and across her pretty face with its textured lips, cinnamon eyes under dark, manicured eyebrows, and shoulder-length auburn hair, he couldn't help but imagine what she would be like in bed.

Teri was feeling a bit of a buzz from the wine and this had the slightly embarrassing effect of making her even hornier than she already was. Her hard nipples now rubbed against her shirt, and she could feel a warm moistness beginning to grow between her legs. But she couldn't help it. This man was simply scrumptious. Besides being easy on the eyes, she also found him to be charming and easy to talk to. It was a cultured kind of charm, almost British in a way, that held back a seething and hungry masculinity ready to burst out if he chose to allow it. He was a real gentleman—yet she could feel something simmering underneath. Something she'd give anything to unleash. This paradox, this polished veneer hiding a voracious appetite, turned her on, and she couldn't help but keep imagining him naked.

After lunch, he held her hand as they walked back to the boat. She sat next to him in the cockpit and admired him as he deftly backed away from the dock and slowly motored out a couple hundred yards offshore before cutting the engines. It had turned into a beautiful day, calm and sunny, and he threw the anchor out and walked back to her with a smile.

"Let's enjoy the day," he said.

"Sunbathe?"

"If you wish."

He headed into the cabin, presumably to put on his swim trunks, and she followed him. "Where'd I put my bikini top," she wondered aloud, but as she brushed past him on her way to the bathroom, he grabbed her arm and pulled her back.

"You won't need it," he said, his voice sounding deeper, more resonant now as he quickly took her in his arms. She offered her lips up and they kissed hard. Within moments, she felt her shirt come off, then her bikini bottoms, and she stood naked wrapped in his arms. His shirt was off, and they were pressed together flesh to flesh, his lips and tongue playing down her neck. He found her breast, and one of his hands pressed her from behind while the other fed her nipple into his mouth. She reached down and unzipped him, taking hold of his large erection, and smiled to herself at his size. "Jeezzz," she breathed.

He backed them into his bedroom but she broke free, said, "Give me a minute," and grabbed her bag. She quickly reached inside and skillfully extracted the small case that contained her diaphragm, then disappeared into the bathroom.

The Heights of Mountains

Russ finished undressing and lay down across the bed on his back. This was easy, he thought. With liberated women, it was always easy, and Teri was most definitely a liberated woman. Just look at the way she plucked her diaphragm out of her bag—like a pro ballplayer plucking his mitt out of his locker—as though she'd done it a hundred times before. And as he lay there on the bed waiting for her to re-emerge, girded for battle, he mused about the sexual revolution. It had been a godsend to men like him—men who pursued the sexual favors of beautiful women. Women like Teri were everywhere now. Young, attractive, and sexually aggressive. Like him, they were just looking for a good fuck. No strings, no attachments, just great sex and a fun time. He smiled to himself at the wonderful neatness of it all.

She came out of the bathroom and crawled across the bed to him where she ran her hand across the curly fur on his chest, briefly kissed him, then slid down until she took hold of his cock and put it in her mouth. With one hand on the stem, her mouth worked slow and then fast, taking him down her throat as far as she could go. He found her clitoris with his fingers and played with her as she sucked his cock, and the growing sensation between her legs caused her to move her ass up so she could straddle his head in the sixty-nine position. They rolled sideways, and he locked on tight, digging his tongue and shaking his head in her wet pussy until she came hard, moaning with a mouthful of cock.

She expected him to cum at any moment, but he didn't. Instead, she found herself flipped around, legs spread wide, with him suddenly full and deep inside her. With his elbows locked, he smiled down at her as he pumped rhythmically into her. She raised her legs up to let him in deeper, and he hit the spot—the spot that hadn't been hit in years—and within moments she came again, moaning loudly, "Ohhh, god… Fuck!... Ohhh, yesss!"

He didn't stop. Her unglued expression fed his purpose, and her rolling, lust-ridden eyes steadied on his face as she stared into his gray eyes. They remained cool and determined, and she yearned to break through, but all she could do was whisper "Don't stop… don't stop!"

Her nails dug into his arms. He was perspiring, his vital, masculine smell filling her nostrils, and she bore into his gray eyes. They remained cool and determined, filled with the concentration of a master craftsman, and in her delirium she desperately craved to break through, to make her unforgettable mark on this man in the same way he was making his indelible mark on her. Only one idea bubbled up to the surface of her consciousness. *"Cum in my mouth!"* she pleaded.

He hummed a grunt to that and picked up his pace. She was breaking through, and she repeated it again— *"Cum in my mouth!"*— this time with an even hungrier plea, and saw that it warmed his eyes. In less than ten seconds, he cried "Now!" and pulled out of her as she quickly curled face first into his groin and took his engorged cock into her mouth. It tasted of maleness and vagina mixed together, and she got ready to receive his load. He exploded in her mouth and she sucked hard, collecting each drop, and swallowed it whole like a delicious raw oyster. She lay there for a moment then looked up at him with dreamy eyes and stuck her tongue out at him to show it was all gone.

She sat in the cockpit sipping on a rum and coke as she watched Russ at the helm. He had the engines at nearly full throttle and the motor yacht cut across the placid water like a giant, graceful swan. She shifted in her chair. She was pleasantly sore between her legs. They had gone at it, off and on, for almost two hours and she was thoroughly relaxed from head to toe in a way she hadn't felt for years.

Russ' right hand played with the throttle while his left hand held the wheel. He gave her a big smile. *Errol Fynn.* That was it, she remembered. That was the old actor he reminded her of. She smiled to herself at that. A handsome man, and always a gentleman. She had tried to break through the polished veneer to that voracious something underneath—maybe almost had—but he remained in perfect control throughout their lovemaking. As a lover, he was more a skilled technician than a man lost to desire. But then again, they hardly knew each other. With more time, she could tap into that unbridled passion. She was sure of it.

But there wasn't more time. Who was she kidding? She could get serious about Russ; he was just about everything she looked for in a man—intelligent, charismatic, successful, he even loved the sea like her father—but she lived in Boston and he lived in California. She knew from personal experience that long-distance relationships never worked. And that assumed he *was* interested in something more than just a fling, which she doubted.

"You okay?" he asked her, slowing down the boat.

"I'm fine."

"You sure? You look sad."

"No, not at all… Just the opposite."

He winked and smiled at her, then opened *Danny Boy* up full throttle.

After they docked back in Redwood City, he held her hand as they walked up to the parking lot. She had a flight home the next morning.

"Come visit me in Boston," she said coolly. "Lobster and craft beer. We'll take in a Red Sox game. My treat."

"It's a date," he said. They kissed, almost perfunctorily, and she got in her car, waved at him, and drove off.

When she got back to Boston and entered her condo complex, she found a large bouquet of red roses on her doorstep. She brought them inside and opened the card. It read, "Teri, to a sweet and wonderful woman. I had a smashing good time. Let's do it again someday soon… P.S. I like melted butter with my lobster… Russ."

She stuck her nose into the middle of the flowers and breathed in deeply. "Yep, a real gentleman," she said out loud.

Chapter 9

C.V. Chandrasekar invited Russ to sit down and then spread his arms out. "How do you like it?" he asked, referring to his office. "I finished decorating last night."

Russ eased himself into the comfortable chair and then swiveled around, taking in the room. A number of framed photos hung on the walls, mostly landscape and architectural sites from around the world, each one expertly done. He remembered that Chandra's wife was a professional photographer.

"Your wife's work?" he asked.

"Uh-huh."

"Very nice."

Chandra made a couple of quick keystrokes on his keyboard and then looked up at Russ. "I take it the meeting with the VCs went well?" he inquired. "Two-dot-one million. Least that's what I heard. Marty hasn't come by to give me the lowdown on it."

"It went well. Marty did his rock star bit and won them over."

"Made an impression, did he?"

"As Churchill said, 'One mark of a great man is the power of making lasting impressions upon the people he meets.'"

"Is that the same Churchill who fought so hard against India's independence?"

"That's the one."

Both men smiled at each other.

"How's your computer working?" asked Chandra.

"Like a charm... One thing popped up in the meeting, though. It doesn't sound like you heard about it... Some guy from World

Markets was grilling Marty about our business plan, and Marty told him he was in negotiations with an international consortium about extending our footprint into Europe. Have you heard that?" (Russ could tell by his expression that he hadn't.) "Well, anyway, when I questioned him about it, he laughed it off and called it 'a creative lie.' Said it would be true… But I was curious if he mentioned it to you."

"No… though it would be part of our logical trajectory. But at least two years out."

"Exactly."

"What did Stu say?"

"Nothing. He was either playing dumb or had no comment."

"Hmm, not surprising. Those two may be cooking something up. Stu isn't always—how do I say it? — forthcoming."

"Agreed."

"But I have heard Marty make claims to fame before. Heard him on the phone with a reporter the other day say we would be turning a profit in less than two years."

"Bloody hell."

"I think you'd agree, it's always better to under-promise and over-achieve than vice-versa… But you know him better than I. Is he prone to tall tales?"

"Hmm," hummed Russ thoughtfully, his mind racing for clues. "Not really. Though, when he gets excited, he sometimes gets a little carried away."

"Yes, I've noticed that—but just as long as he doesn't write checks we can't cash… It bears watching out for."

"Yeah," sighed Russ as he stood up. "I was just curious… Thought I'd check with you." One of the photos had caught his eye and he wandered over to it. "Where's this?" he asked. It was a picture of a long white building with Roman columns and a tall spire.

"St. George's Cathedral in Madras."

"Really? I would have guessed a capital building—not a church."

"Not just any church," replied Chandra with a hint of pride in his voice. "My church. I went there as a child. The Church of South India—also known as CSI."

"You're Christian?"

"Devout."

"Hmm," replied Russ, showing some surprise at that. "All this time, I figured you were…"

"Hindu? Yes, a common mistake. But my family has been active members of the CSI for fifty years. We're a united Protestant church, the second largest in India."

"Huh," voiced Russ, expressing some surprise. "I never would have guessed… All your life then?"

"Well," replied Chandra, winking confidentially. "There was a short time at MIT when I became an atheist. You know, read Dawkins, Gould, and the others—thought I had it all figured out with evolutionary biology. But I had—what's the word? — an epiphany—a revelation that brought me back to the church."

"Don't tell me. Your father threatened to cut off your allowance."

"Not quite," laughed Chandra. "Ironically, it was Information Theory that brought me back to God."

"Interesting… I would have thought just the opposite would occur. Evolutionary biologists tend to lean on Information Theory—helps them explain how the info encoded in our DNA (like five fingers versus four) drives natural selection and survivability."

Chandra leaned back in his chair and smiled broadly. "Ahh, DNA," he replied with an amused twinkle in his eyes. "Let's talk DNA… Are you sure you're interested in this?"

"Sure," said Russ, nodding. He liked Chandra, and he was sure the feeling was mutual. Chandra's manner was so convivial, what with his high, aristocratic forehead, the amused twinkle in his eyes, and the bright yellow shirt that seemed to give off a warm glow. He was an intelligent chap worth listening to, so Russ sat back down, clasping his hands and resting his chin on top of them to show he was ready to listen.

"Very well, then—the abridged edition, without the horse feathers… Fundamental to information theory is the separation of content from conduit. There's the information, then the vehicle that carries it. It's like the fiber optic cable we placed at MFS—the optical fiber is the conduit that carries the light with all the information. Too many evolutionary biologists blur this distinction. They try to make the DNA molecule out to be the information—you know, five fingers versus four—and that way imply life is biochemistry rather than information processing. But there's the crux… the DNA molecule isn't the message—it's just the vehicle for the message. The information comes *first,* which begs the question, where does that information come from?

"And so there I was, a first-year student at MIT, a smart-alecky kid who thought he had all the answers—but who didn't have an answer to that simple question. Where does the information come from? I was stumped—until it came to me in a blinding flash. John, chapter one, verse one… *'In the beginning was the Word, and the Word was with God, and the Word was God.'* There it was, as simple as that. Information is the word, and the word is God. It comes first, and controls the flesh and the world, not the other way around. It doesn't pop up out of random chance or bubble up out of some prebiotic soup. It comes from a Mind, you see… DNA can deliver the information to create our brains, but our brains are an accumulation of proteins that cannot generate the information in DNA. And there was my epiphany… Wherever there is *information*, there is a preceding *intelligence.*"

Chandra finished with a smile, then suddenly added, "I love that word—*epiphany*," before scanning Russ' face to read his reaction. He liked Russ and found him charming and intelligent. They weren't friends, per se, but they had been friendly for years, and he considered him an ally in many things. Religion was probably not one of those many things. It was evident that Russ was a skeptic, maybe even an atheist, but he was also sure that Russ would never allow a difference of opinion to taint their 'friendship.' He was too broad-minded for that.

"Hmm," hummed Russ thoughtfully. "Now I have this image in my head… God sitting at a master terminal, typing in code and creating the program for human existence. It's a lovely image, but not one I can buy into. IBM might be able to program a computer to beat Kasparov at chess, but the thought that a supreme being has programmed all possible outcomes, permutations, and combinations that go into performing just a simple act like scratching your nose, is not scientific, it's a leap of faith."

"Okay," replied Chandra, nodding that he understood Russ' point, "then you must believe that evolution explains it all?"

"I prefer a theory I can put to the test. Evolution is such a theory; I can break down its major premises and test them to be true or false. I can't do that with your theory... When I think of how the human brain works—your brain, my brain—I think of it as a computer composed of programs that process information, and to date only evolution can explain, with data, how that capacity came about."

"That's a reasonable viewpoint... when one is focused only on the output—in the material world."

"Well, *I am* a material girl."

Chandra laughed cheerfully at Russ' joke. "Yes, yes, aren't we all. But let me just say this... The computer (since you bring it up)—a thing near and dear to my heart—offers an insurmountable obstacle to the materialistic trap of evolution. Information Theory shows us that inside a computer, the content, the design of its computations, is independent of its material substrate. You can tell me all you know about the silicon wafer—just like that DNA molecule—but it doesn't help you in any way explain the content of its computations. Which brings me back to that epiphany of mine..."

"You're really making an argument for intelligent design," countered Russ. "Which is a far cry from the Holy Trinity—from an all-seeing father figure that cares about mankind and listens to his prayers. Rather something of a correlation fallacy, I'd say."

"Yes... and I can't help you with that," replied Chandra as he leaned back in his chair and laced his fingers in front of his chest. "All I can do is speak from experience. Once I found God, the rest just flowed naturally. I have a personal relationship with God; he talks to me, cares about me. I *feel* His love... It's not really a thing I can explain to someone who's not felt it themselves, and I don't think you want me to. You'll have me sounding like Ron."

Russ chuckled at that. "He does wear his religion on his sleeve... much more than you do."

"It's a difference in style. You know, he's a minister in his church."

"I didn't know that."

"So, he's concerned with saving souls. Me—not so much. I'll talk to you about my relationship with Jesus Christ—if you're interested—but saving your soul is your own problem."

"I appreciate that."

Russ and Chandra smiled at one another. They'd traversed some potentially treacherous ground. Strong disagreement could have arisen, as it sometimes did in discussions about religion or politics, but they had kept things civil and instructive without being condescending. Both men, as gentlemen, appreciated that. Russ had learned something about Chandra that he didn't know before, and Chandra, for his part, was certain he'd given Russ something to think about.

They talked a little longer. The real reason Russ had popped into Chandra's office was to discuss a problem with turning up the DSLAM in their field trial. It appeared to be a software interface problem. Chandra assured him that they were aware of the problem, that it was a protocol issue, and they'd have a fix for it in a day or two. Glad to hear it, Russ got up to leave.

"A pleasure, as always," said Russ.

"I'll keep you posted." As Russ neared the door to the office, Chandra added, "You know Marty has political aspirations."

"Yeah, I know," replied Russ, pausing at the door. "Governor Madrid… A scary thought."

"I might vote for him. Who knows? My only concern is this: the political animal can sometimes get in the way of the business animal."

"Agreed. I'll keep my eye on him."

"And I'll keep an eye on Stu."

Russ smiled at that, gave a quick salute, and left Chandra's office rather gratified that Chandra didn't trust Stu any more than he did.

Chapter 10

"What'll it be?" asked the bartender.

"Bud."

The gray-haired bartender took his order and quickly returned, setting a cold bottle of Budweiser, along with a frosted glass, in front of Mark. Mark thanked him and slowly poured the beer into the glass, careful not to let it foam up too much. He took a long drink, tasting its crisp lager flavor, then set the glass back down half empty.

He wasn't much of a drinker, but at the moment he needed something to calm him down. His nerves were a little on edge, especially after his go-round with the City Manager an hour ago at dinner.

Mark had come out to Kansas City to find out what was what—the secret to their success—and, boy, had he learned a thing or two. He refilled his glass with the rest of his beer and reflected on recent events.

It started over a week ago in Russ' office. The two of them were reviewing CrestPoint's deployment status. Six cities had been chosen for the field trials; four in California (San Jose, Oakland, Los Angeles, and San Diego), one in the Midwest (Kansas City, MO), and the sixth in Philadelphia. In the six months since Mark came on board, there'd been a mixed bag of success and failure in getting these field trials up and working. The hitch in the get-along wasn't his organization, which was the equipment installation, it was all the upfront stuff like interconnection agreements, franchise rights, licensing, and especially the ordering and construction of collocation space in the Baby Bell's central offices. It had taken four months to get collocation space ready in San Jose, and that was only because it was in their own backyard.

Day-to-day, unrelenting pressure from Marty, Russ, and Stu on SBC and on the city regulators was the only reason San Jose had a working field trial. San Diego and Oakland were close, LA a good month away, and Philly was floundering due to Bell Atlantic's delaying tactics. Kansas City was the exception to the rule.

In KC, not only were all the regulatory issues nailed down quickly, but *three* collocation sites had been completed in less than four months. Installation crews had already completed work and end-to-end connectivity was achieved. This marvelous progress had everyone in their San Jose headquarters wondering what the key to KC's success was and how to replicate it.

The focal point was the City Manager, Stony Bundschuh. Russ had hired him on Stuart Baum's recommendation, and as City Manager he was responsible for a wide range of responsibilities tied to building out the DSL network in Kansas City. This included dealing with city officials, public utility commissioners, and SBC management (since Kansas City resided in the old Southwestern Bell territory). He also oversaw the construction crews, which should have placed him squarely in Mark's organization—but it didn't. Instead, he reported directly to Russ, was "dotted-lined" to Mark, yet was claimed by Stu as his employee since he dealt with regulatory and compliance issues. This feud between Russ and Stu as to where City Managers belonged, whether in Stu's Compliance Organization or Russ' Deployment Organization, had yet to be resolved and the result was a kind of loosey-goosey arrangement that gave Stony Bundschuh, alone out on the banks of the Missouri River, freedom to do pretty much as he pleased.

One other result of this arrangement was that Mark, who should have been Bundschuh's boss, knew very little about him. Until now.

The trip had been Russ' idea. He wanted more information, and he wasn't getting it from Stony. All he could get out of Bundschuh was that their success was due to, one, "a friendly regulatory environment" (which was probably true) and two, "a cooperative Telco management" (which was hard to believe). Adding to this mystery was a complaint from Lucent that Bundschuh was bypassing them and using his own contractors to install the equipment. This piqued Russ' curiosity even further and he asked Mark, as a favor to him, to go out to KC to dig into the matter. If Bundschuh's explanation was all there was to it, validate it. If there was more to the story, find out what it was and bring it back to California so they could benefit from it.

Four days later, Mark flew out to Kansas City and met with Stony Bundschuh. The man worked out of a large office on the seventh floor of a building in downtown Kansas City. He had one employee, an administrative assistant, who was an attractive woman in her mid-twenties. She greeted Mark with a warm smile and showed him into Stony's office. The City Manager got up from behind his desk and came out to shake Mark's hand and offer him a seat. Overweight, balding, with the makings of a double chin, he looked older than his forty-two years. Added to this was a loud, rapid-fire speaking style that made it difficult for Mark to get a word in edgewise.

Overall, the man gave Mark the impression of a well-fed politician, an impression that was only reinforced after an hour of discussion. He touted his success, chalking it up to his ability to work effectively with city officials and SBC managers, but his explanation lacked any details other than to say that these city officials and SBC managers were "open-minded." It was also apparent to Mark that Stony did not view him as his supervisor, dotted line or not. When Mark carefully challenged him as to why he'd bypassed the company's installation vendor and used his own, Stony didn't flinch and smoothly replied that it was the only way to make their aggressive timeline. Mark nodded without commenting.

After their hour talk, Mark asked if there was an office nearby where he could work and make some calls. Stony offered him his office, saying he had meetings with the city and wouldn't be back till 3:00, and extended a dinner invitation to Mark for that evening. Mark thanked him for the use of his desk and accepted his dinner invitation. After Stony left, his administrative assistant (Tess was her name) came in with a cup of coffee—no sugar, light on the cream, just the way he liked it—and assured him with a smile that she was available should he need *anything*.

Having recently worked for SBC, Mark knew all the managers who were responsible for the Kansas City market area, and he called and talked to them along with his local installation vendor to learn all he could about Stony Bundschuh. What he learned was troubling. Mr. Bundschuh was a well-known character around these parts. It turned out that he lied about Lucent not being able to meet his aggressive due dates and instead gave the work to a local vendor owned by his brother-in-law. The SBC managers he talked to, the ones higher up in the food chain, knew Stony but were reluctant to say much about him. Luckily, Mark tracked down an old employee of his, an engineer responsible for Kansas City, who met him for lunch and gave him the straight scoop. "Influence peddling" was the term his old employee used; he couldn't prove it was a bribe, but it included things like box seats to the Chiefs' games, free rooms at the Indian casino, concert tickets, and probably even prostitutes (though he couldn't prove that either). That was the secret to Stony's success.

That evening at dinner, at a swank steakhouse that Stony boasted served up the best T-bone in the Midwest, Mark confronted him with what he'd learned. Stony shrugged his shoulders as he cut into his juicy steak, chalking it up to innuendo and jealousy. He got results, he got things done—that's all that mattered—and Stuart Baum had his back. The man viewed himself as untouchable.

This arrogance, this dismissive smugness, as though Stony was some well-connected wise guy who could act with impunity, angered Mark (a man not prone to anger). The dinner conversation degenerated from there, and in short order, Mark threatened to fire Stony if he could prove bribery or influence peddling. "Knock yourself out, bub," Stony replied as he chewed his steak.

Knock yourself out, bub.

Afraid of his growing anger, Mark got up and left the restaurant without finishing his meal and returned to his hotel where he now sat at the bar drinking a beer.

His anger was dissipating, but in its place returned the black dog that stalked his trail. It was the same malaise that had settled into his soul over a year ago. He hoped this new job would have been a remedy, but instead the malaise had grown worse. Perhaps it just seemed worse, he thought—because of this little episode with Bundschuh—and would wear off. But he knew better. This was a separate thing, like a slow-growing cancer. It was just this vague and growing sense of dissatisfaction with his life, a feeling of restlessness and unfulfillment as though there was something more to life than just his family and his job. He'd heard of men going through "male menopause" who exhibited these same symptoms, and he hoped that's all it was. Maybe all I need to do is buy a sports car, he thought to himself with a wry smile.

He studied the label on his empty bottle of Bud. It was an intricate design that included a square inside an oval inside a rhombus inside a circle, and he wondered if it contained hidden symbols like the dollar bill. His concentration on the beer label was drawn away by a song over the speakers. Country Western music was playing softly in the background but he hadn't given it much notice until now. It was a song by Alabama, and he knew that because his wife liked Alabama and had this CD. He didn't know the name of the song but it had something to do with angels among us.

"He'll take another Bud," said a familiar voice. "Give me a white wine."

Mark glanced over two stools at the woman who just sat down. It was Tess. Her hair was down and she wore a tight dress that accentuated her curved body. She looked like any man's fantasy. Without saying it to himself, he knew exactly what she was here for.

"You look very nice, Tess," he said. "Got a hot date tonight?"

"Depends."

"On what?"

"You."

She smiled warmly at him, and he studied her for a moment. The gray-haired bartender delivered their drinks, and Mark watched her as she picked up her wine glass, delicately took a sip, and placed it back down on the bar with a lipstick stain on the rim. He played out the scenario in his head where he took her upstairs to his room and had sex, but it played out like an old movie riddled with cliches.

He wasn't interested. It was just too barefaced and obvious. Did this Bundschuh joker really think a stunt like this would get him to play along? Unbelievable. This clown was strictly out of the Stone Age.

"It's late," he said.

"Not that late," she replied with a seductive twang.

"Listen, Tess… I'm not interested. Don't pretend you're here by chance, or you found out where I was staying because you got a crush on me. Not buying it…. Shhh—don't say anything. Just listen to me. You seem like a nice gal, so you gotta ask yourself, what do you want out of life? Do you want a career where you're admired and respected—cause this ain't the way to get it. Do you want to marry a good man and raise a family—cause this ain't the way to get it. Playing call girl to Stony's pimp is a dead end. Trust me. You're too smart and attractive to settle for it. Leave this place and do something better with your life."

Tess was taken by surprise at this reaction—coming from a man—so early in her play. She hadn't even leaned into him yet and given him her best come-on. How could he know, she wondered. But he did. It was obvious he was a happily married family man; he radiated decency in the same way some men, like preachers, radiated honesty and modesty. She'd cracked nuts like that before, with a little extra effort, but this one was different. She could feel it. She listened to his words, not even attempting to feign innocence, and nodded at him when he finished.

"That obvious, huh?" she asked.

"Let's just say, I don't believe in coincidences," he replied, getting up off his bar stool. He laid a twenty-dollar bill on the bar. "Drinks are on me."

"Sorry… Mr. Kirkland."

He had planned to simply walk away, but something in the way she said *"Sorry… Mr. Kirkland"* caused him to pause. He took her hand and looked straight into her eyes. "You don't need a guy like Stony in your life," he told her. "You got everything going for you. Do something meaningful with it… Now go home." She glanced away, her cheeks slightly flushing with embarrassment—a gesture that suddenly endeared her to him—and he kissed her hand before walking off.

She watched him walk away. Stony wasn't going to be happy, she thought. But suddenly, she really didn't give a damn.

Up in his room, Mark kicked off his shoes and sat down next to the phone. It was past eleven in KC but only past nine back home. Ronnie would still be up. He called her and they talked for a half hour. He didn't give her specifics about Bundschuh, or tell her about Tess, and instead kept things general, saying he'd found out what he needed to know and didn't need to stay an extra day. He planned to catch a flight home tomorrow. When he hung up, he felt better.

He got ready for bed and turned on the TV. Unable to fall asleep, he lay in bed and surfed through the channels until he found the movie *The Greatest Story Ever Told* and left it there, turning the sound down. He'd seen the movie before and the casting of Max Von Sydow as Jesus always cracked him up. Max looked more like a Viking than the Son of God, and he casually wondered if Max—the Viking Jesus—was a distant relative. There was Scandinavian blood on both sides of his family but especially his mother's side, who could trace her lineage back to the Viking King Harold Fairhair. Maybe ol' Max was a distant cousin… And as his thoughts wandered, Mark began to grow tired and turned off the TV. But he tossed and turned for another hour before finally falling asleep. Towards morning, he had a strange little dream that stayed with him for the rest of the day.

There is a crowd of people. Men are yelling and pulling a young, frightened woman into a circle of people dressed in ancient garb, in robes, like in biblical times. He looks down at himself and sees that he, too, is dressed in a robe. As he nears the circle of people, he sees a tall man standing inside the circle with the woman, who lies prostrate on the ground, and he knows the tall man to be Jesus. And quickly he recognizes where he's at—he's in a scene from the movie The Greatest Story Ever Told—*because the man playing Jesus is the Swedish actor Max Von Sydow. As he gets into the circle, it's confirmed—it is Max—only he isn't dressed like Jesus of Nazareth. Instead, he looks like a Viking warrior, in chain mail, with a cross emblazoned on his front,* and he holds a large broad sword in one hand. His short blonde hair is striking, and his face is clean-shaven (and Mark is sure that their ancestors are related).

The crowd accuses the woman of being an adulterer and demands her death by stoning. Many in the crowd hold a stone in their hand ready to strike. The Viking Jesus bends down, picks up a stone and holds it out saying, "Let he who is without sin cast the first stone." But this falls on deaf ears and the crowd closes in. Mark realizes that this is not the same scene he remembers from the movie, and he waits to see what Max will do. As the crowd inches closer, the Viking Jesus crushes the stone in his hand like a crust of bread, raises his broad sword, and yells out, scattering the crowd in terror. Only Mark is left to witness what the Viking Jesus will do next, and he watches as Max takes the woman's hand, lifts her up, and kisses her hand saying, "Now go home."

The flight was half full and Mark found his aisle seat and sat down. The middle seat was empty but a man about Mark's age sat in the window seat. Mark glanced over at him and said, "How you doing?"

"Good. And you?"

"Good." They both smiled and nodded at one another. The man looked vaguely familiar to Mark but he couldn't place him. He settled into his seat, got out the book he was reading (*Cold Mountain* by Charles Frazier), and waited for take-off. It was a five-and-a-half-hour trip with a short stop-over in Denver.

Once in the air, Mark tried to read but set the book aside when the memory of his dream broke his concentration. Did it have any significance, he wondered? Did it contain hidden symbolism, or was it just a hodge-podge of images stuck together? Probably the latter, since he'd caught part of the movie *The Greatest Story Ever Told* before falling asleep last night. Combine that with the name "Stony" and his little encounter with Tess in the bar, and there was his dream. Nothing more.

The flight attendant came by with the drink cart and he ordered tomato juice. The man next to him ordered the same. Mark took a sip of his drink and glanced out the window. They were passing an array of majestic-looking mountains. The man next to him glanced out at the mountains as well, and as they admired the sight together, Mark commented, "Quite a sight."

The man turned back, smiling at Mark, and spoke clearly over the noise of the jet engines: "And men go abroad to admire the heights of mountains, the mighty waves of the sea, the broad tides of rivers, the compass of the ocean, and the circuits of the stars, yet pass over the mystery of themselves without a thought."

Mark was sure it was a quote. From the Bible, perhaps? But before he could ask, the man gave him the answer.

"St. Augustine."

"Wouldn't have guessed it."

"Yeah, he was quite a character. In his youth, he was a rebel without a cause... Had a live-in lover at seventeen and jumped into every cool religion and philosophy of his day with both feet—the name's Mike, by the way."

"Mark."

"A pleasure, Mark... Then he had his famous conversion, which he writes about beautifully, and becomes this great theologian... What you reading?" (Mark showed him the cover of his book.) "Any good?"

"Yeah... About the Civil War. The story kind of reminds me of the Odyssey. You know, the story by Homer."

"Ahh, Homer... Dante consigned him to one of the more comfortable places in hell, along with the other 'virtuous pagans' like poets and philosophers."

Mark nodded at this and smiled, making a quick assessment of this fellow. He was full of esoteric knowledge, liked to talk, and seemed friendly and affable. And he looked vaguely familiar which, in an odd way, made Mark feel comfortable in his company. He noticed that Mike also held a book in his lap. "What you reading?" he asked.

The Heights of Mountains

"*Mere Christianity*... by C.S. Lewis. I've read it many times—carry it around like an old friend. I like to review my favorite parts every so often." He opened the book, flipped to a page, and quickly ran his finger down to the spot he wanted. "Like this one, for example... 'If you are on the wrong road, progress means doing an about-turn and walking back to the right road; and in that case, the man who turns back soonest is the most progressive man.'"

"Words of wisdom," commented Mark.

"Hmm, yes... for some—if you follow it. I know I did. But it comes at a cost... Where do you work?"

"Company called CrestPoint Communications," replied Mark. "We're a start-up headquartered in San Jose." And without stopping to think about it, Mark began to tell him all about CrestPoint and how he came to work for them. He was led along the way by Mike's probing questions, who seemed less interested in the business end of CrestPoint and more interested in the personal reasons for why Mark left SBC. Why did you leave, he asked. What did you hope to find? Was it as fulfilling as you hoped? Mark did his best to answer these questions.

Suddenly, Mark found himself talking about the black dog that hounded his trail. How he slipped into this intimacy—with a stranger—he couldn't say. All he knew was that he was unloading on this man about his restlessness and feelings of unfulfillment and it felt good. It was not something he could talk to his friends or family about, or even a thing he could confess to his wife (who would have been confused by it or, worse yet, taken it as her fault). And therapy wasn't an option. So, he had no one to talk to about this thing except this stranger in seat 12C who listened intently and seemed very interested in what he had to say.

The two men leaned in close to one another so they could speak softly and still be heard over the noise of the jet engines. A flight attendant came by to ask them about a refill, but she saw them in a deep, concentrated discussion and left them alone.

Mark confessed he had started attending church again. He was Catholic; baptized a Catholic, raised a Catholic, and he and his wife were married in a Catholic church. They had even attended church regularly early in their marriage but, after a few years, found themselves becoming 'Holiday Catholics' and stopped altogether instead of continuing the charade. But recently he had wanted to start up again in the hopes that the Church—the Church that he knew and grew up with—would be the answer to his melancholy. His wife was happy to go with him. His kids? —not so much. But there he was now, sitting in the pew, listening to mass, and searching for… What was the word he wanted? Searching for… *transcendence*. But it hadn't come.

"Because you have not opened your heart to Jesus," said Mike as he looked hard into Mark's eyes.

Mark was slightly taken aback by that comment but tried not to show it. Yet a red flag went up in his head. Was this guy waiting in the weeds all along just to spring his trap, he wondered to himself. He let me confess some deep feelings, in fact encouraged me to do so, and for what? Is he a holy-roller, one of those Jesus freaks you run into at the airport who are always trying to convert someone? God, I hope not.

A voice came over the intercom. 'We've started our descent into Denver. Please return to your seats and fasten your seatbelts."

The interruption gave Mark a break and he took it, sitting back straight in his seat and fastening his seatbelt. The flight attendant came by with a trash bag and he threw away his empty cup. He closed his eyes and felt the plane descend into Denver.

The plane landed, and in short order some passengers got off while others came on board. In the interval, Mark got up to stretch his legs. When the plane got ready to push out, the seat between him and Mike remained empty. Mike sat quietly looking out the window.

After lift-off, Mark remained still, not reading his book or turning his head, as a feeling of discomfort began to grow inside him. A couple across the aisle from him were playing cribbage and he could see the man's hand, and he watched the man play his cards for a while until the silence between him and Mike became intolerable. He might have hurt his feelings, he thought. He hadn't meant to blow him off… He needed to say something.

Mark leaned over to speak to Mike, but almost like a mirror reflection, Mike leaned towards him and spoke first. "Didn't mean to scare you off," he said. "With that comment about Jesus."

"Oh, no, no… It's fine."

"It was just an observation—that's all… Because I've heard your story before. It's my story. Having a loving family, a great job, but still feeling like there's a hole in your soul—that's my story. And I can tell you from experience, that going back to church isn't going to fill that hole. It's like repainting an old house when what you gotta do is tear down the old house, tear it down to its foundation, and rebuild it new. Finding that transcendence you're looking for only comes through a radical and complete transformation of your life. For me, it was accepting Jesus Christ as my savior… But it wasn't easy getting there."

"How did you… get there?" asked Mark. He felt rather obligated to hear this strange man's story. After all, he had unburdened himself on this fellow, shared intimate feelings with him, and Mike had been gracious enough to listen to him. It was only fair that he return the favor.

For the next half hour, Mike told Mark about his spiritual journey. Mark listened, asking only a couple of short questions, both men barely touching the meal that was served to them by the flight attendant as Mike's story unfolded. Many parts of Mike's story rang true to Mark—the feeling of restlessness and dissatisfaction with life despite a happy home life, job promotions, and financial success—and he nodded his understanding. But then came Mike's religious conversion, an experience Mark didn't understand at all, and he listened carefully.

Mike's born-again experience was not triggered by a personal tragedy or any kind of job stress, instead it was collection of smaller, milder straws that finally broke the camel's back. The turning point came unexpectedly. It was evening and he was alone in his den with the Bible on his desk. A feeling of being lost and alone permeated his being; like a heavy weight it pressed unbearably down upon him. Out of nowhere he heard his young son, who was playing in another room, yell, "Pick it up and read it!" So he picked up the Bible, opened it, and started reading, and suddenly, in a profound and personal way, he felt that Jesus was talking directly to him. It was then, at that moment, that he opened his heart to Jesus and felt a power and love like he had never felt before filling up his being. It was the most marvelous experience of his life. When he woke up the next morning, he knew something wonderful had happened to him.

He paused his story for a moment, giving Mark a chance to study his face. It was unmistakable—the man's face was filled with a kind of energetic happiness, and Mark envied him.

"They call that 'giving testimony,'" said Mike. "Invigorating."

"And how did your family take it?"

Mike smiled at the question, almost ruefully it seemed to Mark. "*Yeah*... not good at first," he replied. "It's a radical change for them and they don't understand it. My wife didn't understand it. My family. Friends. They viewed me as some kind of brain-washed cult member. You become an outcast, a stranger in a strange land... But it gets better with time—at least with my wife and family it did. Though I lost a couple friends... They couldn't accept the change."

"I can see that."

The flight attendant appeared, and they gave her their half-eaten meals. Mark leaned back in his seat with his arms crossed and thought about Mike's story. He didn't doubt it; he was certain Mike's story was true, that he had experienced exactly what he said he had experienced. He just doubted it was any kind of path for him.

"I'm curious," said Mike, and Mark leaned back over to hear him better. "Do you feel like someone is trying to tell you something? I mean... You mentioned a couple of dreams you've had lately. Have there been other things? Signs? Maybe a song that keeps popping up on the car radio, or a word or phrase that appears at just the right time?"

"I don't know... maybe," replied Mark truthfully. "I'm certainly not consciously doing that—looking out for signs."

"All I would say is—don't fight it. The world consists of divine footprints, fingerprints, and clues. Just follow them and they'll take you where you need to go... Here—I'd like you to have this," said Mike, handing him the book *Mere Christianity*.

"Oh, no, no… I can't take your book. I'll get one at the bookstore. Keep yours."

Mike assured him that he had more copies back at home and it was no big deal. He laid the book in Mark's lap like a loaf of bread saying, "Consider it a gift of the magi," and smiled warmly.

Seeing that he couldn't turn down the gift, Mark thanked him and held the book in his lap. He stared at the front cover for a moment, flipped it over and read the back, then rifled the pages with his thumb until he caught a page and stopped. He glanced down and read the first thing he found: "Now is our chance to choose the right side. God is holding back to give us that chance. It won't last forever. We must take it or leave it."

Mark smiled good-naturedly at the quote, shut the book, and glanced across the aisle at the couple who were still playing cribbage. The man held three kings in his hand. Without warning, a warm electric shock surged up through Mark's body, causing him to become paralyzed in his seat. His mind instantly fought back against this frightening sensation. He was a man who viewed the world logically, saw things in terms of cause and effect, and at this moment he was mentally scrambling to put his worldview back in order… It's just like seeing a ghost, he thought to himself. Like the time I saw the ghost of my dead grandfather (or thought I did) as a boy, and this same electric shock and paralysis overwhelmed me. This is the same. But different somehow. Is it the start of a religious conversion—like Mike described—right here, right now, on an airplane? He closed his eyes to the thought.

When he reopened his eyes, he saw that the three kings were gone from the man's cribbage hand. The man had played them and taken his points. The warm electric shock coursing through his body suddenly diminished, and Mark moved his hands, effectively breaking the spell. A feeling of relief poured over him.

The pilot announced they were starting their descent into San Francisco. As Mark put up his tray and placed his new book into his satchel, he wondered if Mike had any clue as to what had just transpired. He didn't think so. Mike was bent over, digging into his own bag, and appeared oblivious to it.

After they landed and taxied to the gate, Mark reached over and shook hands with Mike. Their farewell was a fond one, both men expressing joy at having met the other. As Mark stood up to leave, Mike said rather cryptically, "John, one-twelve."

It took a moment, but Mark understood the reference and nodded his understanding. He stepped out into the aisle and followed the line of people deplaning, leaving Mike still seated in 12C. Out in the waiting area, he stopped and lingered, expecting Mike to appear at any moment. He took the opportunity to set his satchel down and fish through it for his car keys, finally finding them stuck underneath his new book. When he looked back up, people were still exiting the gate, but after waiting a good five minutes, he decided to leave. Somehow, he'd missed him.

He made his way to the airport parking lot, then got in his car, paid his fee at the exit booth, and drove towards the freeway entrance. It was quiet in the car, so he turned on the radio. The song *Spirit in the Sky* by Norman Greenbaum was playing, and he reached over and turned it up, laughing cheerfully at the coincidence.

Chapter 11

"We're behind forecast. It's as simple as that, and I don't want to hear excuses." Gwen Novak stood up from her desk on the tenth floor of the AT&T building in downtown San Francisco and looked out the window at the city. She wore a headset with a long cord, allowing her to pace the floor behind her desk as she talked on the phone.

"No, now listen," she continued, her tone dispassionate and all business. "Sometimes the problem isn't the process; it's the people working the process. Don't be afraid to say so—not that I want you to go around pointing a finger at people. We fix the problem, not the blame. But sometimes the problem *is* the people, and our job is to fess up to that, separate the wheat from the chaff, and move those people out and replace them with people who can do the job... Yes, I know that, but at the end of the day, what gets measured gets done. So tell me exactly what the gating factors are... I've heard those before; we've talked about them at length. That's why we have to stay focused on the low-hanging fruit and stop wasting time on pie-in-the-sky alternatives. Stick to our core competency... Look, you know as well as I, Armstrong wants us to own the last mile, and we're not going to do it at this rate. We gotta move the needle... Right. Then do it—I want a full-court press on it. You'll have my full support... Very good. But, bottom line, I need to see those numbers go up next month. Understood? ... Alright then. Keep me posted."

Gwen reached down and pushed a button on her phone set, terminating the call. That went well, she thought to herself. Sometimes you have to rattle a cage or two. Calls like this undoubtedly fed her reputation as a driven, cold-hearted bitch. But as President of West

Coast Operations, that's exactly why they hired her—for her reputation for getting things done. If she were a man, it'd be different; she'd be viewed as tough and aggressive. But regardless, she wasn't concerned about softening her image. Too often it worked to her advantage.

She took her headset off and walked over to the large window that overlooked the city. It was getting dark earlier. Already the high rises were casting long shadows across the busy streets. She'd give herself another hour—clear her emails—then head home to her condo in the Richmond District, order some Chinese food, and relax a spell before DJ came over. DJ was her latest boyfriend, another bad boy fifteen years her junior, who would bring with him his attitude and sweet trouble. The thought of him gave her a tingle.

But now was not the time for such feelings, and she swept the thought of DJ from her mind and got back to business. She sat back down at her computer and accessed her emails, clicking on each one and quickly scanning them before either deleting them or typing out a short response. As she whittled down the list, it struck her once again just how easy this job had become. It was less than two years and already she had it wired. With the VP title and big salary, she had expected more of a challenge, but with her no-holds-barred management style, she swiftly cleared the deck for action and molded an effective team by inspiring some and putting the fear of God into the rest. It was like knocking down ducks in a shooting gallery. And now, less than two years later, it was becoming rote. All she was doing was provisioning dial-tone, for crying out loud. It was like baking cookies.

Her emails completed, Gwen shut down her computer and stood up, arching her back. At five-ten, she was a tall woman, statuesque in figure, with long legs and slightly narrow hips that she tended to compensate for by wearing well-fitted curvy pants or gathered skirts. She wore her beige blonde hair medium length, in tapered layers, with a part in the middle that accentuated her oblong face. She was not beautiful, but her poise and refined manner added to what one would call, even at the age of thirty-nine, a handsome prettiness. Her bright hazel-blue eyes were penetrating, and many a male subordinate had withered under its stare.

The Heights of Mountains

She gathered up her things and closed her office, walking through the nearly empty honeycomb of cubicles to the elevator. Her car sat parked in a gated lot, her spot clearly marked with a sign that read 'Gwen Novak, Vice President', and she got into her dark blue BMW and drove home. Once in the door, she greeted her cat Popeye with a hug and a scratch before going into her bedroom to change.

Her king-sized bed took up a large chunk of her spacious bedroom, and she stripped down to her bra and panties, laying her clothes on the quilted comforter that covered the vast bed. She walked over to her antique oak dresser and opened a drawer, glancing at the three framed pictures that sat on top. These were the only photos she had; the rest of the house was sparsely adorned with reproductions of modern art and contained no family photos except what sat here on her dresser. The largest photo, taken fifteen years ago in her parents' backyard, included her mom and dad, her two younger brothers, along with herself and her husband at the time, Jeff Novak. She was only married to Jeff for a year, but she'd kept his last name because it was infinitely better than her maiden name—Borgenhagen.

There was another photo of just her dad. He's around thirty-six in the picture, back when he was coaching her CYO basketball team, and she couldn't help but always look at it fondly. Her mother wanted her to be a model, but Gwen had other ideas. She wanted to play basketball. So, her dad took her in tow, put up a hoop in the driveway, and proceeded to teach her the game of basketball in his rough-and-tumble style. This included how to post up and block out underneath the basket, and he held nothing back in showing her how to hip check and throw elbows to gain good position. Many an evening she'd gone into the house with bruises on her body and the occasional bloody nose. But it all paid off. A basketball scholarship got her into the college of her choice, where she majored in business, and from there into the Harvard Business School where she outshined her competition while getting her MBA.

The last photo was of her and Russ Chappel, taken about eight years ago when they were dating. Their fling lasted only a few months, but they remained friends and continued to stay in touch with one another.

In the picture, taken on his boat, Russ is shirtless, tan and handsome, and he has his arm around her as they both smile into the camera. She never displayed photos of old boyfriends, but this one was an exception. And it wasn't because she still had a soft spot in her heart for Russ (which she did), but because of her smile—that smile that made her look almost... happy.

She turned her dad's picture down, tossed a black anal plug onto the bed, and then changed into something more appropriate for the evening—a t-shirt and lounging pants. Out in the living room, she ordered Chinese food over the phone, poured herself a glass of Sauvignon Blanc, and turned the TV on to CNBC. Her food arrived twenty minutes later, and she sat on the couch in front of her rustic coffee table eating out of the quart containers with chopsticks and sipping her wine.

Nine o'clock came and went. DJ was late again. There'd be no call, she knew, and when he finally showed up—and he would—there'd be no explanations. She really didn't expect anything different. He was an inconsiderate bastard, exactly the way she wanted him to be, and if he called or made polite apologies for being late, she would have jettisoned him long ago. When he finally showed up at 9:40, she buzzed him in without hesitation.

"Hey, babe," she said as she let him. They kissed briefly on the lips as he blew past her on his way to the living room. He wore a tight, black shirt with a Harley Davidson logo on it, faded blue jeans, and steel-toed boots that made him a little taller than his six feet. She looked him up and down from behind with an appreciative eye. "There's some Chinese food left," she called out after him.

When she returned to the living room, he already had a box of food in one hand and chopsticks in the other. He glanced at the chopsticks in disgust and tossed them onto the coffee table saying, "Gotta fork? I can't eat with those fuckin' things."

She went into the kitchen to get a fork. "Want a beer?"

"Yeah."

She kept a six pack of his favorite beer in the fridge and grabbed one, returning to the living room where she handed him both the fork and the beer. He quickly used the fork to dig into the Mongolian beef, and she sat down and watched him eat. His long, sinewy arms were covered in tattoos, his lean face unshaven, while his dark hair hung down over his ears as he hunched over his food. His eyebrows were as dark as his hair, and his gypsy eyes had a wildness in them that excited her.

She could see he'd been drinking. Probably a few shots of tequila before coming over. But there were no signs of meth use in his eyes or in his appetite. That was fortunate; she much preferred him drunk than hyped up on meth. She could control him more easily. In a couple more beers, he would be right where she wanted him.

Gwen had been hooking up with young men like DJ for years, and she had an eye for the type. It was usually in a bar (though she'd found DJ in a grocery store), and after close study and a short conversation, she could tell whether he fit the bill of fare—young, usually mid-twenties, ill-bred and rough around the edges, with a wildness in his manner that she could manipulate for her own desires. For their part, they always jumped at the chance to be with an older, attractive women who had money and liked to fuck. Once they hooked up, she kept them separate from her public life (never introducing them to friends) and fed her appetite until she either got filled up and bored with them or they started getting too serious. Over the last eight years, there'd been a pack of young men like DJ buzzing in, each leaving his mark, and she went through them like a race car driver went through clutches.

"Got any blow?" he asked.

"No."

He mumbled a rude comment under his breath but she ignored it. His beer was empty, so she got up and brought him a fresh one from the fridge. He'd finished the Mongolian beef and started in on the remains of the fried rice. "You get this from that kook place on the corner?" he asked between bites.

"Hmm."

That was the extent of their conversation. After fifteen minutes, he finished off the leftovers along with two more beers, belching loudly to show his appreciation.

"Must you?"

"I must."

She looked at him, shaking her head, but she could see by his eyes and the sly grin on his face that he was right where she wanted him to be. She watched as he pulled his wallet out of his back pocket, which was connected to his belt by a silver chain, and opened it to count his money. He unhooked the chain from his belt, dropping both his wallet and the chain noisily on the coffee table, and then reached into his other back pocket and pulled out a pack of cigarettes.

"You're not smoking in here," she said.

He glanced at her, his eyes flashing anger. "Then I'll go out on the balcony," he answered, standing up.

"No you won't," she replied, knowing this would be the trigger. "Makes you taste like an ashtray. I hate it."

"I don't give a shit. I'm havin' a smoke."

Now she stood up. "No, you're not. Now get out!"

"I'm not goin' anywhere—fuckin' bitch."

"I said, get out!"

He was standing now, glaring across at her with a menacing stare. She threatened him to "get out or else," and he suddenly laughed at that and shot back, "Or else what? What you gonna do?—nuthin! I ain't goin' nowhere. So shut the fuck up!"

"You'll do as I say," she said as she moved to get past him, but he quickly grabbed her arm and pulled her towards him. His grip was tight and hurt her arm, and she tried in vain to twist free. "Let me go!" she ordered, her eyes showing defiance. He slapped her across the face, then again and again, using his fingertips instead of the flat of his hand (as she had taught him) while she tried to pull away. Quickly he spun her around, bending her arm behind her back and putting her in a choke hold. "Stop talking!" he snarled in her ear. "I'm sick of your shit—givin' me orders. I'm givin' the orders!" He pushed Gwen towards the bedroom door. She let out a whispered shriek, "No—no, let me go!" as he pushed her face first against the wall next to the bedroom.

He pressed up against her and she could feel his erection. He pulled his arm loose from around her neck and slid his hand down the front of her pants, fingering her wet vagina while he breathed heavily into her ear, threatening her with lewd and ugly remarks. She whimpered "no" and "don't," her protests only feeding his growing excitement. Suddenly she felt him let go of her arm from behind her back, moving his free hand under her shirt to squeeze her breasts, and as he did, she spun free, her shirt ripping, and ran into the bedroom. He chased after her, tackling Gwen from behind and onto the bed where the force of his body knocked the air out of her lungs. His body pressed down heavily on her, his hand pushing her face into the quilt, and she turned her head to try and catch her breath.

Straddling her body, he pulled off her lounging pants, then quickly unbuckled and kicked off his own pants, keeping her head pressed into the mattress. "No, please, no," she panted as she felt his knee go between her legs, forcing them apart. He kept up a running string of insults, calling her a "whore" and a "bitch," vowing to "tap that ass" as he worked to spread her legs farther apart. She fought against the attempt, trying to keep her legs together, but he was too strong, and she finally relented, feeling his hard cock plunge deep inside her. He pulled her ass up so he could work from his knees, pounding relentlessly into her while she gasped and moaned.

The first spank sounded like a handclap but the second one was louder. "Harder," she gasped. "Harder!" She'd dropped all pretense of being raped and wanted more of what he was giving out. DJ raised his arm and came down hard, spanking her on the left butt cheek, hearing her cry out in painfilled delight before raising his other arm and spanking her hard on the other cheek. He continued, left then right, each crisp spank followed by a cry of pleasured pain, as he rhythmically plunged himself into her. Abruptly he stopped and reached down, grabbing a handful of her hair, and pulled her head back. She rose up with it, arching her back, and he pulled harder until her face nearly pointed to the ceiling.

She was on the edge—the burning in her butt cheeks, his pounding cock, her neck and back stretched to the limit—she was on the edge. But she didn't give the safe word. It was always their middle name (in this case it was "Jesse," DJ's middle name), and all she had to do was say it for all the pain to stop. But she didn't say it, and at the very moment when she thought it was becoming too much, she felt her orgasm rising up in her and expel itself swiftly like a sneeze. At her stifled squeal, he let go of her hair and her face fell back against the quilt, and when she turned her head sideways he could see a smile.

He continued to fuck her from behind, and she knew it would go on for a while longer. She had chosen well. He was like a prize bull, and there was still one more thing she wanted from him before he came. She stretched out her arm and felt around the quilt until she found the anal plug, grabbing it and handing it back to DJ, who wasted no time in taking it and shoving it into her ass. It filled her to the point of busting, burning momentarily before settling in and exciting the nerve ending inside her rectum. Within a minute, she came again, quick and sneeze-like, but intensified in such a way by the ass plug that it felt like her head was exploding. A moment later, he came inside her, whooping loudly, and then fell, exhausted, on top of her.

He continued to lay there on top of her without moving until she opened her eyes and said sharply, "Get off me." He obeyed her command and rolled off her and onto his back. She found her torn shirt next to her pillow, stuck it between her legs, and walked into the bathroom where she closed the door and turned on the light. In the mirror, she quickly checked to confirm there were no marks on her face. Satisfied, she glanced behind her and saw that her butt cheeks were a bright red. She sat gingerly down on the toilet seat and began to clean herself. It took her a while to get it all. It was odd, she thought, how their cum load was so much heavier when they pretended it was rape.

After cleaning up, she slipped back into her lounging pants, threw on another shirt, and left DJ snoring on the bed as she walked back out into the living room. She couldn't sleep; she was still amped up. It was like the way she used to feel after a tough game of basketball. Her cat

Popeye appeared and rubbed himself against her leg, purring loudly. She picked him up and cradled him in her arms. He was a tomcat with short, reddish fur and one eye missing that he'd lost in a fight before she found him and took him in as her own. Now he was pretty much a tame house cat. He always hid away whenever one of her boyfriends like DJ came over, but he would come out of hiding once her fun was over.

With Popeye in one arm, Gwen poured herself another glass of wine and sat back down on the couch. Popeye curled up in her lap and she played with his ears, sipping her wine, and watching CNBC until nearly midnight before laying down on the couch and falling into a fitful sleep where she dreamed of playing basketball with her dad in the driveway.

Chapter 12

My date glanced around the room to see if anyone was looking at her. That's why I called her 'Starlet Girl'. She was always glancing about like a movie starlet to see if she was being noticed. Whether she was walking down the street, standing in line for coffee or, like now, entering on my arm into the crowded ballroom of the Hyatt Regency, she couldn't help but count up her admirers. But I couldn't blame her really. She was a dead ringer for Playboy's Miss September 1995, and people, especially men, were going to notice her. She even had the same first name as Miss September—Donna—which I found to be an amusing coincidence.

I'd been dating Donna for a couple of weeks now, had sex with her twice, and found her to be rather self-conscious in bed, gushy out of bed, with a daddy complex that accounted for why she was dating a man nearly twenty years her senior. I met her through the advertising agency we hired. She was on their account team as a sales rep reporting to a male account manager and acted more like eye candy than a contributing member of their brain trust. She took an immediate liking to me, but I ignored her come-ons given the fact that she was only twenty-five and acted, at times, like eighteen. But… well, in the words of Winston Churchill: "It is hard, if not impossible, to snub a beautiful woman."

Donna may not have been the type of woman I normally dated, which tended to be more mature and fully-rounded, but her physical looks trumped all cards. At least for the time being. At five foot-four, a hundred and ten pounds out of the shower, and a thirty-four-inch bust, she was delectably shaped. And tonight, she was dressed to kill in an elegant, black cocktail dress that hugged her figure and showed off her soft knees and shapely calves. She wore a black velvet choker, and her buttery blonde hair was tied up in French milkmaid braids, revealing a most kissable neck. Even I couldn't take my eyes off her.

We stood in the entrance area to the ballroom, next to a long bar that was quickly filling up with people, and I introduced Donna to the various employees and colleagues who mingled around with their dates and spouses. This was CrestPoint's first annual 'Holiday Celebration', which was a synonym for 'Christmas Party'. Lori Hunter, our new Executive Vice President of Human Resources and Administration, had insisted that this lavish shindig be called a 'Holiday Celebration" instead of a 'Christmas Party' for reasons of inclusiveness and diversity. Chandra and Ron had argued in favor of keeping a Christmas theme to the gala; Marty and I were ambivalent, while Stu tilted the scales by insisting that the festivities recognize Hanukkah. In the end, Ms. Hunter prevailed and the event was officially dubbed a 'Holiday Celebration'.

"Hey, Russ," called out Marty as he walked up to us with his wife Hana following close behind. He put his hand on my shoulder, squeezing it gently. "You look dapper as always. And who's this gorgeous young lady?"

I introduced Donna to both Marty and Hana. Marty gave her a genteel handshake and said, "Wait... Donna, from Digital Marketing, right? I thought I recognized you. The hairdo threw me. Marvelous dress, by the way." Donna thanked him for the compliment while I glanced over at Hana. She wore an expensive-looking evening gown that was tailored perfectly to fit her petite frame. "And you, Hana, look like a vision in that dress," I commented in turn.

"Thank you, Russ," replied Hana, blushing slightly.

"Where we sitting?" asked Marty. Fittingly, he was in a festive mood, grinning broadly, squeezing my shoulder, and looking every bit of the rock-star CEO in a light blue checkered suit that was offset by a gaudy, red and white Santa Claus tie.

I glanced out at the dinner tables spread in a semi-circle in front of a dance floor and stage, each with a white tablecloth and elaborate place settings, and replied, "Not sure... But we're spread out." The five of us EVPs were not to sit at our own table like some king and his liege lords but instead were to be divvied up around the room. This meant we would have to walk around to find our name card.

"Right, right," remembered Marty, nodding happily.

"We were just about to get a drink," I said. "Want us to get you something?"

"No, we're good for now. We'll hang out here for a while and greet folks—there's Ron and his wife. See you two on the dance floor." With that, he took his hand off my shoulder and turned to greet another couple who had just entered. Donna and I walked over to the bar and ordered drinks.

We were expecting nearly three hundred people at this event. That included almost all our one hundred employees, their spouses and dates, along with a selection of suppliers and contractors we invited to join us. It was meant to be both a holiday celebration and a recognition event, and we'd spared no expense at ensuring it'd be a lavish affair. Marty was insistent on that. At $75,000, there was going to be dinner, dancing, an open bar, free rooms (if you wanted one), a stand-up comedian, two rock bands, an awards ceremony where Marty would play Santa Claus and give out $100 gift certificates, and a game of Trivial Pursuit that would award every guest at the winning table a Sony Walkman. And at that price tag, I expected my Johnnie Walker Red on ice, with a splash of water, to be more blended scotch whiskey than water. A short sip of my drink happily confirmed my expectations.

Donna held her vodka martini and glanced around the room. I greeted several folks who came through the bar area, meeting their partners and sharing chit-chat. Ron Lau and his wife, an earthy-looking woman with a ready smile, stopped to say hi, then ordered sparkling waters and wandered off to find their table. I flagged down Chandra and signaled him to come over. His wife Cherry was a slightly overweight woman with big blonde hair, but she was always classy looking and appeared particularly so tonight dressed in a chic evening gown that seemed to swirl around her body like whipped cream frosting (she'd always reminded me a little bit of Miss June 1967). I introduced them to Donna, and we talked for a bit.

"Is Stu here," I asked Chandra. "I'm curious as to whether he brought his wife. I've never met her."

"Yeah, they're over there," responded Chandra with a nod of his head. He had a glint in his eye as though he was enjoying a private joke. "Can't miss them."

"Who's that?" asked Cherry.

"Stu and his wife."

"Oh… Her name is Miriam. Can't miss her." She glanced at her husband with a similar glint in her eye, revealing that they shared the same private joke.

I was intrigued, but I wasn't going to press them for details. I'd find out for myself.

Donna ordered another martini. I was still nursing my drink, but since I was closer to the bartender, I ordered drinks for Chandra and Cherry. We talked a while longer and then they left to mingle with the growing crowd. Donna was on her third martini.

"Let's check out the hors d'oeuvres," I suggested.

"Sounds yummy."

We walked over to a long table that contained a potpourri of finger foods including jumbo shrimp, Swedish meatballs, prosciutto, and bacon-encased water chestnuts (amongst a host of other goodies). Donna stood in front of it all, martini in one hand, the other on her hip, and scanned the table back and forth. "Jeez, where to begin?" she wondered out loud. I handed her a small plate.

"Start with the shrimp," I said. "You need to eat something. Martinis on an empty stomach are never a good idea."

"Okay, Daddy," she replied sharply. Donna reached down and picked up a jumbo shrimp by the tail, dipped it in cocktail sauce, and ate it in one bite, licking her fingers clean to show she was done. "There, I've eaten something."

"Have some more," I said with a smile while wondering if I was going to have a problem with this woman. Three martinis in less than an hour was rather immoderate; it suggested a lack of judgement, and I didn't like the idea of having to keep an eye on her. I turned my back on Starlet Girl, but the gesture caused her to quickly sidle up to me and hug my arm.

• 127

"You're right, I need to eat something," she said agreeably. I patted her hand and looked up to see Mark and Ronnie on the other side of the table.

"Mister Kirkland, Merry Christmas!"

"Hi'ya, Russ. Merry Christmas. You remember Ronnie?"

"Of course… Hi, Ronnie. How are the kids?"

She smiled back, cool as a cucumber, and gave me a quick report on the state of their two kids without looking me in the eyes. That was fine to hear, I replied with a big smile. I introduced them to Donna, and then asked Mark where they were sitting. "I think we're gonna sit over there," he replied, indicating a table on the west side of the ballroom.

"I'm not sure where they got me," I said. "I haven't looked yet."

"You're over there," said Ronnie, nodding towards the east side of the ballroom. "That table there where the waiter just set down the wine bottle. I saw your name card."

"Oh, great… thanks." I found it interesting that she knew my seat assignment and that the two of them had chosen a table as far away as possible. I wondered if that was her doing.

Though it might have been Mark's doing. Our relationship had become rather strained lately, ever since he returned from Kansas City and reported to me that our City Manager there—Stony Bundschuh—was using bribes and prostitution to achieve his impressive success. I took the accusations to Stu but got nowhere with them; as a lawyer, he dismissed it all by saying that without a smoking gun there could be no crime. In my follow-up meeting with Mark, I told him I couldn't act on these accusations without hard evidence to back them up. He admitted he didn't have hard evidence—just feedback from trusted sources in the area. I let him know that wasn't going to be enough, and I could see the disappointment on his face. I did get an agreement that Stony would no longer use his own installation crews, and I thought this news would assuage Mark's disappointment. It didn't.

Yet, it wasn't like Mark to take things like that personally. I'd worked with him long enough to know that setbacks, mistakes, or personal affronts—related to the job—didn't faze him for long. They were like water off a duck's back. But something was bothering him.

Maybe his marriage was in trouble again, though the two of them certainly looked happy enough.

"Judy!" exclaimed Donna upon seeing one of the sales reps she knew from our office. Judy shouted her name back, and Donna quickly joined her and another sales rep in excited conversation. It reminded me of old cheerleaders reuniting at a high school reunion.

I smiled wryly at Mark and Ronnie as if to say, "Yes, I know she's young," picked out a couple of hors d'oeuvres, said, "Have fun," to the two of them, then walked over to Donna and her friends. They were engrossed in conversation, but when I placed my hand around Donna's shoulder to tell her I'd be right back, they all stopped talking and looked me over in a way I was very familiar with. "I'll be right here," she assured me. I nodded, smiling at the two other women who shot rapid glances at each other like envious schoolgirls.

I set my empty drink down and walked around, picking at the food on my plate while scanning the ballroom for Stu. My curiosity was piqued; I had to meet this mysterious wife of his. I found them sitting alone together at a table, eating from a plate piled high with hors d'oeuvres. He saw me coming and quickly leaned over to his wife and said something, causing her to look up and put me in her sites.

"Stu, there you are. Happy Hannukah. And is this your lovely wife?"

"Yes... Miriam, this is Russ Chappel."

Before I could say, "It's a pleasure to meet you," she quickly said, "Yes, yes. Russ Chappel. My husband has mentioned your name to me." She looked me up and down with her big brown eyes under a fluttering set of false eyelashes. Her face was round and noticeably pancaked with make-up, and she wore her dark hair up in a beehive in a way that made her look like a character out of some sixties sitcom. Her black evening dress seemed a tad too small for a woman who was buxom and broad in the beam, and the neckline of her dress, which revealed only the beginning of a very deep cleavage, was covered by a gaudy necklace that looked like a large, gold bicycle chain around her neck. She wore matching earrings.

"You were at MFS with Stuey," She continued. "I'm *sooo* glad he's out of there. I told him MFS was no good. Don't you agree? The office politics were the worse, but I'm sure you know all about that—"

"We don't need to talk about MFS," interrupted Stu.

"No, of course not," she replied, not missing a beat. "Russ, please, have a seat… You're quite handsome. Somehow my husband *failed* to mention that. And single, too. I bet you have to beat them off with a stick. And you founded CrestPoint with Stuey, and with Marty—Marty's a peach, don't you think? — and together you're going to give us all—what does he call it?—'high-speed Internet' and you're all going to become rich and famous. If I'm lucky, maybe I'll get a new car out of it. I have a '92 Mercedes. Five years old now. Time for a new one, don't you think?"

"I'm sure Russ isn't interested in the year and make of your car," interjected Stu.

"Oh, but I am," I said cheerfully. I saw an opportunity here, an opportunity to get under Stu's skin, and I wasn't going to pass it up. The dynamic between these two was easy to read: she talked, he scolded, and she talked some more. "What kind of car would you like to get?" I asked her.

And off she went, like an emptying balloon, filling the air with her hopes and desires, gilded opinions, off-the-wall observations, and crafty non-sequiturs. Stu squirmed in his seat while I did my best to feed the boiler. ("Is that a Brooklyn accent I detect?"—"What a marvelous looking necklace. Must have cost a fortune."—"I never knew that about Stuey. Tell me more.") Each time she grabbed the bait and ran with it, and soon I was learning a wide array of personal things about her and Stu's life. Stu would interrupt her at times, sometimes severely, but the best he could do was get her to change the subject. Otherwise, he sat there squirming, his face turning redder by the minute.

Unfortunately, my fun ended when Marty's voice came over the PA system welcoming everyone and telling folks to find a table. I got up from my chair and took Miriam's hand in farewell, kissing it lightly while glancing over at Stu. (If looks could kill, I would have gone down in a heap.)

I looked around for Donna but she wasn't where I'd left her, so I found my seat and kept an eye out for her. The large round dining tables were slowly filling up, and I happily welcomed the folks who sat down at my table. Donna appeared, along with her buddy Judy and a date. She kissed me on the cheek and sat down, resuming a conversation with Judy that would last through dinner. I was encouraged to see that Donna no longer held a martini glass.

Once everyone was seated, Marty welcomed us all to "CrestPoint's first annual Holiday Celebration." He paced the stage, microphone in hand, and launched into a rousing speech that recapped the year's accomplishments, thanking everyone in the room for their hard work and dedication.

Marty had every right to crow a little. Heck, we all did. Everything we'd set out to accomplish—securing investors, hiring talent, delivering on promises—in short, giving birth to a new company, had been done. The old adage that 'Starting is easy, finishing is hard' wasn't quite right. There had been long days and hard work, even mistakes and failures, but we'd persevered, learning from our mistakes, building off the failures, and pouring our blood, sweat, and tears into making it work right. As we expected, the Baby Bells fought us the whole way, throwing out obstacles and excuses to keep us from establishing our footprint, but we effectively counterpunched by filing FCC complaints, threatening lawsuits, and even calling in old favors and debts to get them to play fair. Our 'proof-of-concept' was a success; we'd shown our investors that we could build a DSL network by delivering high-speed Internet to small businesses in six key areas in the country. We were even billing some of them.

Overall, I was very pleased with where we were at. There was much more to come in 1998—more market areas to penetrate, a network to expand and a team to grow, and it would be at least another year before we could launch DSL into the consumer market. But tonight, it was time to celebrate. Most start-up companies never made it through the first year. We'd not only made it, we'd made it in style. And tonight was the night to shout it to the rafters.

Marty was doing a good job of that. The crowd was fired up and rocking to his beat. (I knew for a fact that he had hired a political consultant to explore a run for state office sometime in the future, and I think he was practicing his speechifying.) And with Marty, there was always the unexpected. Tonight was no exception. He suddenly stopped his pacing and in a conspiratorial whisper told us to lift up our dinner plates. There we found a fifty-dollar gift certificate. The discovery caused whoops and hollers across the room. Donna and Judy leaped up, squealing in delight, and hugged each other.

Donna had not stopped cheering and yelling throughout Marty's speech and I was getting a little annoyed with her. At this new outburst, I grabbed her arm to keep her from jumping and down but failed, so I handed her my gift certificate in the hopes of quieting her down. This elicited another squeal of delight and she hugged me, covering my face with kisses, a face that was quickly turning red with embarrassment.

Mercifully, she stopped as Marty wrapped up his performance and signaled the waiters to begin serving dinner. Donna sat back down and we all settled in to the first course of our three-course meal. There were both red and white wine bottles on the table and I poured myself a glass of red. Donna had already started in on the white wine and was drinking it like water. She ate very little and talked a lot. I pretended to enjoy my over-cooked prime rib while making conversation with the folks at our table. Donna and Judy got up a couple of times during dinner to go to the bathroom, which gave me a welcome break from their noise.

After dessert, the comedian came on stage and did his act. Most of his material was based on pop culture and current events. There were jokes about George Clooney—People Magazine's Sexist Man Alive winner—Ellen DeGeneres coming out of the closet, Marv Albert's trial for forcible sodomy, Frank Gifford cheating on his wife, and, of course, the escapades of President Bill Clinton. He did a bit about the Baby Bells whining at having to give up space for our equipment, comparing it with stuffing college students into a phone booth, which was rather funny. He got a hearty applause when he finished.

The Heights of Mountains

An awards ceremony followed with Marty playing Santa Claus, and one of the awards went to Stony Bundschuh (we had flown the City Managers in for the event). I wondered at Mark's reaction to that, so I craned my neck and looked across the room at Mark's table. He was talking to Ronnie and ignoring it all. Next came a game of Trivial Pursuit that a table stacked with IT techs won hands down. After that game, the first rock band of the night started playing and folks made their way out to the dance floor.

Donna wanted to dance but I declined, so she raced out to the dance floor with Judy and her date and the three of them danced together. Starlet Girl gyrated seductively on the dance floor, always glancing around at her admirers, and at one point, she and Judy bent down suggestively in front of the crotch of Judy's date as he danced in place. She put on a bloody spectacle, and her antics weren't going unnoticed by people around the ballroom.

I'd misread Donna. Usually my instincts, combined with my keen eye, could tell early on whether a woman was a match for me, or not. But this keen sense failed me this time. Perhaps her Playmate good looks had skewed my judgement, yet I'd dropped beautiful women like her before, women who showed early signs of being self-indulgent or immature, without any hesitation. Perhaps my mistake was her age. She wasn't much older than my son, for Christ's sake, and the twenty-year difference had probably fed my ego. This was something I needed to be cognizant of in the future. Either way, Starlet Girl was a noisy sloppy drunk, and I detested noisy sloppy drunks.

I got up from the table and walked off, stopping to talk with co-workers at the various tables, mingling with others in the bar area, and generally trying to keep my distance from Donna for the rest of the evening. I found Ron and his wife sitting alone at their table and I joined them. They seemed a tad out of place, like out-of-towners riding the subway at night, and the loud music and raucous behavior on the dance floor made them visibly uncomfortable. I swung a chair over to be close to them so we could hear each other over the music, and I immediately congratulated Ron on our success, joking that the five of us—a bunch of outcasts from MFS—hadn't done too bad at launching our own company. Ron and his wife smiled and nodded at this remark, and Ron leaned in close to tell me it was all a part of God's plan and that we should be thankful.

"I don't know about that," I kidded him. "The only plan I see is five smart jaspers starting their own company and making a fortune out of delivering fast-speed Internet to the masses."

Ron nodded and he and his wife smiled politely at me, and for the moment I felt like I'd committed something of a faux pas, so I quickly changed the topic. We talked about our staffing needs for the coming year before his wife gently nudged him and he excused himself, telling me with his congenial good manners that it was past their bedtime and time for them to go home. I wished them both a good evening and walked off.

I met Lori Hunter's partner, a short-haired, serious looking woman like herself, and we talked briefly about biking. Marty was in high spirits and feeling no pain, and he was showing everyone pictures of his six-month-old son and cracking jokes that everybody laughed at. He hugged me numerous times, patting me on the back and calling me "old chap", before his wife Hana, rolling her eyes affectionately, finally dragged him off to their room.

I had secured a room for the night even though the Hyatt was only a short drive down the freeway from the yacht harbor, but I didn't want to chance driving home drunk. When the live music wrapped up just after midnight and the event officially ended, I remained at the bar deciding what to do—go home or find Donna and go up to our room.

As I was debating the situation, two arms came around my neck from behind. It was Donna. I swiveled my barstool around to face her.

"Found you," she said breathlessly. "Thought I'd lost you—wow, what a night! I danced up a storm—that was fun. What you do all night?—Did you see me dancing out there?"

"I did," I said, studying her face. A slight sheen of perspiration covered her face and arms. Her French, milkmaid braids had come loose during the evening, giving her a rather tousled look, and her pupils were dilated and unsteady. She was obviously drunk, and perhaps something more. I'd kept my eye on her throughout the evening, and when she wasn't making a fool out of herself on the dance floor, she and her friends were either huddled together at our table, drinking wine and yakking it up, or they were all running off to the bathroom together.

With her arms still around my neck, she leaned into my ear and whispered, "Are we going up to the room? I'm horny as hell."

I decided not to end it here and risk a scene. I'd take her up to the room, get her settled in, and then politely say my farewells. "Sure," I replied with a slight smile. I took her hand and led her to the elevator.

Once in our room, she made a beeline for the bathroom, and I stood next to the bed listening to her pee and rustle about. I grabbed my overnight bag and set it on the edge of the bed, waiting for her to reappear. When she emerged from the bathroom, she was stark naked except for her velvet black choker and a small purse she carried in her hands. She quickly sat down at the desk, opened her purse, and took out a small, folded-up piece of paper. As she unfolded the piece of paper, revealing the white powder inside (which I knew to be cocaine), she kept up a running dialogue.

"There's a party in room 369. We should check it out later. My friends'll be there. I'm sure other CrestPointers will be there. It'll be hella fun. We'll check it out after. Whaddya say? We'll party here first, then go over there and party some more. First a line of coke. There was a line out of the ladies restroom for lines of coke. All night. A line for lines. Ha, ha, ha…"

I half listened to her talk while watching her cut up the little mound of cocaine with her credit card and lay out two lines on top of the desk. She pulled a dollar bill out of her purse—still talking – rolled it up, snorted a line, then licked her finger, wiping up the residue with it and then reaching down between her legs where she rubbed it into her pussy. Once done, she turned and offered the rolled-up dollar bill to me.

At that moment, with the sheen of perspiration still on her body, the tousled hair, her uninhibited nakedness, and the professional way she handled cocaine, she reminded me of a hooker working on her third trick of the night. I tried to hold back my total disgust for this scene and simply picked up my overnight bag. "No," I said loudly.

My response startled her, and she swung her chair around to face me, her legs spread apart with a look of confusion on her face. She began to speak but I cut her off.

"Listen to me," I said firmly while grabbing a pillow off the bed. I tossed it to her. "Cover yourself up—no, stop talking. Listen. We're done, young lady. Tonight, you made a fool out of yourself, and you embarrassed me. You were carrying on like some out-of-control teenager—the drinking, the drugs, the shoddy behavior. Totally unacceptable. I don't know what you were thinking, or whether you were even thinking at all, but it really doesn't matter at this point. You're not a woman I'm interested in being with anymore. And I guess I blame myself for that. You're too young, too immature, totally lacking in any kind of self-control, and I should have known better… So, put your clothes on, go to your party, do whatever it is you want to do—the room's all yours. I'm going home."

She listened to me with a growing look of shock on her face, and now, having heard it all, she suddenly broke into tears. "My bad, my bad, I know," she spluttered. "I'm *so, so sorry!*" I moved to go but she leaped up from the chair and sat down on the edge of the bed next to me, grabbing my arm. "My bad… I'm *so, so sorry,*" she repeated as the tears streamed down her face. The stress had been too great, she explained between sobs—the pressure too great—from being "with you… the man…Russ Chappel… everyone idolizes you," and she had to find a way to relieve it. She'd been wrong—stupid and wrong—and she knew it.

I stood next to her with her head against my crotch, gently stroking her hair and trying to get her to calm down. She sniffled, cried some more, sniffled again, and I wondered how long I would have to stand here stroking her hair before she calmed down enough for me to leave.

I suddenly realized that she was trying to undo my belt buckle. I immediately stepped back, said "No," but she hooked her hands into my belt and pulled me into her.

"*Please,*" she said, looking up at me with her big wet eyes and her swollen lips while she quickly worked to unbuckle my pants. "*Just one more time—I know you want me—just one more time,*" she pleaded. And now my cock was in her hand, quickly growing hard despite my efforts to fight it. "*See—I knew it!—I knew you wanted me!*" She stroked me until I was fully hard then slid up on the bed, crab-walking backwards until her head hit the pillow, then opened her legs and reached out to me. "*Come to me—now! I know you want me—come on, come on.*"

What the hell, I thought—*Just one more time.* If that's what she wanted then that's what I'd give her. Within seconds, I was undressed and on top of her, and we were going at it with total abandon. No doubt the cocaine fueled her carnal lust. As for me—I funneled my anger into a non-stop assault on her body. Face-to-face, legs up, from behind, sideways, she was insatiable, wanting it *more* and wanting it *harder.* Eventually, she ended up on top, riding me like a bronco buck, for ten—fifteen minutes, until I finally came and she collapsed onto my chest.

I was exhausted. It felt as though my life's essence had been drained from my body, and I closed my eyes with her lying on top of me and dozed off. When I awoke, she was gone.

I got dressed and checked my watch. It was two-thirty in the morning. Donna had finished off the second line of coke and was now, most likely, scoring more of it at the party in room 369. *Adios, Starlet Girl.* As I grabbed my overnight bag to leave, I felt a twinge in my back. I straightened up and tried to stretch it out.

No more twenty-year-olds. I was decided on that.

Book Two

Chapter 1

For the people of CrestPoint Communications Inc., 1998 flew by like the start and end of an intense sporting event. They were busy all year long, sometimes working at a frenetic pace, while never once doubting that they were doing something incredibly important. The long hours piled up along with the seven-day work weeks, but there were no complaints or talk of bailing out. The work was fun and they enjoyed themselves, often without even knowing it, as though they were crusaders too caught up in the noble struggle to notice the hardships they were enduring. When the year ended and another Holiday Celebration was attended—this one larger, flashier, and even more lavish than the first one—people mingled in the ornate ballroom, cocktails in hand, and looked back over the year with pride at what they had accomplished.

And what they accomplished in 1998 wasn't bad for a start-up company that lost $25.4 million on only $922,000 in sales. Those losses were expected; that was the price of future greatness. The good news was, their DSL service was available to businesses in 17 markets, encompassing 36 cities, and there were plans to expand to another 11 market areas by the end of 1999. CrestPoint currently had about 3,400 business users paying an average of $130 a month for service. Cheap and reliable high-speed Internet was becoming a reality.

It was a paradigm shift, and the industry was taking notice. By using CrestPoint's DSL product, even the smallest Internet providers like Telocity, Brainstorm, or Fastcom could get access to a high-speed data system that was more advanced than anything America Online was using. These ISPs were eager to jump on the bandwagon, signing deals with CrestPoint at a rapid pace. And for Marty and his leadership team, they struck while the iron was hot, expanding their footprint, forging alliances with such high-tech giants as Microsoft and Intel, while inking deals with over eighty online connection companies. Money from venture capitalists and investment banks continued to flow in. CrestPoint's payroll increased to 500 employees and their office space at Rio Seco Business Park doubled in size.

1998 was the gathering crest of the dot-com wave, and Marty and company rode that wave along with hundreds of others. Online service companies continued to sprout up, companies like JD.com, PayPal, Cars.com, and Kozmo.com, while in Menlo Park, California, Google.com was founded by two Stanford students. Anything connected to the Internet was golden, and many in these start-ups couldn't wait to go public and become instant millionaires. IPOs turned into marketing events while employees anxiously watched the stock tickers and counted up their fortunes. Of the 379 IPOs in '98, many were Internet-related companies, and many like Inktomi, VeriSign, and Xoom were based in the Bay Area with the granddaddy of them all—eBay—going public in September at $18 a share and closing the year at $241.25 a share.

As the Dot-com boom flourished so did the Telecom boom, the one attracting the other like pollinating bees to a field of bright-colored flowers. There were some 15,000 CLECs nationwide (CrestPoint being just one of them). Technology manufacturers like Lucent and Nortel Networks expanded at unprecedented rates. Worldcom bought MCI, Cisco acquired Netspeed, and everywhere people believed that the sky was the limit.

Some wondered if it could last, but if they voiced their doubts at all it was done carefully, with words couched in euphemisms and qualifiers, so as not to appear a spoilsport. This was characteristic of the year 1998. It was a year of big dreams, big achievements, and big lies. Mark McGuire hit 70 home runs in '98, and if some sports analysts were skeptical of this feat, given McGuire's pumped-up physique, they kept it too themselves. Instead, they sat back like millions of others and cheered as the balls flew out of the ballpark.

Chapter 2

I could hear the anxiety in Marty's voice. It was the same anxiety we all felt. Our two main competitors—Nomad Communications and Pulse Netconnections—had just gone public and raised a combined $290 million in hugely successful IPOs. We had always planned to go public in the summer of '99, but now the heat was on to speed up our timeline as much as possible.

"Look at the publicity they're getting," said Marty, lifting up the business section of the San Francisco Chronicle for all of us to see. "You couldn't buy better publicity than this. They're the lead story on CNBC…"

Marty continued to vent his frustration at our competition beating us to the punch. I was a little more philosophical about it. Sure, we were late to the prom, but we were flush with cash thanks to Marty's talents at raising venture capital, and we were about to launch service into the consumer market. Granted, Nomad and Pulse were enjoying the spotlight at the moment, but they were just opening acts to the headliner—CrestPoint Communications.

I glanced around the conference table to gauge everyone's mood. Ron Lau sat stoically with his hands clasped on the tabletop, listening intently to Marty. No panic there. And Chandra was cool as a cucumber; he leaned back in his chair watching Marty with that amused twinkle in his eyes, and when he noticed me looking at him, he gave me a wink and smiled. Lori Hunter, EVP of Human Resources and Administration, sat staring down at her notepad with a slight scowl on her face. But that scowl was normal. She was a gray, flat, masculine-looking woman who always seemed on the verge of giving us all a proper dressing down. Her demeanor remained that of a menopausal nanny. That brought me to

Stu, who sat fidgeting in his chair like the kid in the classroom who knows the answer and can't wait to be called on.

"And, I think, we need to advance our IPO to April or May," said Marty, coming to the point. "We'll need to confirm this with the underwriters, but I'm confident Morgan Stanley will accommodate our plans. Whaddya think Stu?"

"They will," replied Stu quickly. "And if not, there's a half dozen more out there chomping at the bit to underwrite our IPO. I'm not worried about that. But let's be clear here—as to the impact these IPOs are going to have on us. Besides advancing our timeline, the publicity they're getting out of this—as Marty points out—will give them a bump in subscriptions. It's like a one-two punch, and we need to come right back at 'em—like Mike Tyson"

"And what, bite their ear off?" I asked, taking a shot at Stu's affinity for sports metaphors and hyperbole.

"If need be," replied Stu, taking my quip good-naturedly. "But my point is this: we need to move up our IPO. One, to regain our momentum—and we'll certainly gain it back when we launch into the consumer market—and two, for the money. I know we're sitting on $60 million that Marty and I have raised over the last couple months, but that also represents a debt. We need to speed up our IPO because the public equity market has become a cheaper source of capital than anything we can raise in the private sector."

There were nods of agreement around the table. I found it interesting that Stu was partly taking credit for raising venture capital when it was really Marty's talents and his talents alone that had garnered the cash. One of these days, Stu was going to throw his shoulder out patting himself on the back.

"Looks like we're agreed then," said Marty. "We advance our IPO into spring. Any other thoughts on the matter?"

Stu started to speak again but I cut him off. "We need to be careful how we present this to the industry," I said. "You've gone on record saying our IPO would be in late summer, now we're changing our story. The analysts and trade publications are all gonna wanna know why we changed our plans. Are we panicking? Are we running out of cash?"

The Heights of Mountains

"It's simple," replied Chandra. "We don't want to wait to cash in our winning lottery ticket."

"Exactly," I agreed. "In the words of Churchill, 'We have before us a great opportunity, a golden opportunity, glittering bright but short-lived.' And our message should be this: We came together as a team, surveyed the landscape, and in a calm and collected manner, decided it was in the best interests of our future shareholders to advance our public stock offering. And, no, we're not strapped for capital—thanks to *Marty's* efforts. We make that clear. But to Stu's point, we can't continue to accrue debt when there's a cheaper source of capital at hand."

"It's a strategic decision," added Ron.

"Quite right."

"Couldn't agree more," concurred Marty. "That's exactly how we'll position it."

We all glanced at each other around the conference table, making quick eye contact to confirm that we were all on the same page. This was how we typically voted, like NASA Control with nods and eye contact rather than a show of hands at a PTA meeting.

"One more thing related to the IPO," said Stu. "A logistical issue. A requirement really. We must hire an accounting firm to come in and basically live with us. That's part of the process—and I'll set up a call with the underwriters to take us through that process in more detail—but for now just know that I've engaged Tollerson Accounting to be our auditor. They'll be responsible for preparing all the financial info needed to file with the Securities and Exchange Commission, as well as our quarterly earnings reports."

"Wait now," replied Ron with a look of confusion on his face. "We talk about this before. I thought we were putting out RFP. Then make the decision together."

"So did I," I said.

Stu glanced over at Marty, who showed no emotion, before continuing. "Hmm, yes, we discussed it, but that was before Nomad and Pulse went public and it became obvious we needed to accelerate our plans. So, I moved on it… In a two-minute drill, you don't call a timeout unless it's absolutely necessary, and I didn't think it necessary."

• 145

"It wasn't your call."

"I disagree. As CFO, financial auditing clearly falls under my purview. And Marty was in the loop. I kept him fully apprised of my decision."

"You're missing the point," I said. "It wasn't your decision to make. It should have been the team's decision." I looked over at Marty for help, but he remained inscrutable. "Marty?"

"Yes, *Marty*," echoed Stu.

Marty shrugged his shoulders. "He had my blessing," he replied nonchalantly. "I told him to move on it—and he did. Tollerson is a top-notch accounting firm. None better. So, I'm sure we'll all be happy with the decision."

"But why secrecy?" asked Ron. "Why do we find out about this just now?"

"I can't brief everyone on every little thing," countered Stu.

"It's not a little thing, Stu," I said. "We had a game plan and you changed it."

"I simply called an audible," replied Stu, glancing around the table to see if his witty comeback would elicit smiles. It didn't.

"Okay, it's on me," said Marty, pointing a finger at himself. "I should have communicated better. I gave Stu the go-ahead on this and should have let you all know, but I was caught up in negotiations with Microsoft and meetings with investors and it slipped my mind. Juggling too many balls. But it's done, and we need to move on." He paused and looked first at Ron and then over at me with an expression that expertly mixed contriteness with impatience. "I'll try better in the future to communicate these things… That's all I can say. If you want to discuss it further, then let's take it offline. We still have an important agenda item to discuss."

The "let's-take-it-off-line" remark was Marty's way of saying *shut up and move on*. Very well, I decided. Why Marty was taking the blame for a communication break-down that was clearly Stu's doing, and why he was defending this toad, was beyond me. But so be it. In a way, this brought us perfectly to the next agenda item—a discussion about bringing in a new President to run CrestPoint Communications.

For some time now, there had been a growing consensus among the officers that Marty's role as President and CEO was becoming too much for him. The primary role of President was to oversee the day-to-day running of the business, to resolve inter-departmental conflict, and to insure alignment between strategy and execution. But what Marty enjoyed doing was raising capital, negotiating deals, and exploring innovative ideas. He was extraordinary at these things. Because of this focus, the day-to-day running of the business had taken a back seat. Through his own admission, Marty was not as interested in the minutiae of running CrestPoint as he was in exploiting CrestPoint's potential in the marketplace. He'd given birth to a racehorse and all he wanted to do now was ride it—not feed it, groom it, or clean-up after it.

Marty was open to bringing in a new president. It was understood that he'd remain CEO, and once we went public, become chairman of the board of directors. In principle, we were all in agreement, and now it was just a matter of finding the right person to come in and take over running the nuts and bolts of CrestPoint Communications.

"Then let's move on to that next agenda item," I said cheerfully. "It's the perfect segue." (Personally, I was a little skeptical about how this was going to play out. Marty was not one to give up power this easily.)

"Right then," agreed Marty, taking over the discussion. He quickly recapped the issue, assuring us that he was in complete agreement with bringing in a new President to run the day-to-day stuff, even owning up to the fact that he'd let some things fall through the cracks over the last year due to his busy schedule. "Now we need to beat the bushes for a suitable candidate," he concluded with a charitable smile.

"Someone with a proven track record," said Chandra. "Properly vetted."

"And chosen by us... together," added Ron.

"Yes, assuming Stu hasn't already hired someone, this should be a team decision. *Collectively*," I said.

"Of course, it will be," agreed Marty, pausing for effect. "But who's out there that wants the job?"

"Why do we need to look outside this room?" asked Stu. "Who'd be better suited to take on the role of president than someone who helped found the company and knows how it works?"

"And who might that someone be?" I asked. "You?"

"I think I can make a compelling case."

"I can make an equally compelling case for Ron or Chandra. But let's see—Ron, Chandra, are either one of you interested in becoming President of CrestPoint Communications?"

Ron emphatically shook his head 'no' while Chandra leaned back in his chair with a whimsical smile and said, "If nominated, I will not accept. If elected, I will not serve."

There was laughter at that, and I appreciated Chandra's well-timed quip. It helped my aim. "Like you," I said, looking straight at Stu, "we all have full-time jobs. If Chandra became President, we'd have to find a new CIO. In your case, a new CFO. And don't tell us you could combine both CFO and President in your job description."

"I wouldn't tell you that," countered Stu calmly. "But I'd like to make my case—if I can get a fair hearing... I think I have a workable plan, one that leverages the talents we have in-house instead of going out and bringing in a stranger. May I then... if I can get your undivided attention."

"By all means," replied Marty. "Make your case."

Chandra and I exchanged glances that said it all: if Marty was going to listen, then we were all going to listen, though a sharp stick in the eye would have been preferable. I didn't believe for a second that Marty supported this coup attempt, though what his motive was for allowing this rubbish was beyond me.

For the next ten minutes, Stu made his case to become President of CrestPoint Communications. He knew the company inside and out. He understood the problems and what needed to be done about them better than anyone. There would be no need to bring in a new CFO; they would simply promote Harold Rubin to that position. Stu went on to explain how he as President and Rubin as CFO would be the path of least upheaval and a boon to the company.

Harold (Hal) Rubin had been hired by Stu six months ago as V.P. of Finance. (He was another smoker; Stu seemed to only hire smokers.) So, what Stu's proposal amounted to was a power grab, pure and simple. He would take over as President while his hand-picked man would step in as CFO. That would be two votes on the board of directors. Marty showed no reaction to Stu's pitch, neither nodding nor frowning, and wore his Kabuki mask of inscrutability throughout.

Towards the end of Stu's pitch, Lori suddenly fell into a loud sneezing fit, causing Stu to give her an annoyed look as she got up out of her chair saying, "I'm so sorry—achoo!" and left the room. Thank God for small miracles, I thought. The incident threw Stu out of rhythm, ruining what he'd hoped would be a rousing finish.

There was a moment of awkward silence and I seized it. It was past noon—and that was all the pretext I needed. "Why don't we break for lunch here," I suggested. "Give us some time to digest this… proposal."

"Good idea," agreed Marty. "Let's meet back here at, what, one-thirty. How's that sound?"

Everyone agreed to the break, though Stu looked as though someone had just turned the channel on his favorite TV show.

———

I walked into my office and stood in front of the window, looking out through the blinds. They were slanted in such a way that I could see out but no one could see in. The large oak trees outside were beginning to shed some of their leaves to make way for new ones. A light, misting rain was falling and the cement walkways were wet. I couldn't remember if I had closed the port windows in my bedroom.

"That was cringe-worthy," remarked Chandra as he and Ron entered my office. They didn't waste any time getting here, I thought. That was a good sign.

"Did you have any idea about that?" asked Ron, closing the door behind him.

"None."

We remained standing, facing each other.

"Don't take me wrong," continued Ron. "Stu is good CFO—I just don't want him president."

"I think we all agree on that."

"What about Marty?" asked Chandra. "Do you think he knew about it? Or worse, do you think he supports it?"

"No," I replied firmly. "He may have known that Stu was going to make his case, and allowed him the opportunity to float his balloon, but I'm certain he doesn't support it. He's too politically savvy for that. He knows Stu doesn't have the votes."

"Hope you're right," said Chandra, not looking convinced. "Marty's done some odd things lately."

"Right—for one, having Stu hire auditing firm without our input," added Ron.

It was clear they wanted some assurance that Marty didn't secretly back Stu's bid for president, and as Marty's close confidant, they expected me to give them that assurance. I told them I would talk to Marty before we went back into the conference room. If Marty had no intention of supporting Stu's bid for president, then I would clasp my hands in front of me. No hand clasp meant trouble.

We talked a few minutes longer about potential candidates out in the industry who might be interested in the job, agreeing that he or she needed to be someone with "star power," and the sooner they came on board the better. After they left, I waited a few minutes before walking over to Marty's office. As I approached, his receptionist looked up from her computer screen.

"Hi, Nicole. Is he in?"

"Hi, Russ," she responded cheerfully. "Yeah, go on in. He's with the IT guy—David. Putting in another monitor." Nicole was cute, but she had just gotten married, so she was off my radar. I thanked her and went on in.

Marty and David had their heads together studying the back of a large computer screen. David was one of the tech support guys we'd stolen from the company that installed our LAN system, and he worked almost exclusively for Marty in creating a war room that consisted of linked hard drives and multiple computer screens displaying stock activity, business news, and emails. As I entered, Marty looked up, somewhat startled, and nudged David away with his elbow.

"Hey, Russ," he said. "Grab a seat… Just putting in another monitor."

"Don't tell me. To track your polling numbers."

Marty chuckled good-naturedly at that. "No, not yet. Couple years maybe," he said, turning his attention to David. "We'll pick this up later." He sat down at his desk and waited until David left before speaking. "Don't tell me. Let me guess—Stu's visions of grandeur?"

"Good guess. Do you support it?"

"God no."

"Then why the charade?"

"He asked me if he could make his case and I said, 'sure, knock yourself out.' I told him he didn't have the votes, but he didn't care. He wanted to 'get it out there.'"

"And he did."

"Yeah… It reminded me of once in college; this professor let a student get up in front of the class to make a speech. Even introduced him—said Mister So-and-so has something he'd like to say to the class. So, this hayseed gets up and faces the class—about thirty people—and tells everyone that he's found Jesus Christ, that Christ is his lord and savior, and he's been saved. Of course, he immediately gets booed and hissed but he doesn't care 'cause it's his chance to 'get it out there.' And I always wondered about that professor, about why he let that guy get up and make a fool out of himself. He had to know it wouldn't go well, but he let him get up there anyhow, and maybe the professor felt good about it afterwards, or maybe he didn't. I always wondered about that."

"Now that Stu has *got it out there,* can we move on?"

"Absolutely. I'll nip it in the bud when we reconvene," he replied, looking me straight in the eyes. (I could sense a 'but' coming.) "But you and the others want a new president, so we need to find one—and the sooner the better. Certainly before we go public. If it drags on too long, we'll be forced to start looking at alternatives."

There it is, I thought to myself—exactly what I was afraid of. Marty is leaving the door open, and what those other alternatives might be I shudder to think. It's imperative we find a suitable replacement—now.

"Have you thought about a candidate?" I asked, ignoring his double-talk. "Have anyone in mind?"

"Not off hand," he confessed. "But I know what qualities we should be looking for." He leaned back in his chair and pretended to think out loud about the qualities we needed in a new president. He or she needed to have a proven track record; they had to be smart, loyal, a risk-taker, and a problem-solver. But, no—he didn't have any names, and it was obvious to me that he hadn't given it much serious thought. Unlike me.

I excused myself, telling Marty I needed to grab a bite to eat before we reconvened, and walked back to my office. A big, beautiful idea was germinating in my brain. An idea so captivating that it quickened my walk and got me charged up over its possibilities. If they wanted someone with a proven track record, someone with star power who could come in and take charge, then I had just the person for us. Maybe. If she was interested.

I closed the door to my office, sat down at my desk, and flipped through my rolodex until I found her number. Her secretary picked up on the second ring.

"Yes, let me talk to Gwen. Tell her Russ Chappel is calling."

I was asked politely to hold for a moment, and the next voice I heard was Gwen's.

"*Russ!*" she answered cheerfully. "To what do I owe this honor?"

"Hi, Gwen... Well, I have something of a proposal for you."

"A proposal. Hmmm. What kind of proposal?"

"Not that kind... A business proposal. An opportunity."

"I see... Talk to me."

―――

We resumed our old seats around the conference table and Marty, at the head of the table, waited until everyone was settled before talking. I placed my hands on the table and clasped them as a signal to Ron and Chandra.

"Comic book colors on a violin river," said Marty suddenly. *"Crying Leonardo words from out a silk trombone."*

"The Grateful Dead," said Lori with a quick laugh, having recovered from her sneezing fit. (I hadn't taken Lori for a Deadhead, what with her perpetual scowl and nanny demeanor, but it seems I was wrong.)

"Yep, yep, yep," replied Marty, smiling. "Could never figure out what those lyrics meant… Anyhow, hope everyone had a good lunch… Thought we'd pick up right where we left off, so let me say, Stu, thank you for making your case. It's certainly an intriguing idea—for the very reasons you stated, but at this point I can't afford to lose you as CFO. It's still too early in the growth of our company and you're far too valuable. And I think everyone agrees."

We all nodded in violent agreement while Stu, seeing the writing on the wall, sat passively as Marty let him down easily with a mixture of flattery and hard reality. When Marty finished, Stu thanked us all for listening to what he had to say, clasping his hands in front of him in a mirror image of my own.

"And that's not to say at some point, down the road, circumstances might change," stated Marty. This comment elicited rapid glances between Ron, Chandra, and me. Marty saw our reaction and quickly added, "That's why I think it's vital that we start our search now… And I wanna make sure we're all aligned on the kind of person we're looking for." He jumped up and began writing on the whiteboard, listing the attributes we needed in a new president, reiterating many of the ones he told me in his office, but adding others like "will break down the silos" and "be a thought leader." I noticed Lori writing them down in her notebook. "Any others?" he asked us.

"How 'bout 'walks on water.'" I said, causing Ron to laugh loudly.

"Yes, not a requirement but a preference," quipped Marty. "Any others?"

Each of us offered up a talent or an attribute we'd like to see in our new president, and Marty collected them all on the whiteboard. Lori took the opportunity to emphasize the need for diversity in our search, and Marty wrote it down and underlined it. Stu even added one of his own— "understands business financials'—which was his little swipe at being taken out of the running.

"Very good," commented Marty, as he finished writing and stepped back to review his bullet points. "Pretty close to 'walks on water'. Now we need names." He drew a line down the board and wrote out the heading **Candidates**, then turned around and faced us. "Any ideas?" he asked.

I raised my hand up slightly, pretending to be the timid kid in class.

"Russ, you got a name?"

"Yeah, I do. And I bring you tidings of great joy. It's someone who embodies everything you have listed there." I could feel everyone's eyes riveted on me, and I paused to build the suspense.

"Well?" asked Marty, poised to write the name on the whiteboard. "Who is it?"

"Gwen Novak."

There was a moment of silence as the name sunk in. "You mean Gwen Novak at AT&T?" asked Marty, obviously surprised. I nodded.

"I know her," said Ron eagerly. "She was CEO over at NextGen, then ViaPhone."

"I know her, too, by reputation. And it's a good one," added Chandra.

"A marvelous choice!" chimed in Lori, who was obviously pleased that my candidate was a woman. "But can we get her?"

"She's one of Armstrong's lieutenants, isn't she?" asked Stu rhetorically. "Why would she leave?"

"I take it you've talked to her already and floated the idea," said Marty. "Is she interested?"

"She's open to exploring the idea," I answered honestly. "I'm going to meet her for lunch next week and dangle the bait, so we need to discuss what kind of package we're willing to offer her. If she bites, then I want her to meet with you, Marty, to seal the deal in principle before we bring her in front of this team for final approval."

"Marvelous. I'm crossing my fingers," said Lori. Both Chandra and Ron voiced their support and enthusiasm as well. Stu remained quiet.

"We wish you luck then, Russ," said Marty. I knew Marty better than anyone around this table, and I picked up a hint of insincerity in his voice that the others missed. But I was confident he would come around.

Marty placed his marker down on the whiteboard (he hadn't written Gwen's name up on it) and took his seat. "Lori," he said. "I'd like your due diligence on Ms. Novak. Research her background, make some calls, put together a profile sheet. Right? Okay. Then let's sketch out our offer—salary, stocks—and give Mr. Chappel here something to whet her appetite. For all we know, she may want the moon."

"Not the moon," I replied. "Just a few satellites in Orion's Belt."

―――

I finished up the last of my emails. It was nearly six o'clock and I had a dinner date at seven with a woman who looked like Miss July 1995. It was already dark outside but it had stopped raining. The forecast for the weekend showed cool, in the fifties, with no rain, and I hoped that held true since I was taking my dad and my son out Sunday on my boat to do some fishing.

I was pleased with how the day had gone. In the span of two hours, I had thwarted Stu's power grab, found a viable candidate to replace Marty as president, and strengthened my alliance with Ron and Chandra in a way that could pay dividends in the future. I knew Gwen Novak wouldn't make the move unless she saw it as a challenge wrapped in riches inside a golden trophy, but I was confident I could sell it to her. I calculated my chances at around three to one in winning her over.

The odds of bedding my date tonight were closer to even money. Jenny was a sales rep for Cisco and in her thirties. We'd met a couple of times in vendor presentation meetings and the usual pattern developed—eye contact, smiles, chit-chat to confirm her interest, an invitation to dinner, and eager acceptance. It was a dance I'd played out many times, and it never got old. On our first date, she'd told me all about her marriage and divorce and her eight-year-old daughter. I listened intently to her, looking for the tell-tale signs that fit into my philosophy on single moms. They were all there.

My philosophy on single moms went something like this: show them you are a good listener, gentle, and caring, and they will unlock their treasure chest. But this tendency was subject to the law of gravitas, which stated that most single moms weren't looking for a good time, they were looking for a good husband. Thus, candor was key in navigating these waters—one, to avoid wasted effort on my part and, two, to avoid hurt feelings on her part. I always made it crystal clear that I was not husband material. Many a single mom took heed, but if the occasional one digested my candor and still wanted more of me, then the payoff was worth it since single moms had a certain panache in the bedroom that other women lacked.

The last time we were together, we went biking at Coyote Hills. When we finished up, I loaded her bike onto her car, and she came into me smelling wonderfully of feminine sweat and kissed me hard with her open mouth and tongue. I slid my tongue down her neck, licking her salty perspiration, and felt her give way in my arms. Her right knee pressed up into my groin. Then there were voices—other riders were coming into the parking lot—and we broke apart. She had a Mona Lisa smile on her face, part suggestive, part contentment, and I quickly asked her if she wanted to come back to my boat. Her smile promptly morphed into a look of disappointment as she explained that she couldn't, she had to pick up her daughter, but she was free later in the week for dinner.

Tonight was that dinner date, and I was feeling rather confident that Jenny was the second kind of single mom. My plan was to pick her up at her home in Milpitas and then drive back over to my side of the bay to a nice little Sushi restaurant in San Carlos, which was close to the yacht harbor. After dinner and a couple of flasks of sake, I would suggest she come see my motor yacht and she would readily agree. Once on *Danny Boy*, there would be a tango of words and embraces, followed by kissing and petting, leading to a night of naked passion in my bedroom. It was all part of the dance I enjoyed so well.

The Heights of Mountains

The phone rang and I picked up the receiver in something of a sex-filled daydream. It was Jenny. I swiftly cleared my head and exchanged greetings with her, then listened as she quickly explained that she couldn't make our date—her daughter wasn't feeling well—but hoped we could get together some other time. This last hope wasn't expressed with much conviction, and I sensed a change in the weather. For whatever reason, she had changed her mind about me. I took the cue, sincerely wishing her daughter would soon be feeling better, said goodbye, and hung up.

It turned out she was the first kind of single mom after all.

Chapter 3

We got underway at daybreak and headed out the Golden Gate for an hour's boat ride to the salmon fishing lanes that lay in deep waters past the sight of land. It was just my dad and son. When we hit the open ocean, I looked at my son who sat aft in a chair watching the receding landscape, "What's our heading, Danny boy!" I yelled out.

He swiveled around in his chair and threw up his hands in a gesture of helplessness. "Sorry, Dad!" he yelled back over the sound of the engines. "I lost my compass a couple years ago!"

I shrugged my shoulders to tell him it was no big deal and turned back to the wheel. My dad sat next to me in the cockpit, sipping a cup of Earl Grey, and we exchanged a knowing glance. We both knew he hadn't lost his compass; he had hocked it somewhere along the way to buy drugs.

Once at our destination, we threw out our lines and drifted with the current, waiting for a bite, all bundled up in our jackets and drinking hot tea. It was chilly, in the forties, but it was supposed to warm up into the mid-fifties by noon with no rain. There was a slight breeze from the northwest and the swells were mild, and when the rising sun moved in and out of the clouds, it changed the color of the ocean from gunmetal to aquamarine and back again.

In less than two hours, we caught our limit, which was one salmon per person. They were good size, over 12 pounds each, and my dad gutted them, leaving the heads on, and packed them on ice. As I was stowing away our fishing gear, I sighted a herd of gray whales and yelled out for my dad and son to come see. We watched as the small herd, no more than fifty yards to starboard, swam by, their long gray bodies, speckled white, arcing gracefully up and down.

"We might see a few more of those today," I said. "Let's hang out here for a while. It's not too crowded." There were a couple of charter boats off in the distance, perhaps a half mile away, but otherwise we were alone. "I'll make us something to eat."

"Remember… I don't eat meat," said Dan.

"Right," I replied, remembering that veganism was his latest kick. "How about a PB&J sandwich, junky Jif with grape jelly? I think that's your favorite."

"When I was twelve. But sounds good… Don't forget to cut off the crust."

I smiled at his little joke. It was good to see him in such a buoyant mood. I was looking forward to sitting down with him and my dad and just shooting the bull for a while. We hadn't been together like this in years.

I went into the galley and fixed lunch, making me and my dad ham and cheese sandwiches and my son his peanut butter and jelly. I laid out some chips, cut up a couple of oranges, and grabbed three sodas out of the fridge. With the table set, I called them in to eat and they came in talking about the upcoming Super Bowl, tossing off their jackets as they took their seat in the booth that made out into a kitchen table. I didn't follow football—I was more a baseball fan—but I jumped into the conversation to keep up the good vibe we were feeling.

Dan munched on a chip listening to his grandfather apprise us of the Broncos' chances of winning the Superbowl when he abruptly interrupted and said, "You know, you two can have a beer if you want. It's perfectly fine—I won't fall apart."

"Too early for me," I replied. "Dad, did you want a beer?" My dad shook his head no.

"Okay… I just wanted to get that out there. You don't need to babysit me or walk on eggshells just 'cause I'm an addict. If anything, it puts a focus on it. I mean, when people stop acting normal in your presence, it puts a focus on it. So, have a beer if you want a beer."

I merely nodded and let him talk. In the wink of an eye, Dan had throttled down the good vibe and made us slightly uncomfortable by calling out our behavior. It appears we were guilty of overcompensating, or something like that. This was typical Dan. If he wasn't sullen, his leg beating out a ceaseless rhythm, then he was talking, his nervous energy taking over, hijacking the conversation and driving it in the direction he wanted it to go.

He was twenty-four now and been out of rehab for over a year and a half. From all reports, he'd been clean the whole time. At first, he had lived in a half-way house, then at his mom's, but just recently gotten his own apartment. I'd offered to get him a job at one our vendors, using my influence to place him with a telecom manufacturer in an apprentice position, but he turned me down. Instead, he was driving a Lay's Potato Chip truck stocking shelves in supermarkets. His mom saw this as progress and encouraged me to do the same, and I tried my best to see the silver lining. This hope floated precariously in the right hemisphere of my brain, whereas in the left hemisphere of my brain, where critical thinking resided, sat the inescapable probability that his sobriety wouldn't last. It was like Newton's second law of motion; it was immutable. At some point—tomorrow, a month from now, maybe a year—he would react to an inevitable force. His nature might be at rest for a while, but eventually this force would set him in motion again and he would react by sticking a needle in his arm. I hated myself for thinking it, but it was in his nature, and you can't change your nature. Maybe, over time, you can tire it out, but you can never fundamentally change it.

"This is something they stressed in rehab," continued Dan. "Acceptance. You gotta accept how people are and let them be themselves. If they go out of their way to change their behavior because of you, it doesn't do them any good and it doesn't do you—me—any good. So, I encourage everyone to be themselves. It's a good lesson to learn… I learned a lot of good lessons in rehab."

"Like what?" I asked.

He took a bite of his sandwich. "Hmm, good sandwich, Dad," he said, chewing and swallowing quickly. "Well, for one, I learned what cognitive distortions I suffer from. Like Emotional Reasoning. That's letting my feelings guide my interpretation of reality. So, it can cause me to say things like 'I feel depressed today, therefore my life isn't working out the way I want.' The other is Dichotomous Thinking, which is the same as black and white thinking. That causes me to view things in all or nothing terms. So, I might meet ten new people on my route tomorrow, all of them nice except for one person, who is a jerk towards me. Dichotomous Thinking would cause me to conclude that all people are jerks, even though nine people were nice to me. Make sense?"

"I see what you're saying," I replied somewhat intrigued. (Despite the clinical classifications, there was some truth in it.) Evidently, this was what Dan wanted to talk about—his rehab, his diagnosis, his condition—and he was going to take advantage of his captive audience. He went on to explain other cognitive distortions, giving examples of each, as well as the "rehab process," and seemed to be more focused on relaying this information to his grandfather than to me. This was probably because he rarely saw his grandfather, or talked to him, since his grandmother's death eight years ago. Dan had been very close to his grandmother and her death hit him hard, and since that day he'd distanced himself from his grandfather, who was a painful reminder of his beloved "Gigi." Perhaps now he was feeling some guilt over that and wanted to catch his granddad up on the narrative of his life.

"Did Dad ever tell you about his visit to rehab," Dan asked his grandfather. "No? ... Well, we kinda' bushwhacked him. It was a group session, and I unloaded a bunch of repressed stuff on him. Some of it, I know, was exaggerated, so I wanted to say I'm sorry about that."

"You don't need to apologize," I said. "I survived... anyhow, your mom already apologized. She said if she'd known what was going to happen, she wouldn't have insisted I come."

"*Really!*" reacted Dan with a look of disbelief. "Mom said *that*. Now *that's* funny. Mom was the one who pushed me to set up that session. And it's not like she didn't know what was going to happen. She'd seen

Fala gang up on a parent before. She knew exactly what was coming. So, it's funny she'd say that to you. Huh!"

I took a moment to process this statement. This revelation that my ex-wife lied to me was disconcerting, and I pondered why Jan would have orchestrated an encounter session like that, one intended to humiliate me. I simply replied back to Dan, rather lamely, "Well, that's what she said."

"How's the business coming?" asked my dad, thankfully changing the topic.

"Good… Very good."

My dad knew a lot about my company and followed our growth closely. "Are you buying an ad for the Super Bowl?" he asked.

"God, no," I said, rolling my eyes. "They want $1.6 million for thirty seconds. Out of our price range for now… But we're going public in a few months. That'll bring an influx of cash we can use to expand our network."

"And no doubt make you a multi-millionaire," he said. "Least ways, based on the pattern of IPOs I've seen over the last couple years."

"Very likely. On paper anyhow. But to pocket that money, we have to sustain our success—keep growing, gain market share, and most of all start making a profit. Our stock price will depend on that. So, I won't count my Dickens before it's hatched."

My dad smiled. The Dickens comment was one of his made-up sayings I remembered as a kid. They were usually a British idiom, but he would take the idiom and add his own Americanized spin to it. So, "flogging a dead horse" became "flogging Mister Ed" (after the TV show horse) or "keep your wig on" became "keep your beanie on."

"We're making some changes," I continued. "Bringing in a new president to run the day-to-day business. Launching into the consumer market. Going into more cities…" I gave him a short synopsis of our market penetration to date, the cities we were in, and a few of the obstacles we were encountering. He listened intently while my son grew bored. I could tell by Dan's body language that he wasn't interested in my business, and after a few minutes, he picked up his plate with the

PB&J sandwich on it and left the table saying, "'Scuse me, ol' chaps. I'm gonna check out the whales." We watched him as he walked back on deck.

"He's a lot like your mom," said my dad. "Runs hot and cold."

"Probably why they were so close," I said. My dad nodded thoughtfully at that. My mom, born Dorothy Ann Webb (and called "Dolly" all her life), married my father when she was twenty-six and remained unhappily married to him for forty-one years until she died of liver cancer in 1991. I say 'unhappily' because that was the aura she projected to my older brother and I when we were growing up. Like an artist who feels their talents are wasted painting faces at a kid's carnival, she withheld her best efforts and gave off the impression that she'd rather be somewhere else than where she was. This attitude manifested itself in little ways—in hugs withheld, in comments made under her breath, in the faraway look in her eyes—but also in some big ways. I was in my twenties when my older brother told me that she'd had two affairs and run off once for six weeks when we were little. In all three cases, my father took her back. She was pretty, wickedly smart, and even vivacious when she wanted to be, and he adored her and forgave her everything. He loved her at his own peril, and after all these years, I still didn't know whether to admire him for it or pity him.

She was in her fifties when Daniel was born, and when Jan brought him back to the Bay Area after our divorce, Dolly wrapped her grandson up in a blanket of redemptive love. She was one of those middle-aged women who, knowing they weren't very good mothers, tried to atone for it by becoming exemplary grandmothers. She doted on him, bathed him in attention, and fed him a daily dose of 'you-can-do-no-wrong'. And the fact that they were both alike in temperament—running hot and cold and egoists by nature—only seemed to solidify their close relationship. Daniel was at her bedside when she passed away.

"I used to preach balance in all things, as you did—the Aristotelian Mean—but it didn't take," I remarked rather wistfully. "He'd rather pick a scab than let it heal."

"Hmm," agreed my dad. "Least said, soonest mended."

"Precisely... How's the sandwich?"

"Very good," he answered, and to emphasize the point, he picked up his sandwich and took a hearty bite. My dad, born Sinclair Earl Chappel (and called "Clair" all his life), was second generation British expatriate (with dual citizenships) and an anglophile through and through who read Dickens, admired Churchill, and raised a toast to the Queen every year on her birthday. Otherwise, he was all-American; a graduate of the Naval Academy, Navy veteran, jazz aficionado, lifelong Democrat, and a man who clearly understood his strengths and weaknesses in the same way a captain, who knows his ship, never pushes it beyond its capabilities. He married my mother when he was thirty, and in the early sixties we moved to Foster City—on the water where he could keep his 26-foot Mackenzie—and took a job at the Air Force Satellite Test Center, next to Moffett Field, in a high-security building known as "the blue cube" where they tracked satellites and kept an eye on the Russians.

My brother John was two years older than me and together we grew up in a household that was rigged to challenge the intellect. Both my parents were college graduates and highly intelligent, and our home was a drawing room filled with refined manners, erudite conversation, jazz music, and high expectations. And if my mother remained aloof, watching from the sidelines, my father's compensating energy was ever present, inventing games, designing projects, and finding ways to keep me and my brother engaged and active. From him came my love of the sea, and from him I learned that marriage to a faithless woman was a job for a saint or a fool. He never argued with my mom or, if he did, it was behind closed doors, and the only evidence of trouble were the bouts of silence and the occasional hard stare. They hugged and kissed like actors on the stage, and if there was any passion in their marriage it was kept hidden in their bedroom.

At seventy-nine, he still looked like he could win the America's Cup—that is if he was given a good ship and a skilled crew. He was tall like me, lean, with white hair (what was left of it), white whiskery eyebrows, with a calm and studious demeanor that gave one the image of an English lord or member of the National Geographic Society. We were much alike, though my good looks (if I was allowed to claim such a thing), came from my mother's side of the family and not his. His face was rather hawk-like, and he had long sinewy arms, which gave him the kind of appearance women found interesting rather than handsome.

"Talked to John lately?" I asked.

"Yes, just last week," he replied. My brother was an admiral in the Third Fleet, which put him in different places in the Pacific during the year. He was doing well, my father said. So were his wife and two sons. (I was an uncle but had only seen my nephews a few times over the years.) I told him that was good to hear and hoped that one day soon we could all get together, all the boys, and spend a day like this on *Danny Boy*.

My dad smiled at that hope, then looked oddly into my eyes. "You know, you might have had a sister," he said.

"What do you mean?"

"Your mom got pregnant when you were around five years old—but she got an abortion."

He said this matter-of-factly, like he was relaying directions to a lost traveler, but it didn't take any of the shock out of it for me. It seemed the older I got, the more secrets were to be revealed to me about my mother and father. And this one was a doozy. I didn't know what to say.

"Yeah," he continued, glancing away. "There was some question as to whose child it was… So, she went out and ended it. Told me afterwards."

I studied his face closely but there were no signs of sadness or remorse, just a hard blankness, and all I could manage to say in response was, "Why did you stay married to her?"

With his hands flat on the table, he shrugged ever so slightly, raising both pointer fingers off the table in a gesture that meant, "Because I did, and that's all I have to say about it."

Least said, soonest mended.

Dan walked back into the cabin holding his empty plate. "No whales," he said matter-of-factly. "What'cha talking about?" he asked, sensing a mood of seriousness between my father and me.

"About your grandma," I replied.

"Ahh, Grandma Gigi." He placed his empty plate in the sink and turned back to us, downing what was left of his soda and crumpling the can in his hand after he finished it. "Did I ever tell you what she said to me on her death bed? Her last words?"

"No, you never did," I answered, fairly sure that they were not words of wisdom. But he had our attention, and my dad and I looked at him, waiting.

"She said, 'It was all for nothing.' Then she closed her eyes and died. Just like that."

If he was expecting an emotional reaction to this confession, he didn't get it, as both my dad and I merely gave him a blank look. "Why tell us now?" I asked. "After all this time."

"I don't know," he replied. He grabbed a fresh soda out of the fridge, popped the lid, and sat back down with us. "Guilt maybe. I've been carrying it around inside me like a poison pill for a long time. Guess I needed to finally spit it out."

I simply nodded. My father remained expressionless, drumming his fingers on the table three times before saying, "What's our dinner plans? Let's say we barbecue one of those salmon, with a little butter and garlic, maybe some fried potatoes to go with it. How's that sound?"

My son, who appeared thrown off by the sudden change in topic, managed to say, "Sounds good to me."

I took a deep breath before answering. "I can't. Sorry. I have a dinner date." (Her name was Alicia and she was due on my boat at six tonight.)

"Don't tell me," said Dan in a tone of playful sarcasm. "A Playboy Playmate. Miss January 1990."

My father chuckled at that, and my son took that as a cue to add, "You know my dad—your son—is a regular Casanova."

"I grant you, he's something of a ladies' man."

"Ladies' man. More like a hound dog in heat," laughed Dan.

"I wouldn't say that," replied Dad. He looked at me fondly, as though he was looking at an accomplished jazz musician, and added,

"There's more to it… He's an artist of sorts. Pursuing and winning over beautiful women is his art form—it's the endeavor that best expresses his talents. And fortunately for him, your dad was born with the tools to successfully ply his trade. Just as Sinatra was blessed with a marvelous singing voice, your dad was blessed with good looks and a killer charm that women find irresistible. This gives him the power to create a lifestyle filled with gorgeous blondes, alluring redheads, and captivating brunettes—Did I miss anyone?"

Like the French, I simply shrugged my shoulders in reply.

"Quite… So, let's not cheapen his gifts. My son has an eye for beauty and the means in which to possess it, if even just briefly, and we should admire him for it. It's a gift that won't last forever."

That was the longest speech my father had ever made about me, and I wasn't sure whether I was flattered by it or embarrassed.

Dan tilted his head from left to right, showing us he wasn't sure whether he was buying it or not. "I guess that's one way of looking at it," he said finally.

My cat Clementine appeared out of nowhere and jumped up into Dan's lap to be petted. This momentary distraction gave me the chance to change the subject. "Know what, I'm going to call my date and cancel. We'll barbecue up one of the salmon, fry some potatoes, and Grandpa and I will share a bottle of Chablis—if you don't mind."

"You know I don't," replied Dan happily as he scratched Clementine under the chin.

"It's settled then. Let's start back."

"Won't your date be shattered?" kidded Dan.

"She'll get over it."

"You might have to cross her out of your black book."

"He has a black book?" asked my dad.

"I bet he does. You have a black book, don't you?"

"I take the fifth."

"I knew it."

"I think you're right. He's got a black book."

"Can we see it? Come on, Dad. Break it out. Let's see it."

I stood up. "Have your fun," I said grumpily, but they could tell I was pretending. "I'm gonna fire up the engines and get us underway."

"Ahh, come on, Dad. Show us the book."

"Yeah, Russ. Where you got it hidden."

"Probably under lock and key."

I waved them off as I walked out into the cockpit. I could hear them laughing together at the table. They were having fun at my expense, but that was okay. The good vibe was back.

At the turn of the ignition, the twin diesels roared into action, and I waited for them to settle down to a purr before engaging the throttle. Our heading was east-northeast and we would have the wind to our back the whole way. I would give Alicia a call when we docked. She'd be disappointed, but we'd make it another night. It was rather a shame, though. She was a little dynamo in bed and her particular delight was ribbed condoms (which I kept in a drawer next to my bed along with lubricated, ultra-thin, lambskin, and an assortment of others to meet any occasion). But not tonight. There were other people to think about. I could partake of the pleasures of Alicia or I could forgo the pleasures of Alicia; it was a matter of choice. And I would show my son that I wasn't quite the hound dog in heat he made me out to be.

Chapter 4

Russ first met Gwen when they both worked for AT&T in 1983. They worked on different floors of the same building in downtown San Francisco, each in their own department, and briefly introduced themselves in the elevator one day. Gwen was fresh out of Harvard Business School and had been heavily recruited by AT&T executives who offered her a position in the newly created Pacific Telesis. This was one of the seven Regional Bell Operating Companies formed in preparation of the Ma Bell breakup, and she accepted the position and moved back to the Bay Area where she grew up. Her first week at work she noticed a tall, handsome man in the elevator and they shared eye contact. He stood out from the crowd and wasn't hard to miss, and soon they were nodding and smiling at one another over the heads of the other occupants in the elevator. Then one day, late in the evening, Russ stepped into the elevator to find Gwen alone and quickly introduced himself. They struck up a conversation that lasted on the ride down and out of the lobby and into the parking lot where they said their goodbyes. There was chemistry, they both felt it, but it would be over a year before they started dating.

The first time he asked her out, suggesting dinner and a show, she politely declined. She was fresh out of a divorce and down on men, plus she knew about his reputation as a Don Juan and had no intention of becoming another notch on his bedpost. But over a year's time she learned more about him. From snippets of conversations with colleagues, mutual acquaintances, and even women she knew he had dated, she began to piece together a clearer picture of Russ. For one, he was highly respected and considered something of a wunderkind in the engineering department.

As for the Don Juan image, it appeared there was more to it than that. For one, he had high standards and an eye for female beauty, and as a result, only dated gorgeous women and "model material." She felt rather flattered that he'd asked her out. For another, he had a code; from what she could ascertain through the grapevine, he neither coerced nor harassed women into dating him (in other words, he wasn't a lech), and it sounded as though he took great care to avoid the role of a heartbreaker. And there was this: of the women he had dated in the building, none of them trash-talked him or threw up beware signs. Instead, they all spoke fondly of him long after they stopped dating.

After turning him down, he hadn't tried asking her out again, and after a year's time (and a change of heart on her part), she knew she would have to take the initiative. They continued to see each other in the elevator, still nodding and smiling at one another, and occasionally in the evening they would find themselves alone in the elevator and walk out to the parking lot together. It was on such an evening, when he stepped into the elevator, that she saw an opportunity to make her move.

"Hi, Russ!" she greeted him cheerily.

"Gwen... We meet again."

"And it must stop, or people will begin to talk."

"People *do* talk."

"Yes, they do... Perhaps we should give them something to talk about."

He'd been watching the elevator floor indicator do its countdown, but this comment caused him to cast his eyes over at her and smile. "Hmm, perhaps we should," he replied with a wink. "But we only have four more floors to go. Not enough time to be scandalous."

She sniffed a laugh. "There's always the emergency stop—but then we'd have the fire department to deal with."

"I thought women loved firemen?"

"We do, but one at a time. Not all at once."

"Good point. There goes that idea."

This banter continued on the ride down and out into the parking lot. There they paused, somewhat awkwardly, and she could read a certain anticipation in his body language. She'd piqued his curiosity.

"Has the shelf life on that dinner date expired yet?" she asked boldly.

"It's like a carton of milk, you know, but I think we have a couple days left."

"Gracious, then we'd better move fast. How about this Saturday?"

"Capital."

She knew he would be funny and charming, but once they started dating, she found he possessed a well-mannered grace that had the disarming effect of making her feel like a lady rather than just a woman. She liked that he was taller than her, that he opened doors and pulled out chairs for her, and she appreciated his unique brand of self-assurance which came off as a coolness of mind rather than an annoying kind of chauvinism. Like her, he had a quick wit, but she also discovered that he could talk intelligently about anything; he could talk bricks with bricklayers and rockets with rocket scientists, and with her he was as comfortable discussing modern art as he was basketball. Gwen was fully aware of her power to emasculate men, to out-think them, out-wit them, and with a sharp rebuke or cutting stare, slice their balls off and hold them up for all to see. But she only wielded this power with men she competed against, and with Russ she felt no desire to unsheathe this sword. He moved her in ways she'd not been moved before, and after a couple months of dating him regularly, she found herself precariously close to falling in love with him.

In the bedroom, he lived up to his billing. He was well-equipped with remarkable staying power and always made sure she climaxed before he finished his business. Even in bed, he was the consummate gentleman, and it was this very coat-of-arms chivalry of his that she knew, one day, she'd have to be put to the test. She wanted to be taken, and he would take her—legs up, from behind, flipping her around like a rag doll—but there were times when she wanted more than that—she wanted to be mauled. She had a masochistic itch that, frankly, sometimes needed to be scratched. But she was reticent to push him to that next level.

Early on in their relationship, Russ stopped seeing other women, and at six weeks together, they became a couple, eating lunch together, cozying up in the elevator, and making plans weeks in advance. For Gwen, the time had come. Her love ached to break loose, to relinquish, to submit itself sweetly and painfully to his lust-ridden violence. It was a hope held dear that he would follow her willingly into this realm.

Decided, she quickly tested his resolve. But the outcome was a bust. He did what she asked him to, spanking her, fucking her in the ass, yanking her hair back, but he held back, even quit, if he thought he was hurting her. She assured him it was okay and encouraged him to go farther, but in the end she could see it was contrary to his temperament. It was like trying to make Mr. Rogers talk dirty, and she felt rather ashamed for attempting it. And after a month of trying, she gave up, keeping the hurt and disappointment to herself, and they mutually called it quits.

Upon seeing Gwen for the first time in the elevator, Russ was struck by how much she looked like Miss December 1974, who at five foot ten was one of the tallest Playmates to grace the centerfold of Playboy magazine. He just *had* to get to know her. When they first glanced at one another in the crowded elevator, he instantly felt a connection. And he was rarely wrong about such things; like a gifted mentalist, he could always pick up interest in a woman's eyes without much effort. Over the following weeks, he smiled and nodded at her in the elevator, even introduced himself, but he held off from asking her out until he found out more about her.

What he quickly found out was all good. She was on the executive staff of Pacific Telesis, which was a wholly separate entity from his department (which was fortunate). She was twenty-five, fresh out of grad school, divorced, and already had a reputation for being a highly intelligent and hard-nosed businesswoman. She was the trifecta—single, smart, and stunning—and he wasted no time in asking her out. But to his surprise, she turned him down. Had he misread her? Was she still gun-shy after her divorce? Did she avoid dating company employees? He didn't know, but whatever it was he shrugged it off. As the jolly fisherman liked to say, there was always other fish in the sea.

Over a year later, things abruptly changed. To his surprise and delight, she boldly made her interest in him known one evening in the elevator. He wasted no time in seizing the opportunity, and after a few weeks of dating, he realized there was more to Gwen than just a smart and stunning Playmate look-alike. There was a depth to her character he hadn't expected, and like a newly discovered island, emerald green and inviting in the distance, he swung over and landed to fully explore her. She possessed a lively intelligence, but more than that she possessed an uncanny ability to read cues, to see patterns in action, and to swiftly anticipate the most productive outcome. He recognized these talents because he had them as well, and he enjoyed listening to her and watching her mind work. She had keen insights—from the synthetic cubism of Marcel Duchamp to the triangle offense of the Chicago Bulls—and he found her to be a mansion with many rooms. Without consciously deciding it, he filed his black book away and made her his exclusive lady.

One other key finding, and one that pleased him beyond measure, was this—she enjoyed sex as much as he did. She was sexually aggressive, but not in the way of some liberated women he knew who insisted on taking charge in bed, landing on top, and using him as a warm-blooded dildo. Instead, her aggression translated into a kind of come-and-get-it surrender. She was tinder to his flame; she *wanted* to burn, couldn't *wait* to burn, and he found himself warmed by the fire he could ignite in her. There were times, especially at work, when she could be wound tight, but in the bedroom she became unwound, giving herself up to him in a wonderful way. After two months together, he had to admit to himself he was hooked on her.

But at three months, things took an unexpected turn. Though perhaps he should have seen it coming. For one, all his relationships eventually ended. If they were more than a night out and a roll in the sack, if, like Gwen, they were something more, well then, they always came to an end either by his hand, by her hand, or simply by the laws of inevitability. But this was something different altogether, and he probably should have picked up on it earlier on. Whenever they had sex, he faintly sensed she was leading him somewhere. He couldn't put his finger on it, and quite frankly he was enjoying himself too much to stop and apply cold logic to it, but with each squeal at one of his playful bites, at each cry of delight at one was his impish slaps on her ass, he subconsciously felt her tugging him towards a secret place.

That secret place was finally revealed to him. They were in her apartment, in bed, and were going at it doggy style when she suddenly cried out "Spank me!" He quickly obliged and spanked her. "Harder!" she screamed, and he answered by putting a little more into it. "Harder!" she screamed again. His first reaction was to raise his arm up higher and bring it down with his full force, but he couldn't do it, it wasn't in him, and he held back despite her screams for more, spanking her repeatedly in his own careful way until she finally came and he followed soon after. They sank down on the bed exhausted, took a shower together, and later lounged in their pajamas in the living room without ever talking about what had just happened.

He wanted to take it as an aberration—as a woman in the throes of passion, carried away—but it happened again, this time with an escalating twist that troubled him. She wanted him to fuck her in the ass, and he did. (It wasn't his favorite thing to do; it smelled and caused him to scrub his penis clean afterwards, but he would do it if they asked.) He inserted himself and she moaned with pleasure, quickly pleading with him to spank her and go harder into her, and he worked to please her until he saw the stem of his penis reddening with rectal blood and backed off. "No!" she shrieked. "Don't stop! Harder! Hurt me!—Don't stop now!" But he stopped. He pulled himself out saying, "I can't," and went into the bathroom to clean up.

Her disappointment was palpable, his consternation on open display. And this time they talked about it. She told him it was okay, that she sometimes wanted this kind of rough sex, and if it was okay with her, it should be okay with him. He understood, but the problem was this—hurting women, even if they asked for it, was against his nature. She persisted, encouraging him on as though he were a promising candidate she wanted to recruit into her department. He told her he would try it again.

The Heights of Mountains

But it was no good—the spanking, the choking, the hair-pulling—it was not his bag and he didn't enjoy it. He hoped she'd back off, but she didn't, wouldn't (since the genie was already out of the bottle), and they came to that inevitable impasse. There were a few more dates, both reluctant to admit the obvious, but the leak in their boat was unrepairable and they were listing badly. They sat down together and discussed the situation dispassionately, rationally, as though they were addressing a problem at work, and they both decided to end it. He hid his disappointment from her; for the first time in a very long time, he was saddened by a break-up. It wasn't as though he'd seen marriage as a possibility (bloody well not), but he had hoped that theirs would remain (dare he say it) a love affair for years to come.

Yet, their relationship, now stripped of the burden of sex, continued over the years. They went to lunch occasionally, enjoying each other's company, kept in touch, and they found, to their pleasant surprise, that they were better at being friends than they had been at being lovers.

Chapter 5

Russ found a parking spot two blocks away and walked up California Street to the Tadich Grill where he entered and found Gwen already sitting at a table for two. She stood up and gave him a big hug. As he sat down, a waiter in a black vest and white apron appeared and asked him what he'd like to drink. He ordered sparkling water then looked around the restaurant.

"Haven't been here in a while," he said.

"Still got the best seafood in town," she replied.

He nodded, letting the rest go unsaid. This had been one of their favorite restaurants to eat at when they dated back in 1984 and Russ remembered it fondly.

"What's it been?" he asked. "Three years?"

Gwen paused for a moment to think about it. The last time she saw him in person was at a telecom convention in San Diego where they both sat on a panel discussing the Information Superhighway. That was in '96. "Yeah, about three years ago," she replied. "San Diego, right?"

"Right—San Diego. We went on that dinner cruise sponsored by Motorola. If I remember right, your date looked like a biker gang member. When I first saw him, I thought he'd slipped on board to hijack the ship. I warned security."

"If I remember right, your date looked like a seventeen-year-old hooker with red hair and big tits. I thought of calling the Vice Squad on you."

The two studied each other briefly, then broke out laughing. This was part of their normal repartee—witty jabs laced with sexual innuendo—and each could play the game as well as the other. Despite not having seen each other in three years, they kept in touch with the occasional phone call but more frequently with short, funny emails that commented on everything from pop culture to the latest business mergers. In a strange coincidence, given that they dated the opposite sex prolifically, she was his only woman friend, and he was her only man friend.

The waiter returned with Russ' sparkling water, and seeing that they weren't ready to order yet, he disappeared. "You look smashing, I must say," commented Russ.

"And you're as dapper as ever," she said, returning the compliment. It amused her the way he talked like a Brit. He was always using terms like "bloody" or "smashing" and referring to things as "wonky" or "rubbish." Back when they dated, she kidded him that he should have been born Rupert or Basil instead of Russ. And he looked good—even more handsome than ever. When she first met him, he had just turned thirty and was a gorgeous hunk of a man, looking like he'd just walked off a movie set. But now, fifteen years later, he looked even more distinguished and quietly virile than ever, sitting there with his ruddy tan, those strong cheekbones, slightly cleft chin, and those enlightened gray eyes of his. Yes, she concluded, he was as scrumptious as ever.

"It's unanimous then," he said smiling. "We're the best-looking people in the restaurant."

"It's a heavy burden to bear."

"But we manage... They still have sand dabs?"

"I think so."

They both picked up their menu to peruse the choices, but Russ slyly glanced up and studied Gwen while she read the menu. She hadn't changed all that much since the last time he saw her, and for that matter, she was still the same statuesque blonde he remembered from fifteen years ago. Back then she reminded him of Miss December 1974, another statuesque blond with slim hips and long legs. Gwen didn't have the 38-inch bust but she possessed the same cunning eyes, wide lips, and oblong face that all added up to what he found to be alluringly handsome. Now, at thirty-nine, her hair was shorter, her neck slightly creased, and her cheeks were hardened ever so faintly, but for all that she still radiated a presence and a kind of sexually wrought bearing that he found mesmerizing. One of the things he dug about her then, and dug about her now, was that she wasn't afraid to dress like a woman. Too many women he'd met in the business world, especially women in executive positions like Gwen, thought it necessary to look like men and act like men, dressing in pantsuits and high-buttoned shirts, never crossing their legs or wearing lipstick, thus imitating the very patriarchal society they professed to despise. But not Gwen. She wore skirts and high heels, V-neck sweaters, had her hair done in a way that accentuated her face, knew the right kind of blushes and lipstick to apply, and expected men to admire her. He found her refreshing in that way.

They chatted about some of the menu items, casually changing topics to their favorite TV show (*Frasier*), good books to read (*A Man in Full* by Tom Wolfe), and movies they'd seen and would recommend (Russ went with *The Truman Show,* Gwen with *The Big Lebowski*). The waiter returned and took their order. Russ went with the sand dabs while Gwen ordered the ahi tuna seared rare. She also ordered a glass of Sauvignon Blanc, and Russ decided to join her, ordering one as well. When the wine arrived, Russ raised his glass saying, "chin-chin," and clicked her glass in a toast.

There was a certain etiquette to negotiating big deals at lunch. You never cut to the chase; instead, you sat down, made small talk, ordered lunch, started eating, and then and only then, once both parties were settled in, did the overtures and deal-making begin. For Russ and Gwen, this etiquette was even more necessary given their sexual history together. It loomed in the background like an ancient misfortune they shared, coloring their comfort level and subtly influencing the things they said or didn't say in ways only they would recognize. For them, the memory was bittersweet and required more than a single glass of Sauvignon Blanc to counterbalance.

Gwen already had a fair idea of what they would offer her to become president. She'd done her homework on CrestPoint Communications, knew the bios on each of its officers, and thought they had a solid business plan, at least in the short term. There were a few things she wanted to know and get straight, but she was seventy-five percent sure she was going to accept the position—unless they mucked it up and tried to lowball her. She'd been looking for an opportunity to step into the driver's seat of a start-up company, something cutting edge, a place where she could apply her talents more fully. Working for a behemoth like AT&T had its advantages; it had deep pockets and impressive resources, and her position with them gave her status in the industry. But it was all blocking and tackling stuff and had grown stale. Her real forte was taking a diamond in the rough like CrestPoint, shaping it, grooming it, and making it a plum worth picking for some giant like AT&T or SBC. And here was that opportunity; it had fallen squarely into her lap without even really trying.

Their lunch was served and Gwen watched as Russ took his first bite. "How's your sand dabs?" she asked.

"Good... A little dry."

"So, what's your offer."

Russ chewed his slightly dry sand dab and washed it down with a sip of his Sauvignon Blanc. "Just this," he said, setting his glass back down. "We want you to come in and take over Martin Madrid's position as President of CrestPoint Communications. Marty will remain CEO and become Chairman of the Board once we go public, but the management of the company will fall to you—all the day-to-day stuff, Operations, Sales, Deployment, IT—all of it will be under your lead and direction." Russ paused for a moment and watched as Gwen took a bite of her ahi tuna. She looked at him, chewing thoughtfully.

"How's the ahi?"

"Excellent."

"And here's what we're prepared to offer you."

Gwen listened to Russ while she continued to enjoy her ahi tuna seared rare (it was done perfectly). She loved listening to Russ talk; his voice dwelled attractively between a tenor and a baritone, and his polished speaking style, combined with the timbre of his voice, was like receiving a mental massage. The deal itself—the salary and stock options—were as expected. The salary was handsome, the stock options a little low (given they were about to go public), but all of the perks of the office—a company charge card, a car, and a free cellphone—were added incentives.

Russ finished his pitch and dug back into his sand dabs, waiting on her questions. He thought the deal was a good one and now it was up to her. Her poker face told him nothing and he expected her to dig deeper by asking him about spans of control and chains of command. Instead, she surprised him by launching into her own appraisal of CrestPoint's assets and outlook, talking about market share (which she had a good handle on) and speculating that their biggest problem, besides order flow and billing, was probably dealing with the Baby Bells. Russ told her she was right on all counts. Her appraisal sounded guardedly optimistic, and knowing her as well as he thought he did, that was a good sign.

She had a few questions about burn rate and revenue projections, which he answered, and she wanted to know more about their alliance with Microsoft. That deal was supposed to have been secret, at least until all the particulars were nailed down, but Marty had leaked it to the press, so Russ felt free to give her the lowdown.

"Marty's a bit of a loose cannon," she commented, and without waiting for Russ to answer she added, "If we can get an official, joint announcement out on this Microsoft deal before the IPO, it'll give us a few points on the stock price."

"No doubt," he agreed, rather pleased at her use of the royal "we."

"And the IPO—April or May, right? What's your guess on opening price?"

Russ gave her his guess. She told him it would probably be higher.

The numbers—his guess and her prediction—were mutually satisfying and there was over a minute of silence as they both mused about the future while finishing their lunch.

"I want to come in as President and CEO," said Gwen abruptly.

"Marty won't give up his CEO title. It's not negotiable."

She gave Russ the famous Novak stare but he met it with a charming nonchalance that caused her to blink. She picked up her wine glass, turning it in her hand so the wine caught the light just right, then finished it off with a single swallow before setting it down. "Then I want COO," she said coolly. "So there's no confusion."

Russ understood her concern. It would have been his concern if he was in her shoes. It was a ship full of big egos with highfalutin titles and she wanted clear control of the rudder. President and Chief Operations Officer would give her that. "We can make that happen," he said simply.

"What's next?"

"We meet with Marty—then take your nomination to the officer team for a vote."

Gwen sat in Marty's office and listened to him talk. He was giving her the history of CrestPoint along with his vision of a world where low-cost, high-speed Internet access was available to one and all. Marty spoke like a true believer, but she'd heard it all before and was more interested in getting a read on his character by studying him—his clothes, his body language, even the layout of his office—than at listening to his spiel. He was dressed casual chic in stone-washed blue jeans which were carefully faded, a long-sleeve polo shirt by Ralph Lauren, burnt-orange in color, with the sleeves pulled up to his elbows, workman style, and wore his sandy blonde hair just long enough that it flipped up in the back in a roguish manner. Put together, she thought he came off looking like some inner-city public defender—a man of means dressed down to relate to his clientele.

His office spoke of fastidiousness, from the squared-off chairs around his conference table to the neatly positioned items of stationary on his polished desktop. But there was an interesting counterpoint to this fastidiousness that flashed at her from the artwork on his office walls. (She believed you could tell a lot about a person from the art they hung on their walls.) There was a large, framed illustration of Jerry Garcia as well as other Grateful Dead paraphernalia that adorned his walls, along with a couple of pop-art prints by Andy Warhol. This other half of his office spoke of a liberal viewpoint and a certain bohemian streak that appealed to her. She wasn't a Grateful Dead fan herself, but it was a point in his favor.

When Marty finished his history lesson, Gwen immediately asked, "You said you're launching into the consumer market in a couple weeks… At what price points?"

"I can give you the product sheet on that," replied Marty. "There're different flavors, depending on speed and distance… But, as an example, we'll sell a 160-kilobit line to an ISP like Fastcom for $75 a month. Fastcom will turn around and sell it to the end user for $79.95 a month."

"Not much of a profit margin for Fastcom," commented Gwen.

"If they buy in bulk, they'll pay a little less than $75, but you're right. Since we control the asset, we control most of the profits. That's the beauty of it." Smiling at this last point, he eyed her closely to see if she, too, saw the beauty of it. She neither nodded nor smiled, remaining straight-faced. He wasn't sure what to make of that. If she was trying to come off as a cold-blooded Brunhilde, she was succeeding. But he knew he needed to be careful; his predisposition to dislike this woman could color his perception, and that would be a mistake. She had a formidable reputation, and this whole move to bring her in as President of CrestPoint was in many ways a fait accompli. And that combination—her reputation plus the team's strong support of her—was a rolling boulder gaining momentum. Stopping it at this point seemed unlikely. No, unless she made an unreasonable demand—and he'd have to show it as such—her coronation as president was probably foreordained.

Russ sat next to Gwen and closely watched the interaction between her and Marty. He wasn't sure if they would hit it off. He guessed not, since one was ice and one was fire, and he knew that "hitting it off" was not something Gwen worried about. She didn't become buddies with her employees or colleagues. Marty, on the other hand, was all about camaraderie; he wanted friends and good vibes in his camp before he sallied forth to do battle. But the X-factor here was Marty's resentment, if any, at giving up his President title and the powers that went with it. Despite his rhetoric to the contrary, he suspected Marty wanted to keep the status quo.

"The price seems low," she said. "But I get it. Like Microsoft, you're pricing your product low to build market share." She paused for a moment, then added as an afterthought, "Who keeps the books? Stuart Baum, I take it? He's your CFO, correct?"

Marty told her she was correct, adding that Stu was also their corporate lawyer.

"I don't know him. I know Russ, of course. Both Ron and Chandra to some degree. And I've met Lori before. But Mr. Baum I don't know," she said, telling a little white lie. She'd never met Stu or worked with him like the others, but she knew about him, and what she gathered from her sources wasn't all good.

The Heights of Mountains

Marty assured her that Stu was the best—a top-notch lawyer, one of the finest in the country, and a CFO without peer. Gwen ignored the accolades and cut to the chase.

"Russ told you I want President and COO if I come on board?"

"Yes, he did. Ron Lau is our COO."

Russ waited a moment for Marty to complete his sentence, but when he didn't Russ jumped in, addressing Gwen directly. "We've talked to Ron. He's never been Chief of Operations—at least not in the traditional sense. His focus has always been product management—overseeing the company's product-related activities—and as such, his title will change to Chief Product Officer. Ron is good with this."

"I see," replied Gwen. "Then let's talk spans of control..." She proceeded to outline what she saw as her role at CrestPoint Communications in a blunt and direct manner. Russ couldn't help but chuckle to himself at seeing reality beginning to set in with Marty. His face looked like cold water had hit it as she made it clear that her job was knocking down silos, leveraging synergies, and driving results—not roadshows or entertaining investors (that was his job). Yes, as CEO, Marty would be her boss—he was the vision guy, the thought leader—but the day-to-day operations of the company would be her responsibility and not his. She gave him a few pointed examples of what she meant by that as Marty sat quietly and listened, his demeanor stiffening noticeably. And as Russ watched their interaction, he became sure of one thing. If Gwen came on board, and he was almost certain she would, these two would eventually butt heads. At some point, Marty would step on her toes and Gwen would take exception. When that happened, his money was on Gwen.

Satisfied that she'd made her point, Gwen decided to soften her approach. She'd come into the meeting with a plan to push hard on her stock option plan (she thought it too low) but had changed her mind. Her take on Marty, at least as it pertained to this interview, was that he was looking for a reason to object to her, but she wasn't about to give him one. Anyhow, with the upcoming IPO, she had a much better plan to score more stock options than this one. Now was not the time to poke the bear, so she changed the subject.

"What do you see as the long-term viability of CrestPoint?" she asked. "Are you shooting for an eventual buy-out by one of the Telecom giants?"

"God no!" exclaimed Marty, sounding rather shocked at the suggestion. Without hesitating, he began to paint his rosy picture of CrestPoint's future, and one that didn't include any buy-out by some Telecom giant. Russ jumped in, agreeing with Marty's vision of the future, and together they vigorously made their argument that CrestPoint would one day become a telecom juggernaut on its own. As Gwen listened to them, she found herself keyed in on the interaction between Russ and Marty. It was obvious they were friends. Perhaps there was even a big brother-little brother dynamic at play. But what she found most interesting was the way Marty looked at Russ with puppy dog eyes whenever Russ took over the conversation. That, combined with hand gestures that were a trifle effeminate, would have normally led her to presume he was gay if it weren't for the pictures of his wife and child on his desk (of course, these days, that didn't really mean much).

For his part, Marty was sure he'd made things clear to Gwen about CrestPoint's future. But her question still bothered him. If she thought she was going to come on board and navigate his company into the arms of AT&T or Atlantis, she had another think coming. That was not *his vision*. But abruptly, to his pleasant surprise, she gave out a hearty "Sounds good!" embracing his picture of CrestPoint's future and quickly shifting the discussion over to her staffing needs. If she was one thing, he concluded, she was cagey, knowing when to poke and when to pet. It left him a bit flat-footed. He expected a fight over her stock package but it hadn't happened, and now she'd maneuvered the interview into a de facto discussion regarding her support team. She considered herself hired, and he wasn't sure whether he found that self-confidence irritating or reassuring.

There was one other thing he was sure of; it had become apparent to him over the course of this meeting that something was going on between her and Russ. Affection? Sexual attraction? He wasn't exactly sure, but it was as palpable as the scent of her Yves Saint Laurent perfume. It was common knowledge that these two dated years ago.

But, hell, Russ dated everyone (they came and they went, *they came and they went),* and it was unlikely their affair had been anything other than a casual fling. Yet, he sensed a connection between the two that went beyond just a brief romance, and this six-sense acted as something of a check on his bias against this woman (or at least what she represented to him, which was a loss of power) and helped to oil the works in her favor.

He didn't officially offer her the job of President and COO of CrestPoint Communications; there just came a point in the interview where it became taken for granted. Like the woman who's come about the wet nurse position, she was already breast-feeding the baby before the interview was over. Whether he liked Gwen or not, he thought, was still an open question, but he was confident he could win her over and make her a loyal ally.

At the conclusion of the interview, Marty got up and came around the desk to shake her hand. She stood up to accept his handshake. In her high heels she towered over him, a fact she found amusing and he found annoying.

Gwen met with the officer team the next day and they gave her their unequivocal endorsement. She delivered her two-week notice to AT&T, and a press release went out soon after announcing her new position with CrestPoint Communications. By the first week in February, she was moved into her spacious office at Rio Seco Business Park in San Jose, furnishing it with Scandinavian Contemporary pieces and hanging a collection of modern art prints on the walls. In the parking lot, her space was marked in bold red lettering that simply read **Gwen Novak, President.**

Chapter 6

They were leaving Sunday dinner at his mom's, and she started in on him about the prayer even before they hit the freeway. What was that all about, she asked him—the prayer, at dinner? He shrugged his shoulders in response. His mom had asked him to say grace, just like she did every Sunday when they sat down to dinner, and he had complied. Only this night had been different. Suddenly, he found himself unable to repeat the same old tired Catholic grace ("Bless us, Oh Lord, and these Thy gifts") and instead improvised his own prayer, asking for God's blessing and the forgiveness of their sins, expressing his joy at God's love for them, and pouring his heart into his words in a way he'd never done before. When he finished saying "Amen," he glanced up and saw the looks of puzzlement on the faces of his family.

"What possessed you?" asked Ronnie. "I mean, that was kind'a over the top, don't you think?"

Normally his son and daughter remained quiet in the back seat on the ride home, Brandon playing with his hand-held video game and Lacy listening to music, but they appeared keyed up, tuning in to their parents' discussion. "Yeah, Dad," said his daughter. "Are you becoming a holy-roller or something?"

Mark glanced back at her through the rearview mirror and saw both a grin and a look of worry on his daughter's face. At sixteen, she was filled with teenage angst and typically used sarcasm to express herself.

Ronnie picked up on her daughter's grin and mirrored it, and now his son followed with his own grin. He saw that they wanted to turn it into a joke. *"Yeah, Dad,"* mimicked Ronnie cheerfully.

How could he explain this to them in a way they'd understand, he wondered. It was a moment of inspiration, an impulse triggered by his general discontent and an urge for something new, and once he started, he found the words pouring out of him. "Thought I'd try something different for a change," he said by way of explanation. He came to the freeway on-ramp and accelerated, causing everyone to be pushed slightly backward.

"*That* was definitely different," quipped Lacy, causing both her mother and brother to laugh. He forced a grin, lifting his chin to signal that he got the joke and was done talking about it. The gesture was well-known to his family and it produced the desired effect. Ronnie turned to look out the windshield while Lacy placed her headphones over her ears and his son turned his attention back to his video game.

The prayer *did* feel good, he thought to himself. Like a drink of cool water, it refreshed me. It is probably the first time in my life I ever prayed out loud like that, in front of people, without feeling self-conscious or embarrassed. But it came at a price. Now my family views me as some kind of weirdo.

If they only knew. If they only knew about the black dog that stalked him, or about the utter void he woke up to every morning and the growing desperation that came with it—if they only knew the truth, they wouldn't laugh it off. If they really understood his anguish, it would frighten them. He knew that as well as he knew his daughter's favorite color (red) or his son's greatest fear (heights). So, he kept it to himself. Like a fugitive suffering from a deep wound, he tried to hide it, even though he was beginning to leak blood on the floor.

It had been a year and a half since his religious experience on the plane (he didn't know what else to call it) and, quite frankly, the whole episode had rattled him. He was not a man prone to emotional upheavals; he didn't cry or suffer mood swings. He was steady and dependable, and his experience on the plane was not a welcome one. Since then, he'd kept his head down, working at building CrestPoint's network with an almost fierce devotion to duty. That renewed focus had paid off financially in a raise and bonuses, leading to a new Jeep

Grand Cherokee (the vehicle he was driving now), a new roof on the house, sharp outfits for Ronnie, and a general elevation in their standard of living. But despite the success, the black dog had returned with a vengeance and he didn't know how to shake it. Meds and therapy weren't the answer, for he knew the problem wasn't psychological—it was spiritual. He suffered from spiritual drought, not clinical depression, and only a magic rainfall could replenish him. But where to find it, that was the question. He hoped church would help but it didn't; at first there was a bump up in his spirits, but now it was all rote and ritual. Yet, he continued to attend—Saint Joseph's, every Sunday, third pew from the back—still expecting the cloudburst of Truth to rain down on him at any moment. He continued to wait for it, not knowing where else to look, like some blind man expecting a helping hand at a crowded intersection.

He was a Catholic in name only, and he mused occasionally that it was probably the fault of his Viking ancestry—those brazen, tattooed wanderers who pretended to accept Christianity while continuing to pray to their pagan gods in secret. But the idea that he was being driven by ancient forces, preordained to act in a certain way, was repugnant to him and he rejected it.

Lately, he'd come to the conclusion he was handicapped, spiritually handicapped, by his own intellect, by his logic, by everything he'd grown up with that had taught him to doubt. He knew the answer was not outside himself; it was in his own heart, but opening his heart up to God was tantamount to an overthrow of his intellect. He feared he lacked the tools and the will to unlock his heart. And that was why his prayer at dinner felt so good. For the first time in his life, he had opened his heart, just a crack, and felt the possibilities.

Ronnie continued to stare out the windshield, watching Mark out of the corner of her eye. He looked lost in thought. She wanted to talk about his prayer at dinner and get some insight into his state of mind, but he'd made it clear he didn't want to discuss it. Not that it would stop her; if she wanted to talk about something she would, but she held off for the moment as she collected her thoughts. It wasn't the prayer, per se, that bothered her but the intense look on his face when he delivered it. His brow was knitted in concentration, and then, as he hit his stride and the words flowed, there was a sudden relaxing of his facial muscles followed by an expression of great calm. The only time she ever saw an expression like that on his face was when he finished making love to her, but even that didn't quite match what she saw at the dinner table.

Maybe she was jealous, she thought, but she dismissed the thought as soon as it came into her head. No, what bothered her about the prayer was that it fit into a pattern of quirky behavior she'd seen emerging from her husband over the last couple of months. He'd started reading the Bible every night before going to bed and carried the book *Mere Christianity* around with him wherever he went (she'd thumbed through it once and found it marked up with notes in the margin). Those two things weren't troublesome by themselves (they were Catholics, after all), but with it had come this sort of judgmental or disapproving eye for things. He wouldn't watch her favorite show *Friends* anymore calling it "stylish immorality," and he got up and turned off the TV movie *Stephen King's Storm of the Century*, declaring angrily that it was a "celebration of evil." There were other odd doings, like sticking a Pro-Life bumper sticker on their new car, writing checks to charities she'd never heard of, and sitting for long spells in their garden in the backyard, alone, just thinking. It was all somewhat troubling.

She knew about his restlessness, about that hole in some men that needed filling up, and she really thought that his new job would set things right. And it seemed to her that it did just that—for a while. He worked long hours at his job but came home every evening for dinner, helped the kids with their homework, talked cheerfully about their future, made love to her with his usual passion, and even bragged to her on occasion about his accomplishments at work. It was a good time and had lasted over a year, so what had changed, she wondered. She refused to believe that a loving family and a great job were not enough to make him happy. But something was bugging him and she needed to get to the root of it.

"What was that reading in church today?" she asked him, keeping her voice low. "Something about 'if you have faith and can move mountains, but don't have love, you have nothing.'"

Mark came out of his reverie and looked at her with surprise. "That's Corinthians 13," he replied. "It goes, 'If I have the gift of prophecy and can fathom all mysteries and all knowledge, and if I have a faith that can move mountains, but do not have love, I am nothing.'"

"Mmm, that's it… Wasn't that in our wedding?"

"It was." Rain appeared on the windshield and he turned on the wipers. Her question was leading to something, he guessed. She knew the passage perfectly well and knew it was in their wedding. She didn't forget things like that. "Why you ask?"

"Ahh, I just like that one," she said, smiling. She'd yanked him out of his trance and gotten his attention, and she wasn't going to waste the moment. "It talks a lot about love, about what love should be… Do you love me and the kids that way?" She saw his shoulders twitch back as though jolted by a shock of electricity. It was just the reaction she was hoping for.

"What? Of course—what kind of question is that?"

"I don't know. Just checking. You've been in your own little world lately and you got me worried. What's going on, big guy? Do I need to be worried?"

"No," he answered, vigorously shaking his head. He glanced over at her and saw she was expecting more, but he wasn't about to give her more, not now, not while driving in the rain on the freeway. Thankfully his daughter bailed him out.

"Dad's sign's coming up," she called out. "It's that one there, right?"

Everyone looked out the window as Lacy pointed to the collection of giant billboards that stood in the marshlands on the side of the freeway. There amongst the signs advertising dot-com and high-tech companies was a billboard with a mountain range on it that read 'CrestPoint Communications. Scale the Heights. High-speed Internet Services. Now Hiring.'

"That's it," confirmed Ronnie. They all looked out the rain-swept windows, admiring the billboard. Ronnie turned back to compliment Mark on the sign and noticed that his eyes were searching for something. She glanced back out the window at the billboards, now nearly past them, and saw a smaller sign, still there after all this time, that simply read 'Jesus Saves.' She turned in time to see her husband's face register deep emotion, as though he had just received a secret message from God. He stared out the windshield, having fallen into one of his damn trances again, and her brow wrinkled with concern—and a growing impatience.

"I talked to Cherry the other day," she said loudly, trying to draw him out of his little dream state.

"What?"

"I talked to Cherry the other day," she repeated. By Cherry she meant Cherry Chandrasekar. The two had become friends over the last year, going out to lunch together, shopping, and exchanging gossip. The four of them—her, Mark, Cherry, C.V. (whom everyone called Chandra)—had even dined together and played Trivial Pursuit. In Cherry, she found a kindred soul, a woman who understood what mattered in life, and from her, she learned things about CrestPoint politics that often her husband didn't know.

"She told me that when CrestPoint goes public in a couple months, everyone is going to be millionaires. I told her what your stock plan was and she figured you'd be worth between forty to fifty million dollars… Is that true?"

He took a deep breath, clearing his head, and told her it might be true—if everything went as planned. It was obvious this was what she wanted to talk about. And, yes, it was important; he should have told her about this earlier, but he didn't because there had been other things on his mind. She quickly pressed him for more information and he did his best to answer her questions, confirming her hopes with a large dash of caution. He could see she was more excited about the prospect of fifty million dollars than he was.

Their conversation seemed to organically wind itself down just as they pulled into their driveway. Everyone piled out and rushed into the house to get out of the rain. It was past nine o'clock and there was no school Monday, so the kids wanted to stay up and watch TV. Mom made popcorn and Dad settled into his chair while the kids grabbed their favorite spots and got comfortable. Lacy held the remote and turned on *The X-Files*, which was already underway. Brandon complained that it was half over, and Dad wasn't in the mood for its occult nonsense, so Lacy started surfing channels. After numerous stops, many of them vetoed by Dad, Lacy came to the movie *Indiana Jones and the Last Crusade*, declaring happily, "Here we go. Indiana Jones. I know you like Indiana Jones, Dad." He smiled at her and everyone agreed. The movie was already a half hour in, but it didn't matter (they'd seen it before). What mattered was they now had a show they could all watch together.

Mark watched the movie for a spell, sipping occasionally from the glass of red wine Ronnie had given him. She lay curled up on the couch with the dog. The kids ate popcorn, engrossed in the movie... *The cup of Christ,* he mused. The movie was all about the search for the cup of Christ, and it was rich how the subject fit so neatly into his own pattern of thought... *Jesus Christ... Jesus of Nazareth...* He'd been using his engineer's mind to find Jesus Christ, reading, researching, examining the evidence, and come to the inescapable conclusion that Jesus the man had lived and died. He was even sure the Romans crucified him. But despite all the evidence, he doubted the divinity of Jesus.

There was the block. That was the handicap. He kneeled in church every Sunday watching the priest turn bread and wine into the body and blood of Jesus Christ, and not for one moment did he believe in the miracle of transubstantiation (he was smarter than that). And when he stuck his tongue out to take the wafer, he did so out of an elevated sense of enlightenment, because it was an ancient and profound rite and he was a fellow traveler. Not because he believed. Yet, outside the church, he was an advocate and defender of the faith, encouraging people to open their minds and admit to the possibility of Jesus as the Messiah.

He was a worldly man in church and a spiritual man amongst skeptics. A man in two camps. A dweller on the threshold.

He wanted desperately to see it, and it was right there, just right there in front of him. The block wasn't his education or his twentieth-century sophistication. It was something greater than that; it was something more insidious than that. It was a thing that fed on the world, that devoured love and peace and faith, swallowing it up like so much fodder then vomiting it out in the form of denial and conflict. And it was a thing simply said.

It was the Sin of Pride.

He breathed in deeply at this revelation, his mind fitting the last pieces together. *The Sin of Pride...* This is my great handicap. And maybe *now*, with this knowledge, I can unshackle myself and stride forward. But where to? What comes next? When two and two are added together, the answer can't be anything other than four. It's inescapable. Inevitable. What must come next is recognition of that fact—acknowledgement of the truth: Jesus wasn't just a great moral teacher. If Jesus wasn't the son of God, then he died for a lie...

Mark suddenly ran both his hands through his hair, struggling to make his way clear, trying to trigger a linkage. It was from *Mere Christianity*, a passage he remembered that went something like "If Jesus was merely a man and said the sort of things he did, then he wouldn't be a great moral leader, he'd be either a lunatic or the Devil himself. You must make your choice."

His eyes were closed, and he opened them now and took in the room. Ronnie laid curled up on the couch with the dog. The kids were engrossed in the movie—a movie he had completely tuned out—and suddenly a spoken line of dialogue pierced through his meditation, ringing in his ears, cutting to the core of his being.

"It's time to ask yourself what you believe."

A warm electric shock surged up through Mark's body, causing momentary paralysis—the same shock and paralysis that hit him all those months ago on the plane—but this time there was no panic with it, just acceptance. It was a summons, as plain as day, and he knew he had to get away, be alone, so he could answer it. He waited for the surge to subside then got up, mumbling something about going to his den, and quietly left the room. Once upstairs, he entered the dark bedroom he'd converted into a den and sat down at his desk where he switched on a small reading light and opened the large, leather-bound Bible in front of him.

The Bible was a collector's item, the King James Version, illustrated with pictures by Rembrandt, and he'd resolved at the beginning of the year to read it from cover to cover. He was now at Deuteronomy, and he took the silky ribbon of a bookmark in his fingers and flipped open to where he'd left off, reading the first thing he found.

> *I call heaven and earth to record this day against you, that I have set before you life and death, blessing and cursing: therefore choose life, that both thou and thy seed may live…*

The words were clear—and meant for him—and he rested his forehead against the page and waited for it. He waited for a voice that would speak to him, for a spirit that would fill him up, for something to come and change his life. But it didn't come. For the longest time he waited, *he waited…* but it didn't come. He raised his head and looked out the window at the rain, a feeling of failure sweeping over him. *Why wouldn't it come*, he wondered. *What was he doing wrong?*

A bright light came on.

"Whatcha doin', Dear," asked his wife as she came up behind him and placed her hands on his shoulders. "Comin' to bed?"

"Huh? Just reading… What time is it?"

"Past eleven. Kids are in bed."

"Oh, okay… I'll be in in a little bit."

When she came into the room, she had quickly noticed the intense scowl on his face. It was a look she was familiar with and meant he was deep in thought trying to work out a problem. Her intuition told her it wasn't work related—it was something else—and she wanted very much to talk to him, to get him to open up about it, and now would be the perfect time. Only she hesitated. An odd feeling came over her, a feeling akin to wariness, causing her to have second thoughts. He sat there expressionless, the scowl having cleared from his face, the Bible open in front of him, and normally this would have been the time to press him gently for answers—but something yanked her back. Not now, she thought. At this moment she was sure it was better to leave him alone, so she bent down, kissed him goodnight, told him she loved him, and went off to bed, switching off the light as she withdrew.

Mark listened to her leave the room. Alone again, he picked up his copy of *Mere Christianity,* dog-eared and thumb-worn, and flipped through it unconsciously until he reached the back cover. A notation, faint and in pencil, caught his eye and he raised it into the light to read it. He'd put it there over a year ago and forgotten about it. It was something Mike told him—"John 1-12"—and he quickly set the book aside and flipped through his Bible until he found the passage. He read the words carefully, both verses, 12 and 13, then slid off his chair and onto his knees.

He knew only this—to receive Christ he had to strip away the sin of pride. To be born of God, he had to overcome his ego and come as a supplicant. And now on his knees, Mark prayed the sinner's prayer, acknowledging his sinfulness and inviting Jesus to come into his heart. "Forgive me, Lord. Have mercy on me… Lord Jesus, I believe in you. Please come into my life… Have mercy on me."

He suddenly stood up. He had to get to the garden. The feeling was overwhelming. Something wonderful awaited him there, and he rushed downstairs and out the sliding glass door into the backyard. The back porch light provided a soft glow to see by. It was still raining, a fine mist of a rain, and he followed the narrow path he'd laid down years ago that led into their garden. Once there, he sat down on a wooden bench, not noticing the wetness through his pants, and raised his face to the heavens. And in the garden wet with rain, he opened his heart and felt a great comforting strength begin to well up inside him.

Ronnie had fallen asleep waiting for Mark to come to bed. She was not a frequent dreamer but tonight a dream snuck its way into her unconsciousness, like an intruder into her house.

They are pulled over on the side of the freeway. It's dark and raining and cars are flashing by. "You've got to see this," says Mark excitedly, and he jumps out of the car and comes around to let her out. She's afraid to go with him—it's dark and raining and it looks like they're in the middle of the marshlands—but he's insistent and yanks on her arm. "Okay, okay," she says and turns to the kids in the back seat to tell them to sit still, but they are both asleep, oblivious to what's going on. He pulls her out and they begin running but it's hard to move her legs because they keep sinking into the marshy earth. She realizes now they're by the billboards and guesses he wants to show her the CrestPoint sign, but she knows better—it's for something else—and she's not sure she wants to see it, but he keeps pulling her along, begging her to "come see it." He's flush with excitement, almost wild-eyed, and as they hurry along he sometimes looks like Indiana Jones and sometimes like himself only keyed up and determined. They finally stop. "There!" he yells, and she glances up to see the small billboard that reads 'Jesus Saves'. She's confused. "Where?" she asks, looking left and right and past the sign. "Right there!" he yells, yanking her arm. "What? Where?" she asks again, becoming frightened. "Right there!" he yells again, shaking her arm.

She awoke to him tugging on her arm. He knelt next to the bed wet from the rain. The sight startled her, and she came fully awake, swinging her legs out and sitting on the edge of the bed. He knelt in front of her with eyes that looked drunk or high, his mouth slightly open, and she took his rain-wet face into her hands. "Tell me, darling," she said. "Tell me what's happened."

Chapter 7

Within two years, the break room at CrestPoint Communications had burgeoned into a cafeteria-sized facility designed to accommodate the growing employee population. It resided in its own building strategically centered amongst three other office buildings that CrestPoint had taken possession over the last two years. The modest campus, set within the Rio Seco Business Park, was comprised of rolling hills, manicured lawns, large oak trees, a dry creek bed, and a maze of narrow sidewalks that connected all the buildings to one another as well as to the cafeteria which everyone called "the hub."

In 1999, the hub reflected the tastes and philosophy of a cutting-edge, hi-tech company with an enlightened workforce. There were two foosball tables, a ping pong table, the arcade games X-Men and Mortal Combat (which were played almost exclusively by young men), a bookshelf that stored board games like chess, variations of Trivial Pursuit, Chinese checkers, and Scrabble, along with a table that provided morning editions of the San Francisco Chronicle, the San Jose Mercury, the Wall Street Journal, and a variety of trade journals such as Computerworld, DSL Prime, The Street, InfoWorld, and PC/Computing. There were computer stations where one could surf the web or play solitaire, and mounted at each end of the hub was a large TV that continually displayed CNBC and CNN (or ESPN if there was a popular sporting event on). Besides the different forms of entertainment, there was a Peet's Coffee kiosk where one could also buy bran muffins and scones, a long counter with a sink, microwave ovens, and a large refrigerator packed with food in Tupperware containers, many of them plastered with post-it notes that read 'hands off,' 'Mine' (with the owner's name), or 'eat at your own peril'. There were also vending machines that abstained from your run of the mill choice of candy bars and chips and instead provided an eclectic assortment of goodies such as Drake's coffee cakes, Utz potato chips, and Toblerone chocolate bars.

The hub was the place to take your break, decompress for a spell, play games, enjoy a good coffee, eat lunch, and kibitz with your colleagues. And the hot topic on everyone's minds this morning was the upcoming IPO that promised to make them all millionaires.

"It's May 12th. That's what I heard."

"Yeah, that's what I heard."

"A couple weeks then. That's a Wednesday, right?"

"Right."

"What time does trading open?"

"9:30 eastern, so 6:30 our time, but I'm not coming in at 6:30 to watch it."

"Me neither. It's not what it opens at anyway but what it closes at that counts. But if you download the stock ticker, you can watch it all day, or at least until trading stops."

"Everyone's gonna download it. No one's gonna be working on the 12th. Everybody's gonna be staring at their computer screen figuring out how much money they're worth."

"I know I will."

There was general laughter at this remark between the two men and the woman who stood about twenty paces away from the Peet's Coffee kiosk sipping their java. Another man with a fresh cup of coffee in his hand joined them. "What you guys talkin' about?" he asked. "The IPO?"

"Yep. Couple weeks."

"I know, can't wait."

"Anyone know what our stock abbreviation's gonna be?"

"CPNT on the Nasdaq."

"How do you know all these things?"

"I work for Stu. How else? I hear him and Rubin on the phone with the underwriters all the time. If you don't believe me, go outside and ask him."

They all looked out the large glass windows to see Stuart Baum and two of his employees smoking outside the hub. It was a common site at break time.

"Not without a gas mask… I believe you. CPNT—I like it!"

"What else do you know?"

"Oh… well, let's see. They gotta meeting coming up with Morgan Stanley to set the stock price for opening day. They want it low enough so they get a nice bounce when it starts trading but not too low that they leave money on the table."

"Whaddya think it'll open at?"

"Jeez, hard to say. It could be a ten-point swing. Anywhere from $17 a share to $27."

"Okay, then, for the sake of argument… Let's say it opens at $22 a share."

"And closes at what? For the sake of argument."

"For the sake of argument… Let's say it closes at $35 a share. Certainly in the realm of possibility."

"Certainly."

"Then do your own math. Take your strike price and the difference and start multiplying."

"I'd be worth about $10 million."

"Jeez! *That* was fast."

There was more general laughter at this remark—a laughter that had a distinct undercurrent of excitement to it—as everyone held their coffee cup and did their own calculations in their heads. Another employee emerged from the coffee line and passed by them.

"Morning, Mark."

"Morning, all."

"Talkin' about the IPO."

"The what? Oh, yeah… When's that?"

"The 12th. Least, that's what we heard. Marty's gonna announce it in a townhall when he gets back… We're just taking a swag at what our payouts might be."

"Oh… I see. Good luck with that."

They watched as Mark walked off, rapidly exchanging glances with one another.

"He seemed a bit distracted."

"You haven't heard?"

"Heard what?"

"He found God… He's born-again."

"Yeah, and I heard that he kicked off his last staff meeting with a little speech about how he'd accepted Jesus Christ as his Lord and Savior."

"No shit? Right in his staff meeting? Did he try and convert people?"

"No—not according to Dick Frost, who works for him. He said he just made his testimony—that's what they call it—then went back to business as usual."

"I wouldn't have pegged him as a Jesus freak."

"Me neither."

They stood a moment in silence, digesting this news, then quickly changed the subject back to the IPO.

"Need to be careful, though. You can't make any projections off the first day of trading. That closing price will last about as long as Carmen Electra's marriage to Rodman. Just look at Nomad. It'll drop, then go back up. So we'll see how it all pans out."

"You can't cash in for six months anyhow."

"I don't think anyone's gonna cash in at six months. I'm not. I'm in it for the long run."

"Me, too. For the long run."

"Here's to the long run."

The four of them touched their disposable coffee cups together in a toast to the long run.

Barry got DSL from CrestPoint Communications on the first day it was available. Actually, he ordered it from Telocity—the Internet Service Provider—through an ad campaign that got him first on the waiting list at a discounted monthly fee of $59.99 a month (for six months) and free installation. His parents agreed to the change after he told them they could talk on the phone while he was on-line without any interference, and he sealed the deal by offering to help pay for the service. He was still a manager at Blockbuster Video but had taken up day trading lately, made a few dollars at it, and could afford to be generous. And with a high-speed Internet service like DSL, he could increase his day trading activities and score even bigger wins. It was a win-win scenario.

The whole process was a little convoluted. First, he had to cancel his modem service with AOL. Next, he had to get 'qualified', which entailed them calculating the distance from his home to the telephone central office to make sure he wasn't too far away (he wasn't), then getting a self-installation package that included a router, a battery pack, a splitter box, and an instruction manual that read like a Chinese menu. After six hours, most of it on the phone with their tech support people, he got it installed and found to his delight that his Internet connection was now running at a speed of 160 kilobits per second. He was golden.

As he did most evenings, Barry communed with his friends Mo and Ender on Instant Messenger. Mo was stuck with his modem service because he didn't qualify but Ender was good to go and was simply waiting for his installation package to arrive. Being first with DSL gave Barry a certain stature with his buddies.

"Hey, Trump," typed Ender. "Make a killing today?"

"No," replied Barry. "Quiet day. U set up yet?"

"Nyet. Friday."

"Dont wait for DSL. Set up ur account on Street.com or u can go w/ RagingBull. Theres a ton of investment clubs that cater to asians, blacks, etc."

"Even nerdy white guys," typed Mo.

"Specially nerdy white guys."

"Cool."

"So dont wait," continued Barry. "CrestPoints got an IPO comin up and u want in on it."

"Me and a million others."

"They dont have DSL bro. Thats our lightsaber."

"Which reminds. Phantom Menace end of month. R we standing in line 4 tickets?"

"Thats the plan."

"Line's gonna b a mile long."

"Not if Mo camps out the nite b/4."

"Howd I get elected?"

"Cause ur Mo the Man. Ur Batman, dude."

"Plus u live down the street from the regal."

"That makes more sense. Wish u could order online."

"It's comin, give it time. Pretty soon u'll be able to order anything online. Even a hooker."

"An Amazon hooker! Dude, I luv it."

"Just so she looks like J-Lo."

"Or Angelina Jolee."

"Yum! Hackers. Acid Burn."

"Freakin great."

"You hear? There's a flaw in Hotmail. All u do is type in 'eh' as the password to break into someones account."

"Ender can hack his ex-girlfriend and read her mail."

"Already did."

"Dude. Serious? What u find?"

Ender proceeded to describe in lurid detail what he had found in his ex-girlfriend's email account. After five minutes of breathtaking discovery followed by another five minutes of Q&A, the topic exhausted itself. Though Ender let them know that the security flaw had been fixed and he couldn't get back into her account.

"Bummer."

"Anyhow gotta blow. Lookin 4 a job."

"Use Monster.com."

"I am. Got an interview with sun micro in newark.
"Luck, bro."
"May the force b w/ u."
"U 2."
"Chill."

Barry waited a moment to confirm that his buddies had dropped off before he closed Instant Messenger and went back to what he was doing. It was a sex chat room called Hotime where his handle was Lando, and he passed himself off as a biker from Oakland, a bona fide bad boy with a criminal record, who was into women with tattoos.

Chapter 8

With one week to go before the IPO, the investor roadshows finally came to an end and everyone was back home. The whirlwind tour started in the West, crisscrossed from Chicago down to Dallas and points in-between, and wrapped up with numerous presentations on the East Coast. The team consisted of Marty, Stu, the lead underwriter, Tollerson Accounting, and a floating team of market analysts recruited by Marty who supported the cause (Frank Altobello for one). Marty lobbied hard to have Russ and his cultivated charm join them on the tour but Russ vigorously declined (he had a department to run, after all). He abruptly changed his mind, though, once the tour reached Boston, which just happened to be the home of Teri Starr. Marty could only smile at that; he knew there was an ulterior motive, but a satisfied Ms. Starr and a strong buy rating from her company were all to their advantage.

It was that trip to Boston that Russ sat thinking about while he waited for Gwen's staff meeting to begin. He beheld Teri's face in his mind's eye. She lay underneath him, both having just climaxed, and he studied her pretty face, now serenely relaxed after her orgasm, with a man's appreciation for a woman who sexually satisfies him. Their day together had been first-rate—a Red Sox game followed by dinner at the Union Oyster house—and ended up in her apartment where they wasted no time jumping into bed together. All told they'd had sex a dozen times already, their first time on his boat nearly two years ago, then again on her visits to the Bay Area (ostensibly to interview entrepreneurs but really to hook up with him), and now tonight, and each time she'd given herself completely to him, making him feel splendidly grand.

It was then, as he quietly studied her face, that she opened her eyes, and upon seeing his look of appreciation, took his face in her hands and said, "I think I love you."

"Hi, Russ!" The cheerful hello came from Shavonne, Gwen's personal admin, who carried a stack of papers under her arm. Russ returned her greeting and made small talk with her as she handed him a package containing the agenda and other meeting materials. Gwen came into the conference room followed by Chandra and Ron, Shavonne handing them each a package as they sat down.

Gwen leafed through her package to make sure everything was there. It was. She'd been President of CrestPoint Communications for three months now and her staff meetings were once a week, every Wednesday morning, and were meant to include all the EVPs. She typically didn't invite Marty; as CEO, he held his own board meetings, but today she'd asked him to come in for the first half hour and give them all a summary of his road trip and the status of their upcoming IPO. It was also a way to ensure Stuart Baum's participation. Technically, Stu was her direct report and should have been a regular attendee at her staff meetings, but he went out of his way to avoid them, sending Hal Rubin in his stead.

Marty appeared, loudly greeting everyone, grabbing a bottle of water off the refreshment stand, and sitting down next to Gwen. He smiled warmly at her. Lori came in and sat down, receiving her package from Shavonne. At three minutes past the hour, Stu came in looking like he had better things to do with his day, took a seat at the other end of the conference table, and received his package from Shavonne as though it were an unwanted subpoena. Shavonne sat down and opened her notebook, ready to take meeting minutes.

Gwen welcomed everyone and then quickly kicked off the agenda by asking Marty to give them a summary of his road trip. Marty wasted no time in announcing that the roadshows had gone well—that, if they intended to generate investor interest and market enthusiasm, they had been an overwhelming success. They were treated like celebrities wherever they went. The fund managers and institutional investors—the ones who would be bidding for their stock—clamored to get a seat at their presentations. With a gleam in his eyes, Marty likened the meetings to a church revival and chuckled when he noted that people had to be turned away.

The next part of his summary covered their upcoming IPO. (He was to have a company-wide town hall meeting tomorrow where all of this would be shared—but he would give it to them firsthand now.) CrestPoint's IPO, which would occur next Wednesday, was being underwritten by a syndicate of investment banks, the largest of which—Morgan Stanley—was the leader. All financial information, including first-quarter earnings, had been filed with the Security Exchange Commission. Next Monday, the IPO Team was scheduled to meet and set the opening day stock price. Then, next Wednesday, CPNT would be floated on the Nasdaq, made public, and CrestPoint Communications Inc would transform itself from a private company to a public company. By selling an 11 percent stake in their company, the underwriters projected CrestPoint would net over $300 million in capital and become worth well over $4 billion.

Marty paused to let those numbers sink it. Most of this was not news to the people around the table; IPO process, timelines, stock projections—CrestPoint management did a lousy job of keeping secrets—but he was tickled when Lori dropped her pencil and said "Wow."

"Wow is right," he intoned. "You've all worked hard to get to this point, so I hope you're all ready to become filthy rich."

There was laughter at this remark, though Russ cringed slightly at Marty for throwing out such a jinx as that. Marty seemed to take the cue, quickly reminding everyone in a serious tone to be careful. This was a quiet time right before the IPO and they couldn't afford to slip up. Be careful who you talk to, be careful what you say, and "don't pull an Adam Osborne," which was an allusion to the CEO of Osborne Computers whose bragging led to the implosion of his company right before their IPO.

Gwen asked about the Board of Directors and Marty replied that the board was nearly complete. Besides himself as Chairman, there were all the officers present in the room today along with seven outsiders for a total of fourteen directors. The outsiders included a former commissioner of the FCC, four general partners of prestigious venture capital firms, and two president-CEOs of hugely successful hi-tech corporations. It was an all-star lineup.

Marty's half-hour was up and Gwen thanked him for his time, adding that he was welcome to stay if he wanted. No, he had calls to make, he said and got up to leave while happily quoting lyrics from a Grateful Dead song, *"Fare you well, fare you well. I love you more than words can tell."* This elicited chuckles from around the room.

"We have that call with the investors at one," said Stu abruptly as he started to rise from his chair.

"Have a seat, Stu," said Gwen in her President's voice. "We'll cover your agenda items first. You have plenty of time."

"Yes, yes," chimed in Marty. "Stay here. We have plenty of time."

Stu sat back down with an audible sigh. Gwen eyed him like a hungry lioness and got ready to take a big bite out of his ego. She was looking forward to this moment. It wasn't Stu so much she was fed up with; like Russ, she didn't particularly care for Stu or trust him. It was his whole organization that was the problem; she couldn't get straight answers out of them. It was like pulling teeth. They all shared an attitude of haughty impertinence that she was sure reflected Stu's own attitude towards her, and it was time for a little showdown.

"We still have compliance issues in Chicago," declared Gwen, addressing Stu directly. "It's holding up our consumer rollout. Where are we on that, and what's the plan to resolve it?"

Stu asked what issues those were exactly, and Gwen quickly threw out several examples. He stumbled to give her specific answers and instead tried to pass it all off as trivial. Gwen pressed for straight answers, asking again what his plan was to resolve these problems. Obviously cornered and without answers, Stu announced rather loftily that he'd been out of the office on roadshows ensuring a successful IPO, but that he'd look into it and get back to her.

"By end of day," she said sharply.

"By end of day."

But she wasn't done. She reminded everyone of Marty's warning about being careful leading up to their IPO, adding her own admonishment that CrestPoint—everyone—needed to be "squeaky clean" going into next week. There couldn't be any misconduct or hints of impropriety. To that end, she'd asked the City Managers across the country to give her an account of their spending. Their response was less than stellar, and she had yet to receive reports back from three of them. Stu, visibly incensed at the implication, replied that the City Managers reported to him and were his responsibility.

"That's where you're wrong," shot back Gwen. "You're my direct report, which means they report to me through you. If I can't get them to follow simple directions then I'll replace them with people who can follow directions."

Stu met her withering stare head-on while his mind buzzed at this assault. This woman was trying to pick a fight with him, he was sure of it. But for what reason? To assert her dominance? To show off to the others? She was being provocative and combative (which was a reputation that preceded her), and he wasn't going to stand for it. But now was not the time, he knew. His payback would have to come later. For now he would take the high road.

"Give me their names," he said calmly, "and I'll look into it."

She read off the three names, one of which was Stony Bundschuh, and watched with satisfaction as he wrote them down. She could see she'd rattled him; he was clearly talking to himself in his head. Her killer instinct was aroused but she knew better than to fully castrate a man in front of his peers, especially one as powerful as Stu, so she backed off. There were a couple of other items she wanted to confront him about but instead she turned to Ron Lau and asked him to report on order flow.

Russ enjoyed the show immensely, smiling to himself as he watched Stu squirm in his seat. All talk and no trousers—that was Stuart Baum. And just when she had him, just when he thought she was going to filet Stu's carcass, she let him off the hook. Probably smart of her, he decided, admiring her style.

Gwen listened intently to Ron's report, which acted as a glaring counterpoise to Stu's defensive stumbling. It was precise, articulate, backed by data, and she nodded her satisfaction with it when Ron finished. She appreciated people who quickly got to the point, who caught the ball from her and shot instead of dribbling around with it. Ron was one of those people and so was Russ.

She called a fifteen-minute break, refilling her coffee cup and grabbing a blueberry scone (her favorite) off the refreshment stand. Stu left the room. She half expected him not to return, but when he did, it was with a look of resolve. When she kicked the meeting back off, he asked for a moment and quickly launched into a report on the compliance problems in Chicago and their plan and timeline to rectify them. (He'd obviously spent the last fifteen minutes getting fully briefed on the issue by one of his people.). When he finished, he was visibly pleased with himself at this act of redemption, but she merely nodded and went on to other agenda items.

They were done by lunchtime, and Gwen thanked everyone for their time and watched them get up and leave the room. A productive meeting, she decided, satisfied with herself. She was moving the needle; processes were improving, departments were talking to one another, and by taking Stu down a notch, there was no doubt about who was running the show. She'd come to work today with two objectives—a one-two punch—and she planned to achieve the second one very soon. She was on Marty's calendar for 2:30 today, and that's when she'd deliver her second punch.

Russ leaned back in his chair and stretched his back, tilting his head from side to side to work out the stiffness. He'd been working on his computer since noon and it was now 3:00. He needed a break, and as he stretched his back and cleared his mind, the image of Teri's face floated back up.

I think I love you, she had said. What was he supposed to do with that, he wondered. It wasn't the first time a woman said she loved him, but normally he didn't let it get that far. He could usually tell when a woman was starting to get serious; there were heavy looks, verbal hints, and small tender extra efforts. And when he saw it coming, he jettisoned the pod before things got dodgy and turned into a bloody shambles. It was usually a polite decline of an invitation (no, he couldn't make it, he had another date), or a cooling in his demeanor that did the trick. There was always disappointment—he could see it in their faces, hear it in their voices—but he liked to think that he'd averted a much worse heartbreak.

I think I love you. And he had just smiled, kissed her tenderly on the cheek, and left it like that. He never told a woman he loved her, not really, and he had no intention of starting now. His feelings for Teri weren't love and he wasn't going to lie to her just to keep on having great sex. His personal code forbade it. They had parted on good terms, promising to get together again, but he was sure she could sense the end. And it was a shame—she was a doll, the spitting image of Miss October 1990—and he was going to miss her. But it couldn't be helped.

A perfunctory knock came at his door, which he always left partly open, and Marty burst into the room. "That bitch! That fucking cunt!" he screamed, his face screwed up in rage.

"What!" exclaimed Russ, jumping up from his chair.

"That goddamned, motherfucking bitch!"

"What? Who" Russ had never seen Marty like this and he was alarmed. "Close the door—who are you talking about?"

"Gwen! That fucking cunt," replied Marty, toning his voice down slightly as he closed the door behind him. He immediately began stalking the room, mumbling to himself. *"Ambushed me... traitor... motherfucking bitch..."*

"Calm down, Marty. Tell me what's going on. Gwen—Gwen did what?"

"She stabbed me in the back!"

"Okay, calm down. Tell me what happened… Come on, sit down. Tell me what's going on." Russ came up to Marty and placed his hand on his shoulder. This had an instant calming effect on Marty, and he put his head down and allowed Russ to guide him over to a chair where he sat down. After a few deep breaths, he squeezed Russ' hand on his shoulder and began to speak.

Gwen had just come into his office and demanded another thousand shares of CrestPoint stock. At first, he thought she was kidding, but when he realized she was dead serious, he politely turned her down, reminding her that she had a signed contract—a signed contract that was clear and unambiguous regarding her stock options. She pushed back. Things got testy. Ugly things were said. Finally, she threatened to resign, immediately, if her request wasn't granted, blithely predicting that her resignation right before they went public would have a devastating blow to their stock price.

"And shit, of course she's right," said Marty grudgingly. "The resignation of our company president—now—would be a disaster… Fucking bitch! She's gonna pay for this!"

Russ nodded in sympathy, trying to console his partner. Yes, it was outrageous. Yes, she was out of line. But, as he listened to Marty's rant, he was secretly impressed by Gwen's bold move. Gutsy, he thought. She had them by the short hairs and knew it. He let Marty vent for another ten minutes until he was sure his friend had fully regained his composure.

"Let me talk to her," offered Russ, dead sure that this was the real reason Marty had burst into his office. "See what I can do."

"Yes, yes. Good idea. Talk some sense into her. If anyone can do it, you can. I mean, for Christ's sake, *a thousand shares.* That gives her more shares than you or Stu. Who in the hell does she think she is? Yes, go talk to her."

Russ assured him he'd do just that, commiserating with him a while longer until Marty—who looked like a man who'd blown off steam and was happily relieved—finally got up and left. Russ went straight over to his desk and rang up Gwen's office. Shavonne answered on the first ring.

"Hi, Shavonne. Is she in?"

"Russ? Oh, yes. She's expecting you. Come right over."

He walked to Gwen's office lost in thought. He wasn't mad at Gwen for pulling this stunt. Frankly, he didn't care if she got another thousand shares of stock, or not. It was Marty he needed to pacify, and he could only do that by getting Gwen to back off some. And as he walked over to Gwen's office, he reviewed the cards he'd been dealt. They were pretty shitty. They weren't going to fire Gwen and they weren't going to let her resign—not right before the IPO—and all he had left to play with was their friendship and perhaps her good will. Not much, really. But he would give it his best Churchillian effort. Bottom line, they couldn't have their CEO and President at each other's throats. They wouldn't survive as a company.

He breezed past Shavonne's desk, giving her a wink, and went into Gwen's office, closing the door behind him. She looked up from her desk and gave him a devilish grin.

"*Fortes fortuna iuvat,*" she declared brightly.

"So said Caesar, and we know how he ended up." He saw her shrug at his remark as he sat down, quickly trying to get a read on her attitude from her facial expression. He could see that she wasn't troubled by her actions—no, in fact, it was something other than that. She looked rather gleeful, like she'd just stolen the ball and made an easy lay-up at the other end of the floor. His work was cut out for him.

For the next half-hour, Russ tried every argument he could think of to get her to back off or at least compromise, appealing to her sense of fair play, to the importance of esprit de corps, even reminding her of their days together back with Pacific Bell. It was like trying to bend American-made steel.

Gwen admired his effort. It was Russ at his best—suave, articulate, and charming, his sexy voice coaxing her in the direction he wanted her to go—and she remembered why she'd fallen so hard for him back in the day. Did she still have feelings for him, she wondered—other than friendship? Impossible. But he was a *man*, in some ways like her father, who commanded respect and even, if you were a woman, a certain kind of devotion. It was a shame she couldn't give him what he wanted. At least not today.

About three quarters into his impassioned plea, Russ began to waver as it became blatantly obvious she wasn't going to change her mind. While the words continued to flow out of his mouth, he was simultaneously thinking about how he was going to spin this to Marty. Realpolitik was the only way. They weren't going to let her resign, not one week before their IPO. There was no good way to explain that to the industry or to the investors waiting to bid on their stock. Give her the goddamned shares and move on. He even saw the line of reconciliation he could take with the two of them as his thoughts and words suddenly converged.

"I guess this proves you're a great believer in CrestPoint," he said matter-of-factly. "You don't ask for a thousand more shares in a lemon, right? Marty must appreciate that."

"That's one way of looking at it," she replied. "But I wouldn't worry too much about Marty. He'll get over his little tantrum."

"I'd call it more than a little tantrum. He feels betrayed."

"Hmm… For a vision-guy, he lacks vision." She came forward in her chair, leaning her elbows on her desk, and raised her head in a regal pose like the Sphinx of Giza—at least that's what she looked like to Russ, and it was a pose that told him she had something important to say.

"What do you and Marty think is going to happen here—with CrestPoint?" she asked, not waiting for him to answer. "I'll tell you. We'll go public with great success and everybody will become millionaires—on paper—but it's not sustainable. The RBOCs—AT&T—they're all scrambling right now to get into the DSL market—we've showed them it's possible—and they're gonna come at us like gang busters. So, my friend, besides competing with Nomad and Pulse, now you got the big boys coming after our market share in this hyper-competitive environment. Do you think little ol' CrestPoint's gonna survive that onslaught and emerge independent and victorious? Marty can't possibly believe that—or you. No, the real opportunity for us—the real money—will come through an acquisition. AT&T, SBC, Atlantis—they want into this market now, and they're looking for ways to jump the line and scoop up a company that already has a DSL network built out. And that's us.

My job is to groom this company for a profitable acquisition, to make us a plum worth picking by increasing revenue and keeping our stock afloat until someone like SBC comes along and make us an offer we can't refuse. Then people will have a choice to either stay and keep working in this new subsidiary of SBC, or cash in their fortified shares like you did at MFS and go find something else to do."

Gwen took her elbows off the desk and leaned back in her chair as if to say, "there you are," and waited for Russ to respond. She was sure he would dispute her premise or, at the very least, defend CrestPoint's long-term potential, but he remained silent, studying her.

Russ didn't dispute any of it. It was certainly a possibility—getting bought out—but just not the future he envisioned. The focus of his thoughts was really more on Gwen herself. He knew she was tough-minded, but there was a cold-blooded shrewdness to her that surprised him a little. It was like finding a basement in your house you never knew existed. And it wasn't that he thought her incapable of such cut-throat thinking, it was just slightly jarring to see it on display for the first time.

"You paint a clear picture," he said finally. "I won't dispute it—it's certainly one possible outcome. And I'm sure Marty has considered that outcome as well. It's just that his life essence is being poured into making CrestPoint another WorldCom—a global player—and that's where his mind resides. Anything that messes with his world view will set him off."

"Like a Roman candle, huh?"

"He has his moments," replied Russ with a smile. "He can be a bit of a queer fish at times, but he's a good egg."

Gwen chuckled at this last remark. "'Queer fish,' huh? … Is he gay?"

"Who?—Marty? No… Why do you ask?"

"Ah, just curious. Never mind… Probably misreading him."

This short exchange had the effect of closing the door on their heavy-duty discussion and ushering in a more relaxed, gossipy style of conversation, a style they were both more comfortable with. He noticed a book on her desk and asked her about it.

"*Tycoon*," she answered, holding up the paperback book for him to see. "By Harold Robbins."

"Harold Robbins. I've read a few of us books. Entertaining smut. Haven't read that one yet. Any good?"

"Okay… Not as good as his others. Kinda goes overboard on the smut."

"How so?"

"Well, besides the normal amount of screwing, this one's got incest and a bunch of sadomasochism."

At the word "sadomasochism," there was a heavy pause in their conversation, the word triggering thoughts about their own personal history together. Gwen broke the awkward silence with a question.

"What do you know about this Stony Bundschuh character?" she asked.

Russ swiftly briefed her on what he knew about Stony, adding the information Mark Kirkland discovered about him in '97. All of it—the bribery, the influence peddling—had come from reliable sources but couldn't be proven with eyewitnesses. Stu ran cover for the guy and swept it all under the carpet.

"I'm not surprised," said Gwen. "You heard in the staff meeting—I tried to get spending accounts from the City Managers for just this reason, and Bundschuh was an arrogant little prick about it. He thinks he's bullet proof… But he's not. I'm gonna fire him."

"That'll make my man Kirkland happy."

"Any suggestions for a replacement?"

Russ took a moment to access his mental database, pulling up the memory files for Stony Bundschuh and Kansas City—all the things Mark shared with him regarding the situation there. "According to Mark, any time they need information or something done, they bypass Mr. Bundschuh and go to his assistant. A Tess… Moreland."

"*Tess Moreland.* Very good. Tess Moreland is about to get the phone call of her life. Let Stu stew on that for a while."

They both laughed, and it struck Russ at how quickly the mood had changed since he first stepped into her office. He came to straighten her out. She intended to vigorously fend him off. They had faced off—not as enemies, more like friendly adversaries—but the confrontation had not been without stress, along with the potential for disaster had a wrong word or phrase been spoken. Yet here they were now laughing and joking around as usual. If he'd been played, he'd been played masterfully. She would get her stock options and he, Russ, would spend the rest of the day making Marty accept the inevitable.

After a few more minutes of small talk, Russ got up to leave and Gwen watched his tall, slender frame with its squared-off shoulders stride out of the room. She wondered who he was dating these days—not that it mattered to her. She was just curious.

She reached over to her phone and buzzed Shavonne. "Yeah," she said. "City Manager's office—Kansas City. Get me Tess Moreland on the line."

Chapter 9

Several CrestPoint employees were in their seats by 6:30 am on Wednesday, May 12th, when the Nasdaq opened trading. A newly installed bubble stock-sticker floated in the middle of everyone's computer monitors, displaying CPNT stock with a bunch of zeros behind it. At the bell, CPNT opened at $24 a share. There was a smattering of cheers across the sea of desks in each of CrestPoint's three buildings. Some people—the ones who hired on in '97 and received options with a strike price of $2 a share—were already on their way to making big money.

Work ceased, phones went unanswered, as people sat transfixed on their monitor, watching their company stock steadily climb in price as the day went on. As others arrived at work, they were greeted with jubilant cheers such as "It's at thirty dollars a share!" or "I'm already worth a million bucks!" or "Check it out—check it out! It just keeps going up!" By the afternoon, when trading closed, CNPT sat at $40 a share, up 68%, and CrestPoint Communications Inc was worth nearly $5 billion, exceeding all expectations. Marty Madrid, who wandered around the building hugging everyone he met, now owned stock worth $300 million.

A state of euphoria existed across the company. Parties broke out in each of the major cities across the country where they had offices, especially in San Jose, California. At Rio Seco Business Park, work was officially suspended for the day while people celebrated their new-found fortune. Marty had expected a big day (perhaps not this big) and planned for it with cases of chilled champagne which began arriving at 2:00 pm. Pizzas were delivered along with one hundred Whoppers (half with cheese, half without), twenty buckets of Kentucky Fried Chicken (original and crispy), sushi including forty orders of

California rolls, assorted goodies like Mrs. Fields Cookies (chocolate chip and oatmeal raisin), and a mobile wet bar complete with mixed drinks and blended margaritas manned by a bartender in a vest and bow tie. By 4:00 pm, most everyone was drunk.

The epicenter of the party was in the hub where Marty led the cheerleading while standing on top of a table, tearfully thanking everybody for their dedication and hard work. When Gwen joined the festivities, sipping from a plastic champagne glass, he jumped down from the table and gave her a big hug, spilling her champagne. They both laughed as a loud cheer went up. Everyone knew the rumors—there was friction between the two—but now they were witnessing their reconciliation and it just felt right (money, lots of it, had a way of doing that). Marty clumsily refilled her glass, laughing the whole time, then fluttered off into the crowd to soak in the love. One of the accountants from Finance, an amateur DJ, had set up his sound system and was currently playing *Gettin Jiggy wit it*. Some people were dancing.

There were smaller parties in the other buildings. In building B, Sherry Overfelt from Sales (better known as Sherry-O, who had a reputation for sleeping around), drunk and horny and now worth $4.2 million, was giving men blow jobs in the storeroom. Word quickly got out and an underground railroad of male employees, pretending to chat in the corridor or hanging loose in the doorway, waited their turn. Other women, the ones who became a little crazy after a couple glasses of champagne, scoped out their targets (usually someone in their department they secretly had the hots for), found an empty office or a bathroom stall, and celebrated their new-found fortune with a fast and furious fuck.

Besides the flowing champagne, beer and wine, and mixed drinks in the hub, cocaine now made its appearance. Like forbidden candy, illicit and hip, it came out of pockets and out of purses, providing a delicious high to those who consumed it (some for the first time). In an atmosphere stoked by elation, alcohol, and a lowering of inhibitions, people made no real attempt to hide it. There were lines of coke on desktops and on bathroom counters. Men and women eagerly bent down with rolled-up dollar bills to snort it, arching up as it hit their senses, holding their noses, laughing, immediately chatting with friends around them.

Lori Hunter walked out of her office in building C to go to the bathroom. She passed a small group of people around a desk snorting coke but pretended not to notice. But once in the Ladies restroom, there was no ignoring it. Four young women, loudly talking, crowded around the sinks cutting up cocaine on the marble countertop. Moans and grunts could be heard from one of the stalls as a couple went at it. One woman at the counter yelled out at them to flush when they were done. The others laughed hysterically. Lori froze inside the doorway. The women turned towards her, looking through her as though she was a ghost, and went back to what they were doing. Lori quickly left, found another bathroom, then returned to her office where she closed the door so she didn't have to see what she didn't want to see.

In building A, where Marty's office resided along with the offices of the original EVPs, the celebration was a little more subdued. Small groups of people hung out in office doorways talking happily while sipping champagne. There was no loud music or inappropriate behavior, and cocaine use was nowhere in sight. For that, people went over to buildings B or C or joined the big party in the hub. Building A was like the Vatican where the Pope resided; in it a certain decorum was expected and maintained.

Russ received visitors in his office, each flushed with excitement, each wanting to shake his hand, pat him on the back, and share a glass of champagne. After the fourth wave of visitors, he left his office to go find Marty, Gwen, and a few others he wanted to personally congratulate. He quickly learned that both Marty and Gwen were over at the big party in the hub and he hoped to himself that they weren't duking it out in front of everybody. He looked for Mark Kirkland but found his office empty, the same with Ron Lau, so he changed course and headed towards Chandra's office.

"Hey, Russ!"

He turned to see Stu standing in the open doorway of his office, champagne bottle in hand, signaling to him. "Come on over!" he hollered with an inviting smile on his face. "Have a glass of champagne with us!"

Russ hesitated for a moment, a little surprised by the invitation. What the hell, he thought—it was a day for grand gestures—so he turned and walked over to Stu. As Russ approached, Stu stepped into him and shook his hand briskly, reeking of cigarette smoke. "Hey, old chap, we did it," he said, handing Russ a glass of champagne. "A great day. A great day for CrestPoint—here, come on in. Say hi to everyone." Russ quickly read Stu's face, looking for hidden motives behind this sudden friendliness, but all he saw was sincerity. He followed Stu into his office, agreeing that it was a great day for CrestPoint, and greeted the occupants.

There were two execs from Tollerson Accounting whose names he couldn't remember and Stu's personal assistant Doris Graham, a large buxom woman who wore her dark hair in a beehive, sported gaudy jewelry, and reminded Russ of Stu's wife Miriam. Then there was Hal Rubin, who sat cross-legged in a chair playing with his lighter. Hal was Stu's lieutenant, an expert in corporate finance whom Stu recruited onto his team over a year ago. His face, leather brown from a tanning booth and cigarette smoke, was round and made even rounder by a large forehead, his dark hair having receded to the point where he applied a comb-over and kept it long on the sides in an attempt to compensate for his hair loss. His wide-set eyes always seemed to be looking down when he talked to you, giving the impression he was hiding something. In Russ' opinion, it was the face of a libertine, and he took an instant dislike to Hal the first time he'd met him. Now, over a year later, that opinion hadn't changed.

"Here's to three-hundred and eighty-eight million dollars—net," toasted Stu. Russ joined in saying "Here, here," and clicked his plastic champagne glass with the others. Stu came up next to him and put his arm around his shoulder. "Here's the man," he said, giving Russ a quick squeeze. "Here's the shipbuilder. Marty and I, we just navigate the ship—pay the bills and navigate the ship—but here's the man who built the ship. To Russ!" Everyone in the room raised their glass and repeated, "To Russ!"

Russ smiled and returned the compliment by proclaiming, rather grandiosely, that Stu (and his team) had made today possible by keeping their "eye on the ball." He squeezed Stu's shoulder in return then stepped away from him to raise his glass. "To Stu," he said. Everyone raised their glass and repeated, "To Stu."

Stu thanked them all, agreeing that he and his team had kept their eye on the ball. Today they hit a homerun to take the lead, he continued, embracing another sports metaphor. Now they needed to bring in their closer to lock down the win, which meant doing whatever they needed to do to keep the stock price up. Russ stood and listened as Stu launched into a pep talk, exhorting everyone to "do what's needed" to keep their stock price up. That was the key to winning the game—doing whatever it takes. Stu raised his glass. "To whatever it takes," he toasted loudly.

The others in the room returned his toast with gusto while Russ, who's glass was empty anyway, half-heartedly raised his glass but didn't pretend to drink. (Exhortations like that—"to do whatever it takes"— always made him uncomfortable.) He set the empty glass down on Stu's desk, thanking them for the champagne, and told them he had to leave. He was hoping to catch some folks from his team before they went home so he could congratulate them on their big day.

"Sure, gotta do it," agreed Stu as he followed Russ to the door. He shook Russ' hand again in the doorway and looked him in the eye. "Remember, *whatever it takes*," he said with emphasis. Russ simply nodded and smiled. Stu let go of his hand and watched him walk away, wondering to himself whether Russ could, when the time came, do whatever it took. He doubted it.

Russ could see people in Chandra's office and picked up his pace, but when he came to the open doorway he suddenly stopped, thrown off by the odd scene he witnessed. Chandra's office was filled with people, over a dozen or so, each of them on their knees with their heads bowed, deep in prayer. Russ remained frozen in the doorway, somewhat bewildered at the sight, as though he'd just discovered a secret society and didn't know quite what to make of it.

Ron Lau was leading them all in prayer and Russ, now self-conscious and debating whether he should stay or go, saw Chandra, his head bowed like the rest, peek up and give him a warm smile. He smiled back. This quick exchange of smiles eased his self-consciousness and he relaxed his posture in the doorway and listened in.

Ron was speaking in a clear voice and Russ listened intently to his speaking style, which was rapid and marked by truncated yet efficient sentences that quickly got to the point. It reminded him of what Ron had once told him about how he processed language. According to Ron, when he listened in English, he instantly translated the words into Mandarin in his head, created his response in Mandarin, and then translated it back into English, all in a split second. Russ marveled at this process as he listened to Ron's prayer, which was about this wondrous day and God's blessing, reminding them of the importance of remaining humble and thankful in the sight of God. When he finished, everyone said "Amen" and got up from their knees. Mark Kirkland was one of them.

Upon seeing Russ in the doorway, folks smiled, happily calling out his name and congratulating him as they slowly filed out the door. When Mark came up, Russ gave him a firm handshake and led him off to the side.

"Mark, looking for you," said Russ with a hint of emotion. "Just wanted to say 'thank you' on behalf of Marty, the Execs… everyone. Today doesn't happen without you and your team. You're all top shelf—your whole team, each one of you, and I just wanted you to hear that from me. You've done a marvelous job…" Russ caught himself. He was showing a little too much emotion, perhaps due to the champagne. It wasn't like him (stiff upper lip and all), so he shook Mark's hand once more and left it at that.

"Thank you, Russ. Appreciate it," replied Mark calmly. Russ expected more excitement out of Mark, maybe even a hug, but it wasn't forthcoming. They talked for another minute until Russ, seeing that Mark was rather ill-at-ease at all the compliments, let him off the hook by politely ending the conversation. As he watched Mark walk away, he saw a man who seemed curiously apathetic about the momentous events

The Heights of Mountains

of the day, a day when he—all of them—had just made a staggering amount of money. It crossed Russ' mind that perhaps it had something to do with his religious conversion.

Mark's conversion was common knowledge around CrestPoint but Russ was one of the first to witness it firsthand. Two months ago, in his staff meeting, Mark asked him if he could have a word with everyone before they started. Thinking nothing of it, he granted the request then sat aghast as Mark launched into his testimony, announcing that he had "given his life to Jesus Christ, his Lord and Savior." At first, he thought of cutting him off but remembered the story Marty told him about the college professor, so he let Mark finish his avowal while they all sat and listened in stunned silence. When Mark finished, Russ neither thanked him nor acknowledged his words, ignoring it like an unexpected fit of coughing, and instead quickly launched into his agenda.

But the situation seemed to be in hand. Mark didn't ask for a repeat performance and Russ never received any complaints or reports that Mark was proselytizing in the building. Plus, there'd been no drop-off in the man's work performance. There were signs of change, of course. They were easy to pick up. There was a distinct air of detachment in Mark's bearing, an other-worldliness, a kind of vagabond's serenity that colored his walk and talk and made him look like he'd found *the way*. Russ had seen it all before; he'd come across devout Christians, Zen Buddhists, Jehovah Witnesses, Muslims, Orthodox Jews, Scientologists, even a Satanist, and they all thought they had the answer. Heck, even Chandra and Ron, his cohorts on the board, were men of God. When it came to gods and deities, Russ took them for what they were worth and not a cent more. As long as these people kept it to themselves, he was fine with it.

Ron was seated next to Chandra at his desk and they both stood up to shake Russ's hand. "Congratulations, gentlemen," said Russ. "Quite a day." He paused at the sight of a Bible in Ron's hand and nodded at it, adding, "I guess you could say we 'killed the fatted calf today.'" Both men laughed cheerfully at this as they sat back down. Russ grabbed a chair and joined them.

"I think the better story might be Noah," said Ron. "After hardship and stormy seas, we're at rest on top Mount Ararat."

"That works," replied Russ cheerfully. He glanced over at Chandra who regarded him with an amused twinkle in his brown eyes.

"You're probably wondering what that was all about," said Chandra. "Our impromptu prayer meeting... They're part of our prayer group."

"Prayer group?"

"Sure. It fluctuates between twenty to thirty people. We meet every Thursday morning. You didn't know about us? We had one at MFS."

"No, wasn't aware of it. Interesting... I see my VP is a member."

"Mark Kirkland? Yeah, he joined a couple weeks ago. I've had a couple long talks with him. Interesting man. He's fresh into the light—just had his conversion experience—and he's struggling a little bit."

"Struggling? How so?"

"It's pretty common—what he's going through. When you're born again in Christ, there is this emotional peak—it's transcendent, you're filled with this *power*—but after a while it begins to taper off. It's inevitable—right, Ron?—mostly because your new reality is still bonded to your old life. It can be anguishing. In Mark's case, his radical change is causing marital problems. Even his kids don't understand it. I know this because his wife is friends with my wife and I get all the dirty laundry... Anyhow, it all adds up to what I call 'post-conversion depression.' But I think he'll be all right."

This was all news to Russ—first, this Christian underground in his midst, and second, this emotional crisis of his VP. But these were thoughts for another day; he didn't want to explore them now; he'd rather talk about the $388 million CrestPoint had just netted in their wildly successful IPO. He changed the subject and Chandra flowed with it, changing topics from religion to business as easily as switching stations on a car radio. They chatted a while about their stock price, the Fed, and what the future might bring. Russ shared his little celebration in Stu's office, repeating what Stu said about doing whatever it takes to keep their stock price up ("Sounds like Stu," remarked Chandra), then got up to leave, telling them both he was going over to the hub to find Marty.

The Heights of Mountains

"We'll join you," said Chandra.

"Okay, but I'll warn you. Reports are they're dancing naked in a circle and offering up human sacrifices."

Chandra and Ron both chuckled. "We'll chance it," replied Chandra. "Let's go find Marty."

"Very well then," laughed Russ. "We're off to see the wizard."

———

Mark returned to his office and found three messages on his answering machine, one from Tess Moreland and two from his wife. The one from Tess would be another thank you—a thank you for getting rid of Stony and a thank you for promoting her. He'd already told her it was all Gwen Novak's doing but she didn't want to believe him. She could believe what she wanted; he was happy for her. It was just a week ago when Russ called him into his office to give him the news that Stony was being fired and Tess promoted to City Manager, and he had nodded at the news and said, "Good for Tess." He could tell that Russ expected a cheer or at least a fist pump out of him, but his reaction remained subdued. He held no ill will towards Stony; he simply felt sorry for him, and that night he said a prayer for his soul.

As for the two messages from his wife, he didn't need to listen to them to know what they were about. She wanted to talk about the IPO and celebrate their new-found fortune. No doubt she'd done her own calculation and knew they were now worth $56.3 million. If he talked to her on the phone, he'd have to remind her that it was only a fortune on paper, but it was unlikely she'd listen. Her excitement at this moment would be far too great for any caveats or qualifications to sink in. And her reaction sat in stark contrast to his own, which was restrained and driven by a wholly different set of priorities. She sought to store up her treasure here on earth while he sought to store up his treasure in heaven, and this difference in world views highlighted the growing rift between them, a rift that was breaking both their hearts.

But he knew he must call her, if not for the sake of peace and harmony in their marriage then at least out of consideration for her feelings. He hit the speed dial number for his home and she answered on the first ring, immediately launching in on their great fortune, her joy bursting over the phone like an electrical charge. He listened patiently, a couple of times trying to temper her enthusiasm by telling her the $56 mil was "on paper, not in our pockets" but she was too swept up in the moment to listen. She wanted to know if he was happy. ("Sure.") He didn't sound that happy. ("I am.") Why did it take him so long to call her back?

"The place is a madhouse," he replied.

"I can imagine," she said, laughing happily. At this, she shifted the style of conversation away from a drumbeat and into the smooth jazz rhythm she was so good at, crooning words and phrases that were meant to build him up and make him feel special. Today was because of him. CrestPoint should thank their lucky stars for Mark Kirkland. He'd brought them riches. He had made their family rich.

It was around her third use of the word "rich" that Mark abruptly said, *"It's easier for a camel to go through the eye of a needle than for a rich man to enter the Kingdom of God."*

There was dead silence on the line. When she finally spoke, he could hear the hurt in her voice. "You see, I don't understand it when you say things like that," she said. "Is it meant as a put down or are you just saying it to ruin the mood? Whenever I want to talk about something I think is important, you quote scripture or tell me it's not important, and I don't understand it."

He didn't want an argument, and he felt a wave of guilt sweep over him. He said what he felt and said what he meant, but he also knew he'd splashed cold water on her moment of joy. (It was sad how they found joy in such different things nowadays.) He was merely speaking truth to power, but he wasn't going to push it, he decided—not now, not at this moment—and he told her he was sorry. He didn't mean it that way. In his own way, he was just trying to keep things in perspective.

Sorry. "Let's take the kids out to dinner tonight," he said cheerfully. "Like Vans—some place nice. We'll all celebrate. How's that sound?"

That sounded great, she replied, the hurt gone from her voice like frost from a sun-drenched porch. They chatted amicably for few minutes more, each secretly grateful that a head-on collision had been avoided. When their conversation ended, they both made a point of saying "I love you" before hanging up the phone.

Mark said a brief prayer ("God, please guide me through this time of strife…") then got up from his desk and headed over to building B where most of the employees in his department worked. He wished to avoid the hub for now, which was packed with partiers, hoping to catch at least a few of his folks at their desk so he could congratulate them before they went home. It was expected of him.

He came to the main entrance to building B where he found a piece of paper taped to the door with a note scrawled on it that read, "Beware, all ye who enter here." He took it down and crumpled it in his hand as he entered the building. The lobby was empty but beyond it he could hear a boom box loudly playing *Highway to Hell* by AC/DC. The unmistakable odor of marijuana smoke hung in the air and he frowned at its presence.

The note, the music, the odor—it caused him to hesitate in the lobby. His gut told him he wasn't going to like what he found inside, but it wasn't in his nature to shy away from inequity, especially since his spiritual awakening, so he pocketed his premonition and went inside. What he found quickly confirmed his fears. There were small groups of revelers gathered around desks, all of them drunk and drinking, laughing, talking loudly over the music, some of them bending over to snort cocaine. He looked to his right down the corridor that ran along the east side of the building and saw two men and a woman smoking a joint outside the restrooms. He walked over to them and without rancor or indignation in his voice told them there was no smoking in the building. They regarded him with their glassy eyes, and it took a moment for it to register that he was a VP. Once it did, they quickly apologized, snuffed out their joint, and ambled off trying their best to stifle their laughter.

Farther down the corridor he spied four men standing outside a storeroom. They were talking and laughing while one of them zipped up his fly. He recognized one of his employees in the group. The four were drinking cans of beer but not smoking dope, so he ignored them for now and walked out into the main work area, heading straight to the first group he saw snorting cocaine. He walked up and stopped, his hands locked behind him as he eyed a mirror on the desktop strewn with white lines of coke. The group was engrossed in chatter, seemingly oblivious to his presence, while one of them, a woman wearing her white blouse inside out, got ready to snort a line.

"What's this?" he asked loudly.

They immediately turned to look at him, the woman freezing in mid-bend with a straw poised near her nose. "Ahh… Mr. Kirkland. Hiya!" replied a man he recognized (his last name Grimm or Grimes, from Marketing). "We're celebrating. Join us. Have a line. It's just cocaine—God's way of telling us we make too much money. Go on in. Jill, let him in. Let him cut the line. Ha!" He laughed at his pun while the others laughed along with him.

"You need to stop this now," ordered Mark sharply. "Drugs are prohibited in the building—and anywhere else. It's illegal." He threw a piercing glance at each one of them to emphasize his point, noting their reactions—a combination of alarm and defiance—before adding, "Get it out of here now!"

"Of course, whatever you say," replied the fast-talking man. (Mark remembered him now; he was the Director of Marketing.) "But you can see, everyone's doing it." Others in the group echoed his statement that everyone was doing it, some mumbling angrily. "It's just a crazy day," continued the Director of Marketing. "You know? Stock price goin' through the roof. Everybody rich. People are just goin' a little crazy, that's all."

Mark didn't care about their excuses, doubling down on his ultimatum by threatening to call the cops. That did the trick. The Director of Marketing, still talking fast but now making apologies, urged his friends to quickly obey the order. The woman wearing the inside-out blouse, furious at this turn of events, picked up the mirror of coke, cradling it like a new-born baby, and awaited her instructions from the Director of Marketing. Mark could hear the angry mumblings as he backed away: *"Who's he?"... "A VP."... "No shit!"... "Better listen to him."... "Fuck him."... "He'll do it. He'll call the cops. He's a Jesus freak."... "No shit."... No wonder."... Let's get outta here."*

He didn't need to stay and watch to know they'd clear out, and a warning that the cops were on the way would quickly spread through the building, doing the rest of the work for him. Foolishness, he thought. Just plain sinful foolishness. But not surprising—all have sinned and fall short of the glory of God—and he wasn't going to condemn the world for it. God didn't send his Son to condemn the world; He sent Jesus so the world might be saved through Him. His own salvation had taught him that.

Mark had two directors and thirteen implementation engineers of varying ranks in building B, and he found one of his directors at home and entered his office. His other director was there as well and they both sat talking and sharing a bottle of champagne. Mark came in and congratulated each of them. They were pleased to see him, one of them joking that they were a little surprised that he'd braved shark infested waters to get here. (It was apparent they knew what was going on outside their office.) Mark smiled at the joke, deciding not to share his judgement that anyone (his directors included) who knew the good they ought to do and didn't do it also sinned. Instead, he asked about the rest of his team and was told that most of them were over at the hub.

"Yeah, I guess I'll have to go over there," said Mark. "But I did see Keith in the hallway."

"In the hallway... over by the storeroom? Yeah, you may want to avoid that area."

Mark didn't ask why; he could tell by the glances they exchanged with one another that it was bad news. He nodded his understanding, thanked them both again, and left. A scan of the floor confirmed that the drug use had folded tent and skedaddled, though there was still loud music playing and people drinking. He made a beeline for the storeroom.

As he neared the spot, he saw a young man stumble out of the storeroom door saying, "Dude, she's totally fucked up" as he joined two other men standing outside (one of which was his employee Keith). When they saw Mark, they made a move to leave. "Hold tight!" called out Mark, but only Keith obeyed as the other two rushed off.

"Keith, I was looking for you to…" Mark stopped; he'd intended to congratulate Keith and thank him for his hard work but he could tell there was something wrong. "What's going on here?" He waited for an answer but Keith was silent, his eyes downcast. "What's in the storeroom?" Without waiting for a response, Mark opened the storeroom door. It was dark, so he switched on the light and found a woman sitting on the floor, slumped back against some boxes, unconscious. Keith followed right behind him talking rapidly in self-defense. "It's Sherry Overfelt—from Sales. She passed out. She was giving guys head—but it was her own choice. Nobody forced her—she wanted to—we didn't make her. But she got drunk and passed out—"

Mark could see that she'd passed out from drinking. There were empty champagne bottles strewn about and one clutched in her hand. She was in her panties—her slacks and shoes having been tossed aside—and her blouse was half unbuttoned with one of her breasts hanging out. Mark took a knee next to her and felt her pulse, studying her face. Her short blonde hair was disheveled, her mouth hanging open, and there was dried semen glistening on her cheek and chin.

Keith stood behind him frantically making excuses but Mark ignored him. He knew what his mission was; it was clear—it was to help this woman and turn her away from sin as he had done with Tess in Kansas City. God had put him here in this place and at this moment for just that purpose. "Give me her pants," he ordered Keith, "then go to the restroom and get some paper towels, both wet and dry." Keith immediately did as he was told while Mark put her in a prone position, pulled on her pants, and then lifted her up from underneath her arms into a better sitting position.

She partly came to, her head rolling from side to side, mumbling something about "fourrr mil" and "champay… where's my champay?"

The Heights of Mountains

Keith returned with the towels as Mark tucked her breast back in her shirt and began buttoning her blouse. "You nex'?" she moaned, reaching her hand out towards his belt buckle. ("See what I mean," said Keith.) Mark grabbed her hand, calmly telling her it was okay, and placed it back in her lap as she passed out again. He used the towels to clean her up. When he pressed a cool wet towel against her forehead, she suddenly came to again and looked at Mark. "You nex'?" she slurred. "Gimme-yur cock… Cummm-on."

"No, no more of that," replied Mark, pushing her hand away from his crotch.

"Whaa… can't-git-it up?" she slurred, smiling crookedly at him. She glanced left then right. "Where'sss my champayy?" she asked before losing consciousness.

Mark didn't know quite what to do with this woman other than to guard her until she was sober enough to walk. He told Keith to leave, who didn't need to be told twice to vamoose, and Mark remained on his knees next to her as she drifted in and out of consciousness mumbling about her "four mil" and asking for her "champay." Now completely alone with her, he allowed himself to pray deeply for this woman and ask God to help him reach her. When he finished his prayer, he applied another cool towel to her face, which seemed to help, and when she finally came around, he told her "I'm Mark Kirkland, Vice President of Implementation."

Her eyes widened in drunken wonderment. "Wow," she said, hiccupping. "Wan' me to suck yur cock?"

"No!" he replied sharply. "No more of that. I'm here to help. You passed out."

These words seemed to sober her up slightly. "Ohh, ohh-kay," she answered, glancing left then right. Mark thought she was looking for her bottle of champagne but instead she asked, "Where's my purse?" He handed it to her and she clutched it in her lap, avoiding his eyes. He wanted very much to help this woman, to succor her in God's forgiveness and show her the light, but he didn't know how. What he wanted to tell her was that these evils came from inside and defiled a person, and those that live like this will not inherit the kingdom of God, but he knew his

• 231

words would be lost on her. In her drunken state, it would be fruitless, like trying to write words on the surface of a lake. But he needed to tell her something—something beautiful and true. He felt it in his soul.

He took one of her hands, and she looked up at him in anticipation. "Jesus loves you," he said softly.

She blinked her eyes, laughing suddenly, hiccupped, then turned her head in time to puke on the floor a mixture of champagne, semen, and Domino's cheese pizza.

———

Marty hung up the phone and leaned back in his chair. That made the seventh and hopefully last call of day.

When he returned to his office from the hub, he'd found voice messages from several journalists and news outlets, each one asking for a statement regarding CrestPoint's hugely successful IPO. He dutifully called each one back and gave them a spirited interview, trying to remain humble about his personal fortune while outlining what CrestPoint planned to do with the $388 million they had netted from the IPO ("grow, grow, grow"). It was pointed out by the San Francisco Chronicle reporter that CrestPoint Communications was now in the top 40 on the Chronicle 500 ranking of local public companies, trailing Apple Computer in value by only 15 percent. Marty thanked her for the impressive news and told her it was just the beginning.

CNBC wanted to do a live interview with him tomorrow and the opportunity to go on a national broadcast excited him. He needed to pick out just the right attire—at least from the waist up—an outfit that would speak to his youth and vitality and show he was one of the new breed of CEOs, hip and tuned in to what people wanted. He imagined a corduroy sport jacket, dark brown, over a gold-colored turtleneck sweater would do the trick (and show off his amber eyes). His political consultant was always talking about building name recognition and this interview was a chance to do just that. Maybe he would mention his political aspirations on the air. It was certainly good timing.

What he needed was a press agent. A political consultant was fine for strategizing and helping him build his message, but what he really could use was an aggressive press agent working the phones and increasing his national exposure. There was no reason he couldn't be on the cover of Newsweek or Time. Other hi-tech entrepreneurs had managed it (Gates, Jobs, Andreessen), and there was no reason he couldn't. This was something he needed to look in to.

The phone rang and he saw that it was his wife, Hana. At that same instant, David came through the door. He signaled David to remain quiet as he answered the phone and talked to Hana, following David with his eyes as the young man, holding a champagne bottle and obviously a little drunk, tiptoed over to his leather sedan and sprawled out. Hana wanted to know what time he'd be home. It was hard to say, he told her, watching David pull out his tucked-in shirt to get more comfortable. He had more interviews to do, he explained—more reporters to talk to, more people to thank. It had been a crazy wonderful day and it wasn't over yet. He heard her sigh impatiently just as David, looking deserted on the sedan, sighed audibly as well. The sounds were identical.

Before he could hang up, his wife put their young son on the phone, Ryan, who was almost two and possessed an advanced vocabulary for a toddler. Marty playfully bantered back and forth with him, asking him about his stuffed monkey 'Mishmash' and kidding him about the man in the moon (who Ryan was convinced really did live on the moon). As he talked to his son, laughing freely, he noticed David get up from the sedan and start for the door. "Don't be petulant," scolded Marty, covering the mouthpiece with his hand. "Sit back down and stay put." David did as he was told.

After his son got bored talking with him, Hana came back on the phone and he made his goodbyes, promising to be home soon. He hung up the receiver and studied David, who lay back on the sedan invitingly, his soft eyes returning Marty's gaze. "You've been drinking," said Marty.

"A little… So have you."

"Been drinking water for the last hour," replied Marty, holding up a plastic water bottle.

"Saw you dancing in the hub."

"Imagine you were impressed?"

"Very... When you gonna dance with me?"

Marty hummed suggestively at that while he played out the possibility in his head. Was it or was it not too late to go to his studio apartment on Crestpoint Drive and have sex with David? They'd been having an affair for over a year (the young man's soft eyes, French vanilla cheeks, and Asian good looks had been too much to resist), and his apartment had become their secret rendezvous point. He kept the apartment ostensibly as a DSL test bed (with the rent paid for by the company), but as a residential lab it had pretty much exhausted its usefulness, and now he used it almost solely for his trysts with David. It was only ten minutes away but he'd need an hour, maybe more, with his lover, then there was the drive home. He counted up the time, hoping to make it work, but knew Hana would be counting up the time as well.

"Love to, Sugar Pop," he replied with a dejected sigh. "But it's too late."

David looked at him soulfully, shaking his head. "We can dance right here, Doc," he said, grinning naughtily.

"Here? You nuts?"

"Why not? Everyone else is doin' it. You got people fuckin' in the bathrooms, snortin' coke, givin' head—everyone's gettin' crazy all over the place. Might as well join 'em."

Marty took a second for all the information to sink in. He guessed it didn't bother him—the craziness, the sex in the bathrooms (though he had a problem with the drug use)—it was kind of expected. *"Return of the Archons,"* he joked. "Festival time." David looked at him with puzzlement. "You know? *Star Trek,*" he explained. "The TV show—Star Trek. Spock... Never mind."

"Don't you feel like gettin' just a *little* crazy," crooned David, getting up from the sedan. He began unbuttoning his shirt while slowly gyrating his hips. "Let's dance right here. Or I can come over there and dance… How 'bout a lap dance?"

Marty tried to stifle a laugh but failed. He was secretly enjoying this side of David; he was usually bashful and acted almost deferential, doing what he was told—*everything* he was told—and never taking the lead. But this new aggressiveness sort of turned Marty on. Evidently, owning stock in CrestPoint and drinking some champagne is doing this to people, he thought to himself with some amusement. Anyway, why not? They earned it. I earned it. Going a bit crazy doesn't seem that chancy.

He was still a little drunk, still high from the $300 million, feeling loose and invincible, and the urge was begging to be givin in to.

"Come on, Doc. Live a little."

"Shh… I'm thinkin' about it," answered Marty as he glanced at the clock, at the window blinds, and over at the door. "Lock the door," he ordered, getting up from behind his desk to shut the blinds. "And pour me some of that champagne."

Russ had somehow missed finding Marty all day, and he was nearly ready to give up the search. It was disappointing; the two of them had been there at CrestPoint's conception and nursed it lovingly all the way to this momentous day, yet here he was still looking to give his partner a big high five. They were filthy rich; CrestPoint was flush with cash and set for the future; and everything they'd worked so hard for was coming true. He would have loved to share the glory with ol' Six-gun Marty. But there was always tomorrow.

He just missed Marty at the hub. When he, Chandra, and Ron arrived, Marty had already taken his one-man show to another building, leaving a swinging party in his wake. The three of them were cheered, given glasses of champagne, and patted on the back. It was like everyone's birthday party and wedding reception rolled into one, and he decided to let down his guard, give up his search for Marty for a while, and enjoy himself. He ran into Gwen and asked her to dance.

After breaking a sweat on the dance floor, Russ found a seat at a table next to Chandra. "Here," said Chandra, handing him a bottle of water, "looks like you could use it." Russ thanked him and took a long swig from the bottle, keeping his eye out for invaders. Ever since his spin around the dance floor with Gwen, he'd become a target for every woman, now either tipsy or flat-out drunk, wanting to dance. Every time he tried to sit down, another woman would pull him back onto the dance floor. Adding to this bother was the fact that a few of them wanted more than just a dance, making bold advances in his ear as they danced close to him (one saying he made her hot and bothered, another wanting to show him something in the restroom). He was also pinched in the butt at least twice, but he had fended off their come-ons rather well he thought, and now taken sanctuary at a table with Chandra.

Before he could take another drink of water however, a woman came up and asked him to dance, taking hold of his hand. They had danced before; her name was Shannon, blonde and tall with long legs, who looked a little like Miss November 1981, and he'd made the mistake of giving her an approving eye (and getting caught at it). "Can't," he protested, trying to take back his hand. "Need a break. Maybe later." But she was insistent. Suddenly Gwen appeared and told the young lady she had business with "Mister Chappel." That did the trick and Russ got his hand back.

"You interested in joining me in my office for a taste of Gran Patron Tequila," she offered, smiling. "It's ten years old. Cost me three hundred bucks. And I brought it in just for today." Yes, Russ was interested (he'd had enough of the hub and this was the perfect excuse for a getaway). They left together, joined by Chandra and Ron, and walked over to Gwen's office where she pulled out a bottle of Gran Patron from a little fridge and poured out three shots (Ron didn't drink). Russ found it cool and delicious, sipping it slowly like Gwen and Chandra instead of shooting it down. The conversation quickly turned to the day's events and the company's future, Gwen taking the opportunity to talk about an eventual buy-out. Chandra and Ron didn't seem surprised by the topic, were even open to the possibility, but Russ took a harder line against it. What followed was a lively debate amongst the four board of directors that didn't settle anything but gave them a chance to enjoy the excellent tequila and wrap up the day with a convivial moment together.

It was nearly 7:00 when he left Gwen's office, and he looked around for Marty without any luck. The few people still left in the building had no idea as to his whereabouts, and Russ noticed that Marty's office door was closed. I'll have to get my high five tomorrow, he decided.

Russ collected his brief case and went out to the parking lot. There he found Marty's Maserati still parked in its space. Well, hell, he thought to himself. He's still somewhere around. And with that, he threw his stuff in his Spitfire and went back inside, figuring Marty had to be in his office. He'd give the door a rap and find out.

The door was locked, which was a sure sign that Marty was not in his office, but Russ knocked three times just to be sure. Ready to walk away, he suddenly heard a thump—signs of life—and knocked again. "Hey, Marty. You in there? It's Russ." There was no answer, but when he put his ear up against the door, he could hear furious whispering.

"Marty! It's Russ. Open up." There was another thump followed by a laugh.

"Ahh... Yeah—hey, Russ," came Marty's response from behind the door. "Kind'a busy at the moment. Can you come back later?"

And it hit Russ what was going on—Marty was screwing some babe in his office. Well, it was certainly the day for it, he thought with a laugh. Even Marty, the paragon of virtue, the model husband and dad, couldn't resist celebrating his great day with a shag behind closed doors. This realization gave Russ a sense of satisfaction. Once again, his view of men and women and marriage had been validated.

"No problem. I'll talk to you tomorrow," he replied, trying to hold back his amusement.

"Okay. Talk tomorrow... Thanks!"

Russ sauntered over into a dark corner, found a chair, and sat down, waiting. He was curious to see who this woman was; he had a few guesses, but he wasn't positive. Was it his admin Nicole, he wondered.

She was still a newlywed, but stranger things than that were known to happen, especially after a little champagne. He also wouldn't have been surprised to see Gwen come out of his office. Their so-called "feud" smacked of sexual tension. But he'd just left Gwen in her office not more than fifteen minutes ago, so it seemed unlikely. There were a couple of other women who floated up as possibilities as his anticipation began to grow.

He didn't need to wait long. In ten minutes, the person emerged from Marty's office and his guessing game was over.

Chapter 10

Ronnie Kirkland was not a woman who gave up easily. She didn't give up on her dreams or on the life she wanted for herself, and she wasn't going to give up on her marriage. But her marriage was in a crisis; her family was in a crisis. She couldn't deny it any longer.

Ever since her husband's religious conversion—his "born-again experience"—their life together had been slowly deteriorating. At first, she tried her best to understand his new mindset, listening patiently to his emotional confessions of faith, asking questions, trying to keep an open mind, but soon found herself overwhelmed by his zealousness. The demands of his faith and the pressures it put on her were making her unhappy. What she hoped would be akin to a warm overcoat, something he put on when he was cold but could take off at any time, had turned into a heavy cloak he wore day and night. His passion, his inflexibility, his uncompromising commitment to his new-found faith turned off their friends and alienated family members, and she'd had enough of it.

Part of her frustration were all the changes—in his appearance, in his language, in how he wanted them to live their life. He carried the Bible around with him and constantly quoted scripture. He insisted they change churches to Calvary Memorial Church, which wasn't even Catholic, and he frequently held prayer meetings in their living room in the evening, which had been family time to watch TV. But these things were only trappings; what her husband really wanted, what he relentlessly worked towards every day, was that she and the kids join him in his "new life with Christ." That more than anything caused the growing rift between them. He wanted her to take the leap but she couldn't. He pleaded with her to open her heart, to let

Jesus in, and feel the holy spirit take hold of her, but she found she was unable to, even crying at her failure. Yet, she knew why; even as she wept in front of him at her failure, she knew why. It just wasn't in her. She considered herself religious; she believed in God, but to her faith, prayer, and church-going all had their time and place. It wasn't going to be her entire Life.

And now their daughter was in open rebellion. Their son Brandon, now fourteen, watched and waited, going with the flow, but her daughter, sixteen and already a handful, revolted against her father's transformation. It started with the new church, which she reluctantly agreed to attend, but after ten minutes she stormed out and waited in the car. The final straw came when she arrived home one evening from the movies to find a group of people in their living room, all on their knees, deep in prayer. "No!" she screamed at the top of her voice, running up to her room where she stayed the rest of the evening. After that, she refused to go to church—any church—and threatened to eat alone if Dad kept praying at the dinner table. It was an intolerable situation.

She deeply loved Mark; just how deeply she never realized until now. Maybe that was because she felt so dangerously close to losing him. It was almost as if Jesus Christ was her rival and Mark's complete and unconditional love for Him was tearing them apart. But it wasn't God doing this, she was sure of it. Over the last week, while sitting alone in their garden smoking a cigarette (a thing she rarely did unless greatly stressed out), she had worked it out in her head. The reason was obvious and the remedy was clear, and she ran her conclusions by family and friends to validate it. What was happening was a kind of mental sickness; Mark's zealous devotion to Jesus was a sickness in need of a cure. And in that moment of clarity, she mapped out her strategy to cure him, seeing herself very much like Greer Garson from her all-time favorite movie, *Randon Harvest*, where the heroine tracks down her lost love and brings him back to his right mind.

Convinced of this diagnosis, Ronnie was enlisting allies in her fight to bring Mark back to reality. There were people he admired and respected, people like her father, his mom, their priest at St. Joseph's,

The Heights of Mountains

and others of like mind who she was sure he would listen to. She knew he wouldn't see a psychiatrist so it had to be friends and family. It had to be collective; all the people he respected needed to come at him with the same message and advice (*a balance in all things, see what pain you're causing, find a middle ground*) and together they would bring him back.

And there was one other person she wanted to enlist in her efforts to persuade Mark of his folly. It was a man he regarded as a friend and mentor, and a man, she knew, who had an emotional attachment to her and would help her in this time of crises. Russ Chappel.

Her phone call asking to meet him for lunch came out of the blue. When his admin told him that it was "Mrs. Kirkland calling," he hesitated for a moment, recalling their fling nine years ago and how it had started, finding himself a trifle wary of her intentions. He thought for a moment about having his admin take a message, decided against it, and picked up the receiver. "Hi, Ronnie," he answered cheerfully. "What can I do for you?"

Without wasting time on small talk, she promptly launched into her reason for calling. She needed to talk to him—alone. *About Mark.* He'd gone off the deep end—certainly he'd seen it for himself—and she needed to discuss the situation with him. Russ listened sympathetically but remained noncommittal. Yes, he was aware of Mark's religious conversion but it hadn't affected his work performance, at least not in ways that Russ could tell. Without saying so, he wanted no part in getting in the middle of their marital problems (he'd been down that road before) and tried to evade her attempts to pin him down to a lunch date.

Suddenly she erupted in frustration, telling him that she was seeing a psychiatrist who told her Mark's behavior could be a sign of mental illness, a condition which might worsen over time. There was desperation in her voice—he could hear it, it was palpable—and he felt his resolve to stay out of it begin to fade. If one of his key men (and Mark was certainly that) was suffering from mental illness, then he needed to know about it.

A breakdown, erratic behavior—any of that could have a destructive impact on his organization. He had a duty to hear Ronnie out. Yes, of course, he'd meet her for lunch.

Three days later, he met her in a restaurant in Cupertino, which he picked because it was a halfway point and afforded a level of privacy that something closer to his office would not. She was already sitting at a table when he entered, and she got up and awkwardly hugged him before sitting back down.

"Thank you *so much* for meeting me," she said earnestly. She was dressed down in jeans and a loose sweater and wore very little make-up. Despite her obvious attempt to look ordinary, Russ still found her to be quite a striking woman. They'd run into each other at least a half dozen times over the last two years at company functions, and he couldn't help but note that she still looked like Miss July 1983, only more mature, with a settled-in quality about her.

"*Really*," she added. "You just don't know how important this is to me. I'm *sooo* glad you came."

He raised an eyebrow and smiled.

She didn't want to be misread, not at this point, and his raised eyebrow and smile slightly alarmed her. She hadn't come for *that*. Hopefully he wasn't here under any false pretenses. She simply didn't feel anything sexual towards him; sure, he was handsome (as always), and seemed to get more so as he got older, but whatever flame once burned for him had died long ago. Hopefully, he knew that. She was here for Mark. Russ, on the other hand, was a potential ally, a means to an end.

"I'm not here for that," she said flatly.

"Course not. I didn't think you were... We're here to talk about Mark."

"Yes, thank you."

Her attempt to nip any misunderstandings in the bud triggered a moment of uneasiness between them (she thought it necessary; he thought it gratuitous), but it was alleviated by the appearance of the waitress who introduced herself and took their drink order. They both picked up their menu and scanned the choices, Ronnie making small talk about the upcoming Fourth of July weekend. When the waitress returned, Ronnie ordered a chicken cobb salad and Russ a Reuben sandwich.

Once the waitress was out of earshot, Russ met Ronnie's gaze and said in a business-like manner, "You've got my full and undivided attention. Tell me what's going on with Mark."

"Where do I begin?" she said, leaning back in her seat. But she knew exactly where to begin, and for the next half hour she poured her heart out, pausing only momentarily to receive her salad, take a drink of iced tea, or glance briefly around the restaurant. She'd rehearsed most of what she wanted to say on her drive down, hoping to keep it professional, but once she got started, a string of emotions began to color her language.

What Russ heard was a woman—a wife—at her wits end. Ever since Mark's religious conversion, her husband had changed, *radically*! Their whole life had been turned upside down. All he cared about and talked about was Jesus Christ, *his lord and savior*, quoting from the Bible, praying out loud, emotionally proclaiming his faith in front of family and friends, even strangers. She'd gone to see a psychiatrist, a friend of her parents, who told her that conversions like this were usually triggered by some form of crises, a crisis that typically called into question one's whole fundamental set of beliefs. She couldn't think of any such crises like that at home. Could he, Russ, think of anything like that? (No, other than just the normal grind at work, he answered.) That's what she thought, and that's what she told the psychiatrist, but he went on to say that the "opening" for these kinds of breakdowns could come from a vague and growing sense of dissatisfaction with one's life, in a compulsive need for something more. People like Mark, he said, were "emotionally ill," and their primary motivation for this kind of religious conversion was a search for emotional resolution.

Russ now had questions. Did Mark talk to this psychiatrist? ("No.") So his diagnosis was secondhand? ("Yes.") Did the psychiatrist use the term 'mental illness'? ("No, not exactly, but it was obvious what he meant.") Russ nodded at her answers, pausing a moment to gather his thoughts before continuing. "Obviously I'm not a psychoanalyst," he said. "All I can go by is what I see and hear. Mark comes in every morning and does his job, day in and day out, and he does it very well. Has he changed?

Well, yes. Everyone at CrestPoint knows about his religious conversion, and he's very frank about it. But he doesn't proselytize—at least I've not heard complaints like that—and he hasn't acted, well… crazy, or showed any signs of mental illness. But again, I'm not a psychoanalyst."

He hoped this little speech might ease her worries and he studied her face for any signs of relief. There was none. Instead, she stared back at him with the look of an ER nurse, the ones who can show sympathy one second and dead seriousness the next.

Ronnie hadn't told him everything, or at least not the stuff that proved her point. The evidence of Mark's illness (call it mental, call it emotional, she didn't care what you called it) was overwhelming, and now she saw that she'd have to lay it all out there, no matter how painful it was. "Let me try to explain it better," she said, fighting back a sudden urge to cry. She took a deep breath to compose herself, then continued, dealing out her evidence like cards from a deck.

There was the time she found him naked in their garden, on his knees, crying and screaming out for Christ to save him. He took her to some 'Mana Church', back in the hills of La Honda, filled with a bunch of hippies speaking in tongues. They didn't stay there long (he wasn't *that* crazy) but the next church he found wasn't much better. He brought strangers into the house to pray. He wanted her and the kids to convert as well and his relentless pressure to do so had turned their daughter against him. And there were more examples of his illness. As a husband, well, they still made love, not as much as before, but something was missing, like he was off in Never-Never Land. And money—he didn't seem to care anything about it. They'd gone to a Van Morrison concert and afterwards come upon this homeless guy on the sidewalk asking for money. And what did Mark do? He gave him all the money in his wallet, like a hundred dollars' worth, and tried to give the guy his credit cards before she stopped him in time. I mean, who does that, she asked, but a crazy person. Mark was like one of those Hale-Bop fanatics or a Moonie. That was the best way to describe it.

"I wouldn't call him a Moonie," replied Russ with a chuckle, trying to lighten the mood. "Probably more like one of those Brahmins who reject the material world… to find spiritual enlightenment. I mean, Mark's not one of those guys who's gonna drink the Kool-Aid just 'cause someone tells him to."

"Maybe not. I hope you're right—but who doesn't respect money? This is America, for Christ's sake. *Shit,* I took His name in vain. Good thing Mark's not here; he'd have a conniption… But you know what I mean? It's like the whole IPO business. We became millionaires overnight, but he could care less. And when the hold period is over—what is that, six months, in November, right?—do you think he's gonna cash in? I doubt it."

"Well, I hope not," said Russ quickly. "It would send the wrong message if everyone started cashing in at six months. The market wouldn't take kindly to it." There was more he could have told her about their stock (their 2nd quarter earnings report had been a disappointment, and now their stock had dipped seven points in a week), but he didn't want to talk about CrestPoint stock now. Instead, he wanted Ronnie to get to her point, because he was sure that this was leading somewhere. It wasn't that he was growing weary of her lament. He felt for her, he *really* did, but now the time had come to find out what she wanted from him.

The check came and he paid it. He found her eerily quiet, like someone who had just confessed a deep and dark secret, and he waited for her to say something, knowing she wasn't done yet.

Ronnie was emotionally drained and questioning herself. Had she done the right thing in coming here, in telling Russ about her personal life? She wasn't sure. But, no, she was sure of her strategy to cure Mark, and for that she needed Russ' help.

Russ couldn't wait out her silence any longer. "What is it you'd like me to do?" he asked her, cutting to the chase. "I'm not quite sure how I can help."

"Talk to him," she replied, a tinge of anguish in her voice. "That's all I'm asking. Just talk to him. He respects you. Maybe you can talk some sense into him."

"Sure, I can talk to him, but I—"

"I think if all the people he loves and respects—my dad, his mom, *you*—sit down and talk to him and tell him the same thing, that he's tearing his family apart and breaking our hearts, then maybe he'll come around and see the light, or at least see the damage he's causing and stop. It's possible it could work. That's why I need you to talk to him… Please just talk to him."

There were tears in her eyes as she pleaded for Russ' help, and seeing her tears, hearing her voice, he was suddenly struck by the immense resolve of this woman. To be loved like that by a woman, with this almost ferocious devotion, leading her to take desperate chances and devise schemes to hold on to him… well, it was bloody-well marvelous. He envied Mark. And if he could have let loose an ironic laugh at that moment he would have done so, because now he saw the truth—that their fling nine years ago was never about him or her desire for him. It was about Mark. It had always been about Mark. And it brought a quote to mind, words that embodied her whole relentless love for this man. Was it Shakespeare? Something Cleopatra said to Marc Antony… *"Fool! Don't you see now that I could have poisoned you a hundred times had I been able to live without you."*

"I'll talk to him. I promise."

"Thank you, Russ. That's all I ask." She took a deep breath, managing a smile. "I don't know," she added as an afterthought. "Maybe this is supposed to happen. Maybe it's all part of the plan."

He merely nodded at her comment, silently dismissing her hope of a divine plan. There was no divine plan, he knew. Just a big bang, expansion, and finally collapse. The universe was governed by immutable laws, laws that certainly suggested an intelligence—but not one that cared a fig about petty human dramas like this one. But he kept his opinion to himself.

They got up from the table and he walked her to her car where they hugged goodbye. She gave him a warm, affectionate hug, and in the back of his head, in that part of the man's brain where the male ego refuses to relinquish its throne, he half expected a suggestive scratch on his shoulder. But it never came.

Chapter 11

The fourteen board members sat around the long table listening closely to CFO Stuart Baum review the 3rd quarter earnings report and talk about CrestPoint's financial health. For the most part, it was very good news. Yes, their 2nd quarter earnings had been slightly disappointing and less than projected, but that was based on 3,500 business users paying an average of $130 a month. Since then—with the roll out of the consumer market fully underway—they had over 100,000 household customers paying anywhere from $49.95 to $79.95 a month for DSL service (depending on the speed). CrestPoint's stock was now trading at $34.6 a share, up eleven points since July, and Stu projected sales would come in at $21 million by the end of the year. Not bad for a company that lost $28 million last year on only $928,000 in sales.

Stu clicked on the next slide in his PowerPoint presentation, proudly noting that they had DSL networks in 109 metropolitan areas across the country and were selling their service through 85 Internet Service Providers. Besides their growing market share, they had strategic relationships with Microsoft, Intel, and other high-tech giants, and were in negotiations with the Dutch telecommunication company Teladata International to offer service across Europe, which Marty would brief them on later. Stu's slides painted a rosy picture for the future; despite stiff competition from Nomad and Pulse, the numbers showed strong growth into 2000. There was every reason to believe this would continue—unless the Fed did something crazy like raise interest rates or the Internet craze now sweeping the world somehow fizzled out.

The possibility of those two things happening was highly unlikely, remarked Andy Sikes, who was a former FCC commissioner. Sure, it was possible the Fed might raise interest rates to temper some the exuberance in the market, but it would be minimal and have little impact on what everyone was calling 'the dot-com boom.' As for the Internet craze fizzling out, he added with a knowing smile—well, unless people like his wife stopped buying toys for their grandkids on eToys.com, whose stock just hit a high of $84 a share, then, yes, I guess it could fizzle out. There were a few chuckles and smiles around the table at the remote possibility of this ever happening.

Marty leafed through a magazine in front of him as Stu continued his financial briefing. It was the latest issue of *PC/Computing*, and it had his picture on the cover along with a story about him and CrestPoint Communications inside. Chandra had come into the board meeting with a stack of magazines and handed one out to each of the directors, eliciting some good-natured ribbing at Marty's sake. But everyone saw it for what it was—great publicity for Marty and the company. This was now the third time Marty had been featured in a trade magazine, *DSL Prime* and *Computerworld* being the other two, and he had an interview with a reporter from the Associated Press tomorrow that was likely to be picked up by newspapers across the country.

But Marty wasn't thinking about his magazine story. Instead, his thoughts were preoccupied with a comment Russ made walking into the board room. He, Gwen, and Russ entered the board room together, idly chatting about computer mouses and whether they preferred the wheel or trackball for scrolling. He said he preferred the trackball but complained in an off-hand way that his wasn't working very well. "Maybe you're playing with it too much," quipped Gwen. He laughed at that and replied, "Maybe," enjoying her double entendre, when Russ added "Better get your IT guy to fix it." He shot a glance at Russ to confirm he was joking but caught something else in Russ' face—a look of distaste, almost hidden, as though Russ had swallowed an unappetizing morsel of food.

Marty had known Russ for over eight years and was sensitive to his moods and facial expressions, and he was sure he'd read it right—this look of distaste—despite Russ' attempt to suppress it. And that expression set off a little panic in Marty's head. Did Russ know about his relationship with David, about his bisexuality, about the secret he'd been so careful to conceal from everyone all these years, including his wife? Before today, he would have thought it impossible anyone could know his secret, but the signs that Russ somehow knew about it had just grown exponentially stronger. In the last six months, ever since the day of their IPO, Russ' demeanor towards him had changed, he could feel it without being able to put his finger on it. Had Russ guessed about him and David that night? The signs were converging to an apex; the comment, the expression, the change in demeanor—it was all more than coincidence.

And it worried him. If Russ knew, would he spill the beans to someone? A comment, a slip of the tongue could quickly grow into rumor that could derail his political ambitions (not the fact that he was bisexual, but the lies and deception that came with it, and the divorce from Hana that would surely follow). But no, Russ wouldn't say anything. He was too much of a gentleman. They were friends, and friendship to a man like Russ was an inviolable bond that prohibited him from—

"Marty."

He looked up from his worried reverie to find Stu calling his name.

"About the Dutch venture," added Stu, queuing his CEO who had obviously been daydreaming.

"Right. Thanks, Stu," he replied. "Well done… I was just contemplating this magazine cover. The coat and tie—it's not me. Next time I'm going with a Hawaiian shirt."

"You mean tie-dye," quipped one of the directors. (Marty's affection for all things Grateful Dead was well known amongst the board members.)

"Better yet," agreed Marty, smiling. "And a pair of granny glasses." A few more quips and jests from board members followed this remark, and Marty parried them good-naturedly before launching into his summary on the negotiations with Teladata to provide DSL service in Europe.

Negotiations were going well and he was targeting an announcement in the first quarter of next year. One of the directors asked who would head up this joint venture once it took off and Marty replied that was yet to be determined.

After a few more questions, a yea or nay vote was taken on continuing negotiations with Teledata, and each of the directors quickly voiced a "yea" to make it unanimous (as Marty had expected). With that, he thanked the board and opened the meeting up to new business and general discussion. Bob Wagner, General Partner at a Bay Area investing firm, immediately jumped in to re-express his concerns about the "Year 2000 problem" (and what the media was calling the "Y2K scare"). Was CrestPoint prepared for the millennium bug and the potential impact on their computer systems asked Wagner, who seemed convinced that all hell was going to break loose on 1/1/2000.

Chandra assured him that CrestPoint was fully prepared, calmly explaining that a system crash was highly unlikely. Any potential computer errors, if they occurred at all, would be related to the formatting and storage of calendar data. It was really nothing to worry about and the whole thing was being over-hyped. Ron Lau agreed as did several other directors. Wagner appeared unconvinced that the end wasn't coming but said no more about it.

Gwen jumped in to express her views on the evolution of the telecom industry. 1999 had seen numerous mergers and acquisitions (Ameritech by SBC; Ascend Communications by Lucent, to name a few) and the year 2000 was likely to see even more consolidation as "the hyper-competition," as she called it, began to take its toll, either driving companies out of business or into alliances in order to survive. She could foresee "pooling of interest transactions," like Netscape and AOL, where companies take similar assets and liabilities and sum them together. Certainly, it wasn't too far-fetched to think that CrestPoint and Pulse Net, or CrestPoint and Nomad, all DSL providers, might pool their assets together in a mutually beneficial merger. One or two of us, maybe all three, might become willing targets of a mega-acquisition by one of the telecom giants.

This idea triggered a spirited debate amongst the board members with Gwen acting as ring master. (She planted this seed in the last board meeting—the seed of possibility that CrestPoint might one day merge with another company—and now she was watering it to see if it would take root.) A few were open to the prospect, cautiously expressing their support, while others, like Marty, were vocal in their antagonism to such an outcome for CrestPoint. Gwen spurred the conversation on, cleverly tapping into the intellectual curiosity the topic aroused, greasing the skids in the direction she was convinced they needed to go.

She could see by Marty's face that he was not happy with this discussion, and she expected the stop sign to come out at any moment. And it did. "We've planted the flag on top of the mountain here in the states," he said, abruptly interrupting the discussion, "and after we roll out DSL across Europe, it will be CrestPoint acquiring properties—not the other way around."

There were hums and nods of agreement at his statement from the other board members and the discussion ended. Gwen was satisfied she'd made her point and let it go. Marty glanced at the clock to confirm the time and swiftly went around the table to see if anyone had a quick comment to make. Only Stu had something more to say.

"As you all know," he said, 'our six-month lock out period ends this month and I want to make sure that no one around this table dumps their stocks or sells off a huge chunk of their shares. A move like that, at this point in time, by either one of the officers or a board member, would be deleterious to our stock price. It would be like announcing the sale of your team right before the playoffs and suck the air out of everyone."

The analogy wasn't a particularly good one but everyone around the table got the point, remaining silent and attentive to what Stu had to say next. Stu took their silence as a cue, adding rather grandiosely, "And it would ease concerns, I think, both with our investors and shareholders, if each of the board members took a pledge not to sell off their stock in the foreseeable future."

The request, coming as it did from the CFO, had a disquieting effect on the other directors, and they looked down at their hands or shifted uncomfortably at this inference that they couldn't be trusted to do what was right for CrestPoint Communications. Marty surreptitiously glanced around the table, fully expecting someone like Russ to wittily take exception to this request, but Andy Sikes beat him to the punch.

"I don't think that's necessary," replied Sikes in a grandfatherly tone. "We all agree that dumping stocks can be corrosive, especially if it's poorly timed. But we're all adults here, and a pledge, in blood I'm assuming, seems rather Ivy League-ish. Afterall, we're not college kids and this isn't a frat house." (He got some smiles at this comment.) "I, for one, have no plans to dump my stock and intend to hold on to it as long as our stock stays healthy and continues to grow…" Sikes allowed his voice to fade out as he folded his hands in front of him, punctuating his statement with a patriarchal smile.

"Couldn't agree more," said Marty, clearly reading the body language in the room. "And that's my job—and each of my officers' job—to keep us growing, to keep us a top performing stock on the Nasdaq. Right, Stu? I know that's your focus."

"Absolutely," agreed Stu.

"Excellent. Then I make a motion to adjourn and reconvene next year." The motion was quickly seconded and Marty, having deftly handled the large egos in the room, adjourned the board meeting without further comment. And the fact that no pledge would be given was a relief to more than one board member.

"We've been over this before, Stu," said Russ, his voicing rising in anger. "Our installation cost is *not* $50,000, it's three times that amount. You *know* that. You've seen the actuals and you've seen our reports, and you've heard me talk about this before—yet you continue to use the fifty-K number in our financials. You're understating our costs and inflating our earnings. Bottom line, Stu, that's what you're doing, and you're lucky I didn't bring this up in the board meeting."

"I'm glad you didn't," interjected Marty in a pacifying tone. He had a full-fledged donnybrook on his hands; Russ and Stu—two of his officers, two of his friends—were at each other's throat and he was doing his best to keep them from coming to blows.

Stu quickly responded, repeating points he'd already made. The number was accepted by market analysts, it was the same cost used by their competitors, and it'd been validated by Tollerson Accounting. "Your righteous indignation is *ridiculous*," declared Stu, standing up from his chair. "It's baseless, and your threats meaningless, and I have better things to do than listen to 'em." Russ stood up as well, and the two men eyed each other menacingly. Stu was burlier, barrel-chested like a bar room brawler, but Russ with his superior height towered over him like Reagan over Gorbachev.

"Gentlemen, please," pleaded Marty. "Russ—Stu, come on now. Take your seats and let's talk this through." He watched while both men reluctantly took their seat again, each one trying to hold back their distaste for the other but doing a lousy job of it. Marty shook his head in resignation at this ancient grudge. Perhaps this scene was inevitable, he thought, like two opposing forces colliding, or chemicals, when mixed, triggering combustion—Russ with his cultured charm and code of conduct versus Stu with his driving ambition and shrewd business sense—destined by their properties to hiss and ignite on contact. It was his job to act as a neutralizing agent, and he'd been doing it for over two years, but now he sensed an irreparable rift between these two that challenged even his own inimitable healing powers.

"I'd love to talk this through if I didn't think it'd fall on deaf ears," replied Stu. He'd taken about all he was going to take from Russ Chappel, a man who had no idea what it took to sustain a business. All he knew how to do was play with his erector set, boat around the bay in his oversized cabin cruiser, and, oh yes, seduce women. He had no inkling of the level of commitment it took or what had to be done to maintain CrestPoint's 'strong buy' stock rating.

"He's trying to reverse history," Stu quickly added. "And upset the status quo. The earnings report has already been filed with the SEC, so what he's suggesting is a restatement of our costs—either now or in the future—which would be disastrous. It'd be like Tiger Woods marking a birdie in his book instead of a par. There's no appeal. It's disqualification and go home a loser. Is that what you want?"

"No, of course not," agreed Marty.

"Then you must think you're audit proof," said Russ, interrupting before Stu could continue. The man was growing tedious and he was finding it more difficult to listen to him. What he had hoped to be a Come-to-Jesus meeting where Stu would, if not repent his sins, at least take ownership for them, was turning into the mad hatter's tea party. Though he should have expected it, he realized. Stu was neither an officer nor a gentleman, and his talent for obfuscating the truth was well known. At a fundamental level, the man simply had no clue that a company was built on value—on people, on character—and not stock price.

"The SEC could audit us, even the FCC," continued Russ. "And what do you think they'd find? All our cost data is discoverable—in reports, in my own memos to the two of you. The result would be an embarrassment, a shit storm, and our reputations—especially yours, Stu, would be shot. Is that what you want?"

"No, of course not," agreed Marty.

"Then where do you stand on this, Marty," asked Russ. "Do we correct the bogus numbers or do we continue the charade?"

"Do we commit financial hari-kari or do we stay the course with numbers that the industry accepts?" asked Stu, adding his own spin.

Marty came to rest with both elbows on his desk and studied the two men for a moment. Was there a way to split the baby on this, he wondered... "We'll do what's right for CrestPoint Communications," he answered firmly. No, they weren't going to restate their earnings and, yes, they needed to be audit-proof, certainly. These two things were not incompatible, he assured them. They'd come this far together, from a small studio apartment to a burgeoning business, five bright young men with big dreams, and now was not the time for division. There was too much at stake. To that end, let him work to find a middle ground on this, he pleaded. But not here, not now—but off-line, with each of them separately. Allow him a chance to mend fences.

Both men agreed to this path forward. Marty, visibly pleased by their response, signaled Stu to leave. "Let Russ and I talk," he said. "I'll come see you later. Thanks for your understanding." Stu nodded and got up from his chair, but as he walked towards the door, he couldn't help but leave a parting shot.

"Don't go back in time and rehash the past," he said. "My strong advice is to move forward—*all of us*. It's time to move on."

"Want us to take a pledge on it?" shot back Russ.

Marty dropped his head to hide his amusement and when he looked up Stu was gone. Russ sat gazing at him with a raised eyebrow, and it suddenly struck Marty that the two of them had not sat in his office and talked alone like this in quite some time, at least not since the IPO. And this fact triggered a backdrop of worried thoughts in his head as he tried to address the issue at hand. Russ acted different towards him since the IPO; there was a coolness, a distance that hadn't been there before, and only he could sense it. This change combined with the crack about "your IT guy" fed his suspicion that Russ knew about him and David and somehow, in some way, held it against him.

"Stuuu," he breathed out. "What can I say. He's a force of nature. Only man I know with a law degree and a masters in Economics."

"The only thing he's economical with is the truth."

"Yes," chuckled Marty. "Aren't we all at times… But where would we be without him, or without you? I shudder to think."

Russ knew what was coming—a reasoned defense of Stu's motivations and methods. (He hoped Marty would make the same defense on his behalf to Stu later on.) So, he sat and listened, nodding occasionally, as Marty made the argument that Stu was, after all, not the spawn of the devil but a dedicated CFO with only good—if sometimes misguided—intentions. It was an argument for the status quo, to make nice in the sandbox and de-escalate, and Russ found it all slightly depressing. There was a time, not too long ago, when he could have leveled with Marty, as friends, and come to an understanding (*You want me to ignore this for now? Sure, so long as you acknowledge the risk. Just keep Stu under control.*

Deal? Thanks, good buddy.), but that time had passed. It passed when he witnessed David emerge from Marty's office like Monica Lewinsky from the oval office. And that little episode, which he remembered with crystal clarity, left both an immediate and lingering effect on him. At first, a revulsion, primordial in origin, welled up inside him but he had quickly subdued it, dismissing it as unenlightened, yet even now there was this kind of distaste that lingered. Not because Marty was gay, but on a more personal level at having been, dare he admit it, deceived all these years in their close friendship. Marty's affection, the hugs, pats, and hand touches, were all signs, and if Marty had been a woman, he would have picked up on it long ago. But he hadn't picked up on it, and as a result he felt deceived.

Marty couldn't have guessed Russ' thoughts at the moment even though they ran parallel to his own. He continued to talk, trying to reach his friend and smooth the waters, but he wasn't particularly worried about the current crises; both men would come around, especially Russ who put such store in good manners. No, his real worry remained—did Russ know about him and David? Should he just come out and tell him, he wondered, and let the chips fall where they may? He instinctively rebelled against that idea; it would be like breaking a precious egg. No, it must remain hidden, he knew—a thing behind the curtain that is never mentioned. Just like his love for Russ. And that was the damned irony of it all, he thought. He'd fallen in love with Russ the first time he'd met him, his desire bonding him to Russ in the form of a close friendship, but knowing even then it was hopeless (Russ' dedicated womanizing made it hopeless). So, like the secret of his sexuality, his love for Russ remained just another thing he kept cloistered in the shadows.

Russ' thoughts shifted back to the immediate problem. For the last fifteen minutes, they had discussed the issue at hand, with Marty doing most of the talking, and Russ was ready to accept the fait accompli, fold it up neatly, and take his leave. He didn't really expect anything more. By raising this issue of the bogus cost data with Marty and Stu, he meant to put them on notice and cover his own ass. He'd accomplished that. The possibility that Stu would capitulate or Marty might rise up in righteous anger and demand Stu's resignation never entered his head. It all played out exactly as he thought it would with prevarications on Stu's part and with Marty taking on the role of the overburdened mediator trying to keep the peace. But he would have the last say.

Russ made ready to leave, coming forward in his chair. "Okay, Marty," he said evenly. "I hear you. I'm not going to bring this to the board or bang the drum on it any longer. I'm leaving it with you—but I expect these numbers to be corrected in the 4th quarter report. So talk to Stu… Meanwhile, we'll take the risk that some SEC analyst doesn't call us out on the numbers and have us *really* audited." Russ was to the door now and paused there to make his final point. "There's risk and then there's *risk*," he added, his voice rising on the key word. "And we have to know the difference, so I'm going to believe you know what you're doing by taking this *risk*."

Marty assured him he knew the difference and thanked him for his understanding, promising to talk to Stu about it. Russ nodded and left his office, and Marty glanced up at the ceiling, his thoughts triggered by the way Russ had repeated the word "risk." The inflection in Russ' voice was a dead give-away, and he was sure of it now. Russ knew his secret.

Chapter 12

Every Monday morning I met with Mark Kirkland, my VP of Implementation, to review the week's installation schedule and address potential problems. I started these meetings back in '97 and they were a very effective at identifying bottlenecks and at heading off trouble before it impacted our due dates. These meetings also strengthened my rapport with Mark. There had always been friendliness and mutual respect between us, but these one-on-one meetings every Monday were filled with a common cause and an easy give and take that solidified our bond. Mark always came into my office with a smile, always prepared, always focused, and if he raised any difficulty with the schedule, he almost always had a solution for it. I couldn't have been more pleased; he was everything I had expected and more.

Yet, over the last eight months I'd witnessed a transformation in Mark, not in work performance (he was still on top of his game) but rather in his look and manner. His clothing changed, subtly at first, from slacks, a shirt and tie, and polished Oxfords to blue jeans, flannel shirts, and either a pair of worn sneakers or beat-up Red Wing work boots. His blonde hair, usually close-cropped, was longer now but still neatly combed, and he'd grown a short beard that covered the lower part of his face.

This change in outward appearance was accompanied by a change in his demeanor. At first I read it as an increasing air of detachment, finding his readiness to laugh replaced by a quiet seriousness, and his small pleasantries, wisecracks, and especially his off-the-wall witticisms now shelved and put away. It was almost as if he came into work every morning with a growing disenchantment with the job, and he began to remind me of an actor unhappy with his role who, despite being miscast, was still enough of a trooper and a pro to give it his best effort.

I attributed all this to his religious conversion. His detachment, his other-worldliness, it was all a product of a transformation that seemed to have taken place in the very core of his being, and most everyone, including myself, accepted it as we would someone turning strict vegetarian or changing their political party. As long as he didn't proselytize or pursue converts on company time, there was no harm done, but with a company our size, populated as it was with primarily young, liberal, and college-educated people, a complaint seemed inevitable. And I had finally received one—from Human Resources.

Mark sat across from me reviewing the week's schedule. His voice was precise and dispassionate as he addressed each due date, meeting my gaze while occasionally glancing at his notes, and I wondered how best to broach this HR complaint with him. The whole thing was nonsense but it was official and therefore unavoidable. It all stemmed from the little pocket-sized pamphlet Mark occasionally handed out to fellow employees (I had one). It was a small comic book, the characters rather crudely drawn, that told the story of a man with two lives—one where he sins and is condemned to hell on Judgement Day, and the other where he lives his life in Christ and is ushered into the kingdom of heaven on Judgement Day. A morality tale, amateurishly depicted, which I thumbed through in fifteen seconds then stuck in my desk.

The pamphlet was out of my desk now—exhibit A—as I waited for Mark to complete his report. He seemed unaware of the HR complaint and appeared normal, and by that I meant his new normal—unhurried, almost serene in manner, dressed in his blue jeans, flannel shirt, and work boots. Perhaps this was the 'look' for church elders in his parish, but to me he looked more like someone who'd wandered out of the backwoods of Norway. A Viking Lumberjack, I mused, grinning at the image.

Mark must have caught my grin because he paused, expecting me to interrupt, but when I didn't, he continued his report. After he finished, I complimented him on the thoroughness of his report and the great job his team was doing. In the past, such a compliment would have been reciprocated, leading to comfortable small talk about the company, including the latest rumors and gossip floating around. But that, too, was gone by the wayside. He simply nodded, half smiling, and made ready to leave, which I read as either being overly considerate of my valuable time or a sign that he was entirely indifferent to the value of our meeting. Either way, passive or aloof, it reinforced my view of a man going through the motions. I half expected him to walk into my office one day and tell me he was quitting so he could go forth and spread the word of God. It wouldn't surprise me.

"One more thing," I said, picking up the pamphlet. "I got a complaint about these pamphlets—through HR." (He settled back into his chair, looking neither surprised nor concerned.) "I don't wanna make a big deal out of this but suffice it to say that someone complained to HR who, in turn, brought it to me to address. The official line is no political or religious activism in the workplace. And given you're a VP, it can be construed as management advocating one religion over another. So, in other words, Mark, you'll need to stop handing them out at work. What you do outside work is your own business. Fair enough?

"Sure," he replied. "Sorry for the trouble."

"No problem. As you know, some folks can be… overly sensitive to such things." He nodded thoughtfully at my remark, and I sensed this might be the perfect time to have the 'talk' with him. (Some months ago, I'd promised his wife, in a moment of weakness really, to talk to him about the heavy toll his religious conversion was taking on his family.) But I cringed at the thought. There were two confrontations I'd been avoiding for some time—this one and the other with Marty concerning his sexuality. Both were rife with awkward confessions and raw emotion, and I didn't relish playing out either scene. My inclination was to avoid it. Least said soonest mended, and all that.

"I kinda like the story," I added, opening up the pamphlet. "Though you could use a better artist. Maybe Stan Lee could help."

Mark laughed. It was the first time I'd seen him laugh in a while, and I decided to give it one shot—the 'talk'—and see how it went. If he wasn't receptive, so be it. At least I could say I tried.

"What does your wife think about the beard?" I asked him.

He studied me for a moment as though he was judging my sincerity before answering. "Doesn't like it," he replied. "Nor the boots. Or the flannel shirt."

"Then she's not on board, I take it—spiritually, I mean, with your life in Christ?"

"No… She's Catholic. We were married as Catholics, but I have some problems with the Church of Rome. That and the depth of my commitment has caused some friction."

There it was—my opening—and I took it without much enthusiasm as to where it would lead. But I'd been a supervisor for twenty years, and in that time, I've been coach, camp counselor, psychiatrist, a kick in the butt, and a sympathetic ear. I felt he wanted to tell me his story, and I would practice what I preached and generously listen to it. So, I began coaxing the story out of him with small, leading questions like "Why's that?" or "What happened then?" and found him receptive.

He talked about the problems with his wife and his friends, and the break with his daughter that his "salvation experience" had brought on, not shying away from describing the emotional turmoil it was causing his loved ones. But it couldn't be helped, he explained, and God willing it would all work itself out. Because there was no going back for him. His wife couldn't accept this; she even begged friends and family members to talk to him, to get him to go back to his old life, but it was futile effort on their part. (I kept my best poker face, seeing as I was one of those people.) No, they didn't get it, he reaffirmed, there was no going back. The Holy Spirit had spoken to him, and he was born again with Jesus Christ.

Mark spoke freely about his life and I listened to his story without interrupting him. He skipped forward in time, went backwards, then circled round again to make a connection, pausing at times to find the right word or phrase to describe his feelings, and not quoting the Bible (as I thought he would) but occasionally paraphrasing a passage to make his point. I sensed he was heading towards the moment of his religious conversion, the lightning bolt that explained everything, and I let him go there as you would a crash victim needing to explain how it all happened.

Before his conversion, he explained, there had been a growing sense of dissatisfaction with life, for years really, that he couldn't shake. A loving family, a great job, promotions, stock options—all of it—wasn't enough to shake loose what he called the black dog. (I grinned wryly at that, since it was the same term Churchill used to describe his dark depression.) He hoped it would go away, eventually, on its own, but instead it worsened and came with a thirst that sprouted up inside him like a water-seeking vine. It was a thirst for meaning, for a new life and a new beginning. And he knew the meaningfulness he thirsted for was not to be found in "this world," which was rank with evil and sin, but in something transcendent and greater than himself.

"I tried going back to church," he said, "but it didn't really help. It was like the Peggy Lee song *Is That All There Is?*—trying something new only to find out it lacks any umph, you know? But I knew the answer was God; too many things big and little told me so—signs along the highway, so to speak—they all pointed me in the same direction. But getting there was the challenge. Too many things in this world try and keep us from finding God. Ego, culture, things like a big paycheck and creature comforts, even a woman's love, can keep you from finding God. But once I realized God isn't outside myself, floating around in the ethernet, that he's in me, I just kept at it, praying every day, trying to open my heart to Christ... You know how difficult it is to open your heart—to *really* open up your heart? It's like stripping naked; like shedding every little selfish quirk in your psyche until you lay yourself bare. It's grueling. But for me, it finally happened one night in my den. I was sitting at my desk in the dark, looking out the window at my garden, trying with every fiber of my being to wrench open my heart, when a scribble, hardly legible, sent me to a verse in the Bible that spoke of receiving Him, of getting his power, and becoming born again, not of the will of the flesh or man, but of God, and the words floored me, literally, and I went down on my knees and confessed my sinfulness and asked Christ to forgive me.

"Then the strangest thing happened, and it wasn't a voice, not like in the movies, but this overwhelming urge came over me to get up and go down into the garden—that there I would find my answer.

So I did. It was raining and dark, but I went outside and sat down on a bench, raised my face to the sky, and suddenly without really trying Christ came to me, not in a vision or a dream, but in this kind of quiet unwavering confidence that he was alive in my heart. I laughed with happiness—there in the dark, soaking wet, like some nut job—I laughed with joy. And this power filled me, a power you can't imagine. It was like being plugged into God's wall socket and it filled me up, and I got it, it all made sense—God's creation, life, my place in it—it was all crystal clear to me. It was then and there that I accepted Jesus Christ into my heart and committed my life to Him… and it was, Russ, the most marvelous experience of my life."

With that, he stopped speaking and looked at me, his eyes watering up with emotion, and for a second I thought he was going to cry. I glanced down at my desk, slightly embarrassed for him, and he must have noticed my uncomfortableness because he suddenly laughed and said, "Well, you asked for it, and you got it. Now you can call the funny farm to come pick me up."

"I would never do that," I replied. And I never would. There was one thing I was certain of now; he was no religious fanatic. No doubt there were people at CrestPoint, and probably even his own wife, who thought him one, but I knew better. Zealots didn't make fun of themselves or peal back the onion on their faith. No, he was something different.

Mark smiled, his eyes quickly turning back to normal. "Appreciate that," he said. "More than a few folks think I'm crazy. My daughter for one… Anyhow, that brings us full circle—to my point about not going back. My wife wants me to go backwards, but I can't. She's making it a choice between my faith and my marriage. So, you can imagine the struggle we're having. I don't want to lose her. I almost lost her once before, and I can't go through that again, but I won't go back to my old life either. It would be like closing my eyes to the sunlight."

I cleared my throat. "Hmm, yes," I replied rather clumsily. "I can only imagine… But as you say, God willing, it'll work itself out. You gotta believe that, right?"

"I do."

There was a moment of quiet reflection which I interrupted, telling him that I appreciated his candor and the effort it must have taken to share his story with me. No, it was he who was thankful—thankful for my patience and understanding. I nodded, making a show of picking up the pamphlet and placing it back in my drawer as a sign of trust.

"There's only one thing I need to know," I said. "Are you committed to the job, or are you gonna come in one day and chuck it all?"

He appeared surprised at the question and quickly assured me that yes, by God, he was committed to the job and was in it for the long haul. I smiled, telling him I was pleased to hear that, and he suddenly got up and came across to shake my hand.

As he headed for the door, I felt there was something more I should say. Some words of advice. I'd fulfilled my promise to Ronnie by having a talk with him but I'd not changed his mind or tried to influence him. Not that I would have, but still I felt a need to add a coda to this conversation.

"Take care, Mark. Remember, balance in all things," I said. That felt slightly lame spoken to a grown man (it was something I would have said to my son), so I quickly added, "Don't let your burden get too heavy."

He paused at the door and smiled back at me. "*'Come unto me, all ye that labor and are heavy laden, and I will give you rest,'*" he replied, quoting scripture. "*'For my yoke is easy, and my burden is light.'*" And with that, he gave me a friendly salute and left.

I studied the closed door for a long minute, trying to put his transformation into some sort of perspective. I had heard the term "Jesus Freak" used to describe Mark, which was a person who tossed away everything to devote their life to Jesus, but Mark was anything but a Jesus Freak. Personally, I found religious conversions like this a sign of a weak intellect, but with Mark it seemed different. Having listened to him, I found something lingering, something that bothered me. Perhaps it was the man's poetic sensibility or the fact that he could laugh and cry on the same day. It was hard to say for sure what it was that bothered me about it.

My admin buzzed me to say that Hal Rubin and a new employee were outside my office and wanted to speak with me. By all means, I replied, rather curious as to why Hal Rubin of all people, Stu's right-hand man, wanted to see me.

The door opened and Hal entered, grinning ear to ear, then quickly stepped aside to usher in the most beautiful woman I had ever seen. It's strange the reaction men have when they meet a truly stunning woman, and I had met—and bedded—many gorgeous women over the years, yet in this instance I was like any other man. I swallowed, unconsciously holding my breath, feeling a sudden tingle in my loins and a quickening of my heartbeat. I was immediately aware of my reaction and fought to hide it, clasping my hands calmly on the desk in an attempt to appear unfazed at her appearance.

"Russ, this is Roxanne Lamorte, our new Director of Current Accounting," announced Hal.

"Miz Lamorte," I replied, standing up. "A pleasure to meet you."

She stepped forward and said, "The pleasure's mine" in a mezzo-soprano voice, coppery smooth, and held her hand out to shake. I took it and shook it more than briefly, feeling her warmth radiate up my forearm. When I let go, she gracefully sat down in the chair directly across the desk from me.

I sat back down and glanced over at Hal. He still had that stupid ear-to-ear grin on his face, which was more a leer than a grin, and he seemed to be expecting the same kind of grin from me in return. But I was too busy stifling my own set of emotions to give him the satisfaction of a return grin. I was having a strong, visceral reaction to this woman, and I found the reaction rather unseemly and hoped to hell it didn't show. Flushed cheeks and hungry eyes simply wouldn't do, and I quickly spun the wheel on my internal rudder to put myself on a more even keel.

"And what's 'current accounting'?" I inquired, mildly curious and very business-like. "Never heard of it."

Hal took a seat somewhat back of Roxanne and began to give me an explanation on what 'current accounting' meant—something about the sale of our products and services versus payments made to wholesalers and suppliers—and I half-listened to him, glancing in mock interest between him and Roxanne as an excuse to fully size her up.

The women I rank as the most beautiful in the world are ethereal in a sense; they are women I've seen in movies like Ingrid Bergman, Liz Taylor, and Senta Berger, or women I've admired in the all-out panorama of a Playboy centerfold like Miss January 1972, who I put at the top of my list of Playmates. But all these women paled in comparison to the living, breathing Roxanne Lamorte. For one, she was a true redhead, a tone between strawberry blonde and classic red, ginger in color, matched by her eyebrows which were single brush strokes of burnt orange, and complimented perfectly by a light caramel complexion. Her skin was flawless, smooth and immaculate like Carrara marble, except for an ever-so-light sprinkle of freckles across her nose which acted like the fizz in a gin and tonic. Beneath her expressive eyebrows were a pair of Kelly-green eyes, bright and bewitching in their cat-like cleverness, and I found it difficult not to stare into them. A slightly high and round forehead, almost Oriental in design, rode around her temples to her delicately hallowed cheekbones, which caught the eye and led irresistibly down to her sensuous mouth. Her lips were full, the lower one dominating like the threshold to an inviting doorway, giving her a fertile rather than pouty look. A celestial nose, slightly upturned, centered her symmetrical face, and an elegant jaw line culminated in a splendid heart-shaped chin.

When she entered the room, my eye, which was very good at assessing such things, sized her up at five-four with a thirty-four-inch bust, twenty-three waist, and thirty-four hips. Her figure was shapely, almost a classic hourglass, but more toned and athletic-looking than strictly voluptuous. It suggested aerobics, probably daily, but her graceful movements from the door to the chair, and in sitting down, reminded me of a dancer. She wore a simple dress, dark evergreen, that was sleeveless, hugging her figure down to her waist where it flared out, stopping at her knees. The boat neckline was interrupted in front by two buttons, both left undone, which gave the eye a tantalizingly brief view of her cleavage. She'd slyly hiked up her dress before taking her seat and sat with her legs crossed, but sitting so close to my desk, I couldn't see them. I could only imagine.

"Stu has given us instructions to dig into your installation costs," I heard Hal say as I tuned him back in. "It appears they may be understated and he wants us to validate them so they're accurately reflected in the next earnings report."

"Good to hear," I replied. Of course, my department had been providing detailed cost data to Stu for years, which he'd consistently ignored, but if he wanted to validate it now then so be it. This had to be Marty's doing, and I welcomed the opportunity to officially set Stu straight.

"This is what Roxanne's been tasked with—her and her team," added Hal, giving me that same leering grin. "Course her team is just Roxanne at the moment."

"Yes," she said, jumping in on cue. "Let me know who I can work with in your department and I'll take it from there."

"You can start with me," I replied. "Then we'll see where it goes from there."

"Wonderful. When can we start?" She flashed a smile that was ever-so-slanted to the right (a disarming imperfection), and I smiled back at her. In the short time she'd been sitting in front of me, I confirmed she wore no wedding ring and guessed her age to be in her early thirties. Perfect. I also made a vow to myself to *have* this woman, to put all my talents to work, to woo her, win her, and have her call my name in the throes of passion. She was a living, breathing work of art, a flesh and blood masterpiece, and my desire to hold her naked in my arms was vividly strong, filling my head with schemes and carnal images.

"As soon as you like," I told her, gazing straight into those Kelly-green eyes. "Just check with my assistant and get on my calendar. Best get an hour. You'll need to see our cost data first, and I'll get that to you beforehand."

She was appreciative, expressing her thanks in that mezzo-soprano voice of hers, full and velvety like a clarinet, and I noticed for the first time a fragrance in the air. She was wearing perfume, but it was subtle, a mixture of lily and musk that lingered just enough in the air to pleasantly flirt with my sense of smell. It acted as an aphrodisiac in my head, snapping to life an image of her kneeling naked in front of me, holding my erect cock in her hand, tenderly kissing the tip of it before taking me into her mouth.

Christ! I was losing it. (I wondered if she could read my thoughts. I hoped not, then again, I hoped so.) But this fantasizing, right in front of her so to speak, was rather shameful and needed to stop. Balance in all things, I reminded myself with some amusement. Even in lust.

She was standing up, her hands straightening her dress as she rose, and I rose out of my chair with my eyes all over her. She must have noticed because she raised her chin up and smiled an age-old smile, and at that instant I knew she was receptive. All the signs pointed to mutual interest. She offered her hand to me, saying how nice it was to have met me and how she was looking forward to working with me, and I took her hand lightly, resisting an urge to kiss it, and held it tenderly like a live bird until she slowly drew it back. I, too, was pleased to have met her, I said. I, too, was looking forward to working with her.

I glanced over at Hal to concede his existence and caught him studying me closely. This guy with his round, libertine face and that self-satisfied smile annoyed me and I wished him gone. I watched Roxanne turn and walk out the door, fully admiring her swiveling gait. Right behind her followed Hal, and he paused at the door and glanced back, giving me a wink—a randy, frat-house kind of wink as if to say, "Hey, bro, see what I brought you"—but I ignored him and sat down at my keyboard.

That night I ate dinner alone on my boat and thought about Roxanne. She was on my calendar for an hour Wednesday, in just two more days, and my anticipation was already building. But I knew the pitfalls of being overanxious. Some women, especially discerning women, could read over-anxiousness like a sign pinned to your chest, and it turned them off. And it was never wise to want anything too badly. No, the secret to success with women, and it would be the same formula with Roxanne, was warmth, charm, and an elusive heart; if they found you handsome and amusing but sensed a hole in your heart, the challenge to fill it was almost always too great for them to resist.

A neighbor came on board, a retired colonel of the Coldstream Guards, and we each had a Johnnie Walker Red on ice with a splash of water and played a couple of games of backgammon. After he left, I mixed another drink and sat down to watch the evening news with Clementine in my lap. (One of the news segments had a market analyst boldly predicting the end of the boom early next year). When the news ended, I switched channels and caught part of a 70's disaster movie with Charlton Heston, but grew tired of it, finished my drink, and went to bed. Somewhere in the early morning, I had a dream that spooked Clementine off my bed.

This was a recurring dream I'd been having for a couple of years now. Some elements of the dream varied, different people popped in and out of it and the sub-plots changed occasionally, but the core of the dream remained the same. I am walking along a path that leads to the top of a mountain. Marty usually leads the way with the four of us—Chandra, Ron, Stu, and me—following behind, and inevitably something acts to distract or delay my progress up the mountain. In tonight's version, it was Roxanne with a bang.

She appears magically up ahead of me, on the side of the path, talking to Stu, and he whispers in her ear and they both glance over at me as I approach. I look past them, farther up the path, and see Marty waiting impatiently. "Go ahead and talk to her! But hurry up!" he yells down at me. When I reach Roxanne she is alone, looking beautiful in a hooded cloak, and she offers me something without explanation. It's a small pamphlet, and I take it from her, rather bemused by the gift, and open it expecting to find a religious message inside but instead find it filled with scribbling and numbers that I can't make out. I question its meaning, but she says it's for me and asks me to keep it. I nod and put it in my pocket, obeying her wish, thinking it's all part of a game she wants me to play, so I step up to her, smelling a hint of lily and musk, and pull back her hood to look closely at her face. But it's stone, or polished marble, and I realize with a start that she's turned into a statue. I must be dreaming, I think, but at that moment a loud, god-awful horn sounds, echoing down the mountain, and I look up to see Marty and many others running towards me. "The dam has burst!" they yell. "Run for it!" They race past me, Marty holding hands with David (who has suddenly appeared out of nowhere), pointing up the mountain at a wall of surging water that is raging down upon us.

I struggle to get my legs going, willing myself to run after them, and I'm making progress until I see a man sitting on a rock on the side of the road. At first I think it's my son Dan, but when I get closer I see it's Mark Kirkland, sitting there reading a book, oblivious to the wall of water descending upon us. I yell at him to run but he's content to stay, so I pull his arm to try and force him to flee, causing his book to fall to the ground. He resists my pull, saying "I'm fine right here," and leans down to pick up his book which is not the Bible but a book of poetry. I realize I've wasted precious time trying to save him, and when I look back at the surging wall of water I see it's too late, so I take a knee and brace for its impact.

I woke up to the sound of a boat horn and checked the clock. It was 4:30 in the morning. No one was allowed to sound a boat horn after hours unless it was an emergency, so I got up and looked out the port window to see a cabin cruiser motoring by filled with drunken revelers yelling and laughing. Idiots. They'd likely get fined by the Harbor Master for this stunt, and it would serve them right, waking folks up like this in the dead of night. I found Clementine hiding behind my clothes hamper and picked her up and brought her back to bed with me. But I couldn't get back to sleep, and after laying there for a half hour, I got up and leisurely began getting ready for work, remembering my dream and thankful that Roxanne wasn't a marble statue.

Book Three

Chapter 1

January 1, 2000, came and went and the world did not end. The Millennium Bug that threatened to wreak havoc on computer systems around the world turned out to be another media hype. It was one crisis averted, but another one was on its way.

In the span of five years, the Dot-com bubble had grown to an enormous size fed by the hot air pumped into it from newspapers, magazines, and TV programs like CNBC. Market analysts and hip economists touted the "New Economy," declaring that "The Internet changes everything" and that the old rules could be thrown out the window. Investment houses applied a new Internet math that convinced speculators to invest in the promise of the Internet, eagerly pumping billions of dollars into companies with no earnings simply because they had a dot-com after their name or were in some way connected to the building out of the Information Superhighway. But the old rules have a way of wreaking their revenge; like the immutable laws of gravity, they compelled a return to earth, and in early 2000, the Dot-com bubble was set to collapse.

Gwen Novak saw it coming, in fact, had always seen it coming and had factored it into her game plan from the very moment she accepted the position of President of CrestPoint Communications. Like everyone else around the globe, she had watched the Nasdaq Composite Index rise 400% since '95, but unlike most, she knew it wasn't sustainable. Good things never lasted; a market adjustment, perhaps even a crash, was inevitable. But it wasn't the stock market bubble that drove her thinking. There were runs and droughts in the game, runs and droughts, but what mattered over the long run was the product you put on the floor each night. And CrestPoint's product—DSL, high-speed Internet—was too one-dimensional to win on its own. Already its market share was diminishing. Stiff competition from their main rivals, Nomad and Pulse, was only part of the problem. Now all the big boys wanted in; AT&T, SBC, Atlantis, U.S. West, all of them were announcing plans to aggressively jump into the DSL market, and the time for a game-changing deal was at hand.

It was in their eagerness to get into the DSL market that Gwen saw her opportunity to swing a deal with one of the big boys. CrestPoint already had DSL networks built out in 109 metropolitan areas across the country, each using the Baby Bells own phone lines to deliver high-speed Internet to thousands of customers. The chance for one of them to jump the line by buying up a ready-made network was her golden carrot.

Already in January 2000, Gwen was making discreet inquiries within the telecom industry. A phone call to a CFO or to a key Executive Vice President, and she'd drop the hint, float the balloon, and make it known that CrestPoint was exploring merger opportunities. She was not so much hanging fire as she was betting on the come that one of big boys would roll the dice in her favor. And there was interest—but always with the same caveat: Was Gwen speaking for the CEO? Did she represent the Board of Directors?

Legitimate questions, she'd answer, but not germane to this high-level, what-if discussion. She was merely testing the waters, and if it was warm then all their questions regarding CEO and Board buy-in would be resolved before CrestPoint sat down at the negotiating table. *But make one thing clear*, she would add—she and no one else would be point person in any negotiation to buy CrestPoint Communications.

Some were skeptical, others coy, and for the ones who showed a budding curiosity she pressed her point home: Are you interested in a flourishing DSL network, ready-made and fully functional, and one that you can acquire for a controlling interest to leap-frog your rivals? Yes, they were interested, but they'd have to kick the tires on it, talk about it, and they'd get back to her. So, Gwen waited, feeling somewhat like a GM in the NBA floating a blockbuster trade, wondering which one of the big boys had the balls to make a deal. And when the call came, as she knew it would, she smiled to herself. It was Atlantis—the east coast behemoth, who wanted to go national—and they were interested. Very interested.

The ball was in Gwen's court, right where she wanted it, and now was the time to set some screens, knock down shots, and swing momentum in her favor. She would have to win the board over, get her executive team to buy into it, and Marty had to be dealt with. The first two would be less an effort than the third. The board and her executive team were made up of hard-nosed businessmen who could read the writing on the wall. There was already a growing concern at CrestPoint's mounting debt; the monthly bills from cities, franchise boards, utility commissions, RBOCs, installation crews, and equipment suppliers were beginning to pile up. What paid those bills came out of their revenue stream (should have, anyway, if they were a healthy company). And that revenue came from the Internet Service Providers who sold their DSL to Internet customers. But lately these same ISPs had started missing their payments. And all this—the mounting debt and stressed revenue stream—would present a compelling case to the board to explore a merger deal. She was confident of it.

Marty, on the other hand, was going to be a problem. As CEO and Chairman of the Board, he had the power to scuttle any deal, especially if he saw it as an acquisition or a take-over. The boy wonder still had visions of grandeur that CrestPoint, the company he founded and built up into a national dynamo, would become a global player, one that would acquire and take over other companies—not the other way around. Gwen considered this zeal to be Marty's fatal flaw, and it was a zeal that would have to be tempered or re-directed if a deal was to be struck with Atlantis. Quite frankly, he was a liability that she would have to maneuver out of her way.

But first, she would start with her executive team and then the board, holding one-on-one discussions to broach the idea of "merging" with Atlantis. These would be hush-hush meetings, held behind Marty's back (which was easy since he was wrapped up in the Netherlands deal), and everyone would be asked to hold it close to the vest.

A few things aided her cause. In February, Alan Greenspan announced plans to aggressively raise interest rates, which led to significant stock market volatility. CPNT stock, which closed on May 12th at $40 a share, had fluctuated over time and now, nearly nine months later, was trading at a worrisome $32 a share despite a strong 4th quarter earnings report. Market analysts were changing their tune and advising against technology stocks. Media outlets like Barron's were warning that many Internet companies were running out of cash and on the verge of bankruptcy. To Gwen, this was all grist for the mill.

With her ducks lined up in a row, she started with Stuart Baum. As CFO and Corporate Attorney, he would be key to any merger deal. He was also Marty's confidant, which was a bond she planned to test. To her pleasant surprise, Stu was all in. Not only that, he nearly fell over himself offering his aid and support to her quest. Yes, he said, she had *his* vote. It was the smart move, inevitable, and she could count on him to help push it through. They were allies. She thanked him warmly, reminding him to keep their conversation confidential, especially from Marty, until she was in a strong position to take this to the board. He readily agreed, his eyes showing her that he was all-in on her little conspiracy.

And after Stu left, she sat and thought about how quickly he jumped on board, finding herself slightly amazed at how easy it was.

CHAPTER 2

"I'd love to see how the equipment is installed," said Roxanne. "You know, in a central office, from end to end."

I listened to that smoldering voice of hers, breathing in her intoxicating fragrance, and simply nodded. It was nearly two months since I met Roxanne, this being the third time we'd gotten together in my office to review and discuss installation costs, and despite my best efforts, I was no closer to bedding her than I was the first day I met her. Each time we met, she came dressed to kill and even flirted on occasion, yet she continued to skillfully parry my flattery and smooth advances, remaining enticingly out of my grasp like some lush mansion on a hilltop. Apparently, she was out of my price range.

"It might help, you know, in putting it all together,' she added.

"I'll see what we can do," I replied, running my eyes over her face and neck. She possessed a certain Gallic sensuousness that unsettled me. She was stunning, one of those rare creatures who was a blend of great beauty, intelligence, and aloof charm. Quite maddening really. "I'll talk to Mark Kirkland. I'm sure one of his folks can give you a tour. I think we have a DSLAM going in up in Palo Alto."

She shifted her position in her chair, recrossing her legs, and studied me a moment with those Kelly-green eyes. "Why don't you take me," she asked, her eyebrows rising suggestively. "Maybe combine it with lunch… Unless you're too busy."

That almost sounded like a *come-on*, I thought. Why the sudden change of heart, I wondered, not meaning to doubt her intentions or snub this great opportunity, but rather peeved at my ill luck that this was happening now—now when I was in no position to take advantage of it.

(It was a thing I didn't like talking about. After thirty years of sexual activity and over a hundred sexual partners—always careful to confine my liaisons to women of high quality, not call girls or tramps—I'd contracted gonorrhea. Urogenital gonorrhea to be precise. The clap. And, in a way, it was Roxanne's fault. Just as hunger can lead to theft, my aching gonads led to an act of recklessness. It was at our recent Holiday Celebration—another lavish affair this time at the Bellagio in Las Vegas—where I'd gone to hook up with Roxanne. She had made it known to me she'd be there and would be 'flying solo'. But we talked only briefly that night and danced twice, the second time when it was late and the ballroom nearly empty. It was a slow number, and she crossed the room and tapped me on the shoulder to dance. We stepped onto the dancefloor and she came into my arms, putting both arms around my neck while I pulled her close to me, inhaling her aroma, smothering my lips into her silky red hair, swaying to the music. She was in a skin-tight dress and it was almost like holding her naked, and when I moved my hand down towards her waist I discovered she wasn't wearing panties, and I was thinking *this is it, I'm in like Flynn*. I had an immediate erection and she must have felt it, pressed close together as we were, but when the dance ended, she simply said thank you and walked away and was soon gone from the ballroom. So, there I stood, aroused and erect and left hanging, and maybe I wasn't an addict in need of a fix but I was surely a man in need of *relief*, and I soon found myself in the casino bar with my arm around Sherry, a pert little number from Sales who couldn't keep her hands off me. She reminded me of Miss September 1993, and if that was stretching it, I wasn't in the mood to quibble about it, primed as I was from too many Johnnie Walkers and a permanent hard-on. What followed was a drunken, messy encounter up in her room, and I snuck out right after to go to my own room to sleep it off. Three days later, at work, I noticed a burning sensation while urinating in the restroom. Worried and wondering what was up, I returned to my office to find an envelope marked private sitting on my desk. It was a note from Sherry telling me she had tested positive for VD, that I should get tested right away, and apologizing for the bad news. I left immediately for the doctor's where I tested positive, got a shot of ceftriaxone, and took home both a bottle of pills and a heavy dose of embarrassment.)

"Never too busy for you, young lady," I replied with a smile, turning to my keyboard. "Let's see what my week looks like," I added, pulling up my calendar on my computer that my assistant updated daily. As I looked at my schedule, I ran the timeline through my head. My symptoms had ended but I still had another week of pills to take, then a retest to confirm I was clear. I was a good week and a half away from launching my vessel, so to speak. In the meantime, I was stuck in drydock without a seaworthy ship to pilot.

"Before the end of the week would be great," she said. "That way I can wrap up my analysis and present it to Stu by next week."

I nodded while studying my calendar, thinking about what she had just said. We'd gone over the installation actuals in detail and there was more than enough data for her to confirm that our costs were much higher than what Stu was reporting. But I let this inconsistency go for the moment as I looked for a block of time to give her. It would have to be this Friday, which was still in my no-go period, but an opportunity to spend an afternoon with this sublime beauty, even if it was just to improve my chances, was too good to pass up.

"How's Friday sound?"

"Perfect!" she replied, flashing her disarming smile that was ever-so slanted to the right.

We proceeded to nail down the logistics—time, place, itinerary—and she insisted on meeting me there rather than driving up together. Very well, I told her. I'd meet her Friday at 11am in the parking lot of the Palo Alto central office.

"*Really* looking forward to it," she said in a voice suggesting infinite possibilities. She rose up out of her chair like a prima ballerina, and we exchanged pleasantries before she turned and walked to the door. I watched her five-foot-four frame, all 34-23-34 inches of it, a classic hourglass of a figure toned to perfection, walk out of my office and felt a certain elation for the first time in weeks.

———

I poured over our 4th quarter earnings report as I sipped my morning coffee. The reports included our end-of-year financial statement, including a 1st quarter revenue forecast, which had already been submitted to SEC. Other than a high-level summary presented to the board, this was the first time I'd seen the detailed reports. Stu, who was the king of his domain and ruled it like one, never shared the numbers with me until they went public. Undoubtedly, Marty would have seen them beforehand, and perhaps even Gwen and key board members may have been given a peek, but somehow Stu managed to keep me out of the loop until after the SEC filing.

It didn't take long to figure out why. Stu was still using the bogus cost numbers from 1997. Despite the fact they were severely understated, making our earnings appear better than they were, and despite the fact that time and again I'd warned the numbers were wrong, even getting a pledge from Marty that they would be corrected this time around, they remained virtually unchanged. Oh, there were some cosmetic changes; he added $5000 to the installation cost factor, no doubt so he could say he listened to me, but the actual difference was closer to $100,000, and he knew that. Very troubling.

A few other things troubled me. Marty, my good friend and confidant; Marty, who rode the river with me in pursuing our dreams; Marty, who knew the truth about the cost data and committed himself to resolve the issue—that Marty couldn't be trusted anymore. It was deeply disappointing. And what about Roxanne? The new Director of Current Accounting? Her assignment was to validate our actual installation costs, and we'd done that together in my office, reviewing and dissecting the numbers in detail until she nodded and said my numbers were solid. Did she exercise due diligence by reporting this back to Stu? Evidently not.

I made up my mind to take this to the board. It was the only way to ensure this issue was properly addressed. I'd also brief Gwen on the situation (a step that was probably overdue). But beforehand, I would tell Stu exactly what I planned to do. I would give him a chance to redeem himself by restating our numbers between now, late January, and the board meeting in late March. Part of me worried I was being too gracious. But even a snake-in-the-grass like Stu deserved one last shot at redemption.

It took until the afternoon before my admin was able to get through to Stu. (I was going to have this confrontation over the phone and not in person for fear of punching him in the nose.) He'd been busy all morning, probably avoiding my call since he knew the reason for it, but finally bowed to the inevitable and took it.

"Russ," he said without emotion. "What can I do for you?"

His voice echoed from inside his office. "Take me off speakerphone," I replied.

"It's fine. I'm alone."

"Take me off speakerphone."

There was a pause, then I heard him sigh before picking up the receiver and turning off his speaker. "There. You happy now?"

"You didn't update the installation costs in our earnings report," I said, cutting to the chase. "And that's after I confronted you about this in Marty's office and after you promised to fix it in the next quarterly report. So, at this juncture, I can only assume it's willful—that you're willfully cooking the books to make us look better than we are. Tell me I'm wrong."

"You're wrong," he retorted. "First off, Marty saw this report before it went out and signed off on it, as did Tollerson Accounting. And secondly, take another look at the numbers and you'll see we tweaked your cost numbers."

"Yeah, I saw your *tweak*. It's lipstick on a pig. It doesn't even begin to reflect our actual cost, and you know it. And you can't claim ignorance—you've seen my reports. Even your own people—Roxanne-- have validated my numbers."

"I'm glad you bring that up. Roxanne was tasked with that—validating your cost data—and she's in the process of doing that right now. According to her, she'll be done next week and has a meeting—what?—this Friday with you to wrap things up. You agreed to her audit, or am I mistaken? So, why would I jump the gun and start throwing unvalidated cost data into our reports before that. I wouldn't. It'd be irresponsible."

So that's going to be his play, I thought to myself—claim he was concerned about the cost data all along, which is why he ordered an audit, then pretend to have his hands tied because it isn't completed yet. I can continue to argue this point with him but it'd be like flogging Mister Ed, and it's not why I called him in the first place. I called him to light the fuse. I'm going to give him a chance to come clean or go up with the explosion.

"Here's how this is going to play out, Stu," I said in a stone-cold voice. "Either fix the numbers and restate our earnings or I'm taking this to the board."

"You wouldn't do that."

"You have between now and March to make it right. After that, I'm hanging you out to dry."

There was a pause, then I heard him chuckle as he responded, "Russ, Russ, Russ. Always the knight in shining armor… You're not gonna take this to the board and I'll tell you why: You'd cause a shit storm that would blow us all to hell. You'd make the board members complicit in the charade or fraud, or whatever you're calling it, and force their hand. And if we restate our earnings—what then? I'll tell you what then. Our stocks would bottom out, our investors would panic, and our suppliers would demand immediate payment on the millions of dollars of equipment—your damn equipment—that we bought on credit. We'd default and go into a financial tailspin. And *that's* what would happen—simply because you wanna play fuckin' boy scout."

I really had nothing to say to this nonsense and thought about hanging up, but instead I gave him back an icy silence.

"Nothing to say?" he asked sarcastically. "Didn't think so. You've always been risk averse, Russ. Even back at MFS—never willing to do whatever it takes to win. You think someone like Lance Armstrong wins the Tour de France by quoting the rule book? Think again. He sells out and does whatever it takes to win, which is something you can't understand… Did you see our stock price this morning? Based on our strong earnings report, it's up three points. *Three points!* That's what it's all about—right there—keeping our stock price up and staying relevant. Are you really gonna burn all that down?"

The Heights of Mountains

A quote from Churchill came to mind, and it was the only answer I could give him, "'A kind of palimpsest of jargon and affirmative with no breath, no theme and no facts.'"

"Oookay, whatever that means," he replied. "We can argue about this all day, Russ. But at the end of the day, it is what it is."

"I guess that depends on what your meaning of the word 'is' is," I quipped.

"Ha! Always the funny guy, Russ. Always the quick wit. One of these days it's going to be your undoing."

"I'm done, Stu. I'm warning you, and that's all I called to say."

"*Warning me?* I'm warning you."

"Right." And I hung up.

———

On Friday, I met Roxanne in the parking lot of the Palo Alto central office. She parked her red Acura Integra and got out carrying a notepad. As I recommended, she was dressed in blue jeans, blouse, and tennis shoes, but as it goes with truly beautiful women she looked just as devastating in blue jeans as she did in a Halston dress. I greeted her with a smile, a smile she didn't return, and I immediately picked up a vibe from her that I would call somber. I wondered if it was because of Stu. Part of my intent today was to draw her out—to find out what she had shared with Stu regarding my cost data—but after my heated call with him, he may have put her on her guard.

"I see you're set to go," I said cheerfully. "Blue jeans and tennies."

"I follow directions," she replied dully.

Her reply was devoid of any enthusiasm and I almost asked her if anything was wrong but instead launched into a quick summary of the little tour we were about to take. The Palo Alto central office, I told her, or Palo Alto 02 (oh-two) as they called it, was owned by SBC and housed the telephone switch and other equipment that provided telecommunications service to the surrounding area. As a Competitive Local Exchange Carrier, CrestPoint was a competitor of SBC, and we

• 283

leased space in their office and their phone lines to provide DSL service to businesses and households that were once their customers. In other words, they weren't going to welcome us with open arms.

Finance people tended to be rather uneducated on the interworkings of the telephone network, but she seemed to understand the basics and nodded at what I was saying without taking notes. I steered her towards the main entrance, handing her a badge which she pinned to her blouse, and we went through security and signed in without difficulty. Accessing a central office was a big deal, and my office had called ahead to clear our visit, obtain our badges, and alert our installation crew of our arrival time. Since I was an EVP of CrestPoint, my arrival would have been broadcast far and wide, and sure enough the West Coast President of Lucent Operations was there to greet us.

I knew Wayne Redland from previous encounters (we hired his company to install our equipment), and I introduced him to Roxanne, noticing with some amusement the effect she had on him (and on any man she met). We followed him through a maze of equipment rooms to the collocation area, adhering to a marked path which we were not allowed to deviate from. CLECs were confined to their own space and not allowed into SBC equipment areas, and like one of those TV comedy episodes where the sparring couple divided up the house, we stayed on our side and they stayed on theirs.

Roxanne's somberness was gone and replaced with an almost girlish delight at being in a strange environment. It was obvious she'd never been in a central office before, and I took the opportunity to point out some of the important features. COs (see-oohs) were environmentally controlled environments filled with racks and racks of blinking equipment, lined up in long rows, fluorescently lit, with overhead tiers of horizontal racking piled up with gray and black cables. There were no windows, and subdued lighting along with the blinking equipment which hummed constantly gave one the feeling of being inside a big submarine.

We arrived in the collocation area which consisted of a separate room subdivided by an array of metal cages. CrestPoint was not the only CLEC competing for local service and there were several cages owned by other companies. We had two cages, and in one of them a small crew of men was installing a new rack of equipment. Wayne led us over there and introduced us to three men, all in their twenties, who immediately became self-conscious at Roxanne's sparkling presence. One of them dropped his wrench, apologized, picked it up, and dropped it again.

"I'm going to give Roxanne a tutorial of our network," I said loudly, relieving the poor guy's embarrassment. "She's in our Finance Department, studying our installation costs, and she wants to get a firsthand look for herself. So, don't mind us. We'll try not to get in your way."

Taking my cue, Wayne politely excused himself while the three young men nodded, smiling awkwardly, trying to make eye contact with Roxanne before resuming their work. I had to laugh to myself at their distracted behavior. But who could blame them? In her tight jeans and filled-out blouse, with her red hair tied up in a ponytail exposing her elegant neckline, she was like a glowing angel appearing suddenly before captives in a dungeon.

I explained to her the different components of our network, detailing what was connected to what, and emphasizing all the cost elements that went into installing the equipment. Roxanne seemed genuinely interested and asked clarifying questions, occasionally scribbling in her notebook.

After a half hour, we came to a stop outside the collocation room in a darkened area of the aisleway. "And that, Miz Lamorte, is the end of my tour," I said with a smile. "Any more questions?"

"No... You make it simple to understand," she replied. It was said with affection and I probably blushed a little at the compliment.

"I hope you got an appreciation of all the cost elements involved. That pizza box-looking thing in the equipment rack—the DSLAM—is just one small piece of the overall cost."

"I see that."

"Good. I wish your boss did."

She didn't reply to that and instead frowned ever-so lightly. This piqued my curiosity. I'd intended to wait until lunch to bring up this cost issue with her, but her reaction to my comment about Stu caused me to leap ahead.

"We've spent a few hours together going over my cost data and it's pretty black and white. Wouldn't you say?" She nodded slightly without making eye contact. "Then explain to me why Stu doesn't use it in the company's financial reports."

"I suppose he's waiting on my audit results."

I looked hard at her. At this moment, she wasn't a woman whose beauty I found disarming but instead an employee of CrestPoint Communications who was giving me the run around. "Seriously, Roxanne," I said with an edge to my voice. "You've seen the data, you agree with the data, and you must have briefed him on it—so what's the excuse at this point? He's seen my reports over the last two years. They have the same cost data you've already corroborated. So, again, what's the excuse for not using it?"

She stared down at her tennis shoes like a scolded child, and I thought for a moment she might cop an attitude, but instead she looked up into my face. "I have no excuse," she answered with a tinge of anger in her voice. "Stu does what he wants... I've briefed him on numbers, told him they were accurate—the rest is up to him... I just do what I'm told."

I thought this last statement—*I just do what I'm told*—had a hint of regret in it but I might have been mistaken. In any case, this confirmed my suspicions regarding Stu, and now I felt a little sorry for her. She was just another pawn caught up in Stu's machinations.

"Fair enough," I said, smiling with my lips. "I'm looking forward to seeing your report next week," I added, trying to change the mood. "Whattaya say about lunch? I'm gettin' hungry."

She nodded at this and glanced up at the cable racking overhead. The large black cables that ran along the racks looked like giant anacondas. "Where do they go?" she asked.

"The cabling? To the main frame—thru there."

She glanced where I pointed, thru a narrow aisle of equipment racking, and stepped towards it saying, "I'd like to see it."

"It's out of bounds," I warned her, but it was too late. She was threading her way through the narrow aisle, leaving me to chase after her. This was the SBC part of the office, clearly marked and verboten to CLEC personnel like us, and I had no choice but to get her out of there. I quickly followed her and grabbed her arm before she made it to the end of the aisleway, pulling her away and telling her in a rapid, hushed tone that we had to go back.

"Oh, I'm sorry," she said, turning back. In the narrow aisleway, there was not enough room for the two of us, causing her to have to squeeze by me. She did this face to face, pressing her body up against mine, and in that moment I could feel and smell every luscious inch of her. She lingered just a second under my chin, looking up at me, then said, "I'm so sorry" again before extraditing herself and skipping swiftly away. I took a deep breath, taking in the aroma of lily and musk and her sultry effervescence, then slowly followed after her.

When I came back to the corridor that led to the building entrance, she was nowhere in sight. I went back into the collocation room but she was not there either, guessing now that she must have gone back to the main entrance. Very odd, I thought-- running off like that. Maybe she had to go to the restroom. When I returned to the main lobby, she wasn't there, only a security guard and Wayne Redland who stood by the doors.

"Did Roxanne come through here?" I asked Wayne.

"Yes, she did," he replied. "She looked a little upset about something. I think she was heading for her car."

"Really? Strange. We were just wrapping up our tour when she skipped out." I stood for a moment not sure what to do, probably looking a little bewildered. "Must be in the parking lot," I concluded, walking out the door as Wayne followed me. I found her car gone.

"Hmm, very strange," I said perplexed by the whole scene. "You said she looked upset?"

"Yeah... I hope one of my guys in there didn't say something to offend her. They can be kind'a Neanderthals."

"No. I don't think so. She was next to me one moment then gone the next. I hope she's all right."

"Maybe it was a family emergency."

"Maybe…" Whatever the reason, it was too late to worry about it now. I'd find out what happened once I got back to work. "Well, there goes my lunch date," I added, making light of the situation.

"I know I'm no Roxanne but let me buy you lunch."

Why not, I thought. Vendors and suppliers were always good for a free lunch, and it was better than eating alone. "Sounds good, Wayne. Where you wanna go?"

We agreed on a spot that was within walking distance, and we headed for it talking about the stock market and the Giants' prospect for a good year.

Chapter 3

I walked into Marty's office at 8:10 am with a fresh cup of coffee from Peet's Coffee kiosk, brewed just the way he liked it, and handed it to Marty.

"You're a mind-reader," he said thankfully.

He peeled off the lid and took a careful sip. He looked a little worse for wear, a bit ruffled around the edges, but that was to be expected from a man who'd been working on Netherlands time for the last two weeks. There was nine hours difference—8:10 am here and 5:10 pm there in Amsterdam where his contacts worked—and he had just wrapped up a marathon strategy meeting over the phone. Despite signs of weariness, he seemed rather pleased with the results of his call.

"How'd it go?" I asked.

"Hmm… good," he replied. Another sip of coffee and a chance to brag a little perked him up. "We'll start deployment in Germany and the Netherlands, then move into the UK and France by the end of the year. They can't wait to get going."

"When—March?"

"Yeah, just as soon as we get the I's dotted and the T's crossed and name a management team."

"Exciting stuff."

"Europe is a gold mine," he said briskly. "They're starving for Internet access."

He didn't need to convince me; we were all excited about this deal, one that would give us a global presence and put us back in the headlines. And despite his fatigue, Marty's exuberance at pulling this deal off couldn't be contained. He was like an inventor who couldn't wait to show off the new gadget he'd been tirelessly working on and tinkering with for months. But that was what Marty was so good at—innovation, creation, strategizing and deal-making. He was in his element.

"TelaPoint," he said with an impish grin. "How's it sound?"

He was giving me the name of the new joint venture, a combination of Teledata International and CrestPoint Communications. "I *like it!*" I replied with enthusiasm.

"Thought you would. And you'll like this even more—Martin Madrid, CEO of TelaPoint Communications."

I feigned surprise at this announcement since most everyone, including the board, assumed that Marty would declare himself CEO of this new company. And I was sure he would insist on continuing as CEO of CrestPoint. Without saying so, I knew his dream of being CEO of both companies was problematic at best. For one, CrestPoint's bylaws prohibited it, and unless he could get the board to pass a resolution to support it, his chances were slim at pulling it off. But I would never underestimate Marty's ability to pull off the unexpected.

"Couldn't think of a better candidate," I said. "It's like putting Tony Stewart behind the wheel of a Formula One."

He smiled at the compliment as he put his hand to his face to feel the two-day growth on his chin. "I need to go home. Take a shower, shave, get some sleep... Reconnect with the family."

"You've earned it," I replied, thinking immediately about his wife Hana and what she had to put up with when it came to Marty's full blast endeavors. She was either a remarkable woman or one of those wives of type-A personalities who suffer silently at the neglect and small cruelties. And in her case, there was his sexual ambiguity to contend with, which made me wonder—did she know, did she suspect? I'd not seen his little playmate, David, around lately, so perhaps some reckoning had taken place. But I wasn't interested or indiscreet enough to ask about it.

What I was interested in, what I'd come here for, besides to pat Marty on the back, was to give him a heads-up on my plan to expose Stu's accounting lies to the board. I felt a little guilty about bringing it up now given the high he was on, but it couldn't be helped.

"One thing… before you take off," I added, getting his attention. He looked at me, reading my expression, and raised an eyebrow in expectation. I promptly told him about my encounter with Stu and my ultimatum, leaving unsaid the fact that he, Marty, had promised to resolve this problem but didn't. He listened quietly, blinking sleepily, and waited until he was sure I was done before replying.

"I'm a bit confused," he said slowly. "Stu assured me he fixed your numbers. He even showed me the before and after… so, I'm a bit confused as to why this is still an issue."

"Simple, Marty. The cost factor is a hundred grand off—not a measly five grand, which is what he showed you. It's a sleight of hand."

"I see," replied Marty after a pause, rubbing his chin. "But you know, I mean… it's all about stock price with him—the aggressive accounting and all. It's like heroin. He's addicted to keeping our stock price up—no matter what—and I don't know if I can fault him for…it."

His voice faded off at the end as I saw him blush slightly. He knew about my son, and the heroin analogy was a faux pas that he instantly recognized.

"I suspect the board will fault him for it," I retorted, ignoring his gaffe. "Certainly the SEC."

"Sure, of course… You're right," he answered as though he'd just swallowed an over-sized pill. "What was it you told him—that he has until March to restate our earnings or you're taking it to the board? Then that's what he has to do. No doubt about it… And I'll talk to him to make sure that happens."

"Thanks, Marty," I replied, not believing for a moment that he'd move on this issue with any sense of urgency. All his energy and attention were dedicated to this TelePoint deal. That's why my next stop was Gwen. I congratulated him once again on his deal-making skills, cracked a joke about his ragged appearance, and asked him to pass my affections onto his wife and son before I took my leave.

—

"When you get the Neiman?" I asked her, nodding at the Leroy Neiman print on her office wall. It was a painting of Wilt Chamberlain and Bill Russell going at it. I knew Russell was her all-time favorite player.

"Last week," answered Gwen, swiveling slightly in her chair to face the painting. "Like it?"

"Hmm… It's definitely a Neiman."

"What? You're gonna tell me one Neiman looks just like another?"

"I'd never be so blunt about it, but now that you mention it."

"That's what some say about Pollock, that it's all just swirls and paint splatter."

"Don't know that I'd put Neiman and Pollock in the same class. It's like putting a Big Mac in the same class as a T-bone steak."

"I like a Big Mac on occasion—with a chocolate shake."

"I can't picture you in line at McDonalds paying for a Big Mac out of your Gucci bag."

"Well, picture it, bub, because it happens all the time," she said, laughing. We'd quickly fallen into our easy-going banter, and she swiveled back in her chair to confront me with a playful grin on her face. "Now, did you come here to criticize my artwork or to compliment me on my new sweater?"

I leaned back in my chair in mock attentiveness to examine her sweater. She was wearing a vintage angora sweater, tangerine-colored, that was loose-knit with long sleeves and a low turtleneck. "Hmm, very nice," I said in admiration. "Shows off your hazel-blue eyes."

"That's more like it… Now, to what do I owe this visit to? It's not to shoot the bull. You got something on your mind. I can tell by your face—and it's probably not good."

"You know me so well."

"Remember, I've seen you naked."

"Fortunately, you're the only board member who can say that."

"True," she responded, laughing loudly. "But then, if they'd seen what I've seen, you'd be chairman by now." I shared her laughter. There were times-- and now was a good example—when her repartee seemed to border on flirting. But perhaps it was just my imagination, because in an instant her demeanor shifted noticeably as she regarded me soberly. "Anyhow, what's on your mind?" she asked.

"Right," I said, quickly clearing my head… "It's about our friend Stu."

"*Stu.* What chicanery is he up to now?"

"He's been understating our cost data for years—despite my best efforts to the contrary."

"Why would he do that?"

"To keep our stock price up."

She tilted her head to the side, which was a tell-tale sign she wanted to know more. "We're talking installation costs here, right?" she asked. "The cost to build out the network—your department's cost? But I thought all that was audited and validated by Tollerson Accounting?"

"Tollerson's in Stu's back pocket."

She showed no surprise at this statement and merely studied me for a moment. Suddenly her assistant Shavonne popped her head in the door and said, "It's Atlantis on the line. They wanna talk."

"Ahh, give me a moment," she replied, appearing rather flustered. She hesitated briefly before regaining her footing. "No… tell them I'm in conference and I'll call 'em right back." She looked back at me and I could see that her mind was elsewhere.

"Do you need to get that?"

"No… It can wait," she replied absent-mindedly.

I wondered briefly why Atlantis was calling her and why it had put her head in the clouds. It was almost as if she'd just been told Elvis was on the line. Nevertheless, she was trying to stay on point with me, but before I could resume our conversation, my cell phone rang and I pulled it out of my pocket. "Sorry about that," I said, glancing at the screen. It was Janet, my ex-wife. Odd, I thought. She never called me at work. I quickly sent the call to voicemail and turned off the ringer.

"How 'bout you? Need to get that."

"No… They can leave a voicemail." I stuck the phone back in my pocket and turned my attention fully to Gwen. "As I was saying—" My phone vibrated loudly in my pocket and I dug it out, apologizing again to

Gwen. I saw it was from Jan—she'd called back immediately—and a sense of foreboding caused the back of my neck to tingle. "I guess I need to get this," I said, standing up and stepping away from her desk. I flipped open my phone and took the call.

"Jan. What's wrong?"

Her voice was breathless and filled with panic. *"Danny!"* she cried. "He's been mugged or attacked—I don't know. They took him to emergency. I'm on my way there now. Oh, Russ—he's hurt bad. I think he's hurt bad! They wouldn't say, but I know. I just know."

"Where'd they take him?"

"Where? Emergency. I'm on my way there now."

"No—what hospital?"

"Stanford."

"I'll meet you there." I closed my phone and turned back to Gwen. She was already out of her seat and walking towards me.

"What's wrong?" she asked.

"My son... He was attacked and they've taken him to the hospital."

She took my hand, looking me in the eyes. "You need to leave now," she said. "I'll alert your team that you have a family emergency, and we'll take care of everything here, but you need to go now."

I nodded and let her guide me out her office door, my mind reeling at this news. I was usually calm in the midst of a storm but the thought that my son was injured, maybe badly injured, threw me for a loop. All I knew was I had to get to the hospital—now.

Gwen held my hand and talked to me as we walked out into her reception area. I could hear her voice telling me not to worry, to call her when I found out anything, and to drive safe. I nodded, letting go of her hand, and hurried away as I heard her voice tell Shavonne to get Atlantis back on the line.

I broke every speed limit on my way to Stanford Hospital, making it in fifteen minutes, and found Jan waiting for me in the lobby of the emergency ward. The feeling of dread quickened inside me when I saw her face.

The Heights of Mountains

She came into my arms crying and I held her tight, scanning the waiting room to see a collection of worried, pensive faces, each wrapped up in their own personal dramas, some injured and in pain waiting to see a doctor.

"What do we know?" I asked her.

She stepped back, out of my arms, drying her eyes with a handkerchief, and quickly regained her composure. "Just that he's in ICU," she said. "I've only talked to a nurse. They brought him in unconscious and are working on him now… There's a police officer here, somewhere. He's the one who found Dan and called me after the paramedics came."

"Did they say what's wrong with him?"

"The nurse just said 'head injury'. That's all I know."

"Christ, that could mean anything," I replied, my mind spewing up a number of possibilities that I quickly swept away, trying my best to stay calm. "Come on, let's sit down," I urged Jan, guiding her to a couple empty seats, but as soon as we started to sit, she jumped back up.

"There's the officer that found Dan!" she cried.

I looked to see a police officer emerge through a set of automatic doors that led to the emergency room. He was brawny with a Marine Corp haircut and wore the uniform of a San Mateo County Sheriff. He saw us coming towards him and stepped away from the doors to greet us.

"Officer Addiego," said Jan quickly. "This is Danny's father—Russ. Did you find out anything? Are they still working on him?"

Officer Addiego nodded at me. "Yeah, they're still working on him," he answered matter-of-factly.

Jan began to pepper him with questions about Dan's condition, questions the officer couldn't possibly answer, but he listened to her patiently before responding that we'd have to wait for the doctor to tell us what was going on."

"They told us head injury," I said. "I understand you were first on the scene. What can you tell us?"

"He was unconscious when I found him," he replied impassively. "Blunt force trauma to the head." (*"Oh, God!"* exclaimed Jan in a whispered cry.) "From behind. Probably a pipe or a hammer. They took his cash but left his wallet and ID."

• 295

"A robbery then?" I asked.

"Yeah…" He glanced around the waiting room then moved us into an alcove out of earshot from those sitting nearby. "Is your son an addict?" he asked bluntly.

"No!" cried Jan in indignation. "Why do you ask that? Why are you saying that? Dan's a good boy."

Officer Addiego ignored Jan and looked straight at me. "Yes, he's an addict," I said. "A heroin addict—since he was nineteen. But he's been clean for over two years now. At least as far as I know."

"He's been clean two years nine months," cut in Jan, anger showing in her voice. "He's clean now."

"Why do you ask?" I said, knowing already where this was going. "What do you know?"

He regarded us a moment with an expression that told me he'd heard this all before, then proceeded to lay it out for us in his straightforward, cop-like way. Dan was found in a part of East Palo Alto known as the Heroin capital of the West. It was where you could buy heroin off the street and every addict knew it. The attack on Dan was either a drug buy gone bad or a setup, which was common practice. He'd also found drug paraphernalia in Dan's pockets.

"But I'm not going to do anything about that," he said. "The kid's got enough problems to deal with. Frankly, he's lucky to be alive."

"Thank you, Officer," I said gratefully. Jan stood next to me, wiping her eyes, silent.

He gave me a card with his contact info on it, expressing his sympathy for our misfortune, and cautioned us that Dan's attackers would probably never be caught—not unless the victim regained consciousness and could identify them. He didn't sound too hopeful. I thanked him, shook his hand, and he left.

"Let's sit down," I said, attempting to take Jan's hand, but she pulled it away. Other than our first hug, she had stood apart from me, even stepping away when I attempted to put a comforting arm around her. I could only imagine the heartbreak and disappointment she was dealing with at the moment, so I gave her space and went over and sat down by myself. After a moment she sat down next to me.

"I need to call my dad," I said, fishing out my cell phone. "How about your parents?"

"I need to call them… But I can't right now."

"I'll call them."

"Would you… Thank you."

I got up and went outside to make the calls. There was shock at my news and a ton of questions, and I told them what I knew and recommended they stay put. I would call them as soon as I learned anything new. I returned to my seat next to Jan and gave her a quick summary of my calls. (I'd also called my office to brief them on my situation, asking my admin to alert the management team that I would not be coming back into work for the next couple days.)

We sat in the waiting room in silence. I wanted to ask Jan about Dan's drug use, whether she'd noticed changes or anything suspicious about his behavior, but I let it go for now. The fact that he was using again came as a blow to her and I imagine she was dealing with her own guilt and self-recriminations at the moment. These were emotions I didn't share—the news of his drug use didn't surprise me—and what I felt now was simply worry and fear. Fear for my son's life. A fear, I'm sure, consuming her as well. So, we sat there in excruciating silence for nearly two hours before a doctor came out to talk to us.

He was dressed in surgical garb and stopped to talk to the admitting nurse who quickly pointed us out. We leaped up from our seats and hurried towards him, and as we approached, he put his hand up and said, "Your son is alive."

"Thank, God!"

In short order, he gave us a briefing on our son's condition, his voice both compassionate and clinical as he laid out the facts. It was touch and go when he arrived, but they'd been able to relieve the swelling in his brain and restore his vital signs. He removed some skull fragments from Dan's brain but he would require further surgery by a neurosurgeon to remove what was left. Currently, he was in a coma in ICU, but his heartbeat was strong and his blood pressure near normal.

"And if you ask me about brain damage at this point," he added. "We won't know anything until he regains full consciousness, which won't be for some time... I've seen miracle comebacks after injuries like this before, so let's just wait and see."

"Can we see him?" asked Jan.

"Of course. The nurse will see you in."

I shook his hand and thanked him, and we followed the nurse into ICU, leading us through a maze of partitioned rooms until we came to Dan. Nothing could prepare me for what I saw, and the shock of seeing my son laid out on a gurney-bed with tubes and wires hooked into him stopped me cold in my tracks. He wore a large head bandage and his facial features were soft and relaxed as he lay there in a coma. Jan quickly kneeled next to the bed and held his hand while I remained standing, subconsciously examining the monitors to make sure there were no blinking alarms or red lights the staff might be overlooking.

"Talk to him," said the nurse. "He can hear you... I'll be back in a bit to check on him."

Jan immediately started talking to him while I remained silent, standing at the foot of the bed, trying to process it all. I reached down and touched his foot through the white, coarse blanket, struggling to contain my emotions. How long I stood there, I don't know, but after a while I began to hear the words Jan was speaking into his ear.

"It's not your fault, baby... He did this to you... Oh, Danny, I love you so much. This is mom, I love you so much... You'll be okay. It's not your fault... He did this to you..."

"Who?" I asked her, coming out of my trance. "Who did this to him?"

She turned to look up at me, her face twisted with hate-filled rage. *"You!"* she cried viciously. *"You* did this!"

I wanted to ignore this accusation, blame it on a mother's shock—she was unbalanced and didn't know what she was saying—but instead a cold anger rose up inside me like an artic blast. "You're wrong," I said sharply. "He's here because of choices. His own bad choices."

She sprang up and came at me, hissing *"Choices!"* with her fists raised, but I caught her arms before she could hit me. She was screaming now, *"You! You did this! He was never good enough for you! Never! You drove him to this with your stupid, fucking perfection! He could never live up to you!"*

I held her arms tight, trying my best to hold back her fury, astonished at the complete and utter hatred she felt towards me. The nurse now reappeared and hugged Jan from behind trying to calm her down. Finally, the nurse was able to pull her back and Jan dropped her arms, her eyes still burning into me with malicious contempt. "Nobody's love is good enough for you!" she cried, her voice a choking whisper. "You treat us like shit—go around living your life like some fucking playboy, like James Bond, or something. Like some kind of fucking superstar. But you're not! You're just a thoughtless jerk who uses people!"

"You should leave," said the nurse over Jan's shoulder. "Give her time to calm down… Please."

I nodded and backed away, glancing once more at my son before I left, and walked out into the waiting room and through the doors into the night air. I breathed in deeply and checked my watch, noticing that my hand trembled slightly. It was after 7:00 pm.

Had that anger always been there, I wondered. Had she kept it bottled up all this time? How could she have shown friendship all these years, even made love to me, with all that hate inside her? I couldn't understand it.

I started walking in no particular direction and took out my cell phone. I called Jan's parents first to give them the news, suggesting they come to the hospital to help comfort their daughter. But it was really my father I wanted to talk to. I needed to hear a voice of reason, to talk to someone who's words would be true and straight. After giving him an update of Dan's condition, I told him about Jan's outburst in ICU, and he wisely advised me not to take it personally. I was a good father, he said, and her words were just the result of grief and shock. She was just striking out, and I'd been in the line of fire. That was all. Taking it personal was like getting upset over pouring rain. Once she came to her senses, she'd apologize. Sure, I said—of course he was right, and when I hung up, I felt a little better.

I walked on, lost in my thoughts, and when I finally looked around I realized I'd wandered onto the Stanford campus. Hoover Tower loomed in the distance. I was familiar with these surroundings; it was where Jan and I used to sit and talk when we were students here, and I found our old bench and sat down. It was a crisp night and the campus was nearly empty. The walkways were lit by the soft glow of incandescent lamp posts and an occasional student passed by, hurrying on, carrying a backpack, oblivious of my presence.

How did it come to this, I wondered to myself. My son nearly murdered, my ex-wife blaming me. It seems surreal, as though the laws of physics have been suspended, like I'm caught in the transmutations of a waking nightmare. I looked up at the sky, at the panorama of washed-out stars, and suddenly thought of Mark Kirkland. What would he do in my place? Pray and find solace in his God. But I have no God to pray to. I'm alone—by choice.

I felt empty inside, and if there was any kind of feeling left within me it was one of vacant, bottomless loneliness. It infested itself into the pit of my stomach, rawboned and famished, and would have sucked me into its dolorous vacuum had I let it. But I thought of Danny, my son, and with that thought came a bracing purpose. He needed me. The best doctors, the best care, my helping hand, my love—I'd be there for him. Whatever it took, I would fix this.

I stood up and took my bearings. The hospital was that way—south, back the way I came—and I changed direction and started walking.

Chapter 4

Ronnie hung up the phone and finished wiping down the kitchen counter. It was always pleasant talking to Cherry Chandrasekar; the woman was a wealth of information whose sympathetic ear she could pour her troubles into. Through her, Ronnie got caught up on executive politics, office gossip, and every so often, like today, got a tidbit of hush-hush information. Today's tidbit was the news that CrestPoint was in merger negotiations with one of the giant Telecoms. Cherry swore her to secrecy before revealing this classified info, and Ronnie crossed her heart and hoped to die if anyone heard it from her. What it could all mean, added Cherry in a conspiratorial whisper, was a lucrative buy-out of their eroding stock.

This information should have come from her husband. There was a time when he freely shared office politics and gossip with her, eagerly listening to her opinion on it and any advice she might have. But those days were gone. Now he viewed the passing on of rumor or gossip to be sinful, which included sharing personal information about the important people in their lives. It was Cherry who gave her the lowdown on Russ Chappel's son—not Mark, who's very job had been greatly impacted by the tragedy. With Russ' leave of absence, Mark was thrust into the role of acting EVP, a tremendous increase in responsibility, and all he would tell her was it was the result of Russ' son being seriously injured in an accident. It was from Cherry she learned that his son was attacked during a drug deal, had almost died, and would probably be a mental vegetable the rest of his life.

This news deeply saddened her but she was leery about trying to pump any more details out of Mark. She wanted to call Russ and pass on her condolences but thought better of it and instead sent a get-well card to the hospital signed *The Kirklands*. As for updates on the young man's condition and the extent of Russ' leave of absence, she had to rely on Cherry. And the great irony of Russ' tragedy, she reflected with a bit of morbid humor, was the positive effect it was having on Mark.

Yes, what a double-edged sword it all turned out to be, she mused, still wiping down the counter, unconsciously now, as she thought back over it. Out of Russ's tragedy had come some good, at least for her and her husband. It was almost as if God finally answered her prayers. There was Mark sixteen months ago, then there was Mark now. Sixteen months ago, right after his born-again experience, life was intolerable. It was like living with a madman who heard voices, saw visions, demanding that they all share in his madness together. Their life was turned upside down; by devoting his life to Christ above all else, he alienated family, friends, and put their marriage on the rocks. But now, after stepping into Russ' shoes, he was—and she wasn't going to use the word "normal"—but he was less fervent, more reasonable than before. He'd regained some of his old balance. Gone was the beard, the flannel shirt, the work boots; replaced by a shirt and tie, a sports coat, and a somber determination to fill in for Russ to the best of his abilities. Nearly gone as well were the evening prayer meetings in their living room, though he tried at first, finally surrendering to the harsh reality that there was no longer enough time in the day to keep it up. And that caused friction with his church (thankfully, she thought). Through snippets of conversation with his deacon and church elders, she picked up that they were troubled by his absence, by his distraction from church matters, and were pressuring him to come back into the fold.

And that was the brutal irony of it, she concluded, finally putting her washcloth away. All that she'd done before this to bring him back—the tearful pleas, the implied threats of divorce, the enlisting of friends to her side—had been useless. It had taken a savage blow to a young man's head to change her life back to the better.

Her daughter suddenly appeared. She was still in her robe, which she wore like sackcloth and ashes, and she shuffled softly to the refrigerator, head down, and opened the door to peer inside. After a moment of contemplation, she reached inside and pulled out a can of soda, inspecting it first before re-closing the refrigerator door and shuffling away. Ronnie heard the soda can pop open as her daughter neared the foot of the stairs.

"Finish your homework?" Ronnie asked her.

Lacy started up the stairs, ignoring her.

"*Did you* finish your homework?" she asked again, raising her voice.

Without stopping, her daughter gave her a barely audible "yes" and continued her journey up the stairs and back into her room.

Ronnie sighed. There was a quote that came to her mind, one she'd heard in church that stuck in her head and went something like *"Correct your children, and they will give you peace."* (Funny how she found herself quoting the Bible these days.) But she hoped it was true. Lacy had been suspended three days from school after getting caught smoking marijuana on school grounds. She was grounded two weeks on top of that, which meant no going out, no friends over, no computer, and no talking on the phone. The quadruple whammy.

Lacy, now seventeen, had been acting up for over a year, and to Ronnie it felt at times as though they were at constant war with one another (which was the price you paid for being a parent rather than their friend). They argued about everything—clothes, boyfriends, attitude—and over the last year, Lacy had been caught skipping school, driving without a license, and sneaking out after bedtime. And now it was marijuana. Drugs. It was all eerily similar to my own teenage-hood, she thought to herself, only I didn't have a mother willing to get her hands dirty and battle it out. As a result, I got pregnant at seventeen—Lacy's age—and became an embarrassment to my family.

Ronnie wasn't going to let that happen to her daughter. She wasn't naïve enough to think Lacy wasn't going to have sex at seventeen, so she saw to it that her daughter got a prescription of birth control pills. That was just facing reality; in today's world with half-naked divas shaking their booty on MTV, pop stars groping themselves, and every teenage-orientated TV show or movie calculated to stimulate their hormones, it was a fool of a mother who tried to hold back the tide. If your child insisted on jumping out of an airplane, then you made damn sure they wore a parachute. It was just good common sense, she figured.

Yet, there was one thing that preyed on her mind and kept her up at night worrying. Despite taking the level-headed precaution of getting her on the pill (which Mark had no clue about and would go Old Testament on them if he ever found out), she had a growing dread inside her that Lacy would do something drastic. The pattern pointed in that direction. Teenagers could get overwrought, *especially* teenage girls, and drive themselves to acts of ecstatic desperation. She didn't think attempted suicide was in Lacy's DNA, not for a girl of seventeen who still squealed in delight upon getting an MP3 player for her birthday. And cutting herself (which she'd read about and heard other mothers talk about)—well, she hadn't seen any evidence of that yet. No, what worried her, what acted like an acid on her peace of mind, was the possibility that Lacy would run away—that all this acting out, fighting with her mom, fanatic of a father, groundings and suspensions would accumulate in her head like so much intolerable junk causing her to slip out the back door one night and run off with one of her delinquent boyfriends. And then what? Off to a big city where she'd slip into prostitution and drug abuse, maybe even becoming easy prey to some serial killer. Never to be seen again? God, help me, she said to herself.

She wasn't going to let it happen. She didn't let her husband turn them all into Moonies and she wasn't going to let her daughter run off and ruin her life, even if she had to hire a private detective to spy on her. And she decided one more thing—now that Mark was regaining some of his perspective, it was time for him to step up. Father and daughter had always been close, and Daddy's little girl used to curl up in his lap, play games with him, and run to him for solace or advice quicker than she would to Mom. But that all changed when the modern teenager, with her punk rock music and torn jeans, ran head-on into the Apostle

Mark with his sermons and Bible quotes. Lacy reacted to her father's religious conversion as though it was an act of supreme idiocy, finding it deeply embarrassing and intolerable in the same way she found her cousin Teddy embarrassing—the one with Down's Syndrome, who always talked too loudly and said the wrong things and made a mess.

Maybe that was being too harsh, thought Ronnie, but embarrassment was still the right word. Lacy was embarrassed of her father, and that embarrassment was behind some of her daughter's rebellious behavior (she was sure of it). It was time for Mark to bridge the gap—without preaching, without throwing out guilt trips—it was time for Mark to save his little girl. She'd already planted the seed with him, suggesting he have "a talk" with his daughter, and now Lacy's recent suspension and grounding added pressure on him to take action.

And she wanted it to happen tonight.

Mark sat at the kitchen table eating a late dinner. Ronnie and the kids had already eaten, and he sat across from Ronnie, who was sipping on a glass of white wine, as he slowly ate the spaghetti and meatballs she'd warmed up for him. The kids were up in their room and it was quiet in the kitchen except for the hum of the refrigerator.

"Your church called," she said, interrupting the quiet.

He nodded while chewing his food. She always said it that way, he thought—"your church"—because she didn't consider it her church. *Her* church was St Joseph; *his* church was Calvary Memorial. Despite his efforts to explain to her the problems with the Catholic Church and the beauty of Calvary Memorial (a nondenominational, self-governing, Christian community), and bring her into the fold along with the kids, she balked, making it abundantly clear that she found "his church" too rigid and fundamentalist. It was just one of many divisions between them.

"They leave a message?" he asked after swallowing his food.

"Just to call back. A Gordon Stone."

"Okay," he replied, conjuring up the somber face of Gordon Stone. He was a deacon, chosen by elders to look after the flock, and Mark was sure he was in for a lecture when he called him back. But it couldn't be helped. He loved his church and considered himself a disciple in Christ, but they were pressuring him to choose between his commitment to his job or his devotion to the church. And they didn't even see it that way, he reflected. They didn't see it as a commitment to his job, as his moral obligation to fill in for Russ Chappel in his time of need. Instead, they saw it as spiritual lapse. He was wrapping himself up in the material world and forsaking his church (*He that trusteth in his riches shall fall: but the righteous shall flourish as a branch*), even accusing him of trying to serve two masters (*Ye cannot serve God and mammon*). He disagreed with them, pointing out that no matter what he did, in word or deed, he did in the name of his Lord Jesus Christ, adding that when he worked long and hard, it was for Him and not for men. Deacon Stone was sure to ask him if he was going to teach Sunday School this weekend, and the answer was going to be 'no' (he had too much work to catch up on before Russ returned on Monday), and the Deacon was not going to be happy about that either. Which reminded him…

"Russ is coming back Monday," he told her.

"Really? Wow, that's good news," she replied as a slew of thoughts raced through her head, immediately wondering whether he would regrow his beard, start wearing flannel shirts and work boots again, or whether he'd maintain the balance he seemed to have regained over the last couple months? Her intuition told her that the beard and flannel shirts, along with all the encumbrances that came with them, were gone for good. But only time would tell. "How's his son doing?"

"Better… He's awake and alert, going to start physical therapy."

"That's great to hear." She already knew all this from Cherry, but she pretended otherwise and asked him a few more questions about it. Was Russ coming back full time? Would Mark still need to back him up? What about his son's long rehab process? Mark told her he wasn't sure and that he'd know more next Monday. The fact that he didn't seem too worried about it one way or another didn't surprise her, but she saw an opportunity here to praise him for his sacrifice and, at the same time, prep him emotionally for his talk with Lacy.

"Well, whatever happens," she said tenderly, "you've done a wonderful job filling in for him, and I hope they appreciate your sacrifice…"

Mark listened to her go on about his 'sacrifice', not interrupting her as he would have before by quoting scripture on the real meaning of 'sacrifice', and instead let her warm wave of compliments flow over him. Actually, he hadn't heard her talk like this to him in a while and he found it rather pleasing. But he also knew there was probably a motive behind it, undoubtedly having to do with their daughter. She was getting him in a good mood for the 'talk'. But it wasn't necessary. He'd thought about the talk with his daughter the whole drive home, about her sinfulness and how best to open her mind to the infinite forgiveness of Jesus Christ and how to follow His example. But he needed to be wary. Her heart was hardened against Christ, so he needed to find the right approach—not hip or cool, which she would see right through—but just *honest.*

When Ronnie finished her praise, he replied, "Thank you, dear." It was as simple as that, no more no less, but she saw the warmth in his eyes as he said it. She talked awhile longer about household matters, Brandon's upcoming wrestling tournament, her parents' anniversary, while he sat and listened, sipping his glass of iced tea, nodding occasionally, commenting when needed, until she finally looked up at the clock and said, "You should probably go up to her now, before it gets too late."

"I know," he answered, pushing back his chair.

There was so much she wanted to say to him right now—be nice, be gentle, don't condemn—but she kept her tongue. His past attempts at talking to Lacy did not go well; he preached and she shut down. It was why mom had taken over dealing with Lacy—confronting her rebellion, meting out discipline—and not dad. But now it was time for him to step up, and she had found a quote from the Bible for just this moment and memorized it. She hoped it would speak to him and put him in the right frame of mind.

"Suffer the little children to come unto me, and forbid them not, for of such is the kingdom of God," she recited while he stood up and looked at her in surprise. "Did I get that right?" she asked.

"Yes, it was perfect," he replied with a smile. He noted that she used the King James Version of the Bible instead of his New International Version, but nevertheless, it was well-timed. And of course, it was from the Gospel of Mark. She was clever that way. He came around the table and kissed her on the forehead before starting up the stairs.

He said a prayer to himself as he ascended the stairs, asking the Holy Spirit to imbue him with purpose and to guide his words. He was feeling a little tense, almost as if he was about to make a presentation to a room full of angry shareholders, so he stopped off in Brandon's room first to say hi and talk about school, hoping the detour would calm his nerves. After a short time, he said goodnight to his son and stepped down the hall to his daughter's room.

"Lacy," he said, knocking gently on her door. "It's Dad."

There was no answer, so he knocked again and slowly opened her door. "Lacy, it's me" he announced softly. She was sitting on her bed reading a magazine, head down, and after a moment reluctantly looked up at him.

"I'm in no mood for a sermon," she responded acidly.

"No… no sermons. I just came to talk."

"You mean preach," she replied, dropping her magazine and shooting him a menacing scowl. "You came here to preach to me."

"No, I didn't. But judge for yourself." He sat down in the chair by her desk and leaned back, scanning the walls of her room. If there was any better evidence of his daughter's state of mind, it was on display right here. The four walls of her bedroom were plastered with posters and photos, most showing emaciated, drugged-up punk rockers in torn black clothing, screaming defiantly into a microphone on some dingy stage in front of a crowd of sweaty, half-crazed teenagers. The bands had names like Bad Religion, Rancid, and Sublime, and the posters featured song quotes or mottos that ran from 'Tear it all down!' to

'Oh, yeah, I wanna riot!' The only exception to this onslaught was an 8x10 photo of John Travolta from the movie *Grease* (her favorite movie as a kid) that still hung above her headboard. The fact that this one photo had somehow survived this godless onslaught made him smile to himself.

"Why don't you go talk to Mom?" she asked sarcastically. "If you want to fix something, go fix *that*."

"Why d'ya say that? Mom and I are fine."

Lacy rolled her eyes to show she knew better. *"Really.* That's not what I see and hear. Mom's unhappy, or haven't you noticed."

If Mom is unhappy, he thought to himself, it's because her daughter is acting like a spoiled brat, like some pagan idolator. But he kept this thought to himself. He'd gotten her to start talking without much effort (probably because she was a little stir-crazy), so he followed her lead. "Why do you say she's unhappy?"

"Well, *maybe* it's because she doesn't think you love her anymore. *Maybe* it's because she thinks you love *Jesus* more than her. *Maybe* we *all* think that."

He studied her for a moment, reading the sarcasm and anger that flared from her face like a lit-up billboard. "It's two different kinds of love," he said. "But I love your mother—I love all of you—as deeply and completely as I always have. Maybe even more."

These words seemed to catch her off guard and she relaxed her shoulders noticeably. "Well, you should tell her that," she said simply.

"I will."

Her lips came together momentarily in a smile that quickly disappeared, but he thought he saw in it a note of softening—that the shield wall she'd placed herself behind the moment he walked in the room had dropped ever so slightly. He knew his next question would probably raise it again.

"Why are you smoking dope?"

"*Don't* tell me you and Mom never smoked—and no one calls it 'dope' anymore, Dad. It's called a blunt, or dank, or just weed. But don't tell me you never smoked it as a teenager."

"I won't... But I was never dumb enough to get caught."

She briefly snickered at that, her eyes flashing with a hint of mirth. "I *guess* I'm not as *smart* as you—but you should be happy it's just weed. There's a lot worse stuff goin' round. Hella worse. Maybe not so much at my school, but over at San Mateo High it's like heroin and ecstasy and gangs and shit. It's a mess. You should count your lucky stars or thank Jesus it's just weed I'm smoking."

"Then I'm thankful."

She eyed him suddenly with an expression—part surprise, part suspicion—that reminded him of Ronnie. It was obvious she wasn't expecting that response from him and needed a minute to process it. Without thinking about it, she brushed her blonde hair away from her face in another gesture that reminded him of her mother.

"That's just your religion talking," she said. "Turn the other cheek and all that. See only the good in people. It's a gyp. Don't you think religion's just another drug? That's what Freud said—that it's the opiate of the people."

Freud, he sighed to himself. Pretty quick she'd be quoting Nietzsche and Karl Marx. All the old cliches. But he was bound and determined not to provoke her by attacking her adolescent philosophies. It was better to swim alongside her, gently nudging her to shore.

"Some people believe that," he responded.

"A lot of people, Dad. *Lots* of people think that. They think it's just another drug. That organized religion is a crutch."

"Well, you're right there, dear. It is a crutch. Didn't you know that we're all cripples—me, you, mom—we're all spiritual cripples. And without religion we'd stay that way our whole lives. Religion—God— lifts us up and lets us walk again."

"Hmm, I thought you'd say something like that, but if God is all good and powerful then why do bad things happen? I mean, people do horrible things to each other, you know?"

"I know," he replied, wanting to say more. He wanted to tell her that a person whose inner life is grounded in Christ and set in place is not troubled by the strange and twisted things that people do. But he left it at that.

"It's like that plane that crashed into the ocean a couple months ago," she continued, her eyes boring into him. "All those people, eighty-eight of them, dead and gone. What was their sin? Isn't that proof enough God doesn't exist?"

"I always find it interesting how people use tragedy to prove God doesn't exist," he said. "When good stuff happens—and it happens every moment of the day—they never say, 'See, God must exist.' When a child is embraced by his mother, when laughter erupts from another room, when—I don't know—when a young woman takes the right step instead of the wrong step and it saves her life, nobody ever says, '*See!* God must exist.' Instead, it's always the other way around... Am I preaching? I promised not to preach."

"No... Okay... But let me ask you a question. Just one question. Because it's really something I'd like to know."

"Shoot."

"Why do you have to be so wigged out about it? I mean, people can believe in God and go to church, like Mom and Brandon, but aren't so *extreme* about it. Why do you have to go overboard about it and preach all the time and try to convert people. It's a buzz kill."

He knew the answer to that—that a moderated faith was the same as no faith at all—but he doubted she'd understand that. Instead, he saw a better way to go.

"What if you found an elixir—no, a drug that made everyone happy?" he said, then cut her off quickly as she moved to interrupt him. "Now let me finish. Humor me for a minute... What if, after years of searching, you discovered a drug that made people happy, that filled them up when they were feeling empty, and gave their lives meaning—gave them, every day and every moment, a blissful feeling of transcendence that was better than what any other drug in the world could give them? Let's say this drug is, yes, addictive but has no bad side effects other than it makes you love fuller, allows you to forgive and forget, and makes you want to live in peace with your fellow man. Now, if you owned this drug, let's say an unlimited supply of it, wouldn't you want to give it to everyone—to your loved ones, to strangers, to everyone in the world?"

"What's the street value?"

"It's free."

She sniffed a short laugh and looked at him ironically. "Kay, Dad. I get it. I'd want to give it away to everybody."

"But what if people got mad at you for trying to give it away, or tried to stop you? What would you do then?"

"No, no—I get it. I'd ignore them and keep giving it away... But maybe there's some people who don't want it. You can't force it on them."

"No, you can't. You can't force it on people."

"But that's what you try to do sometimes. Mom would say it, too. It just feels like you're trying to force it on us."

"I can see that, and I'm sorry."

He witnessed her reaction to his apology, and it was as if the two words, *I'm sorry*, were the magic words that opened the vault to her heart. She beamed a smile at him, a child-like smile of triumph that he hadn't seen in years. He saw the look of vindication in her eyes and the surge of forgiveness that followed after it. The shield wall had fallen, completely—he felt it—and their 'talk' suddenly shifted into a daddy-daughter playfulness that filled his heart with joy. They talked about her school, his work, their love of music, and he kidded her about her enduring crush on Danny Zuko while she kidded him about his old man flannel shirts. He lost track of time and when he finally got up to leave, he bent over and kissed her on the forehead, saying "Nite, Lacy-loo" which was his old nickname for her.

"Nite, Daddy."

She hadn't called him Daddy in quite some time and the sound of it, so full of the little girl he loved and cherished, caught him off guard and he slipped quickly out the door before she could see the tears well up in his eyes.

Outside in the hallway, he took a moment to gather himself, breathing in deeply to steady his emotions. He walked unconsciously into the master bedroom, found himself alone there, then walked into the bathroom and turned on the shower and began undressing.

Ronnie was in her usual spot on the couch, curled up with the dog watching Jay Leno's monologue, when she heard the shower turn on upstairs. The sound of the pipes told her it was in their bedroom, which meant that Mark had finished his talk and was getting ready to take a shower. She turned off the TV and quickly got up, telling her dog "bed" which he immediately obeyed by going over and laying down on his bed by the fireplace. Ronnie turned off the lights and headed upstairs anxious to find out how father and daughter had made out together. He was in her room a long time, which was a good sign, but given Lacy's rebelliousness she wasn't holding out much hope.

She passed Brandon's door and went straight to Lacy's where she could see the light still on. She paused there, half-expecting another duel with her daughter's teenage attitude, before knocking softly and opening the door. Lacy lay reclining against her headboard reading a schoolbook, and she glanced up with a calm, collected expression that immediately reminded Ronnie of Mark.

"Gettin' late," she said.

"I know. Soon as I finish this chapter I'm going to bed."

"Okay," replied Ronnie, pleased by the soft tone of her daughter's voice. She wanted more than anything to ask her about her talk with her dad, but something held her back, some odd inflection in the back of her mind that told her not to disrupt this fragile peace with a bunch of questions.

"Nite, honey."

"Nite, Mom... Love you."

That last part came as Ronnie was closing the door and it hit her like a warm, gushing arrow to her heart. There was no sarcasm in the words, no edge or deceit, only truth and a genuine tenderness, and she responded in a way only a mom could respond.

"I love you, too, honey... More than anything... Goodnight, baby."

She gently closed the door, basking in her daughter's smile, and started for the master bedroom, her thoughts filled with only one thing now, one over-powering image—her husband Mark. It was all like a little miracle—this change in Lacy's attitude—and maybe it was temporary, but at least for now it was very real. Because of Mark. Something he said or did made an impact… My husband.

She sat down on their bed, listening to the shower, and thought about Mark. The men in her life came in all shapes and sizes. Her father, aloof and business-like. Boyfriends, each trying to figure out a way to get in her pants. Scott, the boyfriend who nearly raped her, got her pregnant, then went off to other conquests. Father Jeff, her priest, who listened and gave out penance and judged her with his eyes. And her psychiatrist, the one who counseled her about Mark's conversion, telling her it was an emotional malady that needed treatment, suggesting divorce as an alternative and then making a pass at her. Only Mark stood apart. Mark with gentleness and strength. A man who kept his promises and could be trusted. A man who loved God with a great passion, who loved his family with a great passion, and never wavered. This was a good man.

He stood in the shower and let the warm water rain down on his face. A long day, he thought to himself. After this week, Russ returns and I can go back to something resembling normal hours. I hope and pray his son has turned the corner. Children are the joy and heartache of our lives. My own daughter—so mixed up, so turned around. But I think our talk went well, and maybe I made an impact. Yes, I think I did. I mean, she was contrite and trying to get out of the doghouse, so maybe she was playing me, but it felt true. Yes, it was true, and thank you, Jesus, for helping me find the right words to talk to her.

The door to the bathroom opened up and he glanced through the fogged-up shower door to see his wife enter and go to the toilet. She was getting ready for bed but before that she would want to hear all about his talk with Lacy. He'd tell her in bed, he decided, turning his face back to the warm spray, letting his mind empty of all worry. Suddenly, the shower door opened and he felt Ronnie enter the shower and come up behind him naked and silky. She raised up on tip-toes and whispered in his ear, "I love you," then reached around and grabbed his manhood. He was already hard.

The Heights of Mountains

When he awoke, he checked the clock to see it was 3:10 in the morning, then got up and put on a pair of underwear. The room was placid with the dark stillness of nighttime, and he kneeled down to say his nightly prayer but paused first to admire his wife who lay on the bed with her back to him. The sheet was nearly pulled off her, revealing in the tender darkness the soft rise of her shoulder, the sensuous line of her back, and the curve of her hip that led down along her shade-smooth legs. Her undulations reminded him of a sleek mountain range. He watched her breathe for a moment, easy and even, and thought about how much he loved her—then suddenly remembered that he'd forgotten to call back Deacon Stone. It was too late now.

He closed his eyes, feeling a need to do penance, and prayed deeply for forgiveness, his mind quickly finding James 5:16 that spoke to the power of confession and healing. He finished his prayer, as he did every night, asking the Lord to bless his family, naming each one in turn, until he was done and whispered "Amen." He slipped into bed, pulling the sheet back up over his wife's shoulder, snuggled his shoulder into the warmth of her back, and quickly fell asleep.

Early in the morning, at about five minutes before his alarm went off, he had a dream. It was only a snippet, brief but vivid, but he would remember it all day long.

He's in his backyard garden and it's raining, and he has his face turned upwards letting the warm rain shower down on his face. He's content to stand there and let this go on forever, but he hears sounds from the house and glances over to see Ronnie and the kids (who are little, maybe five or six) calling for him to come in out of the rain. But he can't, he doesn't want to, and he calls for them to come out and join him—the rain is for all of us, he says—but they stay put and keep calling for him to come in. He takes a step closer to the house, thinking that will please them, but he remains in the rain.

The alarm went off at exactly 6:00 am, and Mark swung his legs out of bed. It was time to get ready for work.

Chapter 5

It was Monday, March 13, and in two days Marty was scheduled to meet with his Board of Directors to finalize the TelaPoint deal. The press release would go out the next morning with operations starting almost immediately. Marty didn't anticipate any issues. Yes, there'd been a problem with funding that held up the deal for over a month—both Teladata and CrestPoint were to put up $50 million for the joint venture—but Marty had finally secured their end of the funding after some initial setbacks. All was a go. He would be named CEO of the new company and would guide both companies to new heights.

With his door closed, Marty paced his office thinking hard about what was and what was going to be. He was nearly to the top of the mountain and only a major slip-up could stop him from reaching it. In three days, the press release would go out on the TelaPoint deal and he would become a household name; every major news outlet would cover it, from Fox, CNN, ABC World News Now, to BBC News at Ten, CNBC, and The Wall Street Journal. Trade magazines would clamor for exclusives; already The Industry Standard was putting a story together about him entitled 'The King of DSL'. He was looking forward to the whirlwind of interviews that would follow.

His political consultant was confident that the publicity coming out of this, combined with the track record he'd already accumulated—founder and CEO of CrestPoint Communications, self-made millionaire, recognized Internet guru, known philanthropist (through high-profile charities), as well being young, hip and handsome—that all this would give him the star power he needed to mount a run for Governor of California. 2002 was probably out of the question since the incumbent governor, Gray

Davis, was highly popular and would easily be re-elected, and he wasn't going to run against him as a republican. He'd already declared himself a democrat, so that left 2006 and six years for him to hone his image and build up his connections within the state's democratic party. There was serious discussion about him running for State Controller in '02. It would give him practical government experience and position him nicely for a run at governor in '06, but he was still undecided about this strategy.

He was learning fast that image is everything, not that he'd ever doubted it. But the prospect of a successful political career, and the exploits of Bill Clinton, had driven home the lesson that protecting your image, becoming bullet-proof, was all that mattered. It was all about minimizing risks and vulnerabilities and vaporizing anything that could come back to haunt you. Already he had removed David from his life, sending him off to a lucrative IT job over at Apple with strict instructions to move on with his life. Meanwhile, he was pouring new energy into his marriage, bolstering the home front where Hana had been growing suspicious of his extra-curricular activities. The image of a solid family man was key to any political career.

It was all coming together, he reflected, as he paused to look out his office window. It was the road less traveled, a road taken only by the gifted and talented—by the ambitious—and he was well along that road now. And this thought brought to mind some Grateful Dead lyrics that held a special meaning to him. It was about a road, *no simple highway, between the dawn and the dark of night, and if you go no one may follow, that path is for your steps alone.*

He smiled to himself at the lyrics, then quickly lost the mood as another thought popped into his head. There was only one thing that might derail his plans. Gwen Novak. He'd heard the rumors she was courting Atlantis about a merger deal. But without board approval, without CEO—his approval—this courtship was going nowhere. Still, she might pose a problem, even attenuate his message. He was a light beam of hope pulsing through a fiber optic cable, traveling at the speed of light, delivering the goods at the other end. But she might be able to bend the cable and attenuate the flow, maybe even dilute his message. It was up to him to keep the medium straight and true. Once he gaveled the board into session, he'd take control of the narrative and deliver the goods—an international footprint with unlimited growth potential, with Martin Madrid at the helm and no need of corporate takeovers or titan buyouts to insure their bright future. That would put the kibosh on Ms. Novak.

He was feeling confident, maybe even a little cocky, and he smiled to himself at the thought of Gwen's fall from grace. It was payback time. The Board of Directors was prepped and ready; he'd met with each member and secured their vote for CEO of TelaPoint. He had the vision, he had the votes, and when it came to writing CrestPoint's success story, he was about to turn Gwen into a footnote.

Little did he know she was a rockslide coming in his direction.

———

"How's Dan?" she asked.

Gwen welcomed Russ back with a big hug and with the only question that mattered at the moment: How was his son doing? Of course, she already knew the answer; she'd kept in touch with Russ during his ordeal, getting regular updates on his son's progress, and monitoring (for herself) Russ' mental and emotional state. On that point, she was pleased to see that he maintained his usual aplomb, keeping that well-mannered grace and coolness of mind she so admired. But that didn't surprise her; Russ was not the kind of man to fall apart in a crisis.

"He's making progress," he replied, sitting down in the chair that Gwen offered him. She chose a more informal spot to sit, away from her desk, over by the windows where she kept a divan and upholstered chair. She sat down on the divan and studied him as he took his seat. He looked a bit harried around the edges (which was probably something only she would have noticed), but for the most part—at least the front he presented—he appeared to be his old dapper self.

"You know about his surgery," he continued. "They removed the last fragments and part of his skull, but he's out of the induced coma and the swelling on his brain has gone down. He has his own room now where he's monitored twenty-four hours, wears a catheter, but he recognizes us and smiles."

"This is good news."

"Yes," he agreed. There was more to tell, he thought—the brain damage, the loss of speech and motor skills, the likelihood of a lifetime spent in a wheelchair with the mind of a child—but he was in no mood to get into all that. "Some of his movement has returned," he offered, "but it'll take time. Lots of physical therapy ahead… I want to thank you for your support—everyone's support, in fact. It's been marvelous."

"It's what we do," she replied, smiling. "Mr. Kirkland has done a fine job filling in for you. Hasn't tried to convert me once."

Russ knew this last part was a joke and he managed to smile at it. "Yes," he said. "That's good to hear. He's been keeping me posted. Now that I'm back, he can breathe a sigh of relief. I know working for you is no picnic."

She laughed at this, a little too loudly he thought, but she was trying to normalize his return and he appreciated that. It was one of the things he wanted to talk to her about—'his return'—and just what, exactly, it meant. He needed to be back, but he also needed to be with his son, and that meant a balance needed to be struck. Dan was through the worst—he was alive, he was conscious—but the arduous task of recuperation (a mountain in itself) was just beginning and Russ planned to be there every step of the way. That meant no more than forty-hour weeks with the flexibility to plan his schedule around his son's physical therapy. But when he was here—and he would assure Gwen and the entire management team of this—he would be focused and on top of his game.

And as if she was reading his mind, she said, "Well, it's just good to have you back! It's been a bore around here without you… Which begs the question—and forgive me for being blunt, but you know me—how far back are you? Are you back in the starting five, or are you gonna be the sixth man off the bench? Whatever role you want to play, we can accommodate it."

"I appreciate that, Gwen… You're the best," he replied warmly. There was real, deep affection in his voice, she could feel it, and she hadn't heard him speak to her with that depth of emotion for a very long time. It was funny, but it made her happy, and she probably showed it in her eyes as she listened to him lay out his situation. After he was done, she assured him that the hours he was willing to commit and the flexibility he needed in his schedule were both things they could easily accommodate.

Russ dropped his head and there was a moment of awkward silence, which Gwen quickly filled. "There's a board meeting tomorrow, 9:00 am," she said, stepping back into her role of President of CrestPoint Communications. "Do you plan to be there?"

"Yes."

"Good. There's a number of things going on—I'm not sure what you know—but I should brief you on it. Marty will wrap up the TelaPoint deal and be voted CEO."

"As expected."

"What you may not know is that he will be removed as CEO of CrestPoint and I will take his place. That will allow me to complete a merger deal with Atlantis, which will bail out our stock and make us whole again." She stopped there to study his reaction. Not surprisingly, he appeared a little fazed by the news, but that was to be expected. She'd purposely left him till last in her little conspiracy for two reasons: one, because of his family tragedy and, two, because he and Marty were buddies, co-founders of the company, and he was a man who prized loyalty. But it was all moot now; she had all the votes she needed to execute her plan, with or without his support. He could vote no, he could abstain—it didn't matter at this point—but she wished very much to have him appreciate her motives.

Russ took a moment to process this bomb-drop, and after quickly threading together personality traits, comments made, viewpoints expressed, and the state of the telecom market (which was wavering), he found that he wasn't really surprised by it. He always expected a power play of some kind by Gwen, and she'd been candid about her views regarding Marty as CEO and the future of CrestPoint Communications. Obviously, she had the votes or else she wouldn't be so confident. But did Marty know what was coming, or was he going to be bushwacked in the board meeting?

"I guess I'm not surprised," he replied. "And I could ask a lot of questions about how you orchestrated all this, but I won't. I only have one question: Does Marty know what's coming?"

There was an art to lying without lying and when circumstances warranted it, Gwen could tap dance around a question with the best of them. "I'd be surprised if he wasn't," she said. "He knows I've been talking to Atlantis and he's going to try to put a stop to it. He also expects the board will revoke company bylaws, allowing him to hold two CEO positions. But he doesn't have the votes."

He nodded thoughtfully, in that astute way of his, and at that moment she was pretty sure he saw right through her, so she swiftly pivoted her approach by appealing to his good business sense. The Atlantis deal was a godsend, she told him. Surely he'd seen the turndown in the market and the erosion of their revenue base. This deal would turn that around, merging both DSL footprints and pumping millions into their combined operations. But Marty was a hindrance to the deal; as CEO he'd try to put a stop to it. Russ knew this. That's why it was imperative she take over as CEO.

He didn't disagree with any of this, but now he was sure that Marty was walking into a buzzsaw and he didn't like it. But what were his own options here, he wondered. Tip Marty off and start a proxy war? It would be a bloodbath all the way around. Or remain silent and allow this rigged chess game to play out, checkmating Marty but probably saving the company?

A thought suddenly struck him and he asked, "What's Stu's position on this?"

"I have his full support," she replied. "One hundred percent." She found it a bit odd that out of the entire Board of Directors, he would ask about Stu.

"I see... You'll remember—right before I got the call about my son—I was in your office telling you about Stu's manipulation of our cost data. What I didn't get a chance to tell you is I'd given him an ultimatum—restate our fourth quarter earnings or reap the whirlwind. I told him I'd take it to the board."

"You *can't* do that!" she cried, leaning forwards at him like an irate judge. Her cheeks were flushed and he detected a hint of panic in her voice. "Not *now!*" she added quickly. "Not at this point. It's a delicate balance, Russ. Everything—everything is lined up and in its place, and I can't afford a rogue wave knocking it all down. I *absolutely* need Stu's support. Without it, there's no deal. I—we—also need solid first quarter numbers. That'll prime the pump with Atlantis. So any disruption now, any mea culpas or grand gestures, will destroy this deal and put us back in a death spiral. Certainly you see that? And you have my assurance I'll deal with Stu in in the end. If he's playing with the numbers, and I'm sure he is, then I'll put him in the ground—once the merger is signed. Once the merger is signed, sealed, and delivered, I'll deal with Mr. Baum. You have my word. But right now, I need *your* word. I need your word you won't bring this up in the board meeting, that you'll let me handle it. Do I have your word?"

Russ studied her face and wondered at the machinations of man, at the desperate schemes and mad chances, and thought to himself whether it was really worth it or not. The image of his son, lying near death, came and went like a haunting apparition. He knew the answer.

"You have my word," he said.

It was time. Gwen glanced around the table at the other board members and knew it was time. Marty had just completed his synopsis of the TelaPoint deal and its significance to CrestPoint's future, pontificating on their global footprint, on their limitless potential, and on their prospects of becoming the new AT&T, only nimbler, innovative, and more relevant. He presented himself as Chief Executive Officer of their new joint venture and asked the board for final approval. The vote was unanimous, and Marty leaned back in his chair with a big smile. Gwen gave him his moment in the sun, but now it was time, and she felt a slight tingle of excitement before she spoke.

"Congratulations, Marty," she intoned pleasantly, gaining everyone's attention. "And may I say, on behalf of myself and the board, we're all excited about this deal. With you at the helm it's a sure bet TelaPoint will become the premier DSL provider in Europe. With your vision and drive and creative spirit it can't miss. So, once again, thank you, Marty… And now it's time to turn our attention to naming a new CEO of CrestPoint Communications."

"What do you mean?" replied Marty sounding slightly indignant. "I'm CEO of CrestPoint."

"Our bylaws prohibit it," declared Gwen.

"That's easily remedied," said Marty. "The board can override that bylaw. We can take a vote right now if need be."

"We can and we will—if you insist," she answered. "But I think you'll find the board has no intention of overriding the company bylaws."

Marty didn't respond and instead looked around the table. Everyone avoided eye contact with him except for Russ whose pained expression set off a red alert in his head. What was she up to, he wondered. Some kind of power play? A palace coup? Obviously, the bitch had contrived this moment, making promises, cutting deals, maybe even giving each male board member a blow job (he wouldn't put it past her), all so she could bump him out as CEO. And replace him with whom? With herself? Of course, that was it—so she could cut a deal for a buy-out. A merger—no, an acquisition—with Atlantis. Well, he wouldn't let it happen. As majority shareholder, he still held enough power to squash this amateur coup attempt.

"No kidding?" he replied with an ironic grin. "And no doubt you have the votes to replace me. And all for what? So you can cut a deal with Atlantis? A buy-out? Is that what everybody in this room wants? To become some measly subsidiary of Atlantis? They're the very kind of company we quit, the very kind of monolith we rebelled against. Remember, Chandra? Remember, Ron? They're the evil empire. This is no time to surrender or panic. We hold all the cards. TelaPoint is the game-changer. Pan-European DSL. In two years' time, we'll be the one buying up companies. I guarantee it. So don't go down this rabbit hole—I'm not gonna let you destroy CrestPoint… As majority shareholder I won't allow it."

Gwen was sure he'd play the majority-shareholder trump card—and there it was. But she'd anticipated that. "For a CEO, you're not very well informed," she said curtly. "You don't seem to have any clue about what's happening with our company. We're nearly twenty million dollars in debt. We owe investors and suppliers, and our revenue source—the ISPs—aren't paying their bills. Our financial situation is deteriorating. Ask Stu if you don't believe me. And as for our stock price—well, you've seen that. It's dropped fifteen points since our IPO, and it's not going to get any better—not without major help."

"The press release on TelaPoint will pump up our stock," retorted Marty. "As for our debt—we're always in debt. It's normal, like the Mideast Crises. I'll talk to our investors and work it out… There's nothing here that can't be resolved to everyone's satisfaction."

Gwen moved to respond but Andy Sikes cut her off. "If I may," he said firmly. "I'd like to say a few words." As a former FCC commissioner who sat on a number of high-profile boards in the technology sector, Sikes was well respected and a man whose opinion mattered.

"By all means," replied Gwen, yielding the floor to Sikes. All eyes turned in his direction as he proceeded to lay out for the board, in his calm and grandfatherly manner, the hard facts of the matter (which were really aimed at Marty). The market was in a stage of "revulsion," he explained. This happens at the peak of a bubble when investors realize the game is almost up, when they realize the easy money has already been made and it's time to get out. The Dot-com bubble, the tech bubble—whatever you want to call it—was running out of steam. In addition, Japan just entered into a recession, which was triggering a global sell-off of technology stocks. Investors are shifting away from technology stocks over to traditional stocks, and this means that CrestPoint's stock will continue to decline, TelaPoint deal or no TelaPoint deal. And as for borrowing more money, "well," he said, "in a few days—no later than next week—the Fed is going to raise interest rates. You can count on it." He paused at that to see if anyone disagreed with him but no one challenged his prediction, not even Marty.

"So, where does that leave us?" he continued. "A deteriorating market, higher interest rates, both leading to an inverted yield curve. The right move now is a merger. It's not only the right move—but if our first responsibility is to our shareholders, it's the only move…

The Heights of Mountains

Marty, you can use the power of your majority shares to get your way, but that will lead to resignations from the board, cash-outs, and financial hari-kari—no more CrestPoint, no more TelaPoint for that matter—and I don't think that's what you want. Your job now, as I see it, is to lead our international venture while remaining Chairman of the Board of CrestPoint. Gwen Novak will become our new CEO and receive our full support, which will give her the horsepower she needs to hammer out a deal with Atlantis… Does everyone agree?"

There were murmurs of agreement around the table. Marty remained silent. Russ had watched Marty closely throughout this Sermon on the Mount and seen his rock-star bravado begin to wilt. Gwen had sewn this up nicely, he thought—every contingency planned, every countermove anticipated. Personally, he'd already made peace with himself regarding the move—it was the right one—but he couldn't help feeling a little sorry for Marty, not because he was being bumped out as CEO but because he'd been thoroughly out-maneuvered. It was rather mortifying, like getting the ball stripped from you at a key moment of the game. And that sports analogy made him think of Stu—Stu, who always viewed himself as the real power behind the throne—Stu, who made his own grab at CEO—Stu, who now sat quietly making no objection to Gwen as CEO. Russ wondered what he was thinking.

At this moment, Stu's thoughts were calculating the plusses and minuses: Marty out, Gwen in, and a deal with Atlantis that would be a godsend, replenishing their stock, paying off their bills, wiping the slate clean, and covering his ass. He'd gone about as far as he could go in propping up their stock and he needed a Steinbrenner with deep pockets to come in and buy the club. Frankly, Marty was expendable and Gwen was a missile he could guide in the right direction. Together, he and Gwen would cut a sweet deal with Atlantis, allowing him, finally, to get a good night's sleep for a change.

Lori Hunter formally nominated Gwen Novak for CEO. With no other nominations, a vote was taken and passed 13-0. Marty did not vote but raised no objection. What this loss of title meant to his political ambitions, he couldn't tell. Spun the right way in the press release, the impact could be minimal, he thought. But even if his image took a hit, he'd already mapped out a recovery plan in his head; while they sermonized, nodded in assent, and mounted their little revolution, he'd thought through in his light-speed fashion his next set of moves. He wouldn't object to the vote; he'd become CEO of TelaPoint and make his splash in Europe; he'd remain Chairman of the Board of CrestPoint Communications and be ready when the Atlantis deal fell apart, the shareholders panicked, and the board begged him to return as CEO. And if the Atlantis deal didn't fall apart under its own ponderous weight, well then, he'd assist it along.

The next morning, the lead story in the business section of the San Jose Mercury started out as follows:

CrestPoint Starts European Venture

CrestPoint, the fast-growing San Jose firm, which provides high-speed Internet access over conventional phone lines using DSL, teamed up with a Dutch telecommunications firm to offer the service across Europe.

Both CrestPoint and Teladata International plan to pour $50 million into the new venture, dubbed TelaPoint. CrestPoint's chief executive and co-founder, Martin Madrid, 36, is stepping down to run TelaPoint, though he will remain CrestPoint's chairman. President and Chief Operating Officer Gwen Novak, who joined CrestPoint from AT&T in 1999, will take over as CEO.

"The European market is just hungry for Internet access," Madrid said, noting that TelaPoint will initially roll out DSL service to businesses in Germany and the Netherlands, begin testing service in the United Kingdom and France and soon expand to other industrial nations, like Belgium.

CrestPoint stock jumped $4.16, to $29.52, on the news...

CHAPTER 6

⊶❦⊷

In July, after the release of a strong 2nd quarter earnings report, Gwen Novak sealed the deal with Atlantis. The planned acquisition was announced later that month to the press describing the terms of the deal. Atlantis would own 55 percent of the venture, pay CrestPoint's shareholders $335 million, merge both DSL networks, and spend an additional $400 million to expand the combined operations. Teri Starr, an analyst from the Yankee Group in Boston, reported that the agreement was "smart for both companies," giving CrestPoint the cash it needed and providing Atlantis with a strong base of DSL customers.

There was a general state of euphoria in the ranks of CrestPoint Communications. They had seen their stock price erode over the last year, taking a big hit on April 14 (Black Friday), until they saw their stock sitting at $17.32 a share, down 23 points a share since the day of their IPO. But with the Atlantis announcement, their stock rose over 4 points in a day to $21.91 a share. If ever there was a time to sell, it was now, but that was not the prevailing attitude across the company. Like a struggling NBA franchise who were falling in the standings, CrestPoint had just pulled off a trade for Michael Jordan, and now was the time to believe in miracles. Yes, Atlantis was a monolithic giant representing everything they'd rejected, but it had deep pockets and a forward-looking business strategy, and the growing general opinion amongst CrestPoint employees was that they'd be allowed to operate as usual, independently, or at worst as a loose subsidiary, and not as just another bolt in the machinery.

Marty knew better. He sat at his desk viewing his multiple monitors, each one displaying either CrestPoint's rising stock price or airing the opinions of market analysts regarding the announced merger. But

Marty saw it plainly; it was a buy-out, pure and simple. They'd been assimilated by the Borg, and even though Gwen assured him that the TelaPoint venture would be unaffected, he knew that it was only a matter of time before he came under someone's authority and they tried to turn him into another cyborg drone.

All the analyst reviews of the 'merger' were positive except for Frank Altobello from World Markets. He called the news about as exciting as a "king snake eating a mouse' and predicted that Atlantis would find the DSL market a lot less lucrative than expected. "Good ol' Frank," whispered Marty, smiling to himself. Always the doom merchant. Frank could afford to be brutally honest; he'd made his killing with CrestPoint, in and out like some smooth gigolo, and didn't need to carry water anymore. But the man still owed Marty a favor.

Up to now, he'd done nothing to try and scuttle the deal, quite frankly because he didn't think Gwen had the chops to pull it off, but now it was time to act. What he and the board understood, and what Gwen was acutely aware of, was that this deal was not final until Atlantis paid out the $335 million to CrestPoint shareholders, which was to be done in three installments, the first one next month. Plenty of time to work his magic.

The primary tools of that magic lay scattered about on his desktop in the form of financial spreadsheets, each one exposing in small ways the shenanigans that Stuart Baum had been pulling off as their Chief Financial Officer. And he had Russ to thank for it. For over two years, Russ complained about their under-stated costs, entreating Stu to correct the problem, then later threatening Stu with discovery unless the problem was immediately rectified. He himself was dragged into the feud. Fortunately, the TelaPoint negotiations provided him air cover, giving him the distraction he needed to ignore the problem. But now Russ was making noise again and it gave Marty the casus belli to act, not with a show of force but with camouflage and surprise. This information put into the hands of someone who owed him a favor would do the trick.

The Heights of Mountains

Yes, he thought to himself. Accusations will be made in the press, causing Atlantis to pull out. The board will panic. And at that moment, the house will fall on Ms. Novak, the wicked witch of the west, and they'll beg me to come back as CEO to save the company. Then, in the words of Jerry Garcia, they'll be nothing left to do but smile.

His assistant popped her head in the door. "Frank Altobello on line one."

Marty nodded and picked up the phone. "Hey, Frank. Thanks for taking my call."

———

The three men lounged in chairs around the small conference table chatting together while enjoying their morning coffee. Chandra's office caught the early morning sun, unveiling what promised to be another beautiful, sunny day in Silicon Valley. And if the three men didn't find the morning sunlight noticeably delightful it was because they were too busy basking in the glow of the Atlantis merger.

Chandra, Russ, and Ron—three of the founding fathers—made it a point to meet bi-monthly to chew the fat and share their thoughts about the company they started in Marty's studio apartment over three years ago. And though Marty and Stu belonged to this inner circle, they were not included in this huddle for obvious reasons (Marty was too commanding, Stu too obnoxious), leaving just the three amigos, each of like mind and temperament, to collectively read the temperature and predict the weather for CrestPoint Communications. Dominating their chat this morning was the merger and the good it would bring, which was a relief to them all after a year marked so far by falling stock prices, a power struggle between Gwen and Marty, and personal tragedy.

The easy-going discussion touched on Gwen's negotiating skills ("top-notch") to the stock buy-out ("surprisingly generous") to Atlantis's over-lapping DSL operations ("which will have to be sorted out"), and each of them were pleasantly surprised, or maybe it was more like amazed, that Atlantis had agreed to the deal. It finally took Ron to state the obvious and ask the question that was on all their minds.

"The second quarter report did the trick," he said. "Both first and second quarter reports. How Stu pull it off?"

It was a good question given the fact that CrestPoint had been bleeding cash for months. There were debts and unpaid bills, and their dire financial state was well known, which made this merger such a godsend. What did Stu know about subscriptions and projected revenue that they didn't know?

Russ knew the answer to that. He'd been trying to pull the curtain back on Stu for a couple years now but had been thwarted, first by Stu's defiance, next by Marty's empty assurances, and finally by his own promise to Gwen not to rock the boat during the Atlantis negotiations. But now the negotiations were over and all bets were off. Just yesterday, in Gwen's staff meeting, he demanded that Stu hand over the audit—Roxanne's audit—the audit on his department's cost data that had been promised in January but never delivered. Stu hemmed and hawed as usual, even alluding to Russ' leave of absence as an excuse for not releasing it, but Gwen in her inimitable style cut him off and ordered him to deliver the audit results to everyone by Thursday. Tomorrow was Thursday.

"He's cooking the books," said Russ bluntly.

"Think so?" asked Chandra. The long running feud between Russ and Stu was common knowledge, and this wasn't the first time he'd heard Russ challenge Stu's numbers. Their feud had led to a number of tense encounters over the years, in staff meetings and on conference calls, and it was something both he and Ron tried to stay out of the middle of. But he felt compelled to point out to Russ that to 'cook the books', Stu had to run the gauntlet of Tollerson Accounting's review, the inspection of the Securities and Exchange Commission, and finally the scrutiny of a cadre of market analysts. "That's quite a risk," he finished saying.

"*Tollerson,*" scoffed Russ. "They're a rubber stamp." He knew that Chandra was just playing devil's advocate, but it irritated him—that his accusations were so easily dismissed—and he had to catch himself. The stress of his son's medical condition was making him quick-tempered, something which was out of character for him, and it led him to be wary of his reactions.

The Heights of Mountains

"Gosh, I hope not," replied Chandra. "That'd be unethical."

Wouldn't it now, thought Russ, letting his irritation bubble back up. Do I have to spell it out for these two, he wondered to himself. Lay out the numbers, show them the lies firsthand. I guess so since they won't take my word for it.

"I see your numbers," said Ron, who quickly read Russ' tone and body language and felt some sympathy for his argument. "Your cost data from '98 and '99—much higher than what Stu reports. Maybe hundred of thousands difference… But now, growth is incremental. Not big as before, so difference is, I think, much smaller."

"That's true," agreed Russ, thankful for Ron's comment. "But it's a pattern—his willingness to pad the numbers."

"Once a thief…," joked Ron.

"Always a thief. Right. All Stu cares about is stock price. It's the end that justifies the means."

"So, you think there's more going on?" said Chandra, who was now fighting his own suspicions. "That he's committing fraud? That would be… suicidal—even for Stu. Besides the SEC looking over his shoulder, he's obligated to open the kimono to Atlantis. He has to know the risk he'd be taking."

"He knows," assured Russ. "But what of it? He's betting that the stock buy-out will be done and the merger completed before the shit hits the fan. Then it'll be water under the bridge… That's why he supported this deal so strongly. It gets him out from under the sword of Damocles."

There was a moment of silence as the three men reflected on this possibility. It was finally broken by Ron. *"He who makes his ways crooked will be found out,"* he said, quoting Proverbs.

"Well, for one, I pray to God it's not true," remarked Chandra.

Each of them nodded, lost in their own thoughts, and they couldn't help but feel that some of the luster was gone from the Atlantis deal.

When Russ returned to his office, his admin informed him that Gwen Novak and Lori Hunter wanted to see him in Gwen's office at 10:00 am. "Tell her I'll be there," he replied, checking his watch. The meeting was in twenty minutes and he wondered what the urgency was.

He went into his office and sat down at his desk, quickly checking his messages. He was expecting a call back from the Physical Therapy Department at Stanford Hospital regarding his son's progress. That progress was not nearly where it needed to be, and he was not happy with their program. Dan was still practically bed-ridden; he could get up to go to the restroom but only when assisted, and all his exercise, which consisted of arm and leg bends, was done while he lay in bed. He needed to be out of bed, in the gym, trying to walk and build up his strength. Russ wanted the physical therapist to push Dan, to challenge him to make that extra effort, but so far they'd ignored his advice. A large part of the problem was Jan, who argued with him at every turn—about therapy, about medication, about Dan's prognosis—and seemed to want Russ out of their lives. But that wasn't about to happen.

Russ was forming a plan of action to fix the situation. It was something he'd been working out in his head for weeks now, still unfinished, that changed in small ways as new information came in. If the neurologist was right and Dan had suffered brain damage, effecting both his motor skills and cognitive abilities, then intensive physical therapy was required. Probably personal trainers dedicated to Dan's recovery. Perhaps even a house for he and Dan to live in, equipped with a state-of-the-art gym, and designed from foundation to roofbeam to facilitate his son's rehabilitation. *There will be no half-measures*, he thought to himself.

A glance at the clock told him that it was time to leave and walk over to Gwen's office, and he quickly shifted his thought pattern, wondering what this urgent meeting was all about. The fact that it included Lori Hunter, EVP of Human Resources did not bode well. Did it have something to do with one of his employees? Perhaps a complaint had been lodged against Mark Kirkland for preaching at work, for handing out his little pamphlets again after he'd told him to stop. He doubted it; Mark was not one to violate his trust.

Better yet, he thought to himself, *maybe this is about Stu. With the deal virtually done, Gwen is following up on her promise to address the accusations I raised against Stu. They need my corroboration—numbers to back up my charge—before they lower the boom on him.*

That promising thought was in the back of his head as he entered Gwen's office and encountered their somber faces. "Have a seat," said Gwen. She sat behind her desk with Lori sitting directly to her right, and together they made a formidable looking pair.

Russ sat down and regarded the two women. They immediately reminded him of lead detectives in a murder case, and he was going to crack a joke about it but thought better of it. "I'm at your service," he said smoothly. "What's up?"

"A complaint has been filed against you," replied Gwen.

"Me? Goodness. What for?"

Before Gwen could respond, Lori took over. "A sexual harassment complaint has been filed against you by one of our employees," she said briskly. "Roxanne LaMorte, Director of Current Accounting, claims that you groped her—that on January twenty-eighth of this year, in the Palo Alto central office, you sexually accosted her before she broke free and ran to safety. She also claims there was a pattern of intimidation and sexual provocation leading up to this event."

Russ sat stunned for a moment, his thoughts a jumble as he tried to make sense out of Lori's words. *Roxanne?* Roxanne LaMorte… That was the day of the office tour—when she mysteriously disappeared. The following Monday, he'd tried to find out what happened but was told she was out of her office. Then there was Dan and his leave of absence. Since then, he had tried to contact her once to enquire about the audit report, but her office responded that the report had been handed over to Stu and she was too busy to talk. He didn't think too much about it—until now.

"You got to be kidding me?" he managed to say.

"I can assure you, it's no joke," responded Lori, and as Russ met her stare, he could see the deep-rooted malice in her eyes. She's already tried and convicted me, he thought to himself.

"And this was when?" he asked. "Six months ago? Why am I only finding out about this now? I know I was on a leave of absence but—"

"The timing is irrelevant," said Lori, cutting him off. "Women in these cases are often afraid to come forward at first, fearing reprisal or worse. Ms. LaMorte's reasons for waiting to file her complaint are her own. A woman whose been molested or sexually harassed can't—"

"Ms. Lamorte was neither molested or harassed," interrupted Russ. "These are allegations, are they not? Well then, treat them as such and not as proven fact."

"I can assure you I am. They're allegations—serious allegations—and we're treating them as such."

Gwen watched this exchange intently, trying to read Russ' body language. It was obvious he was shocked by the charges and was doing his best to maintain his usual poise, but she could see his anger rising. That wouldn't serve him well and she hoped he could contain it. Frankly, she doubted these charges. For one, she knew Russ, intimately, and it was not in his nature to mistreat a woman. Yes, he had a reputation as a Don Juan—that was well known—but that very reputation was another thing that fed her doubts. He didn't need to hound women; with his good looks and cultivated charm, women went after him (as she well knew). If anything, women pursued Russ, and whether they scored or not depended on his rigorous rating system. Acting like a groping lech was not his style. Yet, Ms. LaMorte was quite beautiful and right up Russ' alley, so who knows? Perhaps he misjudged his attraction (he was pushing fifty after all) and made the wrong move or was over-confident and pounced when he shouldn't have pounced. There was no tolerance for that sort of thing nowadays, and she had to remind herself to keep an open mind and not let her friendship for Russ get in the way of her responsibility.

"It's an official complaint, Russ," said Gwen, "and we're obligated to take it seriously. The complaint amounts to a violation of the company's code of conduct."

"As well as state law," interjected Lori.

"As well as state law," repeated Gwen calmly. "So, Russ, you must understand the position we're in."

"Certainly, Gwen," he replied, glancing over at Lori. She wore her normal gray, genderless pant suit, and she leaned to one side, her holier-than-thou attitude on full display, holding a folder in her hands as though it were a stone tablet. "Is that the complaint?" he asked. "May I have a copy?"

"Course," said Gwen. "But Lori's going to review the main accusations filed against you by Ms. LaMorte."

Russ nodded and sat back in his chair to listen, struggling to show no emotion as Lori energetically read through the main accusations against him. And what he heard was incredible. Roxanne accused him of fondling her, of "pressing me against the wall, squeezing my breasts, and trying to kiss me." Prior to this incident, she related examples of intimidation and unwanted sexual advances that had taken place in his office, each of which he knew to be either gross exaggerations or pure fiction. The whole scene felt Kafkaesque, but he was also well aware of its seriousness. In this inverted reality, he was guilty until proven innocent, and even if this came down to 'he-said-she-said' with no third parties to verify her charges, his reputation would remain tainted for the rest of his career. Bloody fucking hell.

Gwen knew the report by heart but she patiently listened to Lori's read-out, finding her performance a trifle exuberant. It was evident to her that Ms. Hunter relished the role of Judge Judy, which didn't surprise her. Lori was a woman dedicated to the fixed idea that women—all women—are an oppressed class who needed to be freed from bondage. She was a woman perfectly suited for her job, a woman who carried the burden of five thousand years of patriarchal oppression on her shoulders, and a feminist warrior who was dedicated to rooting out male chauvinism and burning it at the stake. Gwen was certain that if she gave Lori the reins, she'd swiftly eviscerate Russ, demand his resignation, then dance on his grave.

Lori was approaching the part in the written complaint where Roxanne called Russ "a creepy old man," and though it wasn't a highlighted quote or even really germane to the allegations against Russ, Gwen was sure that Lori wouldn't be able to resist reading it out loud. Sure enough, she did, and Gwen watched Russ' reaction carefully. He showed no emotion at the quote other than to blink once, slowly, as though he was digesting a bad bit of food.

When Lori finished her summary, she placed the copy on top of Gwen's polished desk and slid it towards Russ. "There's your copy… Any comment?"

He let it sit there for a moment, regarding it like a positive lab test for cancer, before leaning forward and taking it off the desk.

"That's quite a tale, full of sound and fury," he said, glancing through the pages. "Are there any witnesses to support these charges? Or is it just her word against mine?"

"She identified a Wayne Redland from Lucent who was there, and I spoke to him and he confirms that Roxanne left the premises in a hurry looking very upset."

"Did he say he witnessed the alleged harassment?"

"No... he didn't see anything—just her reaction afterwards."

"That's because there wasn't anything to witness."

Russ caught Lori as she glanced over at Gwen and slightly rolled her eyes in a "see-what-I-mean" gesture, and it angered him.

"These things are never done in the light of day," replied Lori. "They're always behind closed doors or in secluded spots, away from witnesses."

"Hmm, just like conspiracy plots," shot back Russ. And at his own use of the word 'conspiracy', his mind suddenly started connecting the dots. What if this was all a set up, he thought—from the get-go? Cooked up by Stu and Roxanne to discredit him? What else could it be? It made perfect sense. But even as that certainty flooded his consciousness, he knew he couldn't use it as a defense without being viewed by both these women as some kind of a con artist trying to talk himself out of trouble. It was something he could float to Gwen offline, but not here, and instead he took another tack.

"Who's doing the investigation?" he asked, cutting off Lori who started to speak. "I'm assuming there'll be an investigation, someone to grill me and take my statement."

"That'll be me," replied Lori.

"No. You've already tried and convicted me. I would prefer someone with a little more objectivity."

"Seeing as you're an officer of the company, and I'm President and CEO," said Gwen, "it's probably my job to conduct the investigation."

"I wouldn't recommend that," replied Lori, clearing her throat a tad nervously. "For one, it's HR's responsibility to investigate this complaint.

And second… well, let's just say there's a history between you two that's well known, and it might appear as a conflict of interest for you to take over the investigation."

"If anyone thinks I can't do my job, they're dead wrong," said Gwen icily, giving Lori the feared Novak glare. There was a moment of awkward silence as Lori met the glare, briefly, then looked away. Having made her point, Gwen backed-off, adding, "But I would prefer it to be someone from HR. You have someone you can assign to this?"

"I do."

"Very well then. And let's have it done discreetly. Gather facts, take statements—but I don't want this leaked to the employee population. It stays in-house. Understand?"

"Of course."

"And in the meantime?" asked Russ, who wasn't about to let this charade derail his duty to CrestPoint (the company he helped found). "Business as usual, correct?"

"Business as usual," repeated Lori sarcastically. "My recommendation is a leave of absence, at least until such time as the investigation is completed and your guilt or innocence established."

"No," interjected Gwen firmly. There was an immediate and somewhat selfish reason she wanted Russ to remain on the job—the merger. He was a key player in the unification of the two DSL networks, and his expertise and influence would be instrumental in the transition. But there was also a simpler reason, and one that Ms. Hunter should have appreciated (but evidently didn't), so she proceeded to spell it out. Mr. Chappel was a member of the Board of Directors, she reminded Lori, and board members were not put on leave, censured, or asked to resign without a majority vote of the board, and they were a long way away from that. So, yes, it would be business of usual until all the facts were in.

Russ watched Lori bow to Gwen's irrefutable logic with a curt nod and no comment. So, he would leave this little court of inquiry and return to his job with a dark cloud over his head and try his best to stay focused. Stu's gambit worked, he thought to himself. At least partly.

I'm not out of the picture but he's got me hamstrung like some circus animal. He thinks it's over for me, that it's the end. But, no, it's not the end. It's not even the beginning of the end.

He slowly rose from his chair, looking straight at Gwen. "I'm sorry for all this, Gwen," he said. "I know it can't be pleasant—having to deal with something like this—and it's a major distraction, but it's no less painful to me, having accusations like this thrown at me from out of the blue. I could stand here and profess my innocence, play out the stereotype of the outraged bully, but I'll spare you that scene. I have my own thoughts about what's behind all this, but I'll keep those thoughts to myself for the moment and simply say I'm confident this will all be cleared up."

"I hope so, Russ," replied Gwen.

The two women watched him turn and walk out the door.

"He's a dinosaur," said Lori, saying out loud what she was sure both of them were thinking.

"Hmm," replied Gwen thoughtfully. "Yeah… a tyrannosaurus rex."

Chapter 7

"It booked this morning," said Stu.

"Excellent," responded Gwen. She was at her desk on the phone with Stu, and the headset she wore left her hands free to lightly pump her fist at the news.

"Yeah. $122 million. Right on time—and none too early."

Gwen didn't add a comment to the 'none too early' part since it spoke for itself. Both she and Stu were painfully aware of CrestPoint's financial plight, and this first of three payments from Atlantis (as part of the merger deal) couldn't have come at a better time.

"It staves off our creditors—Copper Mountain for one, Cisco for another—and gives us some breathing room with the ISPs to pay up their bills."

"Without legal action?"

"I've threatened it in a few cases. Some, as you know, are over three months in arrears. But, yes, we're on the same page. We don't want them bailing out on us, declaring bankruptcy. That's why this payment's crucial. It gives us time back on the clock."

"And puts the ball in our court," she added, completing the metaphor. Gwen was in buoyant mood; the first installment in their merger deal had booked, each of her department heads were working with their counterparts at Atlantis to hash out a transition plan, and her wine club shipment of Chateau Montelena Chardonnay was due to arrive at her door this afternoon. It couldn't be helped that this buoyant mood also made her feel a little generous. "Great work, Stu, and I just want to say I couldn't have pulled off this deal without you. The financials you presented, plus two solid earnings reports—that put us over the top. So, thanks again, and pass my thanks onto your department."

"I will, and it's much appreciated. And let me just say your leadership, coming when it did, made all the difference. We needed a hard ass in the CEO chair."

She laughed at his back-handed compliment. "Don't get gushy on me, Stu," she replied playfully. "We have two more installments to look forward to. Meanwhile, let's continue to leverage our synergies with Atlantis."

"Right, boss."

It was evident by his congenial tone that he considered the two of them 'buddies' now, a view she didn't care to share. One thing she'd learned about Stu, having worked with him on the merger deal, was that he could be a consummate ass-kisser when he wanted to be. And she never trusted ass-kissers, so she kept the rest of their conversation brief, exchanging a few more pleasantries before hanging up. Gwen slipped off her headset and clicked her mouse to activate her computer screen just as Shavonne poked her head in the door to say that Frank Altobello from World Markets was on hold and wished to speak to her. She was familiar with the name—a market analyst and bit of a gadfly—and told Shavonne to take a message. She wasn't in the mood to field a bunch of probing questions about the merger.

Gwen clicked to open her emails, but before she could start reading, Shavonne was back.

"He says it's urgent," she said, shrugging her shoulders apologetically.

"Urgent, huh? About as urgent as the mailman… Okay, what, line two? I'll get it." She put her headset back on and hit line two. "This is Gwen. What can I do for you?"

"Ms. Novak. Frank Altobello from World Markets. Thanks for taking my call."

"Sure. You have questions about the merger?"

"No… I have information critical to your company's survival."

"*Really?* Well then, you have my full attention. What's this information?"

"First off, this information comes with an arrangement—a mutual arrangement that will benefit the both of us. It's info with a hook. Quid pro quo."

"Quid pro quo, huh?" replied Gwen skeptically. (Already she didn't like this guy and suspected he was running some kind of scam.) "You must think you hold the goose that lays golden eggs. Which I doubt. So please come to the point."

"What I hold is information—information that if I release it to the media or hand over to the Securities Exchange Commission will rupture your deal with Atlantis and destroy CrestPoint. It's information that comes from an unimpeachable source, from within your own company, and can be corroborated with hard numbers."

"Who?"

"I never reveal my sources."

"Look, I don't know who you think you are, Frank Altobello from World Markets, but I'm not some wide-eyed virgin fresh off the bus, so don't try to screw me. If you've got some kind of bombshell, then lay it on me. I mean, that's why you called, right? If this info was worth taking to the media or the SEC, you would have done it by now."

"You're right. So here's the deal—I give you the bombshell and you promise not to act upon it for three days. In return, I won't take it to the media or the SEC."

"Why three days?"

"I still own a chunk of CrestPoint stock. With the announcement today that you've received your first payment from Atlantis, that stock will tick up a few decimals, and once World Markets upgrades your stock from buy to strong buy, which I can almost guarantee, it'll probably peak a couple points higher. And that's when I'll sell. In three days' time. After that, you can cover it up, or do damage control. It won't matter to me."

A heavy pause hung over the phone line as Gwen quickly processed this little piece of blackmail. He's done this before, she thought to herself. This isn't the first time he's used market intel to line his pockets. Clever little shit. "Okay, Frank," she said grudgingly. "You got a deal. Three days. Now what do you have?"

In short order, he laid it out for her: he had hard evidence that CrestPoint's earnings reports were a fraud, that they had been doctored to hide rising costs and declining subscriptions and were in violation of the Securities Exchange Act of 1934 and Rule 10b-5. Bottom line, CrestPoint was breaking the law.

Oddly enough, Gwen was not shocked by this news. In the back of her mind, she probably always suspected Stu was massaging the numbers to make them look better than they were. But just that—tweaks and turns and accounting legerdemain (something everyone did), not outright fraud. But at hearing these allegations—allegations neatly leaked by someone high up in her own company—she moved from doubter to believer without breaking stride. And now Russ popped into her head like the answer to a trivia question. He'd made a big deal about the numbers before. Just recently, in fact, in the privacy of her office, he tried to convince her Ms. LaMorte's sexual harassment claims against him had been orchestrated by Stu to keep him quiet. She'd listened politely to Russ's conspiracy theory out of respect and friendship, not really believing a word of it, but now... Well, now she believed him.

"Who gave you this information?" she asked. "Russ Chappel?"

On the other end of the line, Frank briefly entertained the idea of saying yes. He remembered Chappel from a few years ago and thought him an over-confident, smug son-of-a-bitch, with Hollywood good looks who had swept the delectable Terri Starr off her feet. And he wouldn't even need to come out and say it; all he had to do was use a few carefully chosen words and phrases to leave her with the strong impression that she was right, it was Chappel. But at the last second, he resisted the temptation and replied, "I won't play that game—the process of elimination. As I said, I won't reveal my source."

"Fine. You get your three days. But if you think I'm easily put off, you're wrong. I want to know your source. In three days, you get your big payday, so I think you owe it to me."

"Sorry."

"Lou Finkenberg is still an associate partner over at World Markets, is he not? Lou's a good friend of mine, and I'm sure he'd find this little game of yours very interesting. What do you think?"

"And threats won't work either," replied Frank calmly as he thought to himself, *this woman is a bitch and a half and living up to her reputation, but I kind of like her.* "But I'll leave you with this… Who has a motive for trashing your Atlantis deal? Think about it. Who stands to gain from it?" He paused for a moment before adding, "That's all I'll give you. Good luck."

The line went dead, but Gwen didn't need to hear any more. She'd already guessed the name. *Marty Madrid.*

Two hours after her phone call with Altobello, Gwen summoned Roxanne LaMorte to her office. In those two hours, with her door shut and orders to Shavonne not to be disturbed, she played nerf basketball, shooting the small sponge ball at a miniature hoop, retrieving the ball, shooting again, retrieving again, all while she worked out a plan of action in her head to deal with these allegations. Discovery was inevitable, she knew, and it was best to get out in front of it. There would be fallout followed by crises management (which she was an expert at), but first she needed independent attestation. A corroborating source. Stu would never fess up unless she came at him with guns blazing and irrefutable evidence. And it had to be someone she could turn.

Shavonne ushered in Roxanne, who carried a notebook with her and looked slightly anxious at being called into the office of Gwen Novak, President and CEO of CrestPoint Communications. Gwen came out from behind her desk to greet her.

"Roxanne," she said, smiling warmly. "Thanks for meeting me on such short notice. Here—let's sit over here."

"Certainly, Ms. Novak."

"Call me Gwen."

Roxanne nodded and followed Gwen over to a divan and upholstered chair by the large window where they sat down. Gwen detected a note of wariness in Roxanne's body language, so she sought to put her at ease by offering her a soda and making small talk. Roxanne declined the soda, taking a bottled water instead, and crossed her legs while she fielded a few innocuous questions from Gwen about current accounting and how her job was going.

As they made small talk, Gwen studied the young woman closely, making a few educated guesses. She was around thirty, a college grad and dedicated career woman, who thought herself smarter than she really was. Her main attribute was her beauty, and Gwen had no doubt she knew how to use that beauty to her advantage. There had probably been affairs, usually with powerful men that led to opportunities, perhaps even an abortion along the way, and Gwen bet that this young woman had fought at first to hold onto to her traditional family values but in the end had, with a sort of casual regret, thrown them out like a pair of shoes gone out of fashion. But one thing was for sure, thought Gwen—with that red hair, flawless skin, and hour-glass figure, she was the perfect bait to take down our man Russel.

"What do you think of our numbers, going forward," asked Gwen innocently.

"Good. Solid," replied Roxanne. "Especially with the merger. They look good."

Gwen nodded, smiling pleasantly, knowing it was a non-answer and something Stu would have said. She was inching closer to lowering the boom, confident that Roxanne, who was probably a talented manipulator when it came to men, would have no clue on how to deal with a powerful woman who was immune to her charms. In fact, she was counting on it.

Roxanne took a sip of her water and glanced around at the artwork on the walls, recrossing her legs and appearing to relax a bit. Gwen noticed it and struck.

"It has come to my attention, Roxanne, that Mr. Baum has been falsifying company financial records." Her tone was cold, no-nonsense, and it caught Roxanne off-guard who now suddenly uncrossed her legs and sat up straight. "I have the testimony and data to prove it, and once this goes to the SEC, there will be a formal investigation leading to charges and convictions. Stu is gone, either convicted of a federal crime or forced to resign in disgrace. Probably both. And the question becomes, how many others in his department will go down with him—and who is going to play it smart and save their ass by telling me *exactly* the depth of the lies and who's all involved. Is that person going to be you, Roxanne, or you gonna-go down with the ship?" The color had left Roxanne's face. She blinked and looked down at her knees then up at Gwen, the blunt force of Gwen's words having caught her square in the temple. "I… I don't—don't know what you're talking about," she stammered, the fear evident in her eyes.

"Bullshit!" exclaimed Gwen, smelling blood in the water. "I've got the audit you did right here—the one where you lie about our installation costs—so I *know* you're a part of it. Are you gonna deny it?"

"Those aren't my numbers… Stu changed 'em."

That's it, thought Gwen to herself. I have her. "So, Stu changed the numbers and you looked the other way," she said, boring in on her. "That makes you an accomplice and just as guilty as him. But now—right now, right at this moment—you have a golden opportunity to save your ass by coming clean. Give me details, tell me who all's involved, and you avoid termination and the expense of hiring a lawyer. And maybe, just maybe, after I've cleaned house of these assholes, you end up as a VP of Corporate Finance. But you need to decide *now*. It's a life-changing moment, Roxanne, so don't fuck it up."

Gwen paused a moment to read Roxanne's face and could see the wheels turning at a furious pace as the young woman weighed her options. She was teetering on the brink and just needed a final push.

"I don't want this to go to the SEC," she added. "I don't want indictments and I don't want scandal. I want to handle this in-house. Understood? But to do that, I need allies. I need *you*, Roxanne. So what's it gonna be? Do you have the guts to come along with me on this, or do you wanna go down in flames with Stu?"

"With you," replied Roxanne.

Gwen nodded smartly, accepting Roxanne's surrender while finding herself a tad surprised at how quickly the woman folded under pressure. After a few more prodding questions, she got Roxanne to open up and lay it all out for her. And it was worse than she suspected. Though Roxanne wasn't a part of the inner circle of Stu, Hal, and Tollerson Accounting, what she knew was this: besides underestimating installation costs, they were counting operating expenses as capital, booking past-due payments from the ISPs as revenue, and inflating subscriber growth. Roxanne could only prove some of this on paper but not all of it.

"Give me what you can," said Gwen. "And I want it on my desk by 5:00 today." She watched Roxanne nod in obedience before adding, "Thank you for coming clean on this. It's the smart move." She stood up and Roxanne followed suit, and Gwen stuck her hand out to briefly shake Roxanne's hand. "You have some work to do, and I'll let you get to it."

"Okay," replied Roxanne. She put her head down and headed for the door.

"Ah! One more thing," called out Gwen, stopping the young woman in her tracks. "The whole sexual harassment charge against Russ Chappel—it's a bunch of bullshit, right?"

"Yes."

"That's what I thought. You can go now."

―――

Stu glanced up at the clock. It was late, almost 7:00 pm, and he needed a cigarette. He'd gone without one for almost four hours, but it was time well spent. In those four hours, he had called all their creditors and lenders, either making good on their debt or buying time with a partial payment and a promise of more to come. Everyone was happy. That's what an infusion of $122 million will do for you, he thought to himself. I've pulled this company's fat out of the fire—once again—and all I get for it is a pat on the back and an atta-boy from Gwen. If Gwen,

Marty, and the board had any idea, any friggin' clue what I had to do to make this Atlantis deal happen, they'd climb up on a ladder and kiss my ass. But they don't want to know. They just want results. So, someone's got to dig in and get their hands dirty, and that someone is always me.

He was tempted to light up in his office. It wouldn't have been the first time he'd smoked a cigarette late at night in his office, but he decided instead to use the side door and smoke outside. He needed to stretch his legs anyway. He grabbed his pack of Marlboros from his desk door and stood up just as his phone rang. Caller ID told him it was his wife and he let it ring and go to voicemail.

Before he got to the side door, his cell phone rang and he dug it out of his pocket already knowing who it was. His wife. He sighed and walked back to his desk. He knew that if he didn't call her back she would continue to call his office phone then his cell phone, incessantly, until he answered. It made him angry, partly because it interrupted his much-needed nicotine fix and partly because he was in no mood for her nagging. But he decided to get it over with and poked the speed dial button on his phone. His wife, who also had caller-ID, waited until the third ring before picking up, further irritating him.

"What, Miriam," he said sharply. "Why you calling me?"

Gwen came to Stu's office door, which was partly open, and paused to collect her thoughts and review her plan of attack. She'd waited until late, hoping to catch him alone, but when she was ready to enter, she caught the sound of his voice talking to someone and hesitated. A quick peek through the door confirmed that he was alone but on the phone, loudly berating someone. She guessed that it was probably an employee or some cowering CEO over at one of the ISPs (Stu was not known for his delicate touch). Whoever it was, he was dropping F-bombs on them, calling them "stupid," and browbeating them mercilessly. Gwen didn't much care for his bully act, so instead of waiting she tapped loudly on his door and stepped into his office.

"I don't give a shit," he said loudly into the phone. "That's your problem." He noticed Gwen come through the door, signaled to her that he would just be a moment, and continued his one-way conversation.

She nodded curtly and walked into his office, then stopped and stood rather uncomfortably waiting for him to wrap up his call. To hide her discomfort, she glanced around at the pictures on his wall, pretending to take a sudden interest in the exhibit of sports paraphernalia. There were pictures and a pennant of the Oakland Raiders, evidently his favorite football team, and one large, framed picture, prominently displayed, of Al Davis shaking Stu's hand in what appeared to be a luxury box at the Coliseum. (She vaguely recalled that Stu greatly admired Al Davis and occasionally mentioned his name in board meetings.) There was also an old poster of the Bash Brothers—Mark McGwire and Jose Conseco—as well other Oakland A's stuff. She wasn't much of a football or baseball fan—basketball was her sport—and she glanced about for a picture of the Golden State Warriors but found only photos of the New York Knicks. She secretly scoffed at that. Turns out he hadn't gone totally native after all.

He drew her attention back by suddenly calling the person on the other end of the phone "a fat slob" (*who* was he talking to, she wondered). Gwen twirled her finger, signaling him to wrap it up, and he nodded back at her. It's odd, she thought to herself. It's almost as if the other person enjoys his abuse as much as he enjoys giving it out.

"Gotta go," he said. "The president of the company is here... No, I'm not lying. Why would I lie? ... Shut the fuck up. I'm hanging up now... Don't be stupid. You enjoy being stupid? Gotta go... No... When I get there... No... Okay... Love you, too." And with that, he hung up.

The 'I love you, too' startled Gwen, throwing her for a loop. "Who was that?" she immediately asked.

"My wife."

The news that the person he'd been cruelly berating, calling "stupid" and a "slob," and who he nonchalantly replied was his wife, angered Gwen and made what she had to do now a little bit easier.

"I don't think you've been in my office before," said Stu affably. "What do I owe the honor? Questions about the installment booking? It's in the bank and I've already settled with our creditors."

"No."

"Well, have a seat. I was gonna have a cigarette but it can wait. You don't smoke, right? No, didn't think so." He sat down at his desk and looked up at her with growing interest.

Gwen remained standing, her eyes fixed on his face, and gave him the full shotgun blast without warning. "I have two sources and corroborating data that proves you've been falsifying company financial records—No! Don't talk. Listen! —The evidence shows you've been capitalizing operating expenses and lying about our installation costs. It also shows that you purposely over-estimated subscriber growth and booked unpaid ISP bills as revenue. As CFO, you used these gimmicks to artificially inflate our stock price, and as our corporate lawyer you knew that it was against the law. And when the SEC gets their hands on this it will mean an investigation and indictments—your indictment, along with Rubin and Tollerson for fraud."

Stu gripped the armrests of his chair, his anger rising at what he took to be threats from this woman. *Sources and corroborating data,* he thought to himself with a sneer. What a joke. *If she thinks she can intimidate me with this double-cross, she's in for a rude awakening.*

"If that's what you want," she continued, "then play dumb and make out like you don't know what I'm talking about. If not, then play it smart so we can find a way out of this—cause I don't want to see you take the fall for this. It would be a disaster all around."

"*Why, thank you*, Gwen," he replied, his voice dripping with sarcasm. "*That's* generous of you. But let's review a moment… It was *you* who begged *me* for two solid earnings reports. You couldn't pull off the Atlantis deal without them, *remember?* So I gave you what you needed and you looked the other way. And it was *you*, not *me*, who came up with the *gimmick* to have the ISPs roll out an ad campaign for the first-month-free, ramping up subscriptions. Did I count those free subscriptions and book their potential revenue? Goddam right I did. Just as you knew I would. So don't play innocent bystander with me. You're like the head coach who looks the other way when his players shoot up cause he doesn't wanna spoil his winning streak."

Gwen had expected this reaction—the 'your-hands-are-just-as-dirty-as-mine' argument—and she pushed back at him immediately before he gained any momentum. Did he have a memo, an e-mail, even just a witness who wasn't one of his cronies, that proved she knew about his scam? He didn't, she declared. He had nothing that implicated her—just his wild imagination and conspiracy theories that would never hold up in court. She, on the other hand, had Russ Chappel, along with a source in his own department, and another high-profile source that would blow him away.

"You're bluffing," Stu replied angrily. "Who? Who is it?"

"Marty… Marty sold you out."

"Marty! Impossible!"

"Don't yell at me, Stu," she shot back. "I'm not your wife." She leveled her withering stare at him and waited for him the settle down before continuing. "Yes, Marty. The one who never wanted this Atlantis merger in the first place. The one who's been dumping his stock. That Marty." She quickly summarized the call she'd received from Frank Altobello, then paused to let it sink in. He sat looking at her in dazed disbelief, as though he'd been caught with an uppercut and somehow found his way back to his corner. With some effort, he shook off the blow and let his anger take over.

"That motherfucking little pipsqueak," he seethed. "That fucking traitor."

"Exactly."

Stu picked up his pack of cigarettes, patted out one, and lit it up while Gwen watched him carefully. She knew what had to be done and she was sure now that Stu would come along willingly. She wasn't going to demand his resignation; there was too much at stake at the moment to risk a purge. No, they would come clean and restate their 2nd quarter earnings. This would reboot their financial records while at the same time displaying their integrity. Others restated revenue projections, and they wouldn't be the first or the last to do so in this volatile market. She would finesse it with the board, spinning it as overly-aggressive yet well-intentioned accounting practices that, in fairness to all, needed correcting.

And as for Atlantis, she'd take the gamble that being in for a penny, they were in for a pound. Money had changed hands, substantial money, while merger plans and strategies were well underway. She was betting that this machinery, now fired up and inexorably chugging forward, was past the point of no return. Then, once the crises passed and they were safe under the Atlantis umbrella, she would jettison Stu into the icy cold of space. But for the time being, she needed him.

He could tell by her whole posture and attitude—by the way she just stood there regarding him like a rook in her chess game—that she'd already mapped out every move. She was a scheming bitch who wouldn't have bothered coming into his office to make accusations and threaten his job unless it was for one purpose—to bait him and set the hook hard. She didn't want a SEC investigation or a board meeting or his resignation. What she wanted was for him to take a foul and keep playing, and the obviousness of it settled his nerves somewhat.

Stu took a long drag of his cigarette, instantly feeling relief, and blew out the smoke above his head. "So, what do you propose we do?" he asked.

Chapter 8

Three days after Frank Altobello's phone call to Gwen Novak, CrestPoint Communications issued a press release announcing they were restating downwards their financial performance for the second quarter of 2000, lowering revenue from $28 million to $20 million. CrestPoint attributed this move to "bad debt," specifically to the growing number of customers who were not paying their bills. President and CEO, Gwen Novak, commented that "despite the restatement, CrestPoint's business model is sound and our prospects bright."

Market analysts and investment brokers across the country did not agree with Ms. Novak. The prevailing opinion blamed CrestPoint's deteriorating market share and their mismanagement of debt as the culprit, while some took a broader view and attributed their restatement of revenue as further evidence of the Dot-com bust that was occurring worldwide. All of them ventured guesses as to how this would impact the Atlantis merger. On the heels of this reaction, CrestPoint's stock dropped to $12.14 a share.

In the offices of CrestPoint Communications Inc, from their corporate headquarters in Rio Seco Business Park to all points of presence across the country, every employee, each one a vested shareholder, waited in anticipation. The entire leadership team—CEO Gwen Novak, CDO Russ Chappel, CIO C.V. Chandrasekar, CPO Ron Lau, and EVP of HR Lori Hunter—along with the general population of Engineering Managers, Sales Representatives, Marketing Executives, Finance Specialists, Administrative Assistants, clerks, planners, and coordinators all held their collective breath waiting for Atlantis's reaction to the news.

Gwen and Stu did their best to downplay the move with the powers-that-be at Atlantis, calling it a necessary reset of revenue expectations given the unexpected number of Internet Service Providers not paying their bills (some of whom—the smaller ones—had recently declared bankruptcy). There was consolidation happening in the ISP universe and a little patience was required while it worked itself out. Meanwhile, CrestPoint still owned a formidable DSL network, covering 62 cities across the country, a growing presence in Europe, and still represented Atlantis's best option to instantly expand their DSL footprint.

The powers-that-be at Atlantis politely responded that they would assess the situation and get back to them.

Gwen didn't have to wait long. The day after CrestPoint's announcement, her counterpart at Atlantis called in the late afternoon to inform her that the giant telecom was terminating their arrangement. Stunned at their decision, Gwen fumbled with her words, finally managing to ask for clarification ("Did I hear you right?") and asking to know the legal justification behind this decision. The response, cool and measured, sounded as though it was being read from a prepared statement. Her counterpart informed her that Atlantis was invoking a clause in their agreement that gives them an out if CrestPoint experiences "a material adverse change" in its business. She had negotiated in bad faith, failing to disclose the deterioration in CrestPoint's business operations and financial condition, and they had no moral or legal obligation to continue with it.

Angry now, Gwen hotly attacked their decision, calling it irrational and short-sighted, but caught herself when she realized she was sounding like a head coach yelling at a referee for a bad call. She paused to control her anger, finding her expression, and calmly threatened legal action. They would sue, she said. They would force Atlantis to honor their agreement. And it would happen immediately. Her counterpart remained unfazed, alerting her that their formal announcement would go out in the morning, and hung up.

Gwen sat at her desk, still with her headset on, fighting a sickening sensation of rapid descent. She felt as though she was in the cockpit of a jetliner that was suddenly going down, but like a trained pilot there was no panic, just a cool-quick-hard assessment of her options.

It was not in her nature to wilt under pressure; her father had schooled her in roughhouse play, and she knew how give back as good as she got.

She buzzed Shavonne and told her to alert the officers (except for Marty) that there would be an emergency conference call in one hour. In the interim, she began calling each of the remaining board members to give them a heads-up and sketch out her plan for a counterattack. She left one urgent message, two voicemails, and had a brief and to the point conversation with the remaining four. Each strongly agreed with her plan to bring legal action to force the merger.

On the conference call with her officers, Gwen gave them the news without sugar-coating it, hearing Russ say, "Bloody hell." That about summed it up. But there was no time to commiserate with her colleagues. Instead, she launched into their next steps, which included filing a lawsuit to force the merger.

"Atlantis's announcement is due out in the morning," she said, "but I'll counter it with a teleconference stating our strong position to calm our shareholders. Stu, set up a call at once with our law firm to formulate grounds and push for a quick timeline to file suit. Now I need everyone's input on a communique I plan to send out in the morning to all our employees."

Gwen stressed that the communique needed to tactfully balance the bad news with the strength of their position, leaving everyone with hope. Russ and Chandra gave her good advice on wording while all of them promised to follow-up the communique (which would be broadcast across the company via email) with discussions inside their own departments to help calm the waves and maintain a business-as-usual mindset.

"This isn't over," she said firmly. "We will file suit, force Atlantis into a one-eighty, and get back on track. Are you with me?" They all agreed, and she thanked them for their support before terminating the call.

Later that evening, Gwen was still at her desk. She was mentally exhausted but she forced herself to run through her checklist one more time before heading home. In a call with the lawyers, they had laid the groundwork for swift legal action and promised to *get crackin'*. News of Atlantis's announcement had already leaked to the press and she'd deflected calls from reporters by telling them there would be a teleconference in the morning where she would state CrestPoint's position and take their questions. All of the board of directors had now been briefed and she had their unyielding support. The communique to CrestPoint employees was complete and queued up in her email ready to go out in the morning.

She thought about her cat Popeye. He needed to be fed and was probably out of water. With that errand in mind, she shut down her computer and found her purse. The phone rang and she saw it was Marty. This will be short and sweet, she thought to herself.

"Marty," she answered. "I'm about to leave. Make it quick."

"What are you pulling?" he accused her. She could hear the controlled anger in his voice.

"Whaddya mean?"

"You know exactly what I mean. You held an emergency call with all the officers today about the merger—then talked to all the board of directors—without me. *I'm* the chairman of the board. These calls can't happen without me, as you goddam well know."

"What's your point?"

"My point! My fucking point is you're to do nothing about the merger until I convene the board and we work out a game plan. That'll include finding the right leadership to weather this storm."

"It's already been decided, Marty. You're out. You're done. I'm now the chair*woman* of the board." She listened with amusement to his outraged reaction (he had more creative uses for the F-word than a New York mob boss) and waited for him to wind it up.

"Where do you get off?" he demanded indignantly. "Who the fuck do you think you are? What right do you have to do this to me?"

"Ask Frank Altobello."

There was dead silence on the other end and Gwen smiled to herself. "Hmm, that's what I thought... Adios, Marty." And with that she hung up.

Gwen opened her front door and immediately stopped. The lights were on in her living room and she could hear music coming from the stereo. *Shit,* she thought to herself. *Cutter.* That was her latest bad boy—Cutter—and she had no idea how he'd gotten into her condo without a key. Bottom line, she was in no mood for Cutter and in no mood for what he came to give her. She just had one shitty day and all she wanted to do was eat the Thai food she'd brought home, drink a couple glasses of wine, and curl up with her cat on the couch.

At the thought of Popeye, the one-eyed, reddish cat magically appeared at her feet and rubbed himself against her calves. She went into the kitchen where she set down the bag of food along with her purse and keys then bent over and scratched Popeye's neck. She noticed that his food bowl was empty and his water bowl dry, and she quickly refilled both, her lousy mood growing lousier.

After pouring herself a glass of wine, she took a sip and walked out into the living room to deal with Cutter. DJ was long gone but the type—young, ill-mannered, and primitive to the core—still remained. Cutter is what he called himself and what his biker buddies called him, and whether it was his first or last name she didn't know or really care. He lay sprawled out on the couch with one leg on and one leg off, two empty beer bottles on the floor next to him, listening to heavy metal music that gave her a headache.

She walked over to the stereo and turned it off. "How'd you get in here?" she asked.

"You invited me. Hey, turn that back on."

"You don't have a key, so how'd you get in?"

He swung up into a sitting position, eyeing her with a sly grin. "Climbed up your balcony and jimmied the sliding door," he replied. "Piece of cake."

The Heights of Mountains

She glanced over at the sliding glass door and saw that it was open, then turned her eyes back to him. His bare, tattooed forearms rested on his knees and were covered with images of human skulls, ghouls, and arcane numerology. She knew that this one was just a little bit crazy; he had an unhinged kind of fury that could go on like a light switch if she wasn't careful. Normally, that danger excited her, and she could manipulate it to fulfill her needs, but tonight, in her foul mood, she ignored the warning signs.

"That's breaking and entering," she said, giving him the Novak glare. It had no effect on him, and in a slow, foreboding motion, he stood up from the sofa. "So, call the cops," he laughed as he came up to her, his dark eyes revealing a mischievous excitement. He reached down to turn the stereo back on, and as she moved to stop him, he quickly grabbed her wrist, a sneer forming on his lips. His eyes told her he was primed for their rough game.

"No!" she shouted, twisting her arm free from his grip. "No play time tonight, Cutter. I'm in no mood. Get your shit and go." She turned her back on him and began to walk away but he grabbed her blouse and yanked her back, ripping her buttons. He let go, laughing again, only this time without any humor, a taunting kind of laugh.

"Goddam it! You ripped my blouse," she said angrily. "I said, get out! Go! I'm not playing around," she repeated, busily examining the damage to her blouse, fully upset and determined to get him to leave. He ignored her and quickly stepped up into her face, a menacing sneer on his lips, but she didn't flinch or back away. His fingers were in the front of her bra, tugging her hard, his voice hissing "Come on, bitch—you know you want it" but she was having none of it. She'd gone toe to toe with a number of powerful men today, and Cutter, with his gypsy leathers and sneering face, was just an overgrown child in comparison. Without thinking, she sniffed a dismissive laugh, rolling her eyes mockingly, suddenly sensing she'd made a mistake.

His eyes changed in an instant, from noxious dark to a crazed luminescence, and for the first time she felt a twinge of fear. He grabbed her hair and pulled her head back viciously, the spit flying from his mouth as he told her he wasn't going anywhere— "just here, you fucking cunt—laugh at me! —go ahead, laugh some more!"

Her fear was full-blown now as she desperately looked for a way out, and as he put his other hand around her throat, she reacted instinctively and kneed him hard in the groin. He sunk to the ground, a guttural painfilled groan filling the room, and crawled on all fours towards the coffee table. This was her chance to escape, but instead of running for the front door, she backed up to the dining table, glancing frantically about for a weapon. Something sailed past her ear and smashed against the wall. A beer bottle! He'd thrown a beer bottle at her, just missing her temple. "I'm calling the police!" she cried out, reaching for the phone.

Before she could press 9, he was on her, throwing her to the ground and leaping on top of her. He slapped her repeatedly, and not with his fingertips as she had taught him, but with his open hand, slapping her hard as he growled and spitted invectives at her— "Bitch! Fuckin' whore! Keep laughing. Go on, laugh some more."

All she could think to do was use their safe word, and she shouted it again and again without affect while trying to fend off his slaps. He stopped suddenly, then put his knees in-between her legs, forcing them apart, and started unbuckling his belt. "*No!*" she ordered him. "Stop! You fuckin' animal! Stop!" He laughed at her, knocking her hands away as she tried to resist, but she managed to grab a hunk of his hair and pull hard at it. "*Yeow!* Fuck!" he yelled, one hand countering her grip and the other going to her neck where he squeezed until she let go of his hair, unable to breathe and now fearing for her life. "Ha! You wanna see an animal?" he grunted at her. "I'll show you an animal. Bitch!" And at that, he grabbed a handful of her torn blouse, lifting her face towards him, and cocked his fist back.

She saw it coming, the first one, sending a white searing pain through her head, but after that she could only feel the dull thuds of his fists raining down on her face. Before slipping into unconsciousness, her eyes flashed on the small tattoo inside his right bicep that read 666. It's the last thing she remembered.

———

Russ was doing dishes in the galley when his phone rang. He wiped his hands dry and walked over to the phone and picked up the receiver. "Russ, here," he answered.

"*Russs...*" It was a broken voice, filled with anguish, and it almost sounded like Gwen. "Who's this?" he asked. After a pause, the anguished voice repeated itself, *"Russs... I need you."*

"Gwen, is that you? What's happened? Where are you?"

"At home... I need you."

"Be right there," he said quickly. "Whatever's wrong, just stay put. I'm on my way. Okay?" He waited a moment for a reply.

"Okay."

He hung up, grabbed his wallet and keys, and jogged up the long dock to the parking lot where he jumped into his Triumph Spitfire and sped off. She was hurt, maybe badly injured—he was sure of it, he could tell by her voice—and he let out some shaft, pushing his sports car to the limit. He'd already planned out his route; he'd cut up highway 92 to highway 280, then drop down into the City. There was less traffic and less cops that way, and he was sure he could make it in twenty minutes.

As he raced through the foothills up to the main freeway, he thought about what a crazy day it'd been. And it wasn't over yet. Besides the Atlantis deal going belly-up and the conference call with Gwen, there was the email he received—not a call or a personal visit, but an email—from Lori Hunter, informing him that the sexual harassment charge against him had been dropped. There was no explanation, no apology, and he was sure she was disappointed and probably still thought him guilty, but the news was a relief and one less thing to worry about. But now this—Gwen—the formidable Gwen Novak—in desperate need of his help.

Then there was the neurologist at the hospital telling him today that, yes, it was confirmed, his son had suffered permanent brain damage. Traumatic Brain Trauma—TMI, he called it—causing irreparable harm to Dan's cognitive skills. His son would have lasting difficulty in speaking, in processing information, and have the intellectual capacity of a ten-year old, leading to a lifetime of special care. But he didn't want to think about that right now, and he swept his thoughts clean as he took a hard turn at eighty-five miles per hour. Gwen was his focus. She needed him.

When he arrived at her condo, he found the door unlocked and entered carefully, not sure if he should be ready for trouble or not. There was a smashed picture in the hallway, one of her expensive art prints, and he stepped around the glass to get by. He called out her name, waited, then called out again.

"In here," he heard a weak voice answer from another room, and he walked to the end of the hall and looked into the living room. There was a patch of dried blood on the carpet and dreading the worse he followed the trail of blood into the master bedroom where he found her sitting on the edge of the bed in her bathrobe. She held an ice pack to her face, and next to her on the bed was a wadded up blood-stained towel. *"Christ!"* he exclaimed, rushing to the bed where he kneeled down beside her. "What the hell happened?" he asked, examining her bruised and bloody face.

"Thanks for coming," she said, her one good eye opening briefly.

"Of course—of course I came. What else would I be doing, watching *Who Wants to be a Millionaire?*" Now let me see… One of your boyfriends do this?" he asked, his tone gentle and comforting. When she nodded yes, he thought about cracking a joke to lighten the mood but decided against it. "Let me see that," he said, peeking under the ice pack to see a deep gash above her eye. "You're gonna need stitches. We need to get you to emergency." When she nodded in compliance, he noticed her left eye had a broken blood vessel. The asshole had done a number on her, he concluded, but besides a split lip and other contusions to her face, she appeared to be okay. "Are you hurt anywhere else?" he asked.

"No," she lied. She'd been raped but she wasn't going to tell him that—or the nurses in emergency. That would remain her dirty little secret, the final punctuation on her dirty little life.

"We need to get you dressed. You don't want to go outside lookin' like the Big Lebowski." She tried to smile but it hurt her lip. He was asking her questions (Where's your jeans? Where's a sweatshirt?), and she pointed to one drawer, then another, as he gathered up her clothes, pulled on her jeans, removed her bathrobe, and carefully put on her sweatshirt as he quietly and efficiently took over the situation. His presence was comforting; he was kind and gentle and she let him take over, feeling safe in his company, and when he finished dressing her and he reached down, tenderly taking her hands to help her up, she was overcome by his gentleness and sat back down to cry, something she hadn't done in years.

"Don't go blubbery on me, Novak," he playfully ordered.

"It's just… it's just… I'm just so glad you came."

"You kidding me. You're the only woman I've ever almost loved," he half-joked, taking her hands again and lifting her off the bed. He guided her into the bathroom where she wiped her face and brushed her hair, then he found her a baseball cap to wear and guided her past the broken glass in the hallway and out the door.

In the Emergency Room, they gave her twelve stitches, a pain shot, and a prescription of codeine. Besides cuts and abrasions, her left cheekbone was cracked but luckily her nose wasn't broken. Her official story was she'd been mugged walking home from the Thai restaurant but she didn't want to file a police report. The mugger had beaten her up and taken her money (which was true—Cutter had stolen her money but left her car keys) but all she wanted to do now was go home. They released her a little after midnight and Russ drove her home where she laid down on the sofa with an ice pack and watched him clean up the broken glass.

The shot of Demerol had relaxed her, taking away the throbbing pain in her face, and as she watched Russ carefully pick out pieces of glass from the carpet, she decided to tell him the truth—all of it—about Roxanne and Stu (he had been right all along), about the call from Altobello, and about Marty's sabotage.

He listened to her as he picked up the glass and scrubbed the blood out of the carpet, and when she was done, he merely nodded without comment. To him, it was a fitting ending to a crazy day.

"I have a teleconference call with the press tomorrow. 10:00 am," she said abruptly. "I have to be on it."

"Change it to a conference call and take it from here," suggested Russ.

"Yes, good idea, I'll have Shavonne change it to a conference call—but I'm going into the office to take it… I also have to talk to the lawyers."

"You're in no shape to go into the office," he said, hoping to dissuade her, but he could see a fierce determination in her eyes. It was good to see it back.

"No," she replied firmly. "I'm going in—and forget the mugging story. My cover story is a car accident."

"Sure. You're a lousy driver anyway."

"Funny guy."

He offered to stay the night, sleep on the sofa and drive her to work in the morning, but she politely declined, telling him he'd done enough and to go home and get some sleep. She was fine, she was okay, she assured him. "But I'd like you to join me in my office at ten for the call," she asked. Of course he would, he told her, going over to the sliding glass door where he locked and braced it shut. He checked to see if she needed anything else before leaning over and lightly kissing her on the forehead.

"See you tomorrow," he said.

"See you, old chap," she replied, almost cheerfully, and as he walked away a thought occurred to her. "Russ," she called out, and he paused and turned back. "Is it true?" she asked.

"Is what true?"

"That I'm the only woman you almost fell in love with."

―

The lights were off in Gwen's office, no doubt by design, and gave the room a rather gloomy feel, thought Russ. Gwen sat next to him at the conference table wearing sunglasses and a baseball cap. She'd done a remarkable job of covering up her stitches and bruises with small band-aids and makeup, and the sunglasses and hat completed the illusion that she was simply going incognito for the day. Russ joked that she looked like some starlet trying to avoid the paparazzi, and she smiled at the compliment.

Shavonne hovered over them like a mother hen, bringing Gwen water, adjusting the blinds, and getting everything ready for the conference call with the media. The call would be conducted via a gray, starfish-looking device sitting on the table, and Shavonne punched in a number on its keypad to open up the conference bridge. In minutes, members of the press would be calling in, announcing their presence, and Gwen would welcome them and wait until the bridge was full up before kicking off the call with her opening statement.

Russ knew that he wasn't here to answer questions from the press. This was all Gwen's show; he was here for moral support, and he felt rather flattered that she had invited him to sit in. He glanced over and saw her studying her written statement and quickly noticed that her left hand was trembling slightly. He reached over and gently squeezed her hand, and she looked up and smiled warmly at him as the first caller buzzed in and announced his name and press credentials.

By 10:05, the conference bridge was full and Gwen welcomed everyone to the call. "Hi, this is Gwen Novak, CEO and President of CrestPoint Communications, and I have Russ Chappel, our Chief Development Officer along with me... This morning Atlantis announced they were abrogating their legal agreement and backing out of the merger deal with CrestPoint. I will convey our formal response to this unwarranted move then take your questions afterwards."

Pausing only a moment, she launched into their formal reply, stating that they were "stunned" by Atlantis's decision and were "exploring all our options, including legal action." Yes, CrestPoint had been compelled to restate their second quarter earnings due to bad debt—to customers not paying their bills—but this did not entitle Atlantis to terminate either the merger agreement or its agreement to provide interim financing. CrestPoint was prepared to sue Atlantis to force them to complete the merger, but they hoped this would not be necessary and that Atlantis would reconsider their decision, honor their agreement, and avoid costly litigation.

Once she finished, the questions came fast and furious, and Gwen took them head on, keeping the focus on CrestPoint's status as the aggrieved party and on their possible litigation. What was their financial situation, many of them wanted to know, and Gwen assured them that they had more than $120 million on hand and were "currently not in violation of any financial contracts."

Russ sat and marveled at her performance. Eleven hours ago, he thought, she was in the emergency room getting stitched up, a bloody mess, and now here she was—the quick-witted, hard-nosed Gwen Novak—doing her thing and fighting valiantly for the survival of their company. She was a remarkable woman.

When the call ended, she sat very still on the edge of her seat, balancing precariously there as though she'd almost slid down a mountainside but caught herself in time. Russ looked at her without speaking but the expression on his face told her everything she needed to know. She'd risen to the occasion, she was sure of it, and his look of admiration confirmed it. But her good feeling was suddenly eclipsed by a flash of pain in her cracked cheekbone. She'd taken a pain pill three hours ago but it was already beginning to wear off, and she reached into her purse that hung from her chair, pulled out her prescription bottle, and tapped out a large white pill.

Russ noticed her wince in pain then watched as she took her pain pill, washing it down with the bottle of water Shavonne had given her. "I think you made your case," he said brightly, hoping to take her mind off her pain. "Loud and clear. Let's just hope they report it that way."

"Oh, they will," she said, swallowing her pill. "It's a David and Goliath story. They'll eat it up. And when Atlantis sees that public opinion's against them and weigh the cost of litigation, they'll reverse their decision and we'll get back on track."

"Hmm, I'm sure they will," replied Russ, almost believing her.

CHAPTER 9

Peet's Coffee kiosk was closed down but employees could still come into the Hub and get a hot cup of coffee from one of the two Hamilton Beach coffeemakers that sat on the counter next to the sink. It all worked on an honor system; if you were first in, it was your job to fill them up and get both machines percolating. After that, if you poured out the last cup from one of the pots, you were supposed to change the filter, replenish the water, and start a new batch. But that didn't always happen, and people coming in for their afternoon break often found one or both pots empty and cursed loudly at this breach in common courtesy.

What had once been a bustling center of activity was now something of a ghost town, and a sign on the double doors explained why—the Hub was closing in a week. Gone were the arcade games and foosball tables (already sold and shipped out) while the ping pong table had become a collection point for stacks of packing boxes. There was still a bookshelf filled with board games (which nobody played) but the computer stations had been redeployed and only one of the two TV screens still worked, silently broadcasting out CNBC which nobody watched. One could still peruse a copy of the *San Jose Mercury* and *San Francisco Chronicle* but the other subscriptions had been cancelled in the name of 'cost-cutting' along with some of the more esoteric items in the vending machines such as Drake's coffee cakes and Toblerone chocolate bars.

Fortunately, for a small group of employees on their afternoon break, the honor system had worked and they were able to pour themselves fresh cups of coffee. They collected near the coffeemakers, two sipping their java, one stirring in creamer, while two others who'd opted for sodas stood next to the coffee-drinkers talking office gossip.

"I wished I'd known they were selling the foosball tables. I would'a bought one."

"Save your money. You're gonna need it."

"Didn't you sell any of your stock?"

"Hell, no. Did you? Nobody did, and now it's at what this morning?"

"Three dollars and twenty-five cents a share."

"Right. Three twenty-five. Worthless."

"It's hard to imagine that not too long ago we were all millionaires. Course, not like Brent here. Weren't you worth about ten mil right after the IPO? Thought so. Then, *boom*—gone, gone with the wind. Just like that… The whole thing's heartbreaking."

"It's a freakin' Greek tragedy, is what it is."

"You guys are all doom and gloom."

"Not hard to be when you're not sure you're gonna have a job next week. I mean, 20% layoff is—what?—about 250 jobs?"

"Yeah—about. But we all know the drill. You guys came over from SBC, so you know the drill. We owe everyone money—RBOCs, suppliers, cities, everyone—and investors want action. Analysts wanna see a plan. So, what does management *always* do? They announce lay-offs—"

"*Downsizing*, I believe, is the proper term."

"Right—*downsizing, right-sizing*, whatever you wanna call it—it's all part of a plan to cut costs and buy time."

"I heard they're selling off TelaPoint to the Netherlands."

"That puts Marty out of a job. Course, he'll probably go off and start another company. Invent something."

"Heinz already came up with an E-Z squirt bottle, so what's left?"

Everyone chuckled at the joke, the kind of cynical laugh shared by survivors in a leaky lifeboat, but they were all sure of one thing—the brilliant Marty Madrid would somehow come out of all this smelling like a rose.

"But my point is—they're buying time. Meanwhile, we sue Atlantis, force them to honor the merger, or Gwen goes out and finds another buyer. I tell ya, she's gonna pull off a Brandi Chastain."

"Just as long as she doesn't yank off her blouse."

The Heights of Mountains

"Hope she wears a sport's bra. Wasn't she some big-time basketball ball player in college?"

"Yeah. UCLA. I think she was All-Pac-10. Hey, Sandy—wasn't Gwen All-Pac-10 in college?... Yeah, I thought so."

There was a pause in their banter as each of them tried to imagine the imperial and no-nonsense Gwen Novak playing basketball. Another employee appeared, and after filling her coffee cup stepped over to the group and said, "Have you heard the latest?"

"Oh-oh, what now?"

"Pulse Net just announced their own lay-off. 450 jobs. Plus, they're pulling out of some of their markets. They're only gonna focus on their top forty."

This triggered an animated discussion that included a flurry of not-so-surprised comments followed by questions and speculation. What about their other competitor Nomad, someone wondered. Rumors were that Nomad planned to restate their earnings and announce layoffs as well. Everyone was agreed-- it was a general bloodbath.

"Just look at all the dot-com companies that have gone under. Boo-dot-com"

"Pets-dot-com."

"Yeah, it's all a domino effect. They were interviewing some analyst from Merrill Lynch who said the DSL carriers have been clobbered by the markets this year. Mostly because of competition from the Baby Bells and the fact that the Internet craze is turning out to be a lot of hype."

"Nice to know that now."

"It's like that movie *Deep Impact*. We've all been walking around with no clue that a killer comet was on its way to wipe us out."

"That's the one with Morgan Freeman as president, right?"

"Yeah, and Robert Duval."

"All I *know*, I'm not workin' a bunch of overtime without compensation. They lay a bunch of people off and expect us to pick up the slack—but not this time."

"You're salary. You have no choice. Whatcha gonna do, quit?"

"And go back to SBC?"

"Why not?"

"They won't take you back as an employee, but you can come back as a contractor. I know a couple people who've done it. You remember Rick Perez? He did it. Went back as a contractor doing pretty much the same thing he was doing before."

This triggered an open debate regarding the pros and cons of working as a contractor, and by the time it winded down their break was over. Empty coffee cups and soda cans were tossed into the trash and the small group of employees filtered out the door. One employee remained. She emptied and rinsed out the coffee pots, sprayed the sinks clean, and wiped down the counter, worrying the whole time about what she would do if she lost her job.

Barry carried a box from his car into his bedroom, setting it down next to the other boxes that contained his albums, CDs, books, and assortment of clothes. Mo followed behind him with another box.

"Is that the last one?" asked Barry.

"Yep—except for your bike."

"I'll get it later," he said and watched as Mo plopped down in the swivel chair at his old desk, bent over, and plucked a book out from one of the boxes. His other buddy Ender had been a no-show, leaving it to him and Mo to move his stuff back into his old bedroom. Fortunately, his parents had left his room intact, not converting it into a den or guest bedroom, and even the old DSL connection was still active.

The book Mo picked up was a how-to on day-trading, and as he thumbed through it, he asked lazily, "How much were you up?"

"I don't know," sighed Barry philosophically. "About $325,000. That was in March, right before Black Friday. Then I got wiped out."

"I thought you cashed in some of your stock?"

"I did. I still got $5500 or so in the bank, otherwise I'm broke. Most of what I made I traded off and bought more shares. Now all my stock is underwater, sitting at less—a lot less—than what I bought it for."

The Heights of Mountains

"Bummer."

Barry agreed, it was a bummer. As an active day-trader, with accounts through Street.com and RagingBull, he'd had remarkable success buying and selling stock, so much so that he'd been able to move out of his parents' house and into his own apartment. From May of '99 to March of 2000, Barry was on a roll, using his high-speed Internet service and beginners' luck to get in on IPOs for Akamai Technologies, eToys.com, MicroStrategy, and even Value America, making a small fortune on paper. But all those companies had crashed and burned, along with other dot-com or telecom companies he'd invested in, draining his bank account as he attempted to recoup his losses through even riskier buys, leaving him now in August of 2000 with $5500 to his name and no choice but to move back home.

The doorbell rang and Barry ignored it as he rummaged through his things. When it rang again, he yelled out, "Mom! Someone's at the door!"

"I got it!" he heard her yell back from somewhere in the house. The door opened, there was talking, and within seconds Ender appeared carrying a grocery bag.

"You're a little late, dude," said Barry.

"Couldn't be helped," replied Ender. "But I come bearing gifts." He reached into his grocery bag and pulled out a six pack of Heineken beer.

This was a gift indeed—their gourmet beer of choice—which was usually only purchased for special occasions or when one of them was flush with cash. Otherwise, it was cut-rate beer like Pabst Blue Ribbon. (It was even more of a surprise given that Ender had just been laid off by Sun Microsystems.) He handed Barry and Mo each a cold, green bottle of beer and took one out for himself.

"Anyone got an opener?"

"Here," answered Mo who pulled out a medallion that hung on a chain around his neck. It was a small replica of the Millennium Falcon that acted as a bottle opener. He popped the cap off his beer then passed the opener to Barry, and after it made the rounds, he placed it lovingly back around his neck.

• 369

Ender raised his beer in a toast. "Here's to moving back in with the parents," he joked. "Without them we'd be homeless."

"Where you been?" asked Barry, not amused by the toast. "Don't tell us the Green Goblin broke down again?" The Green Goblin was Ender's 1977 green-colored Gremlin, which had a penchant for breaking down at the most convenient times.

"Nah, I wish," replied Ender, taking on a tone of righteous indignation. "I've been on the phone all friggin day trying to get my Internet back up. I can't even get online. Who's your ISP here—Telocity, right?"

"Yeah. Telocity."

"Does it work?"

"It should. My mom uses it to get online. I've been teaching her how to browse. The connection in here should be good to go. I just need to plug in."

"Well, consider yourself lucky, dude, cause there's been a disturbance in the Force and Fastcom's gone to the dark side. Their main office line is disconnected and when you call their tech support line you get a recording that says they've suspended service."

"That's 'cause they filed for Chapter 11," said Barry, who made it a habit to keep up on the latest business news.

"I *know* that *now*," replied Ender, taking a long chug of his beer before launching into his tale of woe. "I called Everyone's Internet in Texas. They're supposed to know what's going on with the ISPs, but all they told me is that they went bankrupt. Duh. Okay, but why is my service down, and they told me to call the PUC and complain, so I did. Ever try calling the PUC? It's like dealing with the Guild—"

"Did you offer them any spice?"

"I wish. I wish I had some spice, a whole bag of it. But no—all you can do with the PUC is lodge a complaint. So I did, and we'll see what happens. Meanwhile, I'm stuck orbiting Hoth unable to jump to hyperspace."

"Just switch providers," suggested Mo. "Go with Telocity like Bare."

"Guess I'm gonna have to."

"Well, here's my advice," said Barry, who had sat down on his bed and now laid back, assuming the role of the wise wizard. "Telocity isn't in any better shape than Fastcom. They might go bankrupt tomorrow, who knows? They both get their DSL service from CrestPoint and resell it to nerds like us, and CrestPoint is in the shitter just like the rest of them. It's the domino effect. Your best bet is to get it from SBC."

"*SBC?* That'd be like buying a Cadillac."

"Nah, I've been checking out their prices and they're just as cheap, plus they got discount specials going on." He finished off his beer and gazed thoughtfully into its green emptiness. "You gotta think of it this way: Your DSL comes in on SBC's line. CrestPoint just rents it and resells it. Now the big boys like SBC and Atlantis got their own service and they're stomping on the little guys, cuttin' out the middleman—and they ain't goin' anywhere. You're not gonna lose service tomorrow cause SBC went bankrupt." He paused to let the overwhelming force of his logic sink in.

"Guess that makes sense," conceded Mo."

"I can try that," agreed Ender, sounding skeptical.

"*Do or do not. There is no try,*" quoted Barry using his best Yoda imitation. "Now pass me another Heine."

Chapter 10

By October, it was apparent to Gwen and the board of directors that Atlantis had called their bluff. After waging a war of words in the press, and after filing a lawsuit in federal court, it was evident to Gwen and the board that their gambit to force the merger back on track had failed. The lawsuit would take years to resolve, and in the meantime, Atlantis made it clear that they were under no obligation to provide CrestPoint interim funding. Gwen railed at that decision, but a spokesman for Atlantis put an end to the debate by stating unequivocally that they disagreed with Novak's claims, adding, "We have terminated our merger agreement. That's our position, end of story."

To nail the coffin shut, Atlantis used the termination of the merger to eliminate the losses they had expected to incur by investing in the CrestPoint acquisition, announcing that they were raising their forecasted profits for the next two years as a result. Atlantis's stock ticked up on the announcement while CrestPoint's stock bottomed out.

In the investment community, the David and Goliath story played about as long as a stale Broadway musical. Investors quickly turned on CrestPoint, blaming mismanagement of its debt and its deteriorating market share for the merger collapse. Some analysts pointed the finger at the one-dimensional business model, not just singling out CrestPoint but Nomad and Pulse as well (who were all floundering). Frank Altobello from World Markets reflected this view, adding salt to the wound when he was quoted as saying, "Everybody seemed to jump on the DSL bandwagon without realizing these companies had no other product to fall back on. Single product companies like CrestPoint were programmed to fail, yet investors poured money into them anyway. Go figure."

Despite the bad news, Gwen was not done fighting. Not by a long shot. She was waging a battle to survive on multiple fronts—in the courtroom, in the media, in board meetings—and she applied every tactic she'd learned over her eighteen years in the game, a game she was well-versed in and played at the highest level.

First, there were aggressive cost-cutting measures that needed to be implemented. This would demonstrate to the industry and to their investors that they were serious about righting the ship and weathering the storm. She held emergency meetings with her leadership team (which no longer included Marty) and asked each of her EVPs to come up with a plan to downsize by 20%. This, in turn, triggered departmental meetings where each of the EVPs tasked their VPs and directors to quickly identify "fat" and "redundancy" and come up with a plan to absorb a 20% reduction in force. This exercise resulted in a list of names—the people targeted to lose their jobs—and was performed with grim efficiency by managers who'd been through this many times before over their career. With the list completed, pink slips went out on a Friday morning along with a month's salary and a thank-you note for their service.

In those same emergency meetings, Gwen brain-stormed with her team on other ways to cut expenses. First on the chopping block was their European venture TelaPoint, which everyone agreed should be sold off. Next came the no-brainers, like ending expense accounts, travel, and office supplies. Other low-hanging fruit included shutting down the Hub (and all its frills) and terminating the lease on Marty's studio apartment.

Even deeper cuts followed. It was Ron Lau's task to slash the advertising budget and drastically scale back Product Marketing. Chandra cancelled the IT support contract, put all software upgrades on hold, and looked for resellers to buy up their unused workstations. Russ saw to it that all growth jobs were stopped, equipment orders cancelled, and the installation contract with Lucent converted into a maintenance-only agreement. Lori, whose department included real estate management, re-worked their lease at Rio Seco Business Park and came up with a plan to consolidate the remaining employees into two buildings. It was Stu's job to terminate their contract with Tollerson

Accounting, though he pushed back vigorously on this move, arguing that their services were still needed, but Gwen insisted. She also insisted that Hal Rubin be included in the lay-off.

It was evident to everyone in these emergency meetings that Gwen could barely tolerate Stu, that he was nothing more to her than a tool she needed to wield in order to fix the CrestPoint engine. In her hard-nosed style, she quickly dismantled his little empire, effectively gutting his 'smoker's brigade' and booting Tollerson out the door. Stu fought against these moves but lost. Gwen had the board's support and all he could do was concede defeat and sulk heavily at the end of the table. But for those who knew him, like Russ, defeat was not something that would sit well with Stu. There was a strong rumor going around that Enron was courting Stu and that he'd soon be off to greener pastures. Russ, for one, hoped the rumor was true.

As Gwen shed expenses, she worked day and night to find other buyers and to convince investors to stay the course, pouring every ounce of her energy into it as if it were a life-or-death struggle. There was something Russ said in one of the emergency meetings that sunk deep into her psyche. It was after a particularly grueling day, a day spent making gut-wrenching decisions about people's lives and future, when Russ put things into perspective in his best Churchillian style: "Don't lose patience and don't lose hope. We have a steep mountain to climb, and there may be fewer of us left when we reach the top, but we're bloody well gonna get there." She had nodded and smiled in appreciation at her dear friend, feeling certain at that moment that she and Russ would bloody well get there.

Russ found a spot to park on Crestpoint Drive and walked up to the studio apartment still wondering why Marty invited him to this rendezvous. "For old time's sake," Marty had said over the phone. "Plus, I have to turn in the key." Russ was both apprehensive and a little curious as to Marty's motive. He'd not seen or heard from him in weeks, ever since

Marty collected his lucrative exit package from the board and gone into exile. His phone call came from out of the blue and with it this mystery meeting.

As he mounted the steps, he could see Marty in the window, and before he could knock on the door, Marty swung it open holding a bottle of champagne.

"Sir Chappel," said Marty cheerily, shaking Russ' hand. "Welcome. Come on in, see what's left of our launch pad. This is the same brand of champagne we shared the night we founded CrestPoint. Three and a half years ago. Seems like yesterday. Thought we'd drink a glass over the body and toast to our new future."

"Oh, what future is that?" asked Russ as he came into the apartment and quickly glanced around. The lease was set to expire in two days and the apartment was pretty much emptied of all furniture. All that remained were two bar stools over by the small kitchen counter where Marty had set two empty champagne glasses. Russ was in no mood to raise a glass 'over the body' of CrestPoint, as Marty put it, considering that he and Gwen and the others were still fighting mightily to keep her afloat. Marty had to know that, so Russ had no idea what future he was alluding to. Given his cheerful mood, he guessed that Six-gun Marty invited him here to tell him all about some new venture he was involved in. Knowing Marty, it was probably another innovative start-up company.

"You already got something lined up?" he asked.

Marty put his arm around Russ' shoulder and led him over to the counter. "What did you expect?" he replied, smiling broadly. "Course I do, and it's something exciting. Here, have a glass with me… I think it'll blow you away. It's definitely cutting edge and can't miss. All this time we've been spinning our wheels on DSL, we were missing the big picture. We just needed to wait a little bit—let the technology catch up with the theory. Internet telephony is what it's all about—IP telephony—and it's gonna be the next big thing." And with that, Marty proceeded to describe to Russ in his exuberant style the beauty of IP telephony. It was all about voice over IP, he exclaimed.

Anyone with a broadband connection could obtain unlimited, flat-rate telephone service with any number they wanted. It would blow the old telephone companies out of the water. It was, he said with a grand flourish, "the ultimate storm of creative destruction."

"Sounds promising," replied Russ, examining the flurry of tiny bubbles in his champagne glass. "IP telephony. Thought it still had its drawbacks. Voice quality problems, right?"

"Solved," declared Marty triumphantly. "I'm working with a team up in Seattle, and we have the problem solved. And much more. Think of an Internet-enabled voicemail system and voicemail-to-email. It's gonna blow everyone's mind."

"It's a start-up then. Got a name?"

"VoiceNet or VoiceCom—haven't decided yet. But I think we'll be able to kick off in a month or so. Already got the funding."

"Well, you're the master at that," complimented Russ as he raised his glass. "Here's to Voice-net or Voice-com, or whatever it's called, and a bright future." He clicked glasses with Marty and took a sip, wondering to himself whether Marty had brought him here to ask him to join in this new venture? God, he hoped not. The one thing he'd learned about Marty through the whole CrestPoint experience was this-- Marty was uncontained energy. In the beginning, he was a whirlwind, full of vim and vigor, a hundred great ideas coming out of his mouth every day, but a genius who got easily bored or distracted. In mechanical engineering, he was a force vector without orientation and, as a result, had no one line of direction. He couldn't see himself working with Marty again.

"Hmm, thanks," replied Marty, sipping his champagne as he studied Russ' body language. He appeared slightly preoccupied, maybe even tired, which was understandable considering the dual burden of CrestPoint and Dan's medical condition that weighed heavily on his friend. This was one of the reasons he'd asked Russ here—to tell him it was all right, that he, Marty, was going to be all right, and to see if his old friend held any grudges against him for how CrestPoint imploded.

"You know," added Marty, "I always thought this place would turn into a shrine, like the Hewlett Packard garage."

Russ smiled and nodded. He was used to Marty changing topics on a dime, so this one-eighty didn't faze him, and he thought he detected a hint of wistfulness in Marty's voice.

"Our dream factory… I really thought we had something here," continued Marty. "I thought we'd captured lightning in a bottle, that DSL was gonna sell like hotcakes and take us to new heights. But we were done in by a hyped-up market, by unfair competition and our own mismanagement." He stopped for a moment to gauge Russ's reaction, and he could see by the raised eyebrow that he touched a nerve. But that wasn't going to stop him from saying what he needed to say. "People stopped believing—turned it into bean counting. You know, I could'a saved that deal. I know you're gonna say I never wanted the merger in the first place, but once it fell through, I could have salvaged it, not with Gwen as CEO but with a clean sweep and an arrangement that would'a saved the company."

"Stop, Marty," said Russ abruptly. "Everyone knows it was you who sabotaged the deal with Atlantis, so don't spin any yarns."

"Okay. All right. I know I'm persona non grata over at CrestPoint, but think about it—when did we start sliding down the mountain? When Gwen showed up. It was always her plan to sell us off, and don't pretend otherwise. You know it's true. She started shopping us around the moment she came in the door. It was always her plan to get some corporate giant to scoop us up and turn us into a minor subsidiary. Then she'd get a sweet payday and move on to her next conquest. Cause that's what she does. Look at her track record."

"I disagree," replied Russ. (He wasn't angry at Marty, he'd even half-expected this little try at redemption, but he had no intention of buying what Marty was selling today.) "The merger was the smart move, the only move, and you were the only one who didn't think so—the only one—and in a snit fit, you went out of your way to blow it up. But don't count Gwen out just yet. She's gonna find a buyer. Wait and see. Then CrestPoint will get back on its feet."

"Ahh, Russ," sighed Marty. (He loved and respected Russ but the poor man was sorely misguided.) "For such an intelligent fellow, you never check your side mirrors. You have a sizable blind spot. What do you think is gonna happen with CrestPoint now? Really? With no merger, no funding, debt up the ying-yang—what do you think is gonna happen? I'll tell you. Within a month, you'll file Chapter 11. A month after that, you'll be forced to close up shop. And a month after that, you'll have a fire sale for pennies on a dollar. Oh, I know Gwen is cutting back expenses, announcing layoffs and all that, but at this point she's just rearranging the deck chairs on the Titanic."

"I have the utmost confidence in her," declared Russ, leaving it at that.

Marty was reluctant to attack Russ' mistaken loyalty for this woman; it wasn't something he wanted to do, knowing it would drive a bigger wedge between them, so he merely regarded Russ with a sad regret. He had toyed with the idea of asking Russ to join his new venture—he could have used Russ' savvy and charm—but there, right there, was the reason why. He was tied too deeply to this woman. For whatever reason—past history, chivalry, *love*—Russ would never break ties with this woman and that made him a liability.

He quickly changed the subject on Russ, telling a humorous anecdote about their early time together at MFS (*"Remember the time..."*) Russ chuckled at the story, welcoming the change in topic, and added a story of his own. This led to pleasant conversation that was part nostalgia, part friendly banter, and it softened the mood considerably as both men sat in the empty apartment laughing and sipping champagne.

"You knew about me and David—the IT guy," said Marty suddenly.

Russ didn't flinch at the remark, guessing immediately that this was one of the reasons Marty asked him here—to clean the slate between them. Marty must fear I hold it against him, Russ thought to himself. But he needn't worry on that score. I dismissed Marty's gay escapades long ago as none of my business, though I feel rather sorry for his wife Hana. Secrets like that always have a way of revealing themselves.

"Yeah."

At this confirmation, Marty studied Russ closely, looking for small signs of insincerity in Russ' face, but he found none and it steadied his nerves. (Popping that question hadn't been easy, but the good mood and champagne had eased the way.) "I've been worried about it," he added lightly. "It was the night of the IPO, right? Yeah, thought so. It was stupid—don't know what I was thinking. But I've worried about it all this time—that it affected our relationship."

"Poppycock."

Marty smiled at Russ with a look of gratitude and replied, "Or, as we say in America, 'baloney'."

Both men laughed and then quickly moved on to another topic, and after another ten minutes of relaxed conversation, Russ said he had to go and check up on his son. He reached out to shake Marty's hand goodbye and said, "*What a long, strange trip it's been.*"

"Ha!" laughed Marty. "That's probably the only Grateful Dead lyrics you know. But I gotta better one for you." He tossed back his head and lightly sang the following lyrics:

> *Goin' where the wind don't blow so strange,*
> *Maybe off on some high cold mountain chain.*
> *Lost one round but the price wasn't anything,*
> *A knife in the back and more of the same.*

When he finished, he came around the counter, and ignoring Russ' outstretched hand gave him a big hug, holding it as long as he could before Russ backed off. He continued to hold on to Russ' elbows, looking deeply into eyes. Russ met his gaze, and he could tell by his eyes that Marty was a little tipsy.

"There's just one more thing I wanted to say," Marty said almost timidly. "And it's taken four glasses of champagne and seven years to say it." He closed his eyes for a moment to muster his courage, then gently squeezed Russ' elbows and said more firmly, "I love you more than words can tell… What I mean is—I've always loved you, Russ… I just wanted you to know that before you go."

"I guess I've always known that."

Marty sniffed an ironic laugh. "Well, what do you know? All this time." He gave Russ the light-hearted smile of a man unburdened by worry, adding whimsically, "I guess it would be pushing it to ask for a kiss goodbye."

"It would."

"Thought so." He let go of Russ' elbows, shaking his hand once more as both men said their goodbyes, and wished each other good luck. And when Russ was gone, he poured out the last few drops of champagne and held up the empty bottle to the light. "Funny," he said to himself just as his cell phone rang. He pulled it out of his pocket and looked at his caller ID.

It was his wife.

―――

Marty's prediction turned out to be eerily accurate. A month after announcing lay-offs and substantial cost-cutting measures, CrestPoint Communications filed for bankruptcy. In the month leading up to the filing, Gwen worked the phones day and night to find another buyer to bail out CrestPoint before they ran out of cash. Her efforts included trying to arrange a $150 million bank loan to keep their day-to-day operations going. When the white knight failed to materialize and the bank loan fell through, time ran out for CrestPoint. After filing Chapter 11, Gwen issued the following statement over the newswires:

"When Atlantis illegally breached their agreement with CrestPoint Communications, it created a funding shortfall. Chapter 11 will provide CrestPoint protection from creditors while enhancing our ability to meet our obligations to customers and vendors by restructuring our financial obligations. Our goal is to reemerge from Chapter 11 as quickly as possible, with a strategic partner and on sound financial footing. By taking this action, we have given CrestPoint the time and resources needed to restructure our business and build for a stronger future."

Industry reaction was I-told-you-so. The same investors and analysts who originally touted CrestPoint as "a sure win" and "a must buy" now pointed knowingly at CrestPoint's staggering debt, calling their bankruptcy "inevitable." Many predicted that CrestPoint would likely emerge from bankruptcy protection in some form because of its massive assets, but that the company certainly wouldn't be owned by the same people. Teri Starr from The Yankee Group issued an analysis that tried to put the bankruptcy into perspective, stating that assembling a talented management team with a great idea (high-speed Internet access) was not enough to guarantee success in an environment strewn with so many obstacles. CrestPoint had tried to scale the heights, but a formidable array of impediments such as hostile Baby Bells, onerous regulatory rules, tight margins, and an over-hyped demand had been their undoing. It was a shame, really.

But filing Chapter 11 did not relieve the tremendous pressure on Gwen to find money to continue daily operations. With public utility commissions across the country threatening to fine them if DSL service to thousands of customers was turned off, Gwen turned in desperation to their existing lenders, securing a commitment of $35 million in "debtor-in-possession financing" to keep service up and running. In addition, she announced that CrestPoint planned to undertake a sell-off of its business and assets, pending approval of an open-bid process by the bankruptcy court. To further calm the waves, she issued a statement saying that the company had no intention of abandoning users of its DSL services.

Gwen wasn't under any illusions that a mere $35 million would buy them the time they needed to find a buyer in bankruptcy court. Their burn-rate was too high. What with the monthly rent in hundreds of central offices, power bills, franchise fees and employee salaries, they were bleeding cash. After another week, she announced a layoff of 75% of their workforce, a move approved by the board which was rubber-stamping every decision she made in hopes of stemming the bleeding.

And just as Marty predicted, one week later, with no source of debt relief in sight, CrestPoint's financial foundation collapsed.

One look out her office window told Gwen that she'd completely lost track of time. It was evening, past 9:00, and she was sure she was the only person left in the building. Then again, she quickly realized, there weren't many employees left. Seven hundred and twenty employees gone, just like that, just with a snap of her fingers. Seven hundred and twenty lives thrown into turmoil.

Her leadership team remained (Russ and the rest) but Marketing and Sales were gone as was Human Resources. All that Lori Hunter lorded over now was one office administrator and a parking spot with her name on it. Chandra and Ron were left with skeleton crews to cover daily business obligations. As rumored, Stu bolted for Texas, taking a fat job at Enron in their Corporate Office, leaving behind nothing but a dispute with the board over his exit package that would one day be settled in court. Roxanne LaMorte was acting VP of Finance, a department that consisted of only a few financial analysts Gwen still needed to crunch numbers for her. Only Russ retained a large part of his organization, since it was his team's responsibility to keep their DSL service up and working. But now even that was just piss in the wind.

Gwen turned back to her computer screen and reviewed the statement she'd been working on all evening. It would go out to all the ISPs in the morning, as well as over the newswires, alerting their partners and subscribers to the cessation of service and the complete shutdown of their network starting tomorrow. She'd spent the last two hours wordsmithing the statement, struggling to get the right tone, but however she worded it she knew its release in the morning would trigger a shitstorm. But it couldn't be helped. They were out of money. It was as brutally simple as that.

Sick of looking at it, she clicked her screen off and pulled a small mirror out of her desk drawer, fighting back a feeling of utter failure that quickly overwhelmed her. She'd been disappointed before, upset after a close loss in college basketball, frustrated by machinations and plots in the board room, and discouraged after her well-laid plans had fallen through, but never ever felt anything like this before. It was as if someone had taken a bat to her ego and beaten it into the ground.

She studied her face in the hand-held mirror. The swelling and bruises were long gone but the scars remained, the scars from another beating, scars that gave testimony to her failed private life. A failure at work, a failure outside of work, there was no other way for her to view that face in the mirror. She was so sick of taking a beating. And at that moment, confronted by a life she thought added up to nothing, she quietly cried.

But self-pity wasn't in her nature, no more than hysteria or fainting or other feminine vapors were, and she quickly composed herself. In quick order, she dried her eyes, pulled a compact out of her purse, and proceeded to freshen up her makeup. When she was done, she felt a little better, and realizing that, she wondered what else she could do to feel better. A glass of wine—or two? Chinese take-out? No, not enough. She needed a jolt, some kind pick-me-up, and there was really only one thing in the world that could do that for her. Russ.

She wished Russ were here. Russ, with his devilish good-looks and easy charm—Russ, with his encouragement and reassuring humor. Always there when she needed him. Always steady and rock solid. The only man she'd ever known who treated her as an equal while still making her feel like a woman. If only he were here.

But she knew better. He was either out on a date or on his boat enjoying a Johnnie Walker Red over ice, waiting for some young beauty to pay him a visit. He might as well be a million miles away, she thought, and with that she reluctantly clicked her computer screen back to life and began proofreading her statement once more. When she was done, she busied herself by saving it and queuing it up to go out in the morning, and it startled her when a knock came at her office door.

Russ appeared as if out of a dream. "Hey, lady," he said cheerfully. "Thought I'd find you here."

"*Russ!*"

Chapter 11

The dinner party at the Boatwright's was something of an annual affair. For the last eight years, Chad and Cindy Boatwright hosted a party on or around his birthday, which featured beer and wine, mixed drinks, catered hors d'oeuvres, and fresh Dungeness crab steamed in a giant pot over an open flame in their backyard. The guest list usually ran around thirty to forty people, mostly married couples, and the adults-only shindig started at four in the afternoon and lasted until midnight. Leaving the kids at home and attending the Boatwright's 'crab fest' was something every guest looked forward to.

The first party had taken place in Hillsborough, the enclave where most of the guests had grown up, gone to school, and become friends. When the Boatwrights bought a larger house in Los Gatos, the dinner party moved as well, and now everyone made the forty-minute drive down the peninsula to attend. It was worth the drive, giving the adults a break from the kids and a chance to catch up with old friends while enjoying conversation, cocktails, and a delicious crab dinner.

The group of friends were in their late thirties to mid-forties, Boomers with children of their own, who owned a home, at least two cars, and either broke even or got a little back on their taxes each year. Ethnically they were diverse, but otherwise they tended to fit a mold which was college-educated, upper middle class, politically liberal, white-collar professionals. About half the women had careers of their own, allowing them to maintain a lifestyle that included private schools for their kids, a time-share in Maui or Tahoe, and a modest portfolio of investments. The other half, the stay-at-home moms, worked or didn't work, usually part-time, depending on their inclinations. The men, many of them mid-level managers, worked in fields ranging from accounting and financial consulting to engineering and information technology, typically spending fifty or more hours a week on the job. Taken as a whole, the men and women who attended the Boatwright's annual crab fest were very much a product of the Bay Area, especially it's pulsating core the Silicon Valley.

Mark and Ronnie Kirkland were once a part of this circle of friends and attended the Boatwright's party every year—until Mark's religious conversion over three years ago. Upon accepting Jesus Christ as his lord and savior, donning the garb of a wild-eyed mountain man, and becoming a vocal evangelist, Mark—along with Ronnie—had been ostracized from the group. Amongst the group, it became evident that Mark no longer fit into their urbane and lively clique, and his banishment was conveyed through the gossip mill, via luncheons and phone conversations, in which friends shared with each other the prevailing consensus that Mark had gone off the deep end, that poor Ronnie was at her wit's end over it, and that divorce was very likely in the forecast.

So, it came as a pleasant surprise when Ronnie received the invitation to the Boatwright's party. Accompanying her surprise was a feeling of vindication given the fact that she'd spent the last year lobbying her friends (the wives), slowly convincing them over coffee or during a chance meeting at the mall that Mark was back to normal, that he'd left his crazy church in the mountains and come back to earth. Not that this was entirely true, she knew. It was true he'd come back to earth by returning to St Joseph's, their Catholic church, but Mark was as devout and passionate towards Christ as ever, it was just that he'd become more private about it.

Mark was not too keen on attending but could see by his wife's reaction she wanted to go, so he consented. In his mind, these were the same people—their "friends"—who had spurned him for his faith, some even going so far as to dismiss him as "hopeless" after failing to convince him of his errors in judgement. Personally, they troubled him not, for blessed were those who suffer for righteousness' sake, but the pain they caused his wife by excluding her from their social circle had weighed heavily on him at the time. Yet, if she was eager to forgive them then so must he, reminding himself what scripture said about forgiveness—*Forgive as the Lord forgave you.*

During the drive to the party, Ronnie debated with herself whether to warn Mark about talking religion. She understood all too well how these things worked; they'd be under a microscope, on parole, so to speak, and if Mark exhibited his old congeniality and didn't sermonize, they'd be welcomed back with open arms. On the other hand, if he started telling them how they could be saved by recognizing Jesus as the Son of God, then they'd collectively turn their backs on him again. She didn't know how to put it to him without making it sound like a warning or a rebuke, two things he did not react well to, so she decided to let it go and allow fate to run its course. Normally, it wasn't in her nature to let things go like this, but of late she'd been thinking a lot about God's plan—God's plan for her and her family. It was a thing she whole-heartedly believed existed. And sometimes it was best just to let God's plan unfold.

A Christian music station played softly on the car radio and Mark listened to it while he drove. Ronnie was quiet; she appeared lost in thought, and he guessed that she was a little anxious about the party and reuniting with their old friends. That was her way—to worry over things like that—but he knew he could usually break the spell by throwing out a light-hearted comment.

"Don't let me eat too much crab," he said in mock seriousness. "You know how I am."

"*You?* I'm the crab fanatic, remember?" she replied smiling.

"Oh, right. I'll keep my eye on you... Did I tell you how beautiful you look today?"

"A couple times. But keep it coming."

He smiled and winked at her. But it was true—she'd put extra effort into her make-up and hair today, even pulling out her favorite summer dress, and she positively beamed. He could go on admiring her forever but he had to drive, and as he turned his eyes back to the road, he caught the lyrics from the song playing over the radio and turned it up. It was one of his favorites.

I don't want to go along with the crowd
Don't want to live life under a cloud
Give me some air and space
And sun on my face
I want to live out loud

He hummed along with it while enjoying the drive. Ronnie became quiet again but he didn't really notice, and after another fifteen minutes of driving and listening to music, he pulled onto the Boatwright's property and found a place to park. There were already a number of cars parked, and when they got out, they heard a woman's voice call out "Ronnie!"

Ronnie turned to see an old friend emerging from a car and she yelled back "Kelly!" The two women skipped cheerfully towards each other, embracing, as the two husbands followed up from behind. Greetings were made, handshakes and hugs, and everyone agreed it was good to see each other again after all this time. The four of them walked through the house and into the backyard where their host Chad, dressed in a gaudy Hawaiian shirt and holding a large pair of tongs in one hand, welcomed them, quickly pointing out the important landmarks like the bar and the bathrooms before stepping forward to shake Mark's hand. "Mark," he said, briefly looking him up and down. "Glad you could make it. We need to catch up. But later, for sure. Right now I gotta help Cindy. Like I said, the bar's thatta way. Have fun." And with that, he was off.

The large backyard was already populated with about twenty people, paired up or in small groups, drinking and talking while an eclectic mix of music (which would include throughout the evening Harry Connick Jr, Classic Rock, Garth Brooks, and a sprinkling of smooth jazz) played unobtrusively over an elaborate sound system. There was a row of picnic tables lined up together under a long, covered pavilion, and twenty paces from that sat an extravagant bar made out of bamboo and tiki wood.

Mark and Ronnie mingled, in some cases renewing old acquaintances, while slowly making their way over to the bar where the bartender—another old friend, Tanner, who always played bartender at these events—poured Ronnie a white wine and handed Mark an ice-cold beer. Mark hadn't asked for the beer but he took it anyway, said "thanks," taking a sip to show his appreciation, and held onto it with the intention of nursing it for the next hour. They talked for a short time with Tanner and then walked over to check out the barbecue pit where the crab would be cooked up in a big steam pot.

Ronnie was pleased. So far, the general inspection had gone well and Mark was passing with flying colors. In each encounter with old friends, she watched closely as their eyes quickly passed over Mark, making their subtle appraisals. She could read their minds; the flannel shirt and jeans were now Dockers and a polo shirt, the heavy beard was now clean-shaven, and when they heard him say he was a "VP with EF&I Services," she caught the slight nods of approval. True, the group's patrician attitude towards her and Mark annoyed her slightly, but she couldn't help but mentally breathe a sigh of relief.

"Hey, Mark!" called out a voice. "Didn't you work for CrestPoint?"

Mark and Ronnie glanced over at the picnic table where two other couples were seated talking. Upon nodding yes, they beckoned him over to join their conversation. They were talking about the Dot-com boom and bust that was currently playing itself out in the stock market, across the media, and in everyone's pocketbook. When Mark and Ronnie came up to the table, the question was repeated: "You worked for CrestPoint, right."

"Yeah," replied Mark. "I started in the spring of '97 and left at the end of 2000, shortly after they went bankrupt." He and Ronnie sat down. They were a friendly group who seemed genuinely interested in Mark's experience.

"Right. Thought so. You guys were a big thing back then—DSL, high-speed Internet. I used to see your billboard along 101."

"We were just talking about the Dot-com bust," another chimed in. "About how all these hyped-up companies like Kosmo.com and Webvan are going bankrupt. It's like an avalanche."

"Weren't there a couple other DSL companies?"

"Yeah, there were," said Mark. "Nomad and Pulse Net. Both went bankrupt. The three of us were in a death struggle for market share.

When I was hired on in '97 to head up their installation program, it was a race to get there first…" And with that opening, Mark gave them a brief summary about his time at CrestPoint, an experience he hadn't talked about to anyone (except Ronnie) for some time. There were the early, hectic days, full of promise, followed by growth and success, then the IPO—the peak—followed by cracks in the dam, growing debt, and finally collapse. "It was a roller coaster ride," he concluded. "But an experience I wouldn't have missed for the world."

"I hate to ask… But what were you worth on the day of your IPO?"

"Fifty-six million," answered Ronnie. This elicited some sympathetic smiles from the others.

"On paper," qualified Mark.

"On paper. But still—fifty-six million. Then you had to watch it drain away to nothing. That's a bummer."

Mark shrugged his shoulders. "Didn't bother me."

His comment triggered a moment of awkward silence as the two couples studied him, surprised at his indifference over losing fifty-six million dollars, no doubt attributing it to his strange religious views. Ronnie noted this and said jokingly, "Well, it bothers me."

Everyone laughed at her quip. Even Mark smiled.

"There were a lot of IPOs like that during the boom," one of them commented.

"What's this about IPOs?" asked Chad Boatwright, who appeared out of nowhere still brandishing a pair of tongs. It was his habit as the host to dip into conversations, make a witty remark or two, then run off to perform one his endless chores that included keeping the beer cold, restocking the bar, checking on the hors d'oeuvres, and seeing to the crab. Given he was a successful broker, the term "IPO" naturally caught his attention.

"We were just talking about all the IPOs during the Dot-com boom. Like CrestPoint—Mark's company. He was worth fifty-six mil then went bankrupt. All because the bubble burst. I imagine some of your clients lost their shirts?"

All eyes turned to Chad. He was considered an expert on the stock market and kind of a financial wizard, and like the old E.F. Hutton commercial, when he talked, people listened. "Yeah," he said with a look of worldly wisdom on his face. "Some did. But they weren't alone. The dimensions of the collapse, which is still going on, have been staggering. I saw a projection the other day that said a half a million people have lost their jobs because of it. Personally, I think that's a conservative number. It's really the decline in the stock market that blows your mind. Take the Dow Jones, what they call the communication technology index—it's dropped 86 percent over the last two years. *86 percent.* Just let that sink in. The declines we've seen are comparable to the great crash of 1929."

"Makes you wonder how the bubble got so big in the first place," said one.

"Greed," said another.

"Greed?" repeated Chad skeptically. "No... I mean, you could say that about any stock market bubble. Personally, I think it was ideology. The Internet became the new religion; it was going to unite the world into a global village. So, when people started investing in dot-com companies and in companies like CrestPoint Communications, they were making ideological investments instead of financial investments. Always a bad idea, and now you're seeing the results. What do you think, Mark?"

"I think that's partly true," replied Mark, surprised at being asked the question. "But at some point, the herd mentality kicked in."

Chad laughed loudly. "Exactly!" he chortled, thrusting his tongs in the air. "And I was one of the herd." Just then, his wife's voice sounded from the house, announcing that his sister from L.A. had just arrived. "Oops, gotta go. Dinner's at seven. Forty pounds of crab, so don't fill up on the Swedish meatballs."

Everyone promised not to eat too many meatballs, and they laughed as Chad skipped off towards the house waving his tongs in the air.

The Heights of Mountains

For the first two hours of the party, Ronnie stayed next to Mark as they mingled and chatted with the other partygoers. Normally, she would have peeled off to go talk to her girlfriends, leaving him to socialize on his own, but admittedly she'd been playing chaperone. But now she had to pee and refill her wine glass, so she politely excused herself from a group discussion about the war in Afghanistan (a topic that bored her to tears) and confidently left Mark on his own.

One of the group, a short, meaty fellow by the name of Jorge, was voicing his strong opinion about the war in Afghanistan and Mark politely listened to him without really taking an interest. Jorge's wife, Rene, who was a slender blonde with a long rectangular face, stood next to her husband agreeing with his opinion and, at times, punctuating one of his remarks with a "fuckin-aye" or a "fuck Bush!" Mark remembered that she liked to swear and particularly found the word "fuck", in its many forms, handy when she wanted to make an important point that everyone should take seriously. Mark couldn't help but find the habit a bit jarring and usually avoided her at parties, but many of the others were amused by her salty language.

Jorge and Rene were part of the Hillsborough crowd that Ronnie grew up with but they were not friends. Out of this group had come a handful of close friends. The Boatwrights had been close friends (Chad was one of his friends who had tried to talk him out of his religious conversion), and after that came 'just friends' followed by 'acquaintants'. Jorge and Rene fell into the third category. Ronnie never talked about them and had never invited them over for a dinner party, probably because of Rene's penchant for dropping F-bombs.

Mark was looking for a way to politely extradite himself from this one-way debate when another man—someone Mark never met before—stepped into the small group, appearing to take interest in their conversation. Mark immediately took the opportunity to introduce himself.

"Hi, name's Mark," he said, extending his hand. "Don't think we've met."

"Name's Max," he replied, shaking Mark's hand. "Pleased to meet you."

Jorge paused his commentary while this greeting took place, looking a bit peeved at being interrupted. When he tried to resume, Mark unintentionally cut him off again by asking, "Max... What's that short for? Maximilian?"

"Yeah. Maximilian. Named after the saint."

"Oh, which one?" asked Mark. "There's two of them—one from ancient times who was beheaded for refusing to fight for the Roman army, and another who was killed by the Nazis."

"Not sure," answered Max, pausing a moment in thought. "I think he was a Polish priest. The last name's Banaszak, so my mom would'a found a Polish saint to name me after."

"That would be Maximilian Kolbe," said Mark, nodding with approval. "Fascinating man. You should read up on him. He ran a monastery in Poland when the Nazi's invaded, providing refuge for Jews and others until the Gestapo arrested him and threw him in concentration camp. Auschwitz. They beat and tortured him but he continued to act as a priest, trying to help as many others as he could. At one point, there was an escape—one of the prisoners got away—and in retaliation the SS commander picked ten prisoners to be starved to death. One of them pleaded for mercy, saying he had a wife and kids, and Kolbe volunteered to take his place. They were put in an underground cell and starved—no food, no water—for two weeks, and each day he kneeled peacefully in the middle of the cell and led the prisoners in prayer. After two weeks, most of them were dead except for Kolbe and, I think, two others, so the guards gave them lethal injections to finish the job. And according to eyewitnesses, Kolbe calmy raised his arm up to get his injection, happily receiving his martyrdom."

"Jeez, poor guy," said Max.

"He probably didn't think himself too poor at that moment," replied Mark with a smile.

"You know a lot about saints?"

"Yeah, done some reading."

"Aren't you the one who joined some loony church up in the mountains?" asked Jorge suddenly. "Where they shake all over and speak in tongues, that kind of thing?"

Mark turned his eyes to Jorge, regarding him calmly. He and his wife stared at him as though he was the Elephant Man on display.

"No, they weren't like that," he replied evenly. "Just non-denominational. Protestant, really… But you're right, it was up in the mountains. Near La Honda."

"That's what I heard, anyway," said Jorge, eyeing Mark back. "That it was kinda looney tunes, with people dressing up like hippies and trying to convert everyone. Isn't that what we heard?" (This question was for his wife, who responded, "Yeah, it was something fucked up like that.") "Are you still a member?" he wanted to know.

"No."

"No? Really? Why's that? Did you see the light, or something?"

Mark wasn't quite sure why this guy was trying to provoke him, but it sure seemed that way. He'd done nothing he could think of to piss him off except maybe interrupt his rant against Bush and the Afghanistan war. That must be it, he thought to himself. This guy needs to be center of attention and I inadvertently cut him off, causing him to react spitefully. Make amends. Remain patient, and please, Lord, don't let me rise to anger. Help me to keep Jesus in my heart.

"Just a parting of the ways," answered Mark.

Jorge glanced around the small circle of partygoers who were listening in, checking to see if they were as curious to hear about Mark's wacky story as he was. The others seemed to lack the same sense of the absurd that Jorge possessed, but the looks on their faces showed him that they were at least curious enough to hear more, and that was all Jorge needed to see to press forward.

"Just like that?" he asked Mark. "Did you give up on religion all together. I'm just curious."

"No, nothing like that. It's a long story."

"Just give us the Reader's Digest version," prodded Jorge. "We're all interested."

If he thought that Jorge was truly interested in the answer, Mark would have gladly explained it to him, but he was pretty sure that wasn't the case. Jorge's manner, his look, and his tone of voice all told Mark that he was not someone who would understand his evolution of faith. And that's exactly what it had been—an evolution, a maturation of his faith. Over time, Mark had grown out of the Calvary Memorial Church, splitting the seams like a pair of worn-out blue jeans. It started as a vague disenchantment with elements of church doctrine and finally crystallized into open protest. He argued with Deacon Stone, sometimes for hours, over interpretations of prophecy, debating passages and their true meaning, and there never seemed to be an end to it. But the final rift came with a doctrine they called 'secret rapture', or a special resurrection and assumption into heaven reserved only for born-again Christians. This doctrine of divine selection, which smacked of predestination, grew to become intolerable to Mark, leading him to search for another church, another house of God where his spirit could flourish and his mind rest assured that God's mercy extended to everyone. And it didn't take long to find it. It had always been there, right in front of him, like a sign on stilts, and he needed only to look up to see it.

"The profound beauty of the Catholic Church called me back home," was all Mark said.

"The Catholic Church?" repeated Jorge sarcastically. "You went from the frying pan into the fire." And without waiting for Mark to defend his statement, he launched into an animated attack on the Catholic Church, citing the sexual abuse scandal as well as the Church's narrow-minded views on birth control and homosexuality. Then there was their stance on abortion, a stance, he claimed, pointing his finger at Mark, that was not only archaic but harmful to women ("Fuckin'-A," agreed his wife.). It was beyond him how any intelligent person in this day and age could be a Catholic.

Mark listened quietly and did not rise to anger. He'd heard all this before, this articulated hatred for the Catholic Church, and run across people like Jorge who viewed the Church as their personal enemy, and he'd become toughened by it like a boxer in training who takes repeated shots to the midsection to harden it. Jorge was far from finished, and egged on by his wife he continued his attack on the Catholic Church, going so far as to equate Catholics with modern day slaveholders, an accusation made more pungent by the fact that Jorge was Afro-Hispanic. Mark showed little emotion; he stood there and took the abuse, thinking to himself about St. Maximilian and Romans 12:14 (*Bless those who persecute you; bless and do not curse them.*)

Having used the bathroom, Ronnie came back out of the house headed for the bar, but a quick check on her husband stopped her in her tracks. He was still with the group she'd left him with but her intuition told her something was wrong. Mark stood motionless while Jorge, whom she considered to be a bigmouth, talked directly at him, even pointing his finger at Mark. It spelled trouble and Ronnie hurried over there. As she approached, she slowed her pace, stopping behind Mark and out of Jorge's line of site, and overheard what sounded like Jorge berating the Catholic Church. A short listen confirmed her fears. They were arguing religion, or at least Jorge was—he was doing all the talking while Mark remained surprisingly passive. She didn't care for Jorge and liked his wife Rene even less, and the fact they seemed to be ganging up on her husband riled her to no end.

She waited for Jorge to take a breath before blurting out, somewhat angrily, "Let Mark talk!"

"Yeah, let's hear from Mark," someone else said.

"You've been doing all the talking," accused Ronnie. "Let Mark have a say."

Caught a little off guard, Jorge responded, "Sure, why not?" adding rather petulantly, "Let's hear what Mark has to say about priests molesting young boys."

At the sound of his wife's voice, Mark glanced back and reached out his hand, and now they stood side by side holding hands. Everyone was looking at him in anticipation.

"I know there are problems with the Church," said Mark. (He paused while Jorge laughed derisively, saying "No shit.") "Just like there are problems with schools and government and other institutions we grew up with. But why is that? —It's because they're run by people and people, God bless their souls, are flawed. A Catholic would say it's because we're born with original sin. But call it what you like—original sin or human nature—I think we'd all agree that people are capable of doing great good or great evil."

"I agree with that," said Max. Mark smiled at him as he caught Jorge and Rene rolling their eyes.

"Right now, the Catholic Church is fighting a number of destructive forces—forces that appeal to the weaker side of our nature—and this, sadly, has had a harmful impact on the priesthood…"

"Is that an excuse for child abuse?" snapped Jorge.

"That's certainly *not* what I said—if you care to listen. What I'm saying is that humans are flawed images of God who can do right or do wrong. All of us—even you, Jorge—has it in them to be either a Hitler or a Mother Teresa."

"I can't imagine Jorge as Mother Teresa," said one of the group, eliciting laughter.

"No, he wouldn't look good in a sari," quipped Rene.

"No, probably not," said Mark, sharing the laughter. "But the potential is there, right? You see, Catholics believe humans have an innate sense of right and wrong, but because of original sin they also have an inherited tendency of the soul to choose poorly."

"Or you could call it the duality of man," said a woman in the group who was a high school principal.

"Yes," agreed Mark, nodding at her. "You can put it that way, but it brings us back to the same place." (He turned now and looked directly at Jorge.) "So, Jorge, I hear you. When you spell out the evil done by priests, I hear you loud and clear. But that evil is just a reflection of the world we live in. It's just a reflection of all of us. The Church admits to this state of man while appealing to our better natures. Who else can say that?"

The Heights of Mountains

Ronnie could tell by her husband's speech pattern that he'd made his point and was done talking, and she came up on the balls of her feet, anticipating Jorge's comeback. So far, Jorge had failed to turn Mark into a comic figure or goad him into an argument, but that didn't mean he was done trying. And when Jorge came back at Mark with an aggressive rebuttal, mocking his points about *original sin* and *reflection of the world* to justify the sins of the Catholic Church, she was to the point of being fed up with it.

"So just let me ask you this," said Jorge. "You're Catholic. Your kids are Catholic. Would you trust your son alone with a priest at your church?"

"That all depends," replied Ronnie loudly. "If you were the priest—the answer's No!"

The others couldn't help but laugh at Ronnie's crude joke, and Jorge flinched back as though he'd been slapped. Ronnie quickly pulled Mark away saying, "Come on, I need another glass of wine," and as they briskly walked away, they could hear Rene say "What the fuck? Did she just say what I think she said?" To which Max replied laughingly, "Yep, I think she did."

When they were out of earshot, Ronnie said, "Can't stand that guy Jorge. He's the one who told all my friends in high school I was pregnant."

"Didn't know that."

"Yeah, he's a big jerk."

"I could probably say something about forgiveness right now—but I won't."

"Smart man."

He gently laughed, giving her a kiss on the cheek as they came up to the bar where Tanner the bartender, drunk and smiling, waited to take their order.

———

They'd left the Boatwright's party early and been driving for about ten minutes before Mark finally said, "That was quite a prayer." They'd both been holding their breath in anticipation and now they suddenly exhaled with a laugh.

"I was inspired," replied Ronnie, pausing a moment before adding, "It felt kind'a good."

"I bet it did."

He was referring to Ronnie's prayer at the crab fest, an act that couldn't have happened without Jorge. Having all sat down at the long picnic table for dinner, Chad Boatwright, as was tradition, welcomed everyone and gave a short humorous speech that ended with a quasi-benediction honoring good friends and good food. "And if anyone wants to say grace," he added jokingly, "Feel free." Without warning, Jorge shouted out that Mark should say grace—that if anyone was "qualified" to say grace, it was "Reverend Mark." Always the gracious host, Chad quickly disarmed Jorge's attempt at making fun of Mark by thanking Jorge for his suggestion and asking Mark in all seriousness whether he would like to say grace before dinner. Mark politely declined, and that seemed the end of it, but before Chad could yell out, "Well then, let's dig in!" Ronnie announced loudly that she would like to say grace. Taken a bit by surprise, Chad signaled her to proceed with a courtly wave of his hand, and what transpired over the next two minutes was less a dinner prayer by Ronnie and more a testimony of her faith as she loudly praised Christ as her personal Savior and shared her hope of knowing Him more clearly, loving Him more dearly, and following Him more closely every day. It was raw and heartfelt, yet tinged with an element of righteous anger, and at one point, she glanced up at Jorge (who stared at her in amazement) and declared, *"Blessed are you when people hate you and when they exclude you and spurn your name as evil, on account of the Son of Man!"* She ended with a gentle reminder that everyone can have eternal life through Christ, said "Amen," crossed herself (as did Mark and a couple others), then raised her head and greeted the awkward silence and embarrassed looks with a defiant smile.

"I think there was a little anger in it," he gently kidded her.

"Maybe just a touch," she confessed. "But those people can be such stuck-up snobs. They all think they just walked out of the movie *The Big Chill*. And people like Jorge and Rene… God forgive me, but they're the worst."

"He forgives you," replied Mark, smiling. Her prayer caught him off guard in a wonderous, spell-binding sort of way and he still felt the glow from it as though he'd just witnessed a small, beautiful miracle. Joy filled his heart, and as he drove along thinking about it, he had to laugh to himself at the exquisite irony of it all. She liked to think she'd mellowed his passionate faith over the years—and maybe she had—but in reality, it was she who'd grown more fervent in her love of God. It was an answer to his prayers.

Ronnie smiled back, thinking about how cheerful and reassuring he always was towards her. She studied the side of his face, and he must have felt her gaze because he quickly glanced at her and winked, and in that momentary glance, like a flash of deep color, she saw the love in his face and it nearly overwhelmed her. She knew he loved her, felt it every day, but in that glance lived an eternal power that told her that they weren't just married, weren't just in love, but were entwined forever like two trees planted side by side that grow into one. The emotion of it rose up in her, nearly turning to tears of joy, but she checked it with some difficulty knowing that her tears would only alarm him. Instead, she held the emotion secure in her breast, captive yet ready to burst, while she watched the headlights of their car cast a lighted path.

They spoke very little for the next ten minutes, listening to the car radio and enjoying the clear summer night, but as they neared the collection of billboards that stood on the side of the freeway, it triggered a reminder in Mark's thoughts.

"I'm having lunch with Russ Chappel next week," he said. "Called me out of the blue the other day."

"Oh... How's he doing?" she asked, already knowing the answer. She still talked to Cherry Chandrasekar on a regular basis and knew that Russ no longer worked and had become his son's full-time caregiver. His son Dan had made great strides in his physical recovery but his cognitive skills had not improved very much after all this time.

"Fine, I guess... He just wanted to talk—not about a job, but just talk. Anyway..."

The billboards were upon them and out of habit they both glanced over at the sign that used to be CrestPoint's. It had been replaced by a bright ad for Burlingame Ford. All the other signs that had advertised dot-com businesses and high-tech firms now promoted car dealerships and appliance stores. The billboard that once pictured CrestPoint's logo of a mountain range now displayed a shiny new truck, and it passed them by quickly. Out of habit, they glanced again at the smaller billboard set off in the back that read 'Jesus Saves'. It was still there but had recently been vandalized, its message obscured by spray-painted obscenities.

"What happened there?" asked Ronnie.

"Don't know. It's been like that for over a week."

"Shame… Who would do something like that?"

Mark didn't answer, but he knew the answer: Many—there were many who would do a thing like that. The world was sharply divided between those who believed in Jesus Christ and those who did not. And many of those who did not believe would do a thing like that.

"I hope they can clean it up and fix it."

"Me, too," agreed Mark.

He had slowed down to look at the billboards, and even though he was in the right lane, the person behind him honked their horn for him to speed up. He looked in his rearview mirror to see headlights tailgating him, and in an instant the car swerved over and sped by, the driver flipping him off as he drove past. Mark smiled wryly, thinking how people like that illustrated his point about a world divided. Ronnie thought something different and made a face at the driver's taillights.

Mark quickly sped back up to match the flow of traffic, and in a short time they were home. Their daughter Lacy, home for the weekend from college, was curled up on the couch with the dog watching a movie. Brandon and his buddy, who was spending the night, were in the kitchen chowing down on leftovers (they were bottomless pits). They all had church in the morning and Mark as lector was scheduled to do a reading at the 8:30 mass and another one at 10:30. After chatting with the kids, he went up to bed and Ronnie followed him a half-hour later. She found him sound asleep, so she quietly got ready for bed and slipped in next to him, molding her back up against his where his steady, rhythmic breathing soon put her to sleep.

Late into the night, at the time when the house lies in tender repose, Mark had a dream.

He is on a platform high above ground, so high it feels like he's on a mountaintop, and he is working to fix the 'Jesus Saves' billboard. There are other people helping him, mostly people from his church, but Ronnie's there, too, as well as his kids, and everyone is helping out by carrying wood, sawing, or hammering new planks into the renovated billboard. It's the middle of the day with a cloudless blue sky, and he stands on the platform and looks out at the freeway filled with passing cars. Some cars slow down and the people inside wave up at him and he waves back. Others speed by ignoring the construction. One car slows down, a car that looks familiar to him, and he can see a woman through the passenger window that resembles Rene. He knows what's coming as she rolls down her window and flips him off, and he chuckles at it, gives her a friendly wave, and wonders whether they drove all this distance just to do that. But he doesn't have time to think about it—someone hands him a board and he puts it in place and hammers it secure, then steps back to assess the work. The sign is coming along nicely. Down below, he can see people moving about, pushing wheelbarrows, and cutting lumber, and one of them waves at him. It's Russ—he waves back—and Russ yells up at him that he needs to talk. Mark signals for him to come up, pointing to a long ladder that leads up to the platform, but Russ seems hesitant and holds back. He points again to the ladder, is going to yell down that it's safe climb up, but someone bumps into him, causing him to catch his balance—

He awoke momentarily at the bump—his wife changing positions—then waited briefly for her to settle down before falling back asleep. When he awoke in the morning, all he could remember of the dream was that it had something to do with Russ.

Chapter 12

When I think back on my time at CrestPoint Communications, especially at the beginning when the possibilities seemed endless and our future bright, I have to laugh at our illusions of grandeur. Marty personified it best that night in his studio apartment when he said that high-speed Internet—built and delivered by us—was going to create a worldwide community, a place where national hatreds would disappear and the world become one. And if Marty was our mad prophet, then we, the four of us (Stu, Chandra, Ron, and me), were equally touched in the head. There wasn't one of us who didn't think about our place in history, that we would one day be remembered for bringing cheap, fast Internet to the masses. It was heady stuff.

It's funny how all the math seemed to add up in our favor at the time. But as Churchill said, "The human story does not always unfold like a mathematical calculation." On one side of the equation was the 'new economy' and its set of ground-breaking rules like 'growth over profits' and 'building market share', while on the other side were the 'facts' that Internet traffic was doubling every one hundred days, that everybody wanted speedier downloads, and that the cost to deploy DSL equipment was only $50,000—all of it hype, half-truths, or downright lies. But we bought into it; like lemmings, we bought into it, and when we realized we were headed for the cliff it was too late to turn back.

Depending on who you read or listened to, the Dot-com bubble began in August of '95 when Netscape, the inventor of the Netscape Navigator Web browser, went public, and ended in April 2000 when the Nasdaq crashed. Of course, history is never as clean and tidy as all that.

The Heights of Mountains

Even after the crash, there were rallies and optimism, but for all intents and purposes the bubble was done. At the mountaintop of CrestPoint Communications and in the corporate offices of hundreds of dot-com and telecom companies, the landslide had begun.

In that boom time between August of '95 and April 2000, online shopping companies and telecom carriers sprouted up like wildflowers after a spring rain. Three hundred Internet companies went public during this time (of which CrestPoint was just one), turning their shareholders into millionaires if only for a fleeting moment. And when the boom collapsed in the classic pattern of a stock market bubble (which some argue is still going on, even now in 2002), it took many of these companies with it. Besides the online shopping companies like Pets.com, Webvan, and Boo.com, others bit the dust. Twenty-three telecommunications companies, including CrestPoint, Nomad, and Global Crossing, all went bust after investing millions in building out the network to carry Internet traffic.

For some, it ended in scandal. WorldCom, Global Crossing, Adelphia, and Enron were all caught in accounting fraud, leading to bankruptcies and even prison time. I like to think that CrestPoint escaped scandal—even if it was by the skin of our teeth. But we didn't escape humiliation. For one, everything we built up—everything that *my* team built up—the DSL equipment in one hundred and nine metro areas across the country, was sold off to AT&T in a bankruptcy fire sale for pennies on the dollar. In the end, the evil empire prevailed. On top of that, industry and the media condemned us for abandoning our customers. It's true that Gwen worked day and night to come up with the money to keep us going, but in the end the banks turned their back on us, forcing CrestPoint to shut down service to thousands of customers. The howl was deafening; we were accused of failing to uphold our moral and legal obligation to protect our customers. I found it personally embarrassing.

Yet, for all that bloody mess, I don't think back on it in terms of what-ifs or missed opportunities. You don't do that with fate. When you combine the allure of the bubble along with the Type-A personalities we assembled at CrestPoint Communications, it couldn't have turned out any other way. It's naïve of me to think that Stu could have acted any differently than he did, or that Marty could have been anything else but Six-gun Marty, or that I with my so-called diplomatic charm could have made it turn out any different. We were all like actors in one of those Greek tragedies where everyone knows the outcome except the players involved.

And those 'players involved' have all moved on in one way or another. Marty, who envisioned himself becoming Governor of California, moved up to Seattle where he helped start VoiceCom. He was run out by his partners, tried starting another IP Telephony company, failed, and is now involved with a nascent company in Bothell working on what he calls "the next best thing—streaming video." I have no doubt it is the next best thing and that Marty, in all his psychedelic brilliance, will find his niche, make his fortune, and enjoy the fame he was born to achieve.

Ron Lau recently took a job with Space X and is helping to build a starship that will take us to Mars. I like to picture him starting the first church on the red planet. Chandra stayed with his first love—Information Theory—and is back in R&D working on data compression and error-correcting codes. He's as 'jolly as a sandboy' as Dickens would say. Stu, on the other hand, was fortunate not to get caught up in the Enron scandal (the accounting fraud having occurred before he got there), but his stay was brief and now he works back east as a corporate lawyer for a firm called Vice Media. It sounds like a perfect fit.

And then there's Gwen—but more about her later.

There are several others I've kept track of through emails and third-party gossip, and many of them returned to the mother ship, taking jobs for less pay back at the Baby Bells where they started out. In 1997 and '98, they ditched companies like SBC and U.S. West for greener pastures over at CrestPoint Communications and now they were begging Scotty to beam them back on board. The irony of it alone is worth the price of admission.

Mark Kirkland, who I've been thinking a lot about lately, took a job as VP over at EF&I Services engineering and installing telecommunications equipment across the country. It's a job right in his wheelhouse, and I'm certain he'll excel at it. There are times, especially after a few Johnnie Walker Reds on ice, when I think that it was Mark and Mark alone who took something worthwhile out of the whole CrestPoint experience.

As for me, I moved on in quite another way, and if there is a compelling argument to be made that things happen for a reason, well then, I guess I'm the walking example of it. Because of CrestPoint, Gwen and I are together again. And because of the fall of CrestPoint, my son Dan can eat and walk on his own. Simply put, if CrestPoint had flourished and become the telecommunications powerhouse Marty and the rest of us had all envisioned, then I would have followed its rise and left Dan's recovery to 'professionals', which means he'd still be in a wheelchair being spoon-fed. That fact is not lost on me.

My full-time job is rehabilitating Dan. I refused to accept the prognosis from the neurologist and other specialists who told me he would never walk again or regain eye-hand coordination, and that his cognitive functioning would remain that of a ten-year old. I bought a house in San Bruno and turned the garage into a gym equipped with balance bars, weights, a treadmill, and other equipment necessary for Dan's physical therapy. Each morning, we wake up, eat a hearty breakfast, and hit the gym for two hours. After a shower, we play mental agility games at the kitchen table like Connect Four, Simon, Memory, and other image and shape matching games. He's gotten quite good at them. For lunch, I usually take him to his favorite burger joint (Nations) and then we walk around the neighborhood, a little farther every day, as he advances in the use of his cane. Then it's a nap, the gym again, and dinner at the house (usually with Gwen), or I drop him off at his mom's for the night. But in the morning, the routine starts again, without fail or excuses, and each day I cajole and push and challenge him to go just a little bit farther than he did the day before. And he meets the challenge cheerfully, never complaining or quitting, always good-natured, always smiling. I'm proud of him.

Gwen is back in San Francisco working for a software company which, I'm sure, she's grooming to sell to Microsoft or Apple or some other big fish. She still has her condo in the City but spends most of her free time with me here at the house or on my boat. We're together now. A couple. And just how my playboy lifestyle and her fatal attraction for bad boys metamorphosed into a gentle and loving relationship, I can't really explain. All I know is that her presence in my life has been a godsend; whether it's her passion in the bedroom or her lively intelligence or her uncanny ability to read situations that helps guide my actions, she's like an angel with long legs. Dan adores her, and her bargaining skills have been instrumental in forging a peace between my ex-wife and me. It's becoming hard to imagine a life without her.

Gwen and I...

Perhaps there's an analogy in nature that explains it, some phenomena in physics where atoms with different properties unite together in a chemical bond to create something greater. Gwen might say it's two artistic styles merging into one, like baroque and modernism blending into expressionism. But it's all rubbish. I prefer not to analyze it or even think about it too much. I've decided to just let it be and accept it for what it is—an anonymous gift.

This was the last voyage of the motor yacht *Danny Boy*. After today, it would become the property of one of the bigwigs over at Oracle. It wasn't even on the market for a week before I got my asking price, and that money would pay off Dan's hefty medical bills and allow me to settle things financially.

Dan wanted to visit the sea lions in Monterey, so that's where I set our course, just the four of us—Dan, Gwen, Dad, and me—as I headed out under the Golden Gate Bridge then south along the coast. It was a chilly morning but the patches of fog outside the gate were quickly burning off and it promised to be a beautiful summer day. It was calm and windless, and the blue-gray ocean was smooth as glass.

The twin diesels hummed in unison as I set our speed at just over 10 knots, giving *Danny Boy* some time to catch her groove before I really opened her up.

Gwen sat next to me in the cockpit, her hair tied back in a ponytail and wearing a wind breaker, a cup of coffee in her hand. She'd brought me a cup as well, black with cream, just the way I liked it, and we sat together sipping our coffee while scanning the horizon. Dan sat aft on deck, in one of the fishing chairs, wearing a life jacket. My dad sat next to his grandson keeping a watchful eye on him. The whole scene gave me a good feeling inside.

We skimmed across the smooth surface of the ocean without a bump or vibration as the early morning fog dissipated, and Gwen reached over and wiped the dew off the face of my glass compass. I smiled at her with my eyes and then checked the newly cleaned compass to confirm our heading. South by southeast. A thought came into my head (I'd recently bought Dan a new compass to replace the one he'd lost or hocked), and I turned aft and yelled, "What's our heading, Danny boy?!"

Dan looked up at me from his seat, smiling, and quickly dug into his pocket to pull out his compass. He looked at it for a moment not sure which way to point it, but his grandfather leaned over to help him, whispering in his ear.

"South southeast!" yelled Dan back to me.

"Right! South by southeast. Steady as she goes!"

I turned back to the con just as a wave of raw emotion washed over me, causing my eyes to water. Gwen must have seen it because she reached over and squeezed my hand tightly. I usually don't get emotional like that, but all the people I loved were here on this boat (the last voyage of *Danny Boy)* and with Dan yelling out like old times… well, it all caught up with me. After a minute or so I was better.

Ten minutes later, Dad and Dan came forward. Dan had to pee, which meant he needed help using the toilet on board, so I took his hand and guided him downstairs into the cabin while my dad took the wheel. Gwen followed us.

I got Dan situated in the toilet head, taking off his bulky life vest, sitting him down, and then told him to call out when he was done and closed the door. Gwen was standing in the doorway to my bedroom and I came over to see what she was looking at. The painting of an English fox hunt was gone from above my bed, having been packed up and moved out a week ago, leaving a rectangular shadow on the wall where the painting once hung. I put my arm around her and asked her what she was looking at.

"If only these walls could talk," she said playfully. "I wonder what they'd say?"

"I'm sorry, but my walls are bound by a non-disclosure agreement."

"What a shame. National Enquirer would pay a fortune for it."

"For me? Nah, I'm a nobody."

"Not in my book, bub," she replied, slipping her arm around my waist and giving me a hug.

"There's only one thing I'll remember about this bedroom," I said. "The night I came and found you in your office—writing up CrestPoint's obituary—and I took you back here and we made love together—again, after all that time… That's what I'll remember."

"Hmm, me too."

I was referring to the night, now almost two years ago, when Gwen had worked late into the evening struggling to write the missive that would end CrestPoint as a company. I had worked late as well, arguing unsuccessfully with suppliers (who we owed millions to) to ship us repair parts, and when I wrapped up, feeling both flustered and disheartened, I walked out to the parking lot and saw Gwen's car. And at that moment, something breeched inside me, and not an emotion as much as it was a sudden and clear awareness of what I needed in my life. I needed Gwen. I went back inside and headed towards Gwen's office, wondering and fearing whether she'd feel the same, but knowing too that it would be all right. And when I opened her door, she called out my name and ran into my arms and we kissed long and hard until we had to come up for air. Things were said—hot, breathless, happy things—and we left together in a trance, back to my place and this bedroom where we made love into the night. There was a great beauty to it, something that went beyond just lust or passion, and I think it surprised us both. Afterwards, we were shaken by its deep emotional impact, and when I awoke in the dead of night to find Gwen sitting on the edge of the bed quietly weeping, I asked her what was wrong. "Never leave me, Russ," was all she said, but it was enough. Something in her voice seemed to go deep inside me. I didn't need to think about my answer. My words just seemed to come by themselves, free and true. "I'll never leave you, Gwen... I love you."

Gwen unzipped her windbreaker and tossed it on the bed, standing there a moment to take in my bedroom and the memories that went with it. She wore a short-sleeved blouse, shorts, and a pair of slip-on sneakers. Standing there like that gave me a chance to admire her form. At age forty-four, she was still a striking woman, tall and statuesque, with long legs that looked like they belonged to a twenty-year old dancer. There was a time when I would have said she resembled Miss December 1974, but I didn't think of her in that way anymore. There was too much between us.

We'd even talked of marriage. Not that I was ready to say I do, but there was a certain cumulative logic to it—like the soil that grows the vine that bears the fruit that produces the wine—that appealed to me. Things had settled in between us. Gone was my roving eye and gone was her kinky sweet tooth (for good, I feel), replaced by a more gentle and appreciative equanimity that we both shared. But we weren't rushing it; instead, we were letting things marinate for a while. I think she sensed a certain hesitance on my part when it came to marriage, something she knew had to be warmed-to over time and didn't need to be pushed. That was another thing I admired about her: Besides her lively intelligence, quick wit, and passion in bed, she possessed a sixth sense about men that most women only pretended to have.

When she turned back to me, she saw the look of admiration on my face and came quickly into my arms, her hazel-blue eyes alive with emotion, and we kissed.

Dan called out that he was done and we broke apart, laughing happily. I went over and extracted him from the toilet head, helping him zip up his pants. He hit the electric flush, which was his favorite part, and carefully watched it run its course, smiling the whole time. The doctors claimed that his constant smiling was a side-effect of brain damage, but like everything else they told me, I took it with a grain of salt. I didn't have much use for specialists anymore. They categorized and cubby-holed everything, and when they were confronted with a mountain, they shook their heads and said it couldn't be moved. But what was it the Bible said about faith moving mountains? That's what I'd done with Dan. I'd moved the mountain—with faith and hard work.

As we passed through the living room, Dan pointed to the spot where my antique sextant used to sit and said, "Sextant," wondering at its absence. I reminded him that it had been packed up and moved to the house, and he nodded his understanding. Most everything I was keeping—my pictures, books, my bust of Winston Churchill, the bar, and a few pieces of furniture—had already been moved out, but I still had my stereo and CD player. It was currently playing *It Might As Well Be Swing* (one of my favorites) by Frank Sinatra and Count Basie, and as we walked through the living room to go back on deck, Frank was crooning about picking a plum out of the tree of life.

We finished visiting the sea lions then anchored in Monterey Bay to eat a late lunch before starting back home. The four of us cozily crowded into the booth that served as the kitchen table and dug into the sandwiches and chips that I'd brought along for the trip.

"Who's reading the book?" asked my dad, nodding to a book laying on the galley counter.

"Me," I answered.

"*Mere Christianity*," he said, repeating the book title. "What possessed you to buy *that* book?"

"A friend gave it to me. I find it interesting."

"Really? You getting religion on me?" he asked with a critical eye. "I thought I brought you up better than that."

Well, he had certainly tried, I thought. Both he and my mom had been vocal agnostics growing up, but especially my dad. He liked quoting George Bernard Shaw and Aldous Huxley, and his clever and erudite logic (which he freely shared with my brother and I) as to why God was a fraud and religion a superstition had been effective on me for most of my life.

"Have you read it?" I countered.

"C.S. Lewis? No, not my cup of tea."

"I've read parts of it," said Gwen. "It's well-written—but I need to read it straight through."

My dad hummed thoughtfully, if rather skeptically. He was in his early eighties now and not quite as spry as he used to be. There was still the lean, tall frame, and the white whiskery eyebrows, but the studious manner that once gave him the image of an English lord had grown rather fusty, giving him more the look of a retired yet venerated college professor.

Whatever he must have thought, he kept to himself and suddenly changed the subject. "Have you heard from Cummins?" he asked.

(He was referring to Cummins Engine Company, who I was currently in negotiations with to sell my patent. It would increase their diesel engine efficiency to over 55%, and I had proven the modifications on my own engines.)

"Not lately," I replied. "My lawyer is running the negotiations. They know the modifications work, so now it's just a matter of paying me what it's worth."

My dad was sure that it would all work out to my advantage while Gwen added that my lawyer needed more leverage. Open up negotiations with another engine company, she suggested—someone like Hino Motors. That would get Cummins off their duff. I agreed it was a good idea and said I'd pass it on to my lawyer.

"Talking of lawyers," said Gwen. "Meant to tell you—CrestPoint's lawsuit against Atlantis finally got settled the other day."

"After two years. Amazing."

"$150 million—enough to cover our outstanding debts and pay off the lawyers."

"It's a moral victory, I suppose."

"For what that's worth," commented Gwen dryly.

"*CrestPoint*," mused my father, saying the name as though it were a famous battle in ancient history. "I really thought you had something there. So did everyone else—at the time. What with fast Internet and low cost. It seemed like a winner."

"It was never going to win," said Gwen, setting down her sandwich, her face turning serious (this was a subject near and dear to her heart). "Marty was a dreamer, and I don't think the original premise was all that sound to begin with. Sorry, Dear, but I don't. It exaggerated the role the Internet plays. I mean, the Internet may help with planning and ordering, but it doesn't turn screws or lay bricks. Wings still need to be attached to planes and airbags installed in cars. The Internet does none of that. Oh, it's got its future, especially for online commerce and entertainment, but that will be left to companies like SBC and Atlantis to provide, companies with deep pockets and a lot of clout. An upstart like CrestPoint never stood a chance—not unless it merged with one of those deep pockets. Which we tried to—but should have done sooner."

"You make a good argument," said my dad, clearly impressed by her little speech.

"There's a little bit of 20-20 hindsight in that, but I don't disagree," I replied. "But I will say that we played our part—CrestPoint and companies like us—we all played out our part in the mania that caused investors to pump billions of dollars into building up the Internet. It's called 'irrational exuberance' and nothing important has ever been built without it."

"*Irrational exuberance*," repeated my dad, amused by the term.

"Yeah, and nothing important has ever been built without it. Just like the railroad or aerospace industries. The Dot-com boom—that whole speculative mania—led to capital investment, a lot of it lost now, but it left in its wake a high-speed network with servers and databases and a plethora of sophisticated software. And now we're seeing the weeding out and the consolidation that always follows this irrational exuberance."

"Like the telegraph," said Dad.

"Exactly... I think at one point, there were fifty telegraph companies all competing for the same routes, and over time they went out of business or consolidated and we ended up with Western Union."

"Here's to irrational exuberance," said Gwen, raising her soda can up in a toast.

"To irrational exuberance!"

We waited for Dan to pick up his can and join the toast. I was sure he had no idea what we were toasting but he liked the whole show of clicking cans or glasses together.

The conversation shifted into more mundane topics—the selling of the boat, how Clementine and Popeye were getting along (they now lived together in my house), and the garage sale I wanted to do in order to get rid of some of my junk. I watched Dan out of the corner of my eye the whole time. He ate his lunch slowly, closely examining each piece of food before eating it. This was especially true of the potato chips which he picked up individually, inspecting both sides for spots or imperfections before either discarding or eating it.

We were discussing the film *A Beautiful Mind* when Dan, who had just finished his lunch, suddenly yelled "Out!" I looked at him in alarm, wondering if he was in pain. His fixed smile was gone, replaced by a look of discomfort, and I could see a growing panic in his eyes. "Out!" he yelled again. He was kind of smooshed between my dad and the wall, and a quick assessment told me he'd become claustrophobic in that tight spot and wanted out. I rather roughly told my dad to get up and let him out of the booth. "Keep your beanie on!" my dad replied as he clumsily extracted himself from the booth to let Dan out. Once out and standing up, Dan quickly calmed down and the smile returned to his face.

"Why don't you take him out on deck," I said to my dad.

"Sure... Wanna go out on deck? Maybe we can see the sea lions. Whaddya say, Danny boy?"

Dan eagerly agreed and Dad took his hand and led him away. "Don't forget his life jacket," I called after him. I really didn't need to remind my dad of that but I said it anyway.

Gwen and I started cleaning up the galley. When we were nearly done, Gwen asked, "Do you think he dreams?"

"Who? Dan? I don't know. Maybe."

"I hope so."

"Me, too." The mention of dreaming triggered something I'd been meaning to tell Gwen. "That reminds me," I said. "Remember the recurring dream I told you about?"

"The one where you can't get up the mountain? Did you have it again?"

"Yeah, that bloody dream. Only it was different this time. Usually—or always—I'm at the bottom, or maybe halfway up, and something sidetracks me or knocks me back and I have to start again."

"Like Sisyphus."

"Like Sisyphus—only this time it was different. This time I made it to the top. Not that I climbed up there in my dream—I was just at the top. It was the same mountain and all, only somehow I'd gotten to the top and I could see everything. It was clear and I could see everything for miles around, the Golden Gate Bridge, the house in San Bruno, even the yacht harbor, and I thought 'How neat is this?' I can see everything. Oh, and you and Dan were there, and I got you to come over so I could show you the view, and we all looked at it together. Mark Kirkland was there, too—why, I don't know—but he was aways off on another bluff and we waved to each other… Anyhow, it was all very vivid and strange."

"That's a good dream… But how'd we all get back down, or did we all just end up living there?"

"Don't know. We were at the top—then I woke up."

"Maybe we'll stay up there for a while."

"I'll see what I can do. Maybe I can talk to the park ranger."

"Who would that be—Sisyphus?"

I laughed at that and we kidded around some more about my dream until we finished cleaning up. Gwen went back up on deck while I stopped by the stereo to change out the CD. When I came out into the cockpit, I was greeted by a glorious summer day. It was in the mid-eighties with a high blue sky, and the ocean all around reflected the same powder blue, giving one the feeling they were floating between two skies. Gwen and my dad had switched places, and she sat aft next to Dan while Dad stood next to me at the wheel. I breathed in the warm sea air and gave him a smile.

"I took up the anchor."

"Right-o," I replied happily. There was a speaker on deck, next to the short wave, and we both listened as Sinatra sang about the summer wind and how it came blowin' in from across the sea.

"Perfect song," he said.

I nodded in agreement as I turned on the engines. They hummed softly, and I let them idle there for a while without revving them up so we could listen to the rest of the song.

"She's a lot like you," said my dad, nodding over to Gwen.

"Really?" I replied. (I'd never really thought about it like that before but maybe he was right.) "You really think so?"

"I do… in a number of ways. It's lucky how you two got back together again. If it wasn't for CrestPoint."

If it wasn't for CrestPoint, I thought to myself with a smile. If it wasn't for a lot of things…

The song ended and I took *Danny Boy* out of neutral, edging us forwards. "It's all a part of the plan," I said.

"That's a pretty way of looking at it," he commented.

I turned the wheel, setting our course for north-northeast. "Yeah," I said, fully engaging the engines. "I used to think that, too."